MANAGING CLIENT-SERVER ENVIRONMENTS:
TOOLS AND STRATEGIES FOR BUILDING SOLUTIONS

MANAGING CLIENT-SERVER ENVIRONMENTS: TOOLS AND STRATEGIES FOR BUILDING SOLUTIONS

John McConnell
McConnell Consulting, Inc.
Johnmc@McConnell.com

For book and bookstore information

http://www.prenhall.com

Prentice Hall PTR
Upper Saddle River, New Jersey 07458

Library of Congress Cataloging-in-Publication Data

McConnell, John W.
    Managing client-server environments : tools and strategies for
building solutions / John W. McConnell.
        p.   cm.
    Includes index.
    ISBN 0-13-127176-8
    1. Client/server computing.   I. Title.
QA76.9.C55M45   1996
004'.36—dc20   95–41165
                                                                CIP

Acquisitions editor: Mary Franz
Cover designer: Jim Walsh
Cover design director: Jerry Votta
Manufacturing buyer: Alexis R. Heydt
Compositor/Production services: Pine Tree Composition, Inc.

The publisher offers discounts on this book when ordered in
bulk quantities.

For more information contact:
    Corporate Sales Department
    Prentice Hall PTR
    One Lake Street
    Upper Saddle River, New Jersey 07458

    Phone: 800–382–3419
    Fax: 201–236–7141
    email: corpsales@prenhall.com

Printed in the United States of America
10 9 8 7 6 5 4 3 2 1

ISBN: 0-13-127176-8

Prentice Hall International (UK) Limited, *London*
Prentice Hall of Australia Pty. Limited, *Sydney*
Prentice Hall Canada, Inc., *Toronto*
Prentice Hall Hispanoamericana, S.A., *Mexico*
Prentice Hall of India Private Limited, *New Delhi*
Prentice Hall of Japan, Inc., *Tokyo*
Simon & Schuster Asia Pte. Ltd., *Singapore*
Editora Prentice Hall do Brasil, Ltda., *Rio de Janeiro*

*This book is dedicated to my wife, Grace Morlock.
Your support makes the difference.*

Contents

Contents

Preface

Client/server computing was our salvation several years ago. It would free us from the tyranny of the data center and its mainframe, place powerful applications on worker's desktops, speed the introduction of new services, and deliver on the promise of distributed processing. Organizations would exploit the steady price/performance breakthroughs of desktop computers and empower their employees with instant access to information anywhere.

The reality has been another matter—client/server computing has proven to be far more difficult than the early boosters expected. Network and systems management has not been up to the task—yet—resulting in excessive administration costs. Promising applications are sitting in development and prototyping laboratories because they cannot be supported and deployed across thousands of desktops around the world.

There are several contributing factors: many vendors have not supplied solid management solutions since they only need to stay ahead of their competitors. Management platform vendors offer the promise of integrated management environments, but most have fallen short of delivering the kind of integration that makes the difference: the ability to access and share data among a set of management tools.

Those who plan, implement, and manage client/server environments, have also contributed to the dismal state of the management solutions. Many expect good management to be included free of charge when they buy an operating system, application, or network device. They have also resisted making the necessary investment in planning, implementation, and ongoing refinement.

Many users are also disillusioned by the siren song of open solutions. The attraction of standards-based interoperable products is strong and should be a significant factor in long term strategic planning. There are several reasons why open solutions have not increased our ability to manage the enterprise.

First, the idea of buying "best of breed" solutions and easily integrating them has proven to be just a worthy concept. The real integration of information, events, and processes takes a lot of extra time and money. Large organizations attain better integration by paying systems integrators and consultants for their expertise.

Second, the idea of interoperability is diluted by the proprietary extensions added to products that support any number of recognized standards. Standard management turns into a lowest common denominator exercise. The administrator can use general-purpose management tools that cannot capitalize on extended features; or choose a set of overlapping point tools that offer higher functionality.

The focus of this book is on what works, what are the practical steps that take an administrator toward a better management environment? Therefore, standards are not emphasized; most books with this focus help developers construct compliant products. This book, in contrast, discusses ways to use management tools, platforms, and frameworks in order to deliver better management as judged by availability, service levels, cost of ownership, management staff productivity, and similar measures.

A solution framework introduces a three-level model with effective management as the highest goal. Effective management delivers business results, not just technology management. Effectively managed client/server environments deliver high service levels, reduced operating costs, and a scalable solution gracefully accommodates growth.

The initial focus examines architectural issues from a practical perspective. Exploring combinations of managers and agents offers alternatives to localize various management functions. The introduction of intermediate agents introduces new possibilities for scaling and intelligent local responses.

Many management functions can be grouped into disciplines such as instrumentation management, event management, inventory, problem management, device management, LAN management, and systems management.

Examples are used to illustrate the ideas. A case study is carried through many chapters showing how the pieces of an effective management solution are assembled and used. Products are also mentioned in places to give real examples of solutions. Mention in no way implies endorsement of any product as a winner—rapid product development will change the relative standings. Rather, take the product examples as indicating interesting actual features and functions.

The management marketplace is changing rapidly. For example, the early SNMP platform leaders are now facing serious challenges from underdogs that have surpassed their technology and are trying to get the market's attention. The quality of management tools is higher because vendors in each niche must still differentiate themselves. Better management tools are being offered by independent software vendors that are exploiting overlooked areas. Systems management is the new battleground with computer vendors raising the ante with new strategies and offerings while independents are also offering integration of point tools.

These promising developments are offset by the reality that administrators must still work too hard to assemble the best management technology, organize it, and transform it into a powerful and effective management solution. This book is written to ease some of those burdens.

This book is organized into four major parts. Part I serves as an introduction to a discussion of the practical aspecs of managing distributed systems and sets the stage for introducing the basic solution elements. Part II deals with infrastructure issues: architectues, instrumentation, and platforms. An infrastructure supports sets of management tools and processes and provides a means for evolving a management environment as new requirements emerge. Part III deals with LAN and systems management. Part IV puts all the individual pieces together and defines a process for building a policy and process-driven management solution.

Acknowledgments

Many people have contributed ideas, insights, and feedback through discussions. Many of those people are clients that have struggled with management challenges in several parts of the world and the United States. Others are in the vendor community and have enriched my thinking by discussing products, competitors, technology, and market trends.

Among those who have helped clarify my thinking while discussing and wrestling with the problems we all encounter in this business are: Asheem Chandna, Jerry McDowell, Dave Mahler, Sanjiv Ahuja, John Burnham, Karen O'Neill, Charley Robbins, Jim Herman, Roselie Buonauro (and the team at NetLabs), David Passmore, Ed Snyder, Marius Abel, David Colodny, Jean Hammond, Nate Kalowski, Marc Schwager, Bill Seifert, Carol Crall, Larry Lang, Bill Erdman, Bill Hawe, Bill Seifert, Andy Gottlieb, Michael Harrison, Michael Skubicz, Dick Vento, Tim Lee Thorp, Gordon Smith, Jeff Case, Vishal Desai, Debra Curtis, Gordon Saussy, Phil Fuchino, Bob Goodman, Joe Skorupa, Abbott Gilman, Dan Simula, Michael DiSabato, and others that I omit with apologies.

Many thanks to Elizabeth Peach who transcribed the early manuscript and helped me meet my timelines.

MANAGING CLIENT-SERVER ENVIRONMENTS: TOOLS AND STRATEGIES FOR BUILDING SOLUTIONS

PART I

INTRODUCING DISTRIBUTED NETWORK & SYSTEMS MANAGEMENT

Chapters 1 through 3 serve as an introduction to a discussion of the practical aspects of managing distributed networks and systems and set the stage for introducing the basic solution elements. Chapter 1 introduces the basic problem set for network and systems administrators. Chapter 2 examines what is really needed for solving the tough problems that administrators encounter every day. Chapter 3 introduces the various players in the convoluted standards efforts.

CHAPTER 1

An Overview

Our ability to build complex networking infrastructures and applications usually outstrips our ability to manage them. We have been struggling to conceptualize and build information-intensive environments that change the ways we do business, learn, entertain ourselves, deal with government, and even shop. Much of the potential promise eludes us because we cannot easily manage the environments we are creating. Unfortunately, the problems seem to arrive more quickly than the solutions we have been promised.

Most organizations are trying to deploy the best networking technologies and applications that they can afford. Our dependence on information continues to grow, without better ways of accessing, creating, and distributing it, we fall behind.

Almost all businesses realize the value of information. Yet, as a consultant, I have seen many exciting client/server applications in our clients' prototyping laboratories that have not yet been deployed. The reasons are similar: there are several full-time support people at the lab to keep the demonstrations going, but deploying the application to several thousand desktops is entirely another matter. The resources and staff are not there, or the tools aren't available, or they don't know where to start. Solid systems and network management solutions are needed to exploit the technologies we use today as well as those we'll employ in the future.

We face a variety of challenges today and the quality of our management solutions will determine, in part, our success in meeting them.

1.1 INFORMATION-INTENSIVE COMPETITION

Almost every business today finds itself under increasing competitive pressures. Global competition, the changing economic environment, and dynamic shifts in the market contribute to these pressures. Information makes a strategic difference: the ability to access,

3

consume, and use information sustains competitive advantage. Workers must access information wherever it resides and share it with others. More organizations are collaborating through their networks, working more closely with suppliers, customers, and strategic business partners.

Networks and computer systems are needed to access, analyze, and distribute the information we depend upon. Organizations must respond more quickly to changes and deliver services and products with shorter cycle times. Effective network management delivers high availability so workers have the access they need. The quality of service is managed so that critical applications perform as expected. Systems management keeps every desktop properly configured with the appropriate software needed. Sound security management protects critical resources from inadvertent or purposeful access.

Reengineering the Business

Many organizations are reengineering their businesses as a response to information-intensive competition. They are changing the structures of their businesses by flattening out management hierarchies and building more fluid and flexible organizations with direct reporting.

At the same time, businesses are also changing their processes—the ways they deal with their customers, the way they design products and services, and the way they deliver them to the marketplace. Project teams, or workgroups, are formed with the appropriate skills from different parts of the organization. Individuals may actually be members of several teams, they are reassigned as projects are completed or their skills are needed elsewhere.

Information flow is critical to fluid, widespread workgroups. Network and computing services allow them to be responsive, creative, and productive from any location. Client/server environments must also be flexible; they must be as malleable and changeable as the workgroups and project teams they support. Network topology, bandwidth, and services will be changed more often in the future. Administrators I have spoken with estimate, for example, that they change 40 to 50% of their systems annually. This heavy burden of management staff time and disruption raises more concerns when the administrators also report that this rate of change is where they "max-out": they lack the tools and staff to keep pace with the changes they really should be performing.

Organizations are demanding that their networking and computing resources be as flexible as their structures and processes. Network and systems managers must be able to alter their structures and services to support dynamic, project-oriented operations.

Internetworking

Internetworking has moved from the research and technical environments into mainstream corporate networking. It has become the foundation from which future networks will evolve. Internetworking has matured into a sophisticated transport system that actually supports many separate network architectures such as TCP/IP, IPX, SNA, DECnet, and others. This multiprotocol transport system has provided extensive interconnection from the desktop into many larger environments. Attachment to the Internet or other services brings information from all over the world.

The simplest level of internetworking begins with the **local** workgroup, interconnecting several sets of Local Area Networks within the same building. The next level extends to the **campus,** interconnecting a set of local buildings. The **enterprise** level interconnects campuses and other sites with wide-area backbone links. Internetworking today is moving into the **intercompany** domain, tying different business organizations together.

The large size and complexity of internetworks strains management capacities. Multiple protocols and multiple technologies add to the complexity of managing traffic flows across many different networks.

Client/Server

The allure of client/server computing has been strong for many years. The price performance breakthroughs of RISC processors offer mainframe-like computing power for the desktop. Intelligent applications directly support workers and make them more productive. High-speed networks link any desktop to information anywhere within the organization or beyond. Companies that successfully deploy client/server computing environments gain a competitive advantage by leveraging their information more effectively.

The introduction of new network operating systems such as Microsoft NT holds promise for a better application environment. The introduction of DCE (Distributed Computing Environment), a technology from the Open Software Foundation, is expected to speed application deployment. Vendors such as Digital, IBM, Hewlett-Packard, Microsoft, and Novell have indicated that they will deliver DCE solutions for their customers, opening the possibility of a true multivendor standard.

Managing a geographically dispersed collection of desktops and servers is a struggle today. The large numbers of systems make Systems Administration the high leverage area for management solutions. Administrators must be able to manage a networked set of clients and servers through the network itself. Desktops and servers must be configured and monitored remotely, software needs to be delivered and installed, behavior should be monitored, and an increasingly complex environment must be protected and secured.

1.2   THE MANAGEMENT BARRIER

The need for better management of the communications and computing resources of an enterprise is apparent. The solutions have been slow to arrive, however. Most administrators of systems and networks are still frustrated with their management solutions and capabilities. *Head-to-Head: Customer Satisfaction with Management Products*, a survey we conducted of 220 organizations, showed that administrators rated their overall satisfaction with management solutions as slightly higher than "only adequate." Individual management tasks and processes such as asset/inventory management fell below the only adequate mark.

Delivering good solutions is a challenging task for management vendors. Vendors of network devices, systems, and applications as well as Independent Software Vendors are under pressure to address management problems in multiple areas.

The Manager's Challenge

Network and systems managers today face challenges in several major areas including complexity, change, service delivery, and the cost of ownership. Each area has significant problems to address, which also means there are substantial opportunities for those who solve them. Some management tools address these areas directly while others affect them indirectly.

Complexity   The complexity of the manager's job seemingly increases on a daily basis. Growth, multiple technologies, and new applications are the major contributors to complexity.

Unchecked growth is forcing management solutions past their limits. Organizations we work with estimate continued network and systems growth even in the face of downsizing. Fewer remaining workers must be leveraged by better information services. Many of our customers project LAN segment growth rates from 50 to 200% in a two-year span. The growth in interconnection devices such as bridges and routers will keep pace. The number of managed elements grows rapidly, straining the capacity of staff and tools.

Many organizations are not yet remotely managing all their computer systems through their networks, when they do, the number of managed elements will increase by orders of magnitude. There will be dozens to hundreds of computer systems to every device such as a hub or router. Each desktop or server will have multiple components such as video cards, coprocessors, monitors, and the like. The number of applications and files in thousands of computers will strain the capacity of current management tools to simply keep track of everything.

Most organizations have a collection of heterogeneous technologies that must be coordinated and orchestrated into a cohesive environment. Management tools are spotty: some do a fine job managing a part of the environment, while other parts are barely covered. The introduction of switching introduces new technologies to the current collection of networks.

The emergence of virtual workgroups will be based on a switching fabric that interconnects traditional LANs. Groups will be defined on a functional basis rather than by physical attachment. Managing such a fluid environment requires more sophisticated management tools.

Also adding to complexity is increasing interconnection of local, campus, enterprise, and intercompany networks. More complicated topologies are difficult to trace and understand. The introduction of new high-speed switching technologies, such as ATM and LAN switching, also increases complexity. LAN and backbone switching will combine traditional datagram services with new switched virtual circuits. Connections and routing policies must be coordinated.

The geographic distribution of computing resources within an organization also makes the manager's job much more complex, since there is no single site that contains the managed resources. The data center now is on everyone's desktop, rather than behind glass walls.

Change   We discussed the rates of change needed to support a reengineered enterprise. Higher rates of change are not sustainable with current management tools and practices.

The network and computing resources must be adapted quickly to support a team-oriented organization. This need for managing continuing change places the burden on the network and systems management infrastructures. The creation of virtual workgroups also requires great changes in reconfiguration and tracking resources since physical connectivity is less important.

Organizations are being merged, sold, or reorganized into different business units. The mix of technologies, staffs, and management tools may change rapidly, taxing the capacities of the best network and systems management teams.

Service Delivery   Network and systems administrators are being evaluated on their ability to deliver services. Simply managing a device, communications link, or server will not suffice: network users need a consistent level of service for maximum effectiveness. Availability and quality are the defining parameters for networked services.

Service delivery is increasingly important as organizations depend on their networks for supporting mission-critical activities as well as more mundane, but equally important, tasks such as messaging. A service focus demands better tools that allow the administrator to manage a service, such as messaging, rather than a technology.

I recall one client who was greatly annoyed with his network management team; he would inquire about delays in sending messages from New York to Tokyo, and his management team would cite network statistics such as link utilization to indicate that operations appeared satisfactory. At one level, they actually were: the low utilization probably meant that the network management group had few problems to deal with. However, the service wasn't being delivered and the company's ability to carry out its business activities was compromised. The reverse situation could also hold. A high network utilization would not be a problem to the business unit that was still getting an acceptable level of service. The network management team might be alerted to address the utilization levels before service was affected.

Network administrators will need new tools that allow them to address service delivery. As in the case cited above, they need to monitor service levels rather than the behavior of the basic technology. Application level information must be collected and presented so that the application behavior can be understood. Administrators will make adjustments that protect service levels and keep the business operating effectively.

Cost of Ownership   The cost of network and systems ownership has become a more important concern. Studies by the Gartner Group, The Index Group, and Strategic Networks Consulting have shown that costs for network hardware and software are less than 20% of the life cycle costs. A large portion of the costs goes for management and administration. Reducing these costs delivers a bottom-line impact for the business.

Resources are a severe constraint for most network and system administrators. Spending pressures are forcing them to find new solutions. Growth cannot be accommodated by adding more management staff to match growth. The growth rates are too steep, and staff members are too expensive, difficult to train, and hard to keep. Management staff must be leveraged through consolidation and the use of intelligent remote management tools. More management tasks must be automated so that staff are freed from repetitive operations. Controlling the costs of configuration, changes, operations, and user support are key ingredients in a good solution.

Improving the cost effectiveness of the network and computing services that they manage is also important to the administrators. Higher network and system availability, better service quality, user support, and other aspects of solid management are reflected in the bottom line and in rewards for the management teams.

Building effective management solutions is a challenge for any organization. Coping with complexity and change while optimizing shrinking resources is a demanding job. Many organizations are changing their priorities, focusing on their core competencies and obtaining other products and services that they need. Managing distributed systems is a core competency for any organization. The actual day-to-day tasks can be turned over to an outside vendor, but each organization must develop its strategy, evaluate its options, and keep tight control of essential information resources.

1.3 SOLUTIONS

The major challenges have been described, the means to address them are still evolving. This book focuses on practical steps to consider when you are building or modifying a management environment. We will focus on what can be done, what trade-offs are involved, and the future directions of management technology. There is a minimum of time spent on the emerging management standards, mainly because they do not directly deliver solutions today. We will use examples of current products to illustrate what is possible and to give an idea of real choices. Mentioning a product does not imply an endorsement, rather the goal is to give you an idea of possibilities and useful features. I recommend that you encourage any vendor to incorporate features that will be useful.

CHAPTER 2

What Managers Want

What makes a good network and systems management solution? Good solutions depend upon more than good technology; they also need realistic perspectives and the appropriate organizational structures. Network and systems management solutions probably need more perspectives and organization than technology. We are somewhat constrained by the available technology. Unless we develop our own we must choose from what is available to us. However, the perspectives and organization are under our control and we can choose those which suit our needs and wait for the technical solutions to mature if necessary. This approach builds the foundation for a robust solution that delivers more value with time.

Systems and network managers need new management solutions that address a dynamic, complex client/server environment and allow them to do their jobs better. This chapter describes the general solutions we need; most of the rest of this book focuses on how to deliver the solutions discussed here. The most important aspects of good solutions can be described, and particular products will encompass these qualities to varying degrees. Actually, there are several levels of management solutions that must be addressed.

2.1 SOLUTION LEVELS

Each level of a solution addresses different needs for an organization and delivers different types of value. The levels are interdependent. Each depends upon those levels underneath it: managing for survival transitions to managing for efficiency and then to managing for effectiveness.

Survival

The most basic level is managing for the survival of systems and networks. Little progress can be made until networks and systems are usually available to support the activities of the organization. Survival issues revolve around fault management: detecting, isolating, and resolving problems as quickly as possible. Other aspects of survival include a help desk for fielding user queries, reports, and complaints. A problem-management, or trouble-ticketing tool, is also essential for tracking problems through to resolution.

Managing single LAN segments is becoming tractable through the use of structured wiring schemes and manageable devices. Structured wiring rarely fails, so physical problems are minimized. Intelligent hubs, bridges, routers, and switches are available with redundant power supplies and hot-swappable modules. These design features reduce the impacts of failures since failed modules are replaced quickly without disrupting the device itself.

The remaining problems are at the internetworking level. Tracking problems across a set of interconnected segments is still very difficult. Several different types of networks may be in the path between a client and a remote server. The management tools that trace paths and correlate behaviors in different environments are still maturing and remain more of an art than most administrators feel comfortable admitting.

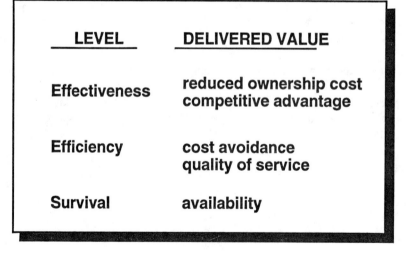

LEVEL	DELIVERED VALUE
Effectiveness	reduced ownership cost competitive advantage
Efficiency	cost avoidance quality of service
Survival	availability

Each solution level delivers increasing value as higher levels are incorporated. A lower level supports those above it.

FIGURE 2–1   Solution levels and outcomes

Efficiency

The focus shifts once our networks and systems are available most of the time. The management goal shifts to getting the most out of these expensive resources. Performance and configuration management become more important, and administrators want to understand their environments and modify them to get more throughput and reduce costs.

We need a set of tools that help us to increase the efficiency of our networks and systems. For example, we need to optimize servers and clients in order to get the most from our applications. At the same time we need tools that analyze the flows of traffic between systems and networks to identify potential network bottlenecks and determine the appropriate actions. Modeling tools help us to anticipate the effects of growth or changes before they cause us trouble. Profiling, or baselining, tools are needed to observe trends and forestall troubles.

Unfortunately, good management is more than managing the technologies, as difficult as that is.

Effectiveness

Managing for effectiveness shifts the focus from keeping technology (networks, devices, systems and applications) running efficiently to delivering results for the organization. Effective management solutions produce business outcomes. Well managed networks and systems increase productivity, support business processes, reduce exposure to revenue loss, and increase competitive advantage.

For example, a site can be connected with two links to the corporate backbone. Survival issues are addressed through redundancy and using different physical paths for each link. If a link fails, there is still connectivity and availability of services. Efficiency becomes relatively simple as well; the remaining link can be filled with traffic.

The effectiveness issue presents itself at this point in the scenario because there is half the normal capacity on the link to the backbone. How do we insure that this diminished link capacity is assigned to the mission-critical applications? Can we keep the key business processes operating throughout the failure? Or do we use the capacity for low priority tasks that should have been postponed? Managing at this level incorporates **policy** into the management system.

We need to describe, review, and modify policies for the management system itself. The policy decisions must be embedded in the management system itself since it is unrealistic to expect harried management staff at a console to make these types of decisions. Effective management is receiving increasing attention and more sophisticated tools will be appearing.

Strategic tasks at this level include capacity planning so growth is accommodated without business disruptions caused by lack of systems or network capacity. Security management is required to protect critical business information as well as private, personal information held by the organization and by the network users. Vendors such as SSDS are actually extending the network and systems management technologies into managing the business processes themselves as we shall see in a later section.

2.2 INFORMATION MANAGEMENT:
NETWORK MANAGEMENT IS EASY, BUT . . .

The real obstacle to more effective management solutions is the inability to manage information more effectively.

In principle, management operations are quite simple, both from a conceptual and an operational viewpoint. Most management operations consists of two basic types of functions: a GET and a SET. The GET operation allows a management application to obtain information from a managed element. This information can include operational status, statistics such as number of users, CPU utilization, and so forth. Unsolicited reports of a change in status of a managed resource are also included. The complementary operation, SET, involves a management application changing information in a remotely managed resource. A SET can alter the behavior of the managed element, such as inactivating a communications interface, reinitializing a server, or activating a new application. It is what occurs between the GET and the SET that determines the quality of a management solution.

An apocryphal story that I have heard in several places illustrates the point. One day, all operations came to a halt in a busy factory with a complex assembly line. The assembly line wasn't working and goods weren't moving through the factory. The factory manager was becoming quite distraught; irate customers were phoning for their orders; raw materials for the assembly line were piling up on the loading dock; and all the workers were standing around idly waiting to get back to work. At last, the factory manager called in a consultant.

The consultant walked around for awhile, observing things and inspecting different parts of the assembly line. Then after several moments of reflection, the consultant took a hammer and hit a particular valve: the assembly line immediately started working. The factory manager was, of course, grateful and relieved. He thanked the consultant profusely, and went back to his duties.

A while later, the bill arrived from the consultant. When the manager opened the bill, he found out that the fee was $1,000. The manager was quite irate and fired back a terse letter stating: "This is an unreasonable fee. I need a complete breakdown to justify this type of expense." A while later, a new bill came from the consultant with an itemized set of charges. They read:

Hitting the valve:	$ 1.00
Knowing the right valve to hit	$999.00

This is exactly what we need from our management tools and technologies: the ability to understand the situation quickly, an accurate determination of the problem, and the correct course of action to quickly restore service to its highest level. In the story, the consultant managed the information: she collected and analyzed it and an accurate and useful action resulted.

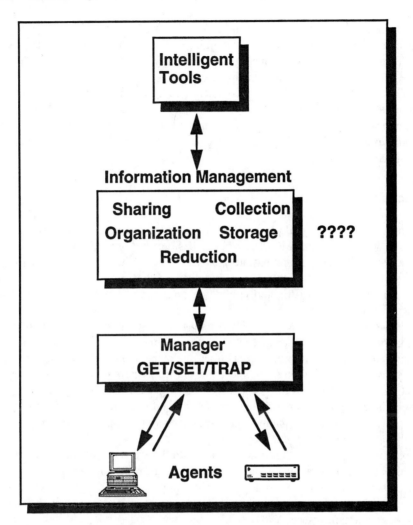

Information management is the key to better solutions. The intelligence of management tools depends on the quality of information they use.

FIGURE 2–2 The "Real" Network and Systems Management Problem

Unfortunately, most of the good information-processing tools that we have in our management systems today reside in the brains of our administrators and operations staff rather than in the tools and technologies they deploy. Better management solutions will require better information management capabilities.

Our network and systems management products need to manage information at multiple levels. Some parts of the information management effort are more mature than others and some are just beginning to be addressed. We'll examine the different aspects of managing information, starting with the simplest levels and progressing to more complex, sophisticated functions.

Collection

The most basic level is collecting the information that we need to make the appropriate decisions when situations arise. Most of the basic operational information and statistics that we need are collected from remote agents and intermediate agents (the chapters on architecture and instrumentation cover these entities). We can consider all of the embedded agents throughout our distributed computing environment as the sources of real-time management information.

However, effective enterprise-level management solutions depend on other types of information that the agents cannot provide. For example, a comprehensive management solution requires other information such as inventory and asset information, corporate data (personnel files, telephone numbers, and so forth), warranty information, contract information, and contact information. These other types of information are distributed in multiple databases throughout the enterprise. A good collection scheme must be able to tap into these different information sources, as needed, to support the management operations that are being carried out.

Other information in the form of **knowledge bases** is appearing. The bases are collections of information about certain products such as a router or an application. Management tools browse these knowledge bases when they need specific help in solving a problem. Management staff also use knowledge bases to respond to their customers, the network, and systems users.

Reduction

The flood of raw management information can be overwhelming, especially in large environments. As a case in point, one organization I worked with reported that their worldwide client/server network generated over one million events monthly. In addition to unsolicited reports, large volumes of operational information flow back to management centers, with reports of utilization, error rates, number of concurrent processes, and other types of measurements.

Administrators have several options for reducing the information volume. They can distribute local collection and processing functions, they can adopt a management-by-exception approach, and they can transform information into more valuable forms.

Local information collection with intelligent instrumentation (see Chapter 6) reduces information close to its source. The collection function also incorporates **testing** which selects information for forwarding. Because wide-area backbone links are typically much slower than the Local Area Networks they interconnect, any increase in management traffic may have an adverse effect on the applications activities. Selective forwarding reduces the impact of management traffic and keeps the capacity available for business activities.

This flood of management information can overwhelm many of the current management products in use today. The organization with a million events found that 10,000 or 1% required immediate attention, the other 99% was logged or discarded. **Managing by exception** reduces the number of events that require staff attention. Automatic sorting of incoming management information and the selection of the most relevant or important information saves staff time and insures that significant events are not overlooked. This selected information can be used to activate the appropriate management applications, change the graphical display to alert operators, or can cause notifications through such means as electronic mail or messaging pagers.

Information can also be transformed to make it more valuable. For instance, a system may report a problem. Usually the MAC (Media Access Control) or IP address is provided. Neither address may be helpful to the management staff as they prepare to respond to the problem event. If the incoming information were **transformed** by looking it up in a database so that the system name, system location, type, owner, and other data were available, the team could respond more quickly and appropriately.

Organization

Management information must also be organized so that it can be easily manipulated and the appropriate information can be accessed quickly and accurately. The trend is toward organizing much of the management information with an **object-based paradigm**. In this type of perspective, each managed resource can be represented and modeled as an object. Objects are defined for each class of resource to be managed.

Instances of objects model a real resource that is being managed. Each object instance has attributes, operations, and notifications. **Attributes** are dynamic and static values that represent such things as operational status, ongoing statistics, and long-term information, such as manufacturer, serial number, or vendor contact. These attributes generally reflect the current state of any managed elements and can also be used to change behavior.

Actions define the types of functions that each object is capable of carrying out. For example, an object modeling a server might include actions for such things as reinitializing the server, doing a virus check, or performing a diagnostic on the disk system. **Notifications** are unsolicited messages from the object reporting changes of state or condition. For example, the server might have notifications for such events as a security violation, a disk failure, or excessive memory utilization.

Incoming information from remote agents must be associated with the appropriate objects, and the information they contain must be modified as needed. Different types of management information structures support an object-oriented perspective, while others, like SNMP, work on a simpler structure organized around tables of variables. The particular organization of the information at this level is probably more important to the application developers than to end users. High quality management applications hide most of the details of the information structure from the administrators, presenting information and options for action instead.

Storage

The collected information must be stored in some type of repository so that it is available to sets of management tools. The construction of a robust management repository is still in the future; most of the solutions available today are highly fragmented, unfortunately.

Most management systems today operate with isolated islands of management information. Many management applications retain most of their information in private files or databases, rather than in a single management repository, even when they stress their "integration" with a management platform. For example, management platforms contain a certain subset of the management information generally relating to topology and operational status. Other information, such as inventory information, is stored in separate databases in other parts of the enterprise.

In all likelihood, a single management repository will be very difficult, or worse, to construct. One obstacle is the many management data sources that are required, such as personnel. Incorporating all of that data into a single repository is too large a task and may introduce security and privacy concerns for the enterprise. There will be information in many of the corporate databases that is confidential and not necessary for management activities.

We are beginning to see the foundations of a structure that provides a single logical repository comprising multiple databases at different locations. The use of an object request broker provides an intermediate step whereby the named objects are first located and then the appropriate access mechanisms at any given site are used to obtain the needed information. This type of approach is more scalable since data can be distributed in multiple locations.

It is also more robust in that any given location still maintains its control over the contents and integrity of the data that it is responsible for. In the examples we've been using, a database administrator for the personnel database may set access control such that management applications can only obtain a strict subset of all the information contained in the personnel files. This type of architecture supports a new generation of distributed repositories that facilitate the construction of better management solutions. The ability to manage and access information in multiple sites through a single interface will be most welcome.

Many enterprises are considering a two-level data repository scheme, containing both real-time, volatile information, as well as long-term data. Examples of volatile information would be operational status and statistics such as utilization, number of users, error counts, and so forth change over relatively short time intervals. Real-time information is volatile and thus does not require stringent levels of backup, protection, and other services. Some of it lasts for only a few minutes and the management system can repeat the collection if the information is lost. The access mechanisms can be straightforward and very efficient since the requirements are relaxed.

Long-term information includes such things as serial numbers, warranties, and other information that tends to be constant or changes infrequently. This information must be protected and conserved even if there are failures within the management system itself. Backup, consistency checks, concurrency controls, and other features provided by robust database management solutions are required for the longer-term management information.

The advantage of a two-level store is the possibility of getting good optimization for both levels. For example, the volatile real-time information could be stored in a data base with access mechanisms that are very quick and efficient. Quick access is necessary to obtain data and perform diagnostics and evaluations as quickly as possible. Sometimes fast access must be traded against issues of integrity, fault tolerance, and so forth.

IBM is an example of a two-level store with their NetView mainframe management product. The Resource Object Data Manager (RODM) is a real-time data store handling the volatile information. It is basically a mapped memory address space without any database access machinery surrounding it. This provides for very quick access, but also exposes the management system to loss of information with system crashes or interruptions in service. RODM is supplemented with a long-term data store, known as Infoman, which keeps configuration, warranty, and other types of information. Infoman is basically a database application, thereby taking advantage of more stringent access controls and fault tolerance built into the database services themselves.

The two-level data store also poses the problem of integrating access to both levels. Some applications may deal entirely with RODM or Infoman, while others may need information from both sources. A uniform access mechanism that bridges these two different types of environments may be very difficult to build. The other alternative is that each management application will need to know the characteristics of the information so that it can go to the appropriate level of storage managers. This is another issue that the request broker can address for management tools.

Sharing

Placing all the management information in a logical repository is a necessary, but not sufficient, step. The real value of collecting management information into a single repository is that it increases the ability to share, or leverage, that information. Any tool with the appropriate access privileges can get the information it needs to provide higher quality solutions. One of the limitations in many of today's solutions is that the tools do not have access to all the information they need in order to make effective decisions and to provide more help for the management staff.

One common scenario, unfortunately, is that staff members use a management tool to obtain some raw information or an analysis. Then the staff members input the information into another tool and carry out another step. The results are then manually entered into a third tool and so forth. This gets the job done, but at the cost of longer service outages, staff frustration, and the possibility of errors being introduced.

What is really needed to facilitate sharing is a common data model—a uniform and consistent schema whereby any management application can access all the types of information it needs. A common data model allows applications from different vendors to work together more easily since they all understand the same ways of describing relationships between objects, object attributes, and associated information, such as asset or warranty information. This type of common data model is one of the missing pieces in management solutions today.

There are many activities underway today to develop common data models for different management platforms. For example, IBM published its SystemView data model several years ago, although it has not become a widely accepted approach. Other platform vendors, such as Hewlett-Packard, IBM, Sun, Cabletron, and NetLabs, are all developing common data models for their own specific management platform products. Many of the third-party vendors are working, as well, to assist in the definition of these models.

However, each of these models will undoubtedly be different in ways that restrict their interoperability. If this occurs, there will be an added burden to third-party vendors who will have to reengineer their applications to support each platform's common data model. An industry-wide common data model is probably too much to hope for, especially in the near term. However, over time the models will converge to something much more consistent and uniform among the different platforms.

Information Management Summary

There are a lot of things to consider when we tackle the issue of managing the management information. Without strong information management capabilities we are reduced to extensive manual procedures to overcome the fragmentation of the data. Many of the following chapters offer ways to manage the information more effectively.

Information management is one way to evaluate and compare different types of management applications. Most tools have a set of presentation features with choices of formats and graphics. Transforming raw information into more useful information is a key characteristic of good tools. The administrator usually has a range of customizing options to make the presentations as comfortable and familiar as possible.

Better information management is shown by the ability to relate information from multiple sources into a comprehensive perspective. For example, a problem management system with case-based reasoning can compare a current problem with past problems to find similarities and extract information that speeds resolution.

2.3 INTEGRATION: THE HIGH-VALUE DIMENSIONS

The ultimate goal of going through the steps of collection, reduction, organization, storage, and building a common data model is to allow managers to leverage their information more effectively.

The words "integration" or "integrated" have been so overused that they are almost useless for understanding the differences in competing products. Early "integrated" management products usually implied more functionality than they delivered. Almost any new management product somehow works the term "integrated" into its product description or implies that the product is part of an integrated solution. Different levels and definitions of integration also add to the confusion; defining the value of integration may shed some light on the differences in value.

Network and systems administrators have been awaiting the arrival of integrated management solutions. The ideal of high-value integration has yet to be realized, but the needed elements are appearing. Administrators expect an "integrated" management solution to offer advantages such as a single management repository, management tools that work together, uniform interfaces, and process coordination.

Value Metrics for Integration

Value certainly depends on perspective. Hands-on administrators value tools that allow them to be more effective and productive by simplifying processes and automating activities. Others in the organization may be interested in return on investment or increased competitive advantage. Effective management environments will return value from any perspective. A way of determining the relative value of various integrated approaches is to relate them to timeframes. Some products offer good value in the short term, while others offer increasing benefits over time. The latter offer the highest-value integration that allows administrators to continually improve their management environments.

Consolidation and Consistency

Some of the initial claims for integrated network management provided low-value integration for short-term gains, but little in long-term increases in capabilities. For example, the introduction of the network management platform led to overblown claims that the dawn of integrated network management had indeed arrived. Actually, the early platforms really offered **consolidation** rather than integration. Multiple element management systems could be consolidated into a single hardware platform and console. These applications, however, were not integrated in any way: each had its own display formats, database, commands, and functionality.

The introduction of graphical user interfaces (GUIs) was heralded as another breakthrough in integrated management. The value of a common graphical user interface can certainly be demonstrated through its ability to deliver **consistency**. Operators had a common way of interacting with various applications· however, the applications rarely shared data and often were still in separate windows.

High-value integration addresses the major management challenge: information management. Higher value integration organizes and leverages information to save time and improve service. Event, data, and domain integration are the foundation for higher value solutions.

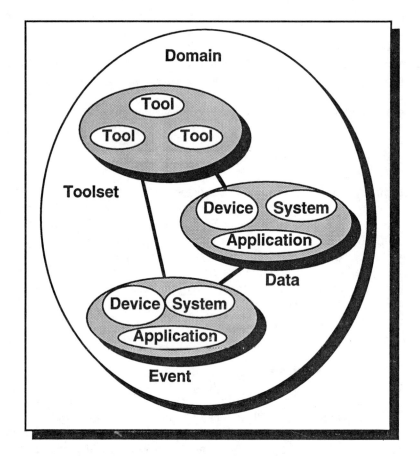

Integration is a multi-level problem. Event integration organizes events, data integration allows sharing and tools are integrated. Domain management integrates different management areas.

FIGURE 2–3   The levels of integration

Toolset Integration

A highly valuable type of integration is the management toolset itself. An integrated set of management tools will be able to work together in a consistent way to deliver a greater value than if they were separated. Tools can be integrated to deliver management processes rather than point solutions. Toolset integration depends on several of the information management capabilities discussed above.

Event Integration

Event integration is the heart of the management infrastructure. The volume of events is reduced through the mechanism discussed in information management, above and in Chapters 6 and 7. All events can be collected and filtered in a uniform fashion.

Management tools can also use events to activate other applications as necessary: the aptly named NerveCenter of the NetLabs DIMONs platforms is a good example of event integration. This capability allows administrators to build a chain of management tools that are activated in the proper sequence.

Data Integration

Data integration is another term for managing management information with a common logical repository and a common data model. All management information is available to those tools that need it.

Domain Integration

Event and data integration add substantial functionality to a single platform; however, domain management will be the scalable solution for enterprise-wide managed environments. Event and data integration must be extended between management platforms so that distributed management can be introduced. Manager-manager protocols are maturing, and all the major platform vendors are either supporting or will support integrated domain management.

Integration Summary

The good news is that higher value integration is coming; the bad news is that no single vendor is providing it all today. Each platform vendor is developing a proprietary common data model (an oxymoron in itself); ISVs will still be forced to reengineer their applications. Functional integration requires extra work; there is no simple "snap-in" for various tools yet. Network planners and administrators must continue to press for higher levels of integration; it will be a while yet before they enjoy the benefits.

2.4 AUTOMATION: MULTILEVEL OPPORTUNITIES

Automation is a general term that describes replacing or supplementing tasks that would ordinarily be carried out by a staff member. Some automation may be simple, such as sending a notification when a failure occurs or translating a MAC address to a host name or office location.

Other types of automated tools are very complex—carrying out analysis and making informed suggestions to guide the staff. Expert systems capture the experience of experts and carry out many tasks without supervision.

Adding more automation is one way of keeping abreast of growth and change. Operators are more productive when they are freed from repetitive, time-consuming tasks. Many activities can be initiated without direct intervention by the staff. Some high-value examples of automation can be found in more intelligent instrumentation and constructing automated management processes described in Chapters 6 and 19, respectively.

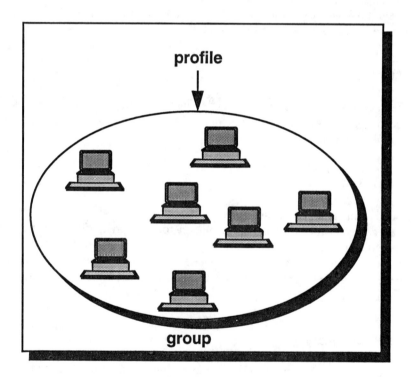

Automation increases productivity by replicating staff actions. In this case the same configuration profile is applied repeatedly to all members of the group.

FIGURE 2–4   Replication

The advent of general-purpose expert systems is still in the future. There are good tools that offer sound advice, such as the Hewlett-Packard Traffic Expert, but the promise of full-blown artificial intelligence is unfulfilled. Many expert systems offer great value by incorporating knowledge bases captured from human experts and exploiting a computer's ability to search them quickly for the appropriate criteria.

Other expert systems are very expensive and often require extensive data input and tuning before they produce helpful insights for administrators. Other levels of automation can offer significant value today by freeing staff and simplifying more complex tasks.

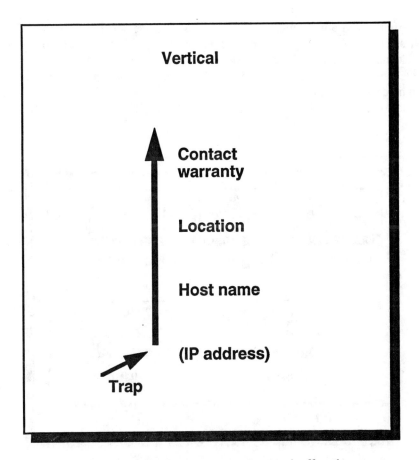

Vertical automation improves point tool effectiveness. In this case automatic lookup routines add value to the information and bring more information to staff.

FIGURE 2–5   Vertical automation

Replication

Automation can make many tasks simpler, especially when they must be repeated frequently. For example, it saves tremendous amounts of staff time to have a standard desktop configuration that includes applications, access privileges, default servers, default printers, and other information. New desktops can be configured automatically whenever they are added. Another valuable approach is to change the standard configuration and automatically update all the systems with one management operation.

Vertical Automation

More efficient and effective automation depends on being able to utilize the information that has been collected and organized in the repository. Individual management tools can be made more effective with automation. For instance, a server management tool can receive a management event that indicates that CPU utilization is dangerously high. Automated procedures can query the server user tables and automatically provide the management staff with a list of users and their applications and the loading that each is causing.

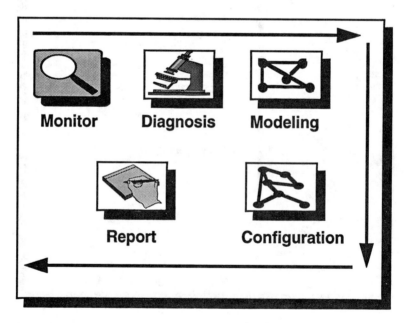

More powerful automation allows an administrator to
sequence sets of tools that implement management
policies and processes.

FIGURE 2–6   Horizontal automation

Providing this information automatically saves staff time and delivers a clearer picture of the situation and the possible options to correct the problem.

Horizontal Automation

Horizontal automation introduces opportunities to build more value into management solutions. Individual management tools can be linked together automatically with one tool to produce results and information that can be automatically used by other management applications, as necessary. For example, a diagnostic application can determine a particular fault and then automatically populate a trouble ticket with the system type, specific details of the problem, system location, and so forth, before automatically launching a problem management application.

This flow of information between the applications will actually take place in the logical repository; the real glue will be the common data model that enables every application to find the information it requires.

2.5   ADMINISTRATION

Management systems themselves must be administered in a similar way to all the resources that they are helping to administer and manage. The most important types of administration for a management system include monitoring, configuration, and access control. Without these types of tools for the management system, administrators will not be able to provide consistent and appropriate coverage for their environments.

The management system itself must be monitored in order to determine when its resources are being oversubscribed. For example, the number of TRAPs or events that a given management platform, intermediate agent, or other element can handle is determined by the processing speed, memory resources, and other processes being supported on that particular hardware environment. A high volume of events or TRAPs may lead to some events either being inappropriately discarded or significant delays in responding to critical situations. Solid management solutions will allow an administrator to set appropriate thresholds to determine when the event volume is beginning to exceed the capacity of that particular element to respond. Such an event or TRAP can be sent to the management system itself to alert the administrator to an imminent situation. A further extension of that could be feedback into the management system itself so that it could, for example, change its event-filtering rules to log lower priority events and insure that processing and response are available for the most serious events that are being reported. This could also be an opportunity to look at the flow of events and determine if the rules have been set incorrectly, allowing too many low-priority events to consume resources, or that it may be an appropriate time to consider placing an intermediate agent "downstream" to aggregate and filter events before they are delivered to this particular element. Without these types of monitoring tools, administrators will essentially be flying blind in terms of their ability to configure their management operations to respond appropriately.

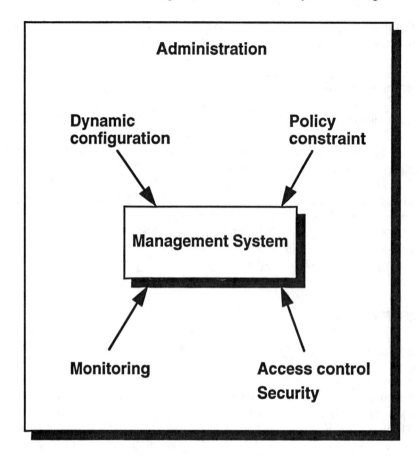

The management system must also be managed with the same types of tools.

FIGURE 2–7   Managing the management system

Configuration

Management systems use considerable resources such as high-performance processors, extensive amounts of memory, large amounts of disk storage, and sets of applications and tools. Just as with any other complicated application environment, the resources must be configured appropriately so that they are in harmony and provide the level of response and capability necessary for adequate management. For example, using high-speed processors with low-speed disks would probably cause performance degradation. In a similar way, the amount of memory must be adequate to support the set of resident processes as well as providing adequate buffering to ensure a smooth and steady flow of information between memory and secondary storage. Disk storage systems themselves must be configured to meet the demands of high-performance management systems. For example, mirroring may be required in order to provide nonstop and fault-tolerant operation. If a particular disk drive fails, a copy of the data is available on the mirrored volume and management operations can continue while repairs or replacements are being effected. High-performance disk systems may also require striping to provide higher speeds of access to the data and lower delays in transfers. Adequate directory space and storage space must be provided so that operations can continue without significant interruptions.

A key determinant of the quality of a management solution will be the ability to reconfigure and restructure the management system while it continues operation. In those organizations that require a 24 × 7 management coverage, systems cannot be brought down for significant amounts of time while the administrator sets tables, checks configuration parameters, and restarts the management environment. The addition of intelligent, adaptable instrumentation (see Chapter 7) will mitigate this problem to some extent since the instrumentation can still collect and hold information while elements "upstream" are being changed or repaired. This, of course, is a stopgap measure, which can provide some level of comfort and safety but is not a foolproof or long-term solution.

Access control and security mechanisms are also critical. Security mechanisms relate to the protection of the management system itself. The management system must be protected from outside, or inside, attacks since taking control of the management system, in a sense, allows an intruder to take control of the corporate information and computing resources. Once the management system has been compromised, attackers could access information they are not entitled to see, or they could just create havoc by changing device settings to cause traffic routing problems, taking devices out of service to reduce service quality and availability, and generally creating a great deal of havoc in the computing environment. Security mechanisms would include encrypted passwords for all staff who are accessing information as well as the same types of intrusion detection mechanisms that are being rolled out to protect clients and servers carrying out company applications.

Access Control

Another level of administration is simply the access control mechanisms provided for the management system itself. Administrators, especially in large environments, will have a staff of people assigned to do different tasks or to handle different parts of the managed environment. Administrators need the capability of determining and constraining the actions that each staff member can take. A typical scenario would have staff members sitting at management consoles, or using their laptop computers as the case may be. When they identify themselves to the management system, they would be provided a view of the resources they are responsible for managing, the sets of tools they are allowed to use to manage those resources, and constraints on the information that they are allowed to access or change. The access control mechanisms must be multilevel in order to provide the granularity of control and protection that will be necessary. For example, junior staff members may be able to monitor critical devices and to do simple analysis. However, making significant changes to key device configurations may be restricted to more senior technical staff who have the appropriate expertise to make the right types of decisions. Another aspect of access control is that the management information itself must be restricted and constrained to the appropriate staff members. For example, a junior staff member who is responsible for managing bridges and routers has no need to look at detailed application information or the activities of the corporate management team. In a similar way, much of the accounting information, data flow information, and so forth can be considered private to the organization itself and not subject to open scrutiny. This is similar to how companies operate now; financial or human resources information is not openly available to any one in the company who would like to look.

2.6 BUILDING PROCESSES

A common data model and single logical repository facilitates the sharing and leveraging of information among the different parts of the management system. The addition of other technologies, such as event management, allows administrators to construct processes. Processes are fundamental to most of the management activities that we carry out on a daily basis.

Processes are defined as collections of tools and staff that are employed in the appropriate sequence. An effective process depends on sequence in much the same way that using the telephone does. For example, it is possible to make some telephones ring by punching in the appropriate number of digits; however, to get a specific phone to ring requires entering those digits in the proper sequence. Many management processes could be highly automated by sharing management information more effectively.

An example of a management process is the periodic checking of network device configurations. A management tool reads each device configuration and checks it against the expected configuration. Any differences trigger further actions, such as reloading the appropriate configuration and issuing a report for the administrator. If unauthorized changes occur frequently, then further steps may be taken to identify the cause or to educate staff. Automation makes these processes easier to implement and monitor. Further details of process design are provided in Chapter 18.

Information management comes into play again. The configuration management tool must be able to access the standard configurations as well as the current configuration in each device. It must also have access to report generating tools and any other tools necessary for following up on frequent problems.

2.7 POLICY

Building policy constraints into automated processes leverages management information in newer, more valuable ways. Policies reflect a business-oriented perspective that is unique to each enterprise. Incorporating policy information allows the administrator to design management processes based on business requirements and constraints rather than simple technical criteria. Policy-based management will be highly effective and will provide the ability to manage complex technology for sustaining and supporting business objectives rather than managing the technology itself. This will represent a substantial change in the types of value that can be delivered by any management solution.

As an example, the server overload mentioned in the vertical automation discussion can be dealt with in several ways. One strategy would simply be to restrict more users from accessing that server. Another approach might be to arbitrarily remove a certain number of users and thereby reduce the server's load. From a policy perspective, the appropriate solution might be application-based: determining the application mix and selecting the mission-critical applications for continued processing while reducing or cutting off the nonessential applications.

Defining mission-critical applications and the policies for allocating resources, preemption, and prioritization allows a management tool to make much more intelligent decisions. Policy must be embedded into the management system, and policy information must be available to all the applications and administrators who need it. It will not be effective or appropriate to depend on management operators and staff to make decisions about the critical activities of their organizations.

All these levels of information management must be addressed in order to provide a comprehensive solution. As these problems are confronted and dealt with, the quality of the management solutions and the value they deliver will increase. All of these levels are necessary in order to ensure that our management applications and operations staff will be able to hit the correct valve as quickly as possible in any circumstance.

2.8 CHARACTERISTICS OF EFFECTIVE SOLUTIONS

Management solutions evolving toward the effectiveness level exhibit some consistent characteristics. Some of these characteristics are also found at other levels, but are not as fully developed.

Leveraging the Management Staff

A key element of any effective solution is its ability to leverage the management staff. Continuing growth and complexity can only be addressed by making each staff member more effective. Each staff member must be able to manage more elements and more complexity or support a larger set of network and systems users.

Automation is one way of increasing staff productivity by relieving them of many repetitive tasks. Centralized management organizations also improve leverage since staff can monitor and control larger numbers of elements.

An essential indicator of increased staff leverage can be found in the time spent on different management tasks. When working with clients, I ask for task breakdowns—the amount of time spent in various areas. One interesting question is "What tasks aren't you doing?". Usually the answers indicate neglect of strategic areas.

Administrators admit that fire fighting takes so much of their time that they have little left to focus on capacity planning, evaluating new technologies, tuning the management systems, and optimizing the systems and networks they manage. Effective solutions free staff from the more mundane tasks and give them time to focus on the strategic tasks that really bring value to the organization.

Cost of Ownership

Cost of ownership includes the hardware and software purchase prices, communications facilities and management staff salaries for operations, planning, user support, administration, and supervision. Most of the life cycle costs for networks and computer systems is taken by administration, support, and operations.

Effective management solutions reduce these costs in several ways. Organizations optimize the expensive resources they use, minimizing spending for excess capacity.

Effective Solutions

Leveraged Staff	**managing more/staff more time for strategic tasks**
Cost of Ownership	**cost avoidance cost reduction deferred expenditures**
Bottom line Impacts	**productivity gains better customer service competitive advantage**
Legacy Management	**incorporation of all resources**
Scalability	**handles increasing growth**

These attributes define an effective management solution. Most also provide better technology management as well.

FIGURE 2–8 Characteristics of effective solutions

Using improved management processes reduces staff costs by shortening times and replacing staff labor with automation. More accurate information allows administrators to plan for future growth and anticipate potential problems.

Bottom-line Impacts

Effective solutions will also have demonstrated impacts on the organization's bottom line. Determining these impacts is more difficult for some organizations than for others. Some measures such as productivity are notoriously difficult to pin down, while others such as revenue loss can be defined in great detail.

A simple way to start with productivity is to consider availability of systems and networks. Productivity can be easily estimated by looking at the salaries of people who cannot use networks and systems to carry out their tasks. Usually, most people can do other tasks while waiting for service to be restored, so a degree of dependence must be estimated. I use the degree of dependence and 100% to give a range of an average productivity loss to maximum impacts. These numbers add up quickly. In one recent case, we estimated that our client was losing a maximum of over $32,000 per year per segment for each 1% downtime on an annual basis.

Other dimensions of productivity are much harder to measure. For example, most organization believe that well-managed networks and systems make it easier for team members to collaborate and move projects along more smoothly. However, these subjective perceptions are hard to quantify.

Revenue losses are easy to estimate in some organizations, and almost impossible for others. For example, an airline reservation network knows that it sells 1,500 tickets per second at peak travel periods. A minute of downtime can mean a large potential loss. Often, these customers will try later and buy the same tickets, making the case that the loss may be minimal. One credit card organization we worked with knows that they authorize over a quarter million dollars a second at peak periods and most customers will use another card if they cannot respond.

Other businesses may not have activities that directly generate revenue. For example, a group of software designers usually doesn't sell its products directly to customers through a network. In other cases one part of the organization may be involved in generating revenue, while other parts design products and manage the business itself.

Leveraged management staff also contribute to the bottom line since they are focusing on the longer-term strategic tasks that eliminate future problems and offer graceful growth and incorporation of new technologies. Reduced ownership costs also add to the bottom-line results.

Legacy Management: Incorporating All Elements

SNMP has won at least the short-term battle as the open management standard. However, most managers must also deal with legacy equipment, which incorporates proprietary

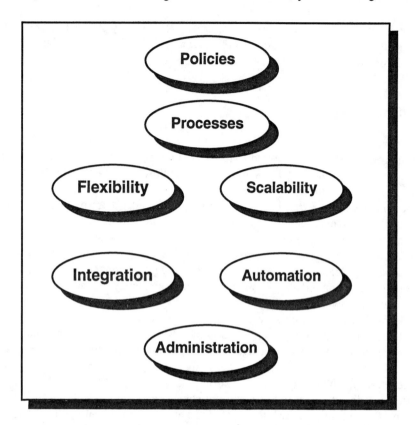

These elements are needed for an effective solution. They deliver more than better business outcomes, however. They also improve our ability to manage the technologies.

FIGURE 2–9   Effective management solutions

agents or, in the worst case, no agent at all. Management solutions must support legacy equipment while moving forward to embrace standards as much as is realistic.

Many products offer a proxy that can translate from legacy to standards or vice versa. These are handy for incorporating older technologies; however, they may also suffer from a lowest-common-denominator problem when certain functions cannot be fully translated.

Scalability: Staying Abreast

Network environments continue to grow and management solutions must keep pace. The environment often grows in a nonlinear way, while good solutions must grow incrementally if costs of ownership and operation are to be contained. Management solutions must deal with growth in desktop systems, servers, networks, applications, and traffic volumes at the same time.

Flexibility: Meeting New Challenges

Flexibility is another important aspect. The management system itself must be reconfigured, reorganized, and possibly relocated. Continued business reengineering changes the organizational structures and business processes, and the management systems are expected to facilitate these changes. Coping with change is easier when the management system can be restructured as necessary.

2.9 SUMMARY

Network administrators need to deliver effective solutions that actually impact the ways that their organizations conduct their business. Policies must be described and embedded into the management system so that they can be enforced and implemented automatically.

Effective solutions depend upon information management; information must be collected, reduced, organized, integrated, and shared. Integration of the information occurs at several levels, the most important being the common repository and the common data model to facilitate information sharing among a set of tools.

Now that we have the requirements in mind, we can turn our attention to the practical issues of building a solution. The next chapter discusses standards and then architectural issues are addressed in Chapter 4.

CHAPTER 3

Standards

This chapter is very short and isn't essential for a practical perspective. Standards are usually positioned as the panacea that soothes our frustrations. Constructing a management solution requires some attention to the practicalities of standards, but few of us, fortunately, need to read the volumes of specifications that the standards efforts produce. This chapter looks at the important standards and relates the efforts to each other. Some architectural terms are used here as well as in Chapter 4.

Standards have always exerted a strong attraction for customers. The primary benefit is interoperability between products from different vendors, which simplifies the construction and integration of disparate types of environments. An active standards-based market drives prices down, forces vendors to innovate continually, and gives the buyer investment protection since there are many sources for products. A wide range of choices is important to allow the customer leverage rather than dealing from a disadvantaged position of being locked into a proprietary solution. These are indeed powerful reasons to seek out and adopt the appropriate standards.

Standardized products also offer the possibility of general-purpose tools. For example, a single tool could manage all computer systems that use standardized management agents and information. This would relieve administrators who use a set of point tools to manage different types of systems such as UNIX, Novell NetWare, IBM OS/2, Microsoft Windows, Banyan Vines, and others.

Standards, however, also have some possible disadvantages. One of the major ones is that standards do not protect against vendor lock-in strategies. The introduction of proprietary SNMP MIB extensions and other types of proprietary enhancements are used to provide a value-added differentiation. If customers come to depend on the proprietary extensions for the foundation of their management solutions, they will, in a sense, be as locked in as with any other type of proprietary approach. However, proprietary extensions encourage innovation and differentiation through quality, a counterbalancing strategy to the trend toward commoditization of standardized products.

Standards may also not be able to drive innovation since they may constrain certain directions of development. Typically, many of the breakthroughs in any technical field comes from a nonstandard innovative approach rather than embellishing an established framework to milk the last increment of optimization. The one major thing that standards cannot do by themselves is provide solutions.

These discussions about advantages and drawbacks have valid points on both sides; often there is little discussion, but heated, partisan struggles that have little to do with delivering solutions. A brief survey of the most important management standards will let us judge for ourselves their value in solving real-world problems.

3.1   STANDARDS OVERVIEW

Multiple management standards are available including SNMP (the Simple Network Management Protocol), CMIP (the Common Management Information Protocol), DMI (the Desktop Management Interface of the Desktop Management Task Force), DME (the Distributed Management Environment), and OMNIPOINT. Administrators should look at all the competing standards issues carefully.

Although we often speak of SNMP or CMIP management, the reality is that standards by themselves do not allow us to manage anything. Today's standards, whether from official standards bodies or de facto groups such as the Internet Engineering Task Force (IETF), are simply basic frameworks upon which solutions are constructed. Current management standards have several related parts: information structures, protocols, APIs, and functions.

Information Structures

Management information structures are the rules for packaging management information so that all elements of a management system can understand it. Naming is one important aspect of describing management information. Network devices, clients, and servers are complex systems; each contains many individual components. An intelligent hub, for instance, has different modules that contain their own processors, memory, and status indicators for routing, bridging, and switching communications servers and other functions. Servers have multiple disk drives, user accounts, and communications interfaces. Naming is necessary to find or change each unique piece of information. Names are usually a series of integers that allow an application to traverse a tree of management information.

MIBs

Management information is organized in an MIB—a **Management Information Base**. The MIB is a collection of static and dynamic management information as well as descriptions of relationships between elements. The MIB is an abstraction: the actual mechanisms for storing and accessing its contents are not explicitly defined. Each management system builds its own schema, access mechanisms, and storage management facilities. Management systems must protect MIB contents in case of management system failures and other types of disruptions.

Status information includes items such as the manufacturer and serial number. Dynamic information describes the actual real-time behavior of a resource. There are several general data types that are used.

Counters   Counters describe operations that are characterized by values that change in a single direction. For example, the count of the number of packets transmitted by an communications interface is monotonically increasing. Counters reach a maximum value and then cycle to zero as they continue monitoring operations.

Gauges   Gauges describe operations that can change in more than one direction. A gauge is used to monitor a server's CPU utilization, for example, which can increase or decrease. An elaboration adds **tide marks,** which capture the maximum or minimum gauge values.

Thresholds   Thresholds are values that are used to detect situations that require attention. A gauge may have several thresholds associated with it, for exceeding a maximum value or falling under a minimum value. Good threshold management prevents hysteresis; a gauge value remaining at the threshold level would trigger an unending series of reports. Most thresholds are implemented so that the value must fall by a certain amount before a new event is triggered.

The above variables represent dynamic values; they change quickly over time. Other MIB variables are more static, including information about the location of equipment, warranties, serial numbers, and software versions, for instance. More complex information structures demand complicated data storage and management services to support them.

Standardized MIBs are in place for SNMP, OSI, and DMTF; ongoing work incorporates new technologies and functions through new definitions. Proprietary management information structures, such as the NMVT (Network Management Vector Transport) for IBM SNA networks, are found in many environments. Complete management solutions must also accommodate these types of "legacy" information models as well.

Planners must be ready for the proprietary MIB extensions that all vendors include. The major drawback to multiple proprietary extensions is the difficulty in writing a generic resource management application that can gracefully incorporate multiple incompatible extensions. This forces network and system managers to buy many point tools, each of which is specially tailored to exploit a proprietary extension. A large set of point tools is confusing to the staff since they may use an incorrect tool to solve what they think of as a generic problem. Integration between and among network and system management tools is also complicated by the numbers of tools doing almost the same function, but using very different conventions and procedures.

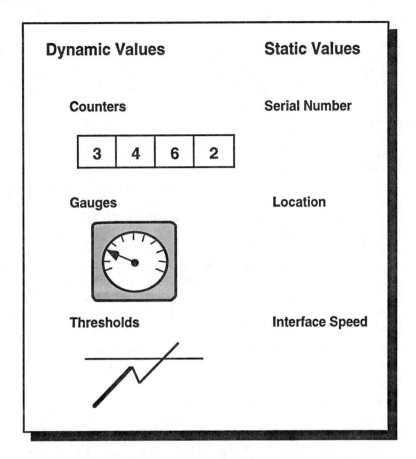

The Management information Base holds the
information that describes a managed resource. MIB
variables such as counters and gauges are dynamic
while others like serial numbers are static.

FIGURE 3–1   MIB structures

Hide the MIBs!!

MIBs are very important; however, their details should remain invisible in most cases.
MIBs are complex since they hold information about a complex environment. In fact, MIBs
were designed for applications to search and manipulate in place of humans. As a case
in point, any SNMP MIB variable is identified by a string of integers, such as
1.3.6.2.7.6.4.3. A program uses these integers to easily traverse a simple tree, beginning
with its root. The tree is traversed to find particular instances of MIB variables. Although

such a naming scheme is simple for an application to parse and trace, it is not friendly to a system administrator. Tracing through the tree itself may be cumbersome even with graphical tools that work with pulldown menus at each branching point.

Good management applications must shield an administrator from any direct contact with the MIB. The management application itself should help select the appropriate MIB variables and transform raw information into more useful processed forms for the administrator to use. Only an expert troubleshooter requires direct access in extreme circumstances. Products that emphasize their ability to navigate the MIB are indicating that they lacked the effort to build tools that make such navigation tasks unnecessary in the first place.

Another factor that dictates the hiding of MIBs behind better management application is their increasing complexity. Simple MIBs contain variables reflecting actual operational status, packet counts, error counts, and so forth. More sophisticated MIBs, such as the RMON MIB, use more complex variables that control other parts of the MIB. For instance, the RMON MIB has interlocking capabilities so that different applications can coordinate their changes to MIB variables. MIBs will become increasingly complex to provide more appropriate information and solutions. However, the increasing complexity will outstrip most administrator's ability to understand and remember all of the particular functions, interlocks, and constraints with the more sophisticated MIBs.

MIBs are proliferating at a rapid rate as new elements are incorporated into a management framework. In the SNMP world, MIBs are defined to extend management to newly developed technologies as well as to fold in existing equipment that was not originally designed for SNMP management.

Summary—MIBs

The battles over the particular information models appear to be tilting in favor of the object-oriented frameworks. The real value will be in the applications that can take information from different sources, integrate it, and use it in a way that provides a more effective solution. The ability to organize the information is one of the key requirements of a successful management solution.

It does appear that object-oriented technology will simplify the developer's task by allowing more reuse of written software, simpler development environments, and faster time to market. Historically speaking, however, the computer industry has seen improving application development tools since the first assembler was written over thirty years ago. It's not clear from the customer's perspective that all these improvements in the developer's lot have led to more creative, original, and valuable applications for the customer.

Protocols

Management protocols allow information exchange between parts of the management system. Protocols have packaging rules defining the structures of all exchanges—where the control fields and data are located, allowed values, and other rules. Protocols also have rules controlling the dialog, who initiates an exchange, how errors are reported, and the appropriate responses for various situations.

Application Programming Interfaces

Application Programming Interfaces (APIs) are used by management applications to access services. Standard APIs simplify the design of management applications and attract Independent Software Vendors with a larger potential market. APIs defines the procedures for communication, the parameters that are exchanged, and responses to requests. However, the important APIs are the ones provided by the management platforms. The major attraction of standard APIs is easier porting of management tools between different environments: a standard API reduces the amount of customization that is needed. Standard APIs should attract more Independent Software Vendors since they offer a larger market opportunity. Customers win by having a larger selection of tools on the computers of their choice, in theory.

Functions

Standards also describe certain functions that are performed by the management environment. Some functionality is minimal, such as the SNMP Get and SET operations, which allow a manager to obtain or change information in a remote agent. The object-based operations in the OSI management standards define a range of complex functions such as testing, filtering events, and logging information.

We'll do a very quick review of the important standards efforts in network and systems management.

3.2 SNMP

The **Simple Network Management Protocol** has won the short-term battle for dominance: it has succeeded dramatically and is the de facto worldwide standard for managing heterogeneous networking environments. It would take an extensive search to find any LAN devices (hubs, bridges, routers, and switches) that do not offer an SNMP agent and management tool. SNMP has spread to other environments such as SNA (IBM's System Network Architecture), Frame Relay, and ATM. Even the telecommunications carriers, staunch advocates of CMIP, have introduced SNMP management interfaces for their network services. Rapid evolution and aggressive incorporation of new MIB definitions has kept SNMP moving forward in terms of its ability to manage more complex and varied environments.

Basic Architecture

The design goals of SNMP were focused upon the creation of simple and cheap agents that offered the following advantages: simple agents were reasonably robust with few places for failure, and simple agents were also inexpensive to implement, thereby attracting many vendors with a low investment for significant market opportunity. Further, cheap and simple agents used fewer resources in the devices in which they were embedded, reducing their impact on performance and throughput.

The manager-agent architecture centers around simple agents feeding basic information to a sophisticated and powerful manager at a remote site. Agents communicate with the managers through an information structure centered on the MIB (Management Information Base).

Management actions are carried out through changing MIB values. For example, a server could be instructed to disconnect all users by setting a variable defining the number of allowed active processes to zero. When the agent detects that change in the MIB variable, the appropriate actions are carried out to complete the remote management request.

Poll/Response

Managers and agents communicate with a simple transaction-based poll/response mechanism. The manager initiates most of the activities and uses time-outs to detect possible lost requests. Agents respond to requests to supply MIB variables or change them. Agents also send unsolicited TRAPs to indicate sudden changes in state that require immediate attention from the remote manager.

While a poll/response style of communication is simple, it does not scale well. Polling a growing numbers of agents consumes more network bandwidth and adds processing loads to the manager. (Chapter 6, "Instrumentation," covers this issue.) Intermediate agents have been introduced to accommodate larger numbers of agents. More intelligent agents are being offered to provide more effective management operations.

The MIB

The SNMP MIB contains the management information for a resource. The MIB is a simple, tabular data store. SNMP uses simple variables to model a managed resource. A communications interface has static information describing the type, media, manufacturer, and other parameters that do not change. Other variables track the number of packets transferred, transmission errors, discarded packets, and other operational information. A system with multiple interfaces would have the variables organized as rows in a table, with each row representing a single instance of an interface.

The SNMP MIB contains simple variables such as integers, counters (a quantity that continues to increase monotonically, monitoring the number of packets through a communications interface, for example), gauges (integers whose value can change in either direction and with variable magnitudes), strings, and object identifiers.

Status

SNMP has proven itself as an open, interoperable standard with hundreds of vendors offering products. However, interoperability suffers from the proliferation of proprietary extensions to the standardized MIBs. These proprietary extensions, while adding extra value to management solutions, also lock customers into the vendor. Only the vendor's management applications can exploit the features in the proprietary extensions. Proprietary extensions will continue to grow as vendors continue to differentiate on management capabilities.

SNMP continues to evolve with the creation of new MIBs that incorporate new technologies and environments. For example, there are MIBs for monitoring and managing DECnet Phase IV Networks, SNA Network Addressable Units, Frame Relay, and ATM Services with many more MIB definitions under development (see the references at the end of this chapter). The proliferation of MIB definitions fuels the continued incorporation of new and emerging technologies into an SNMP management framework.

The introduction of SNMP Version 2 has addressed shortcomings in the initial SNMP specifications. In some ways, SNMP was too simple for large-scale enterprise management. For example, SNMP Version 2 can now be used across multiple transport networks, as well as the traditional TCP/IP Internet. For example, SNMP could be used to manage devices and resources across a proprietary NetWare IPX network, an SNA network, or even an OSI network.

Version 2 also supports a bulk transfer feature, making the transfer of large amounts of information much more effective than with SNMP Version 1. The old poll/response cycles require many transactions in order to move a large object, such as a routing table with hundreds of entries. A single bulk transfer request, in contrast, could move the entire table with one operation.

Version 2 also added security mechanisms, supplanting the simple community string idea of Version 1 (basically an open password). Version 2 provides different authentication mechanisms to verify the identity of agents and managers before any management operations are carried out. Additional privacy is provided by encryption mechanisms that protect the management information from interception. The major problems with the acceptance of the security mechanisms revolve around both technical and political issues.

SNMP Version 2 has been slow to enter the marketplace because of several factors. The first is the political issues involved in the export of cryptographic algorithms. It is an unenforceable restriction, but it stops major vendors and corporations from providing and using Version 2. There is also more complexity in the authentication and security mechanisms which have given some vendors pause when they consider potential performance impacts. The major obstacle may actually be that Version 2 is not fully compatible with the initial version of SNMP.

The technical issues center on the resources required to carry out complex encryption and authentication procedures, which may result in performance degradation or price increases for manageable devices. The political issues revolve around legal constraints covering exporting encryption technology across national boundaries. Any type of open framework must be able to work in a multinational environment with the ability to share such things as encryption technology and keys.

3.3   OSI/CCITT STANDARDS

International standards have been developed by the Organization for Standardization and the Consultative Committee on Telecommunications and Telephony. Often known by the protocol name, CMIP, these standards cover a large number of areas including object models, interfaces, and functions.

Basic Architecture

The international standards also use a manager-agent architecture. The difference from SNMP is that the agents have considerable intelligence. They can collect information, test for conditions, and carry out tasks locally. They are under the ultimate control of a remote manager, but they are considerably more complex.

Communication

Communication can use a poll/response mechanism. Smarter agents also allow for management by exceptions. The agents monitor activities and signal the remote manager when important events occur.

The MIB

In contrast, CMIP uses an object-oriented approach, building abstractions of managed elements, such as devices, computer systems, or applications. The internal operations of an object are invisible to the applications that manage them. New objects can be easily created from existing objects as new needs arise. For example, a generic server object could have many descendants, all having the same basic characteristics of a server, but having extensions that define them for particular vendor products, implementations, or characteristics. Objects are also discussed in the information management section of Chapter 2.

Status

CMIP has been the main competitor to SNMP as an open standard. The OSI/CCITT specifications enjoy the status of "officially" endorsed standards. These standards have been slow to market—a common shortcoming with the entire suite of OSI standards. Further, these standards have been tied to OSI standard networks, although there is no sound technical reason for this exclusivity.

Telecommunications carriers are adopting CMIP as a means of managing their complex hierarchical switching networks. CMIP is well suited for this restricted environment and most major carriers are already underway with their management plans.

A more complex intelligent agent may pay off in the future in terms of scalability (see Chapter 6, "Instrumentation"). However, this complexity also dictates a much more difficult and expensive implementation for CMIP agents. The additional agent resources that are required may also impact the performance or the price of the managed element.

CMIP will continue to grow slowly, finding acceptance in particular vertical markets. However, general widespread adoption is hindered by the lack of quality products and the fact that in many environments new CMIP products will have to displace established SNMP solutions.

Vendors that have invested heavily in CMIP are taking another approach—repackaging the entire effort as a value-added solution, OMNIPoint.

3.4 OMNIPOINT

OMNIPoint is a set of specifications developed by the Network Management Forum, a consortium of management vendors and government agencies. OMNIPoint aims to educate users, encouraging them to write procurement requirements and requests for proposals that mandate OSI-based management solutions.

Basic Architecture

OMNIPoint doesn't define new technical standards, it focuses on packaging the pieces instead. The basic OSI management framework is used as the OMNIPoint infrastructure.

Contributions are in higher-level definitions of **ensembles.** An ensemble is a collection of functions and requirements that deals with a particular management requirement. Ensembles have been defined for areas such as reconfigurable circuit assignment, configuration management, and alarm surveillance, with more to come. The ensembles and functional requirements are very helpful since they define particular steps, processes, and functions that must be included for a good management solution.

Another strong point of the OMNIPoint specifications are the process-flow descriptions that outline detailed steps for doing problem management, change management, and other types of tasks. Complex procedures are simplified by detailing specific steps and choices. Standard procedures can be created and offered by a variety of vendors.

OMNIPoint also has several limitations that must be considered. One is the focus toward managing telecommunications networks. Many of the initial ensembles and object definitions support the kinds of services that telecommunications carriers provide, such as provisioning, reconfiguration, path tracing, and so forth. Many other functions that would be necessary for managing an internetwork or a LAN environment have not yet been specified.

Another drawback is the continued emphasis toward selection of OSI-based products. This is retarding the momentum to some extent because many administrators have not yet been able to see demonstrated value from CMIP-based products.

Although the Network Management Forum has acknowledged the existence of

SNMP and talks about transition and coexistence strategies, there is still a predominant OSI focus. The longer term value OMNIPoint offers is in the definition of processes and functional requirements. Many solutions can be designed to provide this type of functionality and insulate it from the details of whether the information structures are SNMP or OSI-based.

In any case, good management applications will support multiple information frameworks since a heterogeneous environment is a reality.

3.5   DME

The Distributed Management Environment (DME) was sponsored by the Open Software Foundation. The goals were to (1) define the appropriate framework for managing distributed systems and networks; (2) to have a technology "bake-off" to find the best components for the framework; (3) integrate all the pieces into a coherent product; and (4) license DME to vendors who would incorporate it into their products.

Basic Architecture

DME used an object-based framework that supports a complement of distributed applications such as PC management, software distribution, licensing, and printer management. Open APIs would attract third party management tool vendors to build a wide selection of DME-compliant products. SNMP management would also be provided.

Status

DME has floundered and has the potential of completely disappearing. The Open Software Foundation appears to be withdrawing its support and leadership for the integration of the CORBA (Common Object Request Broker Architecture) technology into the distributed management framework. Without this crucial piece of technology, the rationale for DME collapses and it has no demonstrated value to customers.

Many vendors have adopted DME concepts and their products are providing some of the functionality DME promised. Consolidation of platforms has simplified the task for ISVs; there are fewer platforms that they must port to. The market and technologies are passing DME by.

3.6   DMTF

The Desktop Management Task Force is a vendor consortium that wants to standardize management interfaces and formats for computer systems with the DMI. (See Chapter 16, "Managing Computer Systems.")

Status

The DMTF has completed the basic specifications, and vendors are designing standard information formats for different components such as systems, printers, servers, applications, and others. Important computer manufacturers such as Hewlett-Packard, Sun Microsystems, IBM, Digital, Dell, AST, and Compaq have plans to incorporate DMTF. The major operating systems vendors Microsoft and Novell are also endorsing DMTF. There are several obstacles to DMI's success: the major one is to have the significant players fully comply with specifications so that the promised array of systems management tools and manageable components will be delivered for all major desktop and server platforms.

It is too early to proclaim DMTF a success, but they are on schedule and are addressing a painful management problem. We will probably depend more on vendor consortia rather than the official processes (a disconcerting thought).

3.7   THE OFFICIAL PROCESS IS BROKEN

The official international standards bodies that supported the development of CMIP and its attendant framework use a process that is no longer suited to the world we live and work in and the environments that we must manage today. In particular, the limitations of the official standards process can be shown in these following examples.

The development time for CMIP and the attendant ISO management framework has spanned over ten years and the work is not yet completed. This leads to vendors dominating this slow and expensive process, surely a conflict of interest. Vendors want ways of securing their markets, and commodity-based standard products will not suffice.

Much of the official standards work is not subjected to public scrutiny or feedback until late in the process, resulting in further work to address shortcomings that were not detected earlier. Further, a standard is adopted before there is any proof of concept. There are no prototypes constructed and large, complex standards are adopted without the certainty that they can actually be implemented in an effective and economical way.

Even if products can be implemented to the CMIP standards, there is still no guarantee that they will actually interoperate. Designing and testing for interoperability is a complex, poorly understood task that requires a great deal of time and money. Waiting until the end can seriously delay the introduction of products that could exploit these standards.

In Contrast

The SNMP development, in contrast, was supported by the IETF, the Internet Engineering Task Force, which oversees the development of standards for the Internet community. The IETF asked for proposals for a management solution for the Internet and allowed all the contenders a period of time to build solutions, demonstrate their value, and collect allies and supporters within the community.

As a study in differences, these are how the results compared to the CMIP effort. The initial SNMP specifications were completed in a period of two years, and products were introduced almost immediately. The Internet community required several things before SNMP was adopted as a standard. The first is that at least three implementations be successfully completed to demonstrate that the specifications themselves are clear and unambiguous. This further demonstrates the feasibility of building products based on these standards and identifies any problems that the specifications may introduce.

A further step to standardization is a demonstration of interoperability between the independent implementations. Before something becomes an Internet standard, it is constructed, it is debugged, and proven to be interoperable. Quite a contrast to the official standards creation process.

The initial simple goals of SNMP attracted a large community of vendors willing to take a low risk opportunity in order to participate in a potentially large market. The rapid introduction of interoperable products, as well as the aggressive extension of MIB definitions, has allowed SNMP to rapidly move beyond its initial niche.

Another improvement that the Internet process offers is an open and public development of Internet standards. The Internet drafts and the RFCs (Requests for Comments) are available on many public Internet sites. A relatively silly idea is rapidly exposed to the ridicule of the Internet community and adjusted quickly. This provides higher quality solutions with early detection of oversights.

In comparison, the official process is relatively closed. These types of forces and factors continue to keep the international standards lagging behind the areas that really need addressing. The widespread introduction and acceptance of an OSI-based management framework is many years away, if it occurs at all. It is more likely that CMIP, SNMP, and other types of management protocols will continue to coexist for an indefinite time.

3.8 THE REAL VALUE

The real value is not in the standards, but in the applications that use the management information. Much of the information processing, organization, representation, and logging functions are carried out independently of whether an SNMP or a CMIP agent reported an event. Sophisticated applications originally developed in the SNMP world can be modified to accept a different type of structured information. Administrators will continue to focus on the pragmatic: finding solutions that save money, improve quality of service, leverage their staffs, and move the organization forward.

CMIP must still prove itself by placing products in real networks and proving that they can deliver substantial value. CMIP may have some advantage in the emerging switched environments where such features as multiple object selection, scoping, and filtering can be exploited for switching. Many of these functions are not as easily applied to the current connectionless Internets.

Standards are important for long-term planning. SNMP is the standard for short-term solutions. DMTF has a good chance to standardize desktop management. Administrators and planners must trade between moving toward a solution that addresses immediate needs and waiting for products based on official standards. There are advantages in solving problems now; the savings achieved with effective management can lead to a short time for a return on investment. Management technologies can be upgraded as needed. There are also the dangers of moving too soon as several early OSI champions learned; the market evaporated and vendor plans were scaled back.

Summary

Standards are important for the long-term perspective, and any organization should try to position itself to exploit any advantage they might offer. However, administrators have been burned by being "religious" rather than pragmatic such as those who were on CMIP years ago and had no products to work with. Look for what you can buy and what you can use. Nonstandard products that solve a tough problem may pay for themselves in a short period of time while standards mature.

The reality is that SNMP is the victor and there are plenty of management tools and managed products that use SNMP. CMIP will never be the panacea; it may have a restricted role for managing internal networks for telecommunications vendors. The systems management area is still settling. Proprietary solutions abound while DMI is trying to get a foothold.

REFERENCES

Internet Engineering Task Force RFCs and Work in Progress

[1612 PS] R. Austein, J. Saperia, "DNS Resolver MIB Extensions," 05/17/1994.

[1611 PS] R. Austein, J. Saperia, "DNS Server MIB Extensions," 05/17/1994.

[1593 I] W. McKenzie, and J. Cheng, "SNA APPN Node MIB," 03/10/1994.

[1573 PS] K. McCloghrie, and F. Kastenholz, "Evolution of the Interfaces Group of MIB-II", 01/20/1994.

[1567 PS] G. Mansfield, and S. Kille, "X.500 Directory Monitoring MIB," 01/11/1994.

[1566 PS] N. Freed, and S. Kille, "Mail Monitoring MIB," 01/11/1994.

[1565 PS] N. Freed, and S. Kille, "Network Services Monitoring MIB," 01/11/1994.

[1559 DS] J. Saperia, "DECnet Phase IV MIB Extensions," 12/27/1993.

[1514 PS] P. Grillo, and S. Waldbusser, "Host Resources MIB," 09/23/1993.

[1512 PS] J. Case, and A. Rijsinghani, "FDDI Management Information Base," 09/10/1993.

[1461 PS] D. Throop, "SNMP MIB extension for MultiProtocol Interconnect over X.25," 05/27/1993.

[1447 PS] K. McCloghrie, and J. Galvin, "Party MIB for version 2 of the Simple Network Management Protocol (SNMPv2)," 05/03/1993.

[1446 PS] J. Galvin, and K. McCloghrie, "Security Protocols for version 2 of the Simple Network Management Protocol (SNMPv2)," 05/03/1993.

[1445 PS] J. Davin, and K. McCloghie, "Administrative Model for version 2 of the Simple Network Management Protocol (SNMPv2)," 05/03/1993.

[1444 PS] J. Case, K. McCloghrie, M. Rose, and S. Waldbusser, "Conformance Statements for version 2 of the Simple Network Management Protocol (SNMPv2)," 05/03/1993.

[1443 PS] J. Case, K. McCloghrie, M. Rose, and S. Waldbusser, "Textual Conventions for version 2 of the Simple Network Management Protocol (SNMPv2)," 05/03/1993.

[1442 PS] J. Case, K. McCloghrie, M. Rose, and S. Waldbusser, "Structure of Management Information for version 2 of the Simple Network Management Protocol (SNMPv2)," 05/03/1993.

[1441 PS] J. Case, K. McCloghrie, M. Rose, and S. Waldbusser, "Introduction to version 2 of the Internet-standard Network Management Framework," 05/03/1993.

[1389 PS] G. Malkin, and F. Baker, "RIP Version 2 MIB Extension," 01/06/1993.

[1382 PS] D. Throop, "SNMP MIB Extension for the X.25 Packet Layer," 11/10/1992.

[1381 PS] D. Throop, and F. Baker, "SNMP MIB Extension for X.25 LAPB," 11/10/1992.

[1369 I]   F. Kastenholz, "Implementation Notes and Experience for The Internet Ethernet MIB," 10/23/1992.

[1368 PS] D. McMaster, and K. McCloghrie, "Definitions of Managed Objects for IEEE 802.3 Repeater Devices," 10/26/1992.

[1289 PS] J. Saperia, "DECnet Phase IV MIB Extensions," 12/20/1991.

[1231 DS] E. Decker, R. Fox, and K. McCloghrie, "IEEE 802.5 Token Ring MIB."

[1214 H]   L. Labarre, "OSI Internet Management: Management Information Base," 04/05/1991.

[1213 S]   K. McCloghrie, and M. Rose, "Management Information Base for Network Management of TCP/IP-based internets: MIB-II," 03/26/1991.

[1158 PS] M. Rose, "Management Information Base for Network Management of TCP/IP-based internets: MIB-II," 05/23/1990.

[1157 S]   M. Schoffstall, M. Fedor, J. Davin, and J. Case, "A Simple Network Management Protocol (SNMP)," 05/10/1990.

Working Groups

AToM MIB (atommib)
   To join: atommib-request@thumper.bellcore.com
Bridge MIB (bridge)
   To join: bridge-mib-request@decwrl.dec.com
Character MIB (charmib)
   To join: char-mib-request@decwrl.dec.com
DECnet Phase IV MIB (decnetiv)
   To join: phiv-mib-request@jove.pa.dec.com
FDDI MIB (fddimib)
   To join: fddi-mib-request@cs.utk.edu
Frame Relay Service MIB (frnetmib)
   To join: frftc-request@nsco.network.com

Host Resources MIB (hostmib)
  To join: hostmib-request@andrew.cmu.edu
IEEE 802.3 Hub MIB (hubmib)
  To join: hubmib-request@baynetworks.com
Interfaces MIB (ifmib)
  To join: if-mib-request@thumper.bellcore.com
Mail and Directory Management (madman)
  To join: mailserv@innosoft.com (body: "subscribe ietf-madman")
Modem Management (modemmgt)
  To join: majordomo@Telebit.com
Remote Monitoring (rmonmib)
  To join: rmonmib-request@jarthur.claremont.edu
SNA DLC Services MIB (snadlc)
  To join: snadlcmib-request@apertus.com
SNA NAU Services MIB (snanau)
  To join: snadnaumib-request@thumper.bellcore.com
SNMP version 2 (snmpv2)
  To join: snmp2-request@thumper.bellcore.com
Token Ring Remote Monitoring (trmon)
  To join: rmonmib-request@jarthur.claremont.edu
Trunk MIB (trunkmib)
  To join: trunk-mib-request@saffron.acc.com
Uninterruptible Power Supply (upsmib)
  To join: ups-mib-request@cs.utk.edu
X.25 Management Information Base (x25mib)
  To join: x25mib-request@dg-rtp.dg.com

Network Management Forum

OmniPoint Series
Morristown, NJ, USA

CCITT (Consultative Committee on Telephony and Telegraphy)

Series X.700
Geneva, Switzerland

PART II

MANAGEMENT INFRASTRUCTURE

The second part focuses on management infrastructure issues. Chapter 4 discusses the architectural alternatives that dictate the range of choices for building an effective management environment. Chapter 5 introduces General Widgets, Inc., a pseudonym for an actual organization. General Widgets will be used as appropriate examples in following chapters. Chapters 6 through 10 discuss basic management disciplines that are needed: instrumentation, event management, automated discovery, problem management, and inventory management.

The role of the management platform as an integration point for management tools is covered in Chapter 11. Part II concludes with Chapter 12, where actual platforms are discussed.

CHAPTER 4

ARCHITECTURE

This chapter covers the basic architectural issues involved with determining the types of management elements, their deployment, and choices for structuring the management environment. The architectural principles discussed here will guide some of the basic choices in building an effective management solution.

4.1 MANAGER-AGENT ARCHITECTURE

The manager-agent approach is the basic foundation of standards-based and proprietary management architectures. Managers and agents are management system elements that play different roles. However, managers and agents can change their roles within the management system.

Agents—the Worker Bees

Agents are the basic workers in the management environment. Each agent is engineered for the particular resource that they help manage. Agents usually have at least two logical parts: one that is interfaced to a specific type of resource and the other that provides a standard means of communicating through a management protocol and an information structure. Only the standard portion is visible to the rest of the management system. The agent converts the standard commands and information into forms that allow the resource-specific portion to monitor and control the resource. One agent may access operating system tables and configuration files while another reads internal hardware registers.

Agents are mostly passive and are controlled by a remote manager. The simplest agents await instructions from the manager before carrying out any task, while more so-

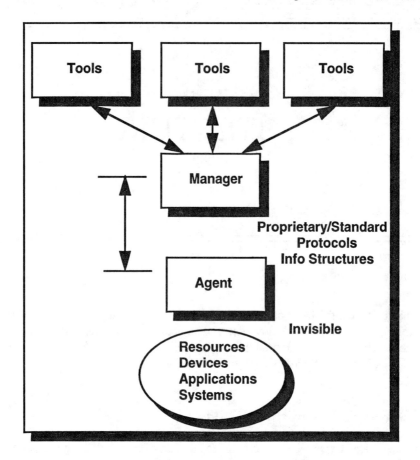

Management tools interact with an agent. Manager and
agent use a protocol and information structure to
exchange information. The agent's interaction with
managed resources are invisible.

FIGURE 4–1   Managers and agents

phisticated agents have a degree of autonomy. Even sophisticated agents are ultimately
constrained by the remote manager, however.

Agents supply management information as requested (such as an SNMP GET request). They extract the requested operational information, whether from device registers
or software tables, and package it according to information structuring rules (SNMP, OSI,
etc.) before delivering it to a remote manager. Sophisticated agents can continuously
monitor a resource and report exceptional conditions to a manager. The agent monitors

selected operational parameters and compares against predefined thresholds or other types of criteria. When the criteria are satisfied, the agent signals the manager that these predefined conditions have been satisfied. The manager still controls the agent's actions by selecting threshold values or other conditions for reporting.

Agents can also modify the behavior of a managed resource under direction of the manager (the SNMP SET or the OSI SET or ACTION). More sophisticated agents can take automatic local action without waiting for a remote manager to intervene. This trend will emerge to free the central manager from micromanaging details. It will also increase the ability to scale management solutions for large environments since some processing is performed by each agent rather than by a single manager.

	Simple Agents	Intelligent Agents
Cost	lower	higher
Performance impact	lower	higher?
Bandwidth	higher	lower
Scaling	poorer	better
Local decisions	no	possible

Each type of agent offers advantages and drawbacks, there is a balance between processing and bandwidth.

FIGURE 4–2   Agent trade-offs

Agents only act on their own if exceptional conditions arise; these situations require prompt attention from a management application. A failure of a disk drive on a critical server, for instance, must be reported as quickly as possible to minimize the impacts of such a failure.

There are trade-offs to be considered between the simplest agents and their more sophisticated descendants. The simplest agents, such as those specified for SNMP, provide raw information to a remote site and change information as instructed. Simple agents are inexpensive to implement and do not consume many resources themselves. Lower resource consumption reduces the chance of the agent degrading performance of a managed resource.

The drawback with a simple agent is that some other management element must process the information and make decisions for the agent. This involves more management traffic between a simple agent and its remote manager. Also, a remote manager usually controls a group of agents and must have the capacity to handle all their decisions. Increasing the numbers of agents places more burdens on the remote manager.

Smarter agents are able to provide more local collection and processing. Actions can be carried out locally without direct involvement of the remote manager. Increasing local agent activities reduces the communications between manager and agent, thereby reducing bandwidth consumed for management purposes and the loads on the manager. As more powerful processors, cheaper memory, and sophisticated ASICs (Application-Specific Integrated Circuits) are added to products, agents will become more intelligent and autonomous without degrading performance.

Managers

Managers are the active components in the system, directing the activities of collections of agents. Managers are responsible for packaging a request to an agent, carrying out the communication, retrieving the expected or requested information, and passing it to the requesting application. In actuality, managers are driven by the management application toolset and are merely a utility for communicating with the remote agents in order to obtain the information or cause the intended actions.

The management tools, or the staff using management tools, actually make the decisions about what information is required or what actions must be undertaken. The manager simply passes the information between a management application and the appropriate remote agent. So the manager is nothing more than a utility to support a wide collection of management applications.

Manager-Agent Deployment Options

Managers and agents may be deployed in real environments in many ways. Combinations allow for different types of management structures and partitioning of functions that best meet the demands of any organization.

Multiple managers can communicate with any agent, offering the ability for functional partitioning. For example, an operational manager may contain tools that carry out fault, performance, and configuration management functions since they are so closely coupled. A separate manager could be used to collect accounting information and process it separately. In the same way, a separate security manager in a physically protected environment could be used to monitor and collect security violations as well as assist in the distribution of security-related information to each agent.

Other types of multiple manager schemes can also be employed so that a backup or standby manager is known to the agent. In that case, the failure of the primary manager does not disrupt management operations significantly since the agent will simply switch to the secondary manager and continue reporting as necessary.

Multiple Agents

Networking devices and computer systems are becoming more complex. Often a system or device is a collection of other elements. For example, an intelligent hub is not simply a smart repeater anymore. The same chassis contains bridging modules, routers, switches, and file servers, with other new components to be added on an ongoing basis. Each of these individual components is in effect a separate, independent device with its own management agent. Servers may contain add-in boards for routing or network monitoring while desktops can contain FAX or video cards.

Complex products can have multiple agents for all the different components they contain. From a communications point of view, however, there is only one IP address for that device. Such things as the SNMP Multiplexer (SMUX) is one mechanism that allows multiplexing a data stream between a set of agents in a device and a single remote manager.

A manager may also control and monitor a set of distinct agents. This is the common structure that initial manager-agents solutions used.

Multiple Managers

There are situations where an agent can have multiple managers. For example, an agent may forward operational status and event reports to one manager while sending security-related information to another. Organizations may want separate managers to deal with different types of management tasks with the same agent. Multiple managers may also be used to provide a higher degree of management availability. If an agent loses connection with one manager, it can direct subsequent reports to another on standby. A more reliable delivery mechanism will help this type of operation; the connectionless, nonacknowledged UDP traffic may be lost without notification.

Proxy Agents

Proxy agents are required when there is equipment that does not support the standardized management information structures and protocols used by the organization. Much of this so called "legacy" equipment will remain in operation for many years and must be accom-

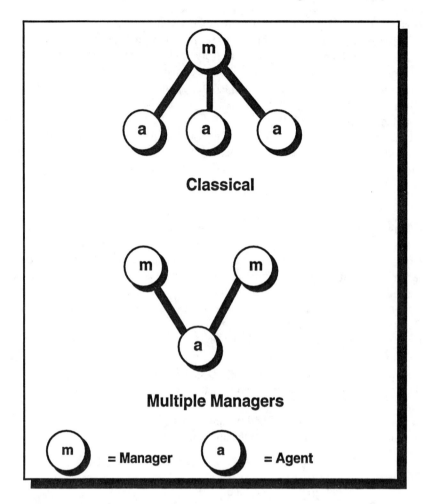

The classical approach uses a manager to direct a set of agents. Multiple managers can also oversee a single agent.

FIGURE 4–3   Manager-agent deployment

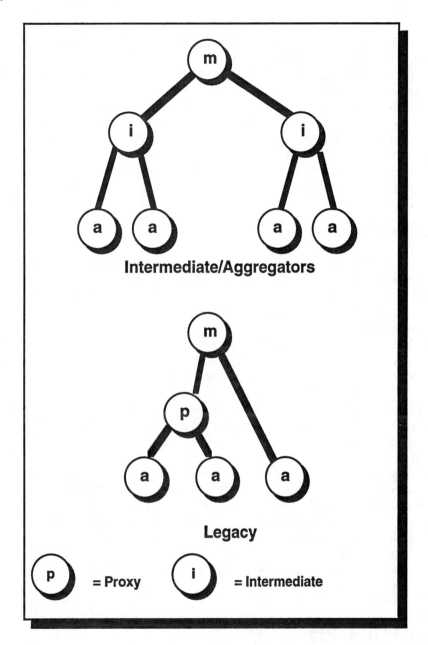

Intermediate agents can aggregate information for a manager while proxy agents offer translation.

FIGURE 4–3   *Continued*

modated into any enterprise-level solution. A proxy agent is basically a translator that maps information from a proprietary management system into whatever management standards the enterprise has selected.

For example, an SNMP proxy translates SNMP MIB variables into their appropriate counterparts in any type of a proprietary information framework. In the same way, the SNMP proxy agent would translate SNMP directives into the appropriate proprietary commands and responses. Although proxy agents allow easier incorporation of proprietary or legacy equipment, the proxy approach typically suffers from a lowest common denominator problem. Only the lowest or the least functional mappings can be supported. Much of the richness from either the proprietary or the SNMP side may be lost because there is no appropriate way to translate it into a lower level of functionality and representation.

Intermediate Agents

Intermediate agents are appearing in many architectures as a way to address some of the scalability and bandwidth problems. Intermediate agents are placed between simple agents that are embedded in devices, systems, and applications, and remote management sites. Of course, intermediate agents can be layered themselves if additional levels of data consolidation are needed.

Intermediate agents handle local management activities, such as polling and data collection from simple agents, helping to scale the solution. For example, an intermediate agent at the end of a wide-area link eliminates all the polling traffic that would be needed for each individual agent. Without an intermediate agent at the end of the wide area link, many individual poll/request cycles would consume a larger proportion of scarce bandwidth. Many wide-area links are up to 200 or more times slower than the LANs they interconnect, becoming a potential application-level bottleneck if management traffic is too heavy.

Intermediate agents across Wide Area Networks may also reduce costs when many WAN services are billed on a usage or connection time basis. The intermediate agent only forwards information to the remote manager when there is something that requires further attention. The majority of local polling activities usually find no problems and that bandwidth is saved. Intermediate agents will take on more functions in the future.

There are many combinations of managers and agents that are used in real environments. The next section discusses a formal way of describing the different types of management activities that can be performed.

4.2 FUNCTIONAL AREAS

Management tasks and processes can be organized into one or more functional areas. The basic functional areas were defined as part of the OSI management framework and have been accepted as a common way of describing tasks for any management environment. The functional areas are fault, configuration, performance, security, and accounting management.

Fault Management

Fault management is self-defined, it is involved with all those tasks and processes required to maintain network and systems availability. Fault management involves detecting and reporting faults to the appropriate management site. Faults are detected through polling and other types of monitoring operations, as well as by collecting unsolicited reports of trouble. Fault management is basically a survival level management function.

Fault information must be logged so that longer-term analysis can be applied to determine the relative failure rates of different network and systems components, the mean times to restore service, and other types of information. Logging is very useful for understanding the fault management process.

Once a fault has been detected, the cause of the failure must be quickly identified so that the necessary actions can be initiated to restore service. Testing and diagnostic tools are needed to pinpoint the problem as quickly as possible. Repair and resolution procedures must be followed in order to replace a failed component or take other steps to restore it to normal activity. Finally, appropriate testing procedures must be followed before the failed element is restored to service.

The remaining functional areas address the efficiency and effectiveness concerns.

Configuration Management

Configuration management deals with the information that describes the state of all elements in a complex network environment. For example, a router has information describing each communications interface, the protocols that are to be routed, and the necessary routing metrics for relaying traffic. A server, in contrast, has information describing each user account, the file system, available memory and disc space. Individual systems contain host names, IP addresses, subnetwork masks, and other parameters. Managing this collection of information and keeping it optimized and accurate is a crucial task. Configuration management becomes more important as the environment becomes more complex.

Some faults are caused by configuration errors while other configuration errors may affect the performance of various elements. For instance, a client that has a small packet size configured for file transfers will not deliver good performance, nor will it use network resources effectively.

Proper configuration is not only essential for each element, but sets of elements must also be configured for harmonious cooperation. Clients and servers must work together by using the same versions of software and the same protocols. Bridges and routers must cooperate in moving traffic between different networks. Administrators need better tools for configuring collections of elements.

Periodic testing is another part of configuration management. Remote elements must be checked to ensure that their configurations have not been changed inadvertently or by intention. Establishing standard configurations (as much as possible) simplifies configuration management and facilitates some types of troubleshooting.

Configuration management also involves the collection of inventory and change information so that longer-term processes, such as tracking assets and keeping track of versions, can be accomplished. Moves, adds, and changes are still one of the most difficult and time-consuming operations carried out by most staff.

Performance Management

Performance management focuses on maintaining or improving the quality of service of networks and client/server systems. Performance management has a real-time component and longer-term functions.

Real-time operations involve monitoring and reporting, using many of the same functions and information sources as the fault management functions. Administrators must define threshold levels for network utilization, server utilization, error rates, response times, and other criteria so that they can determine the actual performance levels of managed elements.

Actions must be taken when performance levels fall below expected levels. Reconfiguration or reallocation of resources may be necessary in order to maintain required service levels. If additional resources cannot be found then lower priority applications may be suspended to ensure that mission-critical applications receive the resources they require. Performance levels must be restored as quickly as possible; administrators need tools that give them information and options for bringing the service quality back to required or expected levels.

Performance monitoring is a multilevel operation that needs more integration. Users may complain about delays in sending messages or transferring files. Administrators who only monitor network activity such as packet volume may not be able to relate these data to the user complaint.

The longer-term aspects of performance management deal with such things as capacity planning and modeling. Capacity planning is an ongoing process of collecting activity profiles over time in order to determine the trends, such as increasing network utilization application mixes, protocol activities, and so forth. Network planners use this information to anticipate resource shortages and take appropriate actions before they actually occur. Administrators who cannot spot trends are placed in situations where they cannot respond appropriately when performance problems arise. Even slow, steady growth will strain networks and systems over time and consume all the initial slack in resource usage.

Modeling or simulation is another part of performance management. Administrators can use tools to model their network in order to determine ways of optimizing performance, minimizing latency, or making overall capability more robust. Modeling changes in topology or the introduction of new applications such as multimedia gives the network planner information about the possible impacts and ways to mitigate them. Modeling reduces the chance that a change will have unexpected catastrophic consequences.

The best modeling tools accept actual operational information collected by such things as RMON probes. This information can be input directly into the model so that the results approximate the managed environment more closely. Other modeling tools use standardized profiles of devices and traffic patterns to provide a more generalized, but possibly easier and less expensive set of options.

Interactions

Although fault, configuration, and performance have been described as separate functions, they are actually closely interrelated. Fault, performance, and configuration management activities actually overlap frequently in the real world. For example, a particular
fault may start to cause problems for the other two areas.

A failure may cause performance levels to fall below an acceptable level. This initiates performance management actions while fault management continues to pursue the
problem, isolate the cause, and restore service. The performance management functions
may require help from configuration management services in order to reroute traffic or
bring on additional provisioned circuits.

In a similar way, a fault may be related to a configuration error and may require a
change in a device or network configuration in order to resolve the problem. Also, some
performance problems may be related to inadequate or improper configuration, requiring
the appropriate types of cooperation to understand and resolve the problem.

Accounting

Accounting management is becoming more important for many organizations. The basic
function of accounting management is collecting information on resource usage. Usage
information can be based on different types of criteria—individual usage, usage by a department, usage across wide area facilities, usage by application, usage by volume, and so
forth. This information can be used in many ways by an organization; some will use it for
charging users while others will use it for planning purposes.

Treating Local Area Networks as "free" in some sense has been a common practice.
There were installation costs for a LAN as well as ongoing management expenses. LANs
are often treated as overhead and users have not been charged for their usage. Users could
take as much capacity as they desired, the only constraints being the fairness built into the
access control mechanisms.

Many organizations are considering charging for LAN usage as new switching technologies are introduced. Different workgroups will use different amounts of bandwidth
and the charges can be adjusted accordingly.

Wide-area backbones are another matter, however. The communications circuits are
tariffed on a different basis. Traditional leased lines were based on a fixed charge while
newer services such as Frame Relay, Switched Multimegabit Data Service, and Asynchronous Transfer Mode are moving toward a usage-based charge. More backbone traffic
increases costs by requiring more fixed fee links or higher usage charges. Charge back for
wide area services is common: users, or departments, pay for their proportionate share of
the costs.

Many organizations will not use accounting information for direct charge backs, but
will use the information instead as a complement to some of the long-term planning tasks
discussed under performance management. Other accounting mechanisms are used for
making network usage patterns more realistic. In many organizations, the end-users do

not necessarily understand the economic impacts of broadcast, messaging, and other types of potentially abusive network activities.

Accounting is becoming more essential as business practices continue to change. Many organizations contain autonomous business units that are independently responsible for their own profits and losses. These units want to monitor expenditures closely. When they share resources such as backbone networks, they only want to pay for their share.

Security

Security management entails protecting the networking environment and the management system itself. One part of security management is the distribution and maintenance of all security-related information, such as authentication keys, passwords, access control codes, and user accounts. This information is distributed in multiple places in a client/server environment and it must be monitored and protected.

The organization's resources must be protected at many levels. Key information on clients and servers is protected by multilevel access codes that control access to different information and determine the allowed actions such as reading, modification, and deletion. Setting access controls on switches as well as router and bridge filters can be used to restrict access to different networks. Some types of intelligent hubs can be equipped with access control features to provide privacy and prevent eavesdropping.

The management system itself must be secured from intrusion and tampering by unauthorized parties. Authentication mechanisms may be needed so that different elements of a distributed management system can verify the identity of their partner before taking actions. Management information may be encrypted to protect it from interception. Captured management information can offer insights into internal operations of an organization.

Security management also involves defining particular products and capabilities that help to make networks and systems more secure. The adoption of selective repeating in hubs, access control information on switch ports, the Kereberos client-server authentication mechanisms, and so forth will simplify and strengthen the security management functions. Sensors can be used to detect intrusion in a remote site or equipment tampering.

Security violations must be detected and reported to the appropriate management site so that corrective action can be taken as soon as possible. Configuration management functions may be invoked to isolate a compromised portion of the managed environment until the problem is resolved.

4.3 MANAGEMENT DISCIPLINES

A more productive way of looking at functional areas is to take the standard ISO functional areas and refine them to specific management disciplines. I find that these disciplines make it easier to identify particular functions, tools, and problems that need to be solved. Each of these disciplines can span multiple resources and multiple areas. For example, problem management can take care of problems related to failures in hardware, software, desktops, servers, or network devices. There are finer granularity functions that extend beyond the common fault, configuration, performance, security, and accounting management areas defined by official standards bodies.

Problem Management

Problem management is a superset of the fault management functions. There are many other types of problems that network administrators and the users they support may encounter. For example, not having the appropriate version of application software is as much a problem to the user as the failure of a network device. There are further problems that can be associated with lack of resources, misunderstanding of procedures and processes, or simply lack of information in how to proceed to use the network and its systems in an efficient and effective manner.

Particular functions that fall under problem management are the **Help Desk**, a means of being the first line of contact for network and systems users. The Help Desk fields the calls, assigns problems to the appropriate management staff, and helps users while the problem is being resolved.

Trouble ticketing is another aspect of problem management whereby problems are reported, logged electronically, and monitored until they are resolved. The most capable problem management systems provide mechanisms for comparing past histories to find similar problems and thereby speed the resolution process. In addition, trouble ticketing applications can use automated escalation procedures that automatically generate a call for more resources and expertise to help when critical problems that are not solved within a given time period.

Instrumentation Management

Instrumentation management will be covered in detail in a Chapter 6. Part of the tasks of instrumentation management include selecting the appropriate instrumentation for different resources: network devices, LAN segments, WAN backbones, desktops, servers, applications, databases, and information. Another key part of instrumentation management is trading off the impacts of fine, granular monitoring with resource and bandwidth consumption. The goal, as we shall see in the future chapter, is to build intelligent adaptable instrumentation systems that can successfully funnel information to the appropriate management tools so that the environment can be made more manageable.

Event Management

Event management is a broad discipline that provides the mechanisms for collecting events and other types of reports of unexpected conditions in a uniform and consistent manner. A major aspect of event management is the automated processing of events to select those that require further attention. Filtering and correlation are complementary approaches to shifting through the flood of information for the important reports. Other mechanisms must be able to allow administrators to change filtering and correlation criteria and rules. In addition, event management systems must link the events to the appropriate management tools, procedures, and processes that can respond to them in the appropriate way.

Inventory Management

Inventory management is key in complex internetworked environments. The number of devices, desktops, servers, and other resources can grow quite large and in a dynamic environment these elements are moved rapidly and often. As the environment continues to grow, the financial investment of the organization can be substantial. Administrators must be able to collect information from all of their resources; keep track of the numbers, locations, versions, and other information about all the things they are responsible for managing.

Asset Management

Asset management is an extension of inventory management that focuses primarily on the financial aspects of managing a set of expensive resources. Although quite capable desktop systems can be had for a mere few thousand dollars today, organizations that have thousands or tens of thousands of systems have still made a significant financial investment in resources. Asset management can be used to monitor service levels, to relate particular resources with service contracts, levels of service agreements, service level performance, rate of failures, and warranty information.

Software Management

Software management covers the automated delivery of software to desktops and servers spread throughout the organization including those in homes and in mobile laptop computers. In addition to delivery, software management includes the appropriate installation of software in each target system as well as adequate reporting schemes to follow the installation and delivery process. Administrators have automatic scheduling tools so that software can be delivered without requiring human presence and intervention.

Workload Management

Workload management is a discipline that balances the available computing resources against the computing and application requirements of the organization. Administrators use scheduling mechanisms to insure that regularly executed applications receive the resources they need so that their results are delivered in a timely fashion for the organization. Further types of scheduling allow the specification of dependencies between different applications or application steps as well as reporting and monitoring tools to follow the process.

Data Management

Managing the information that is part of a client/server environment includes standard functions such as backing up and saving client and server files so that data is not lost in event of a failure. Archiving is a mechanism whereby data that has not been used for a certain amount of time (therefore, becoming stale) is migrated to less expensive media such as magnetic tape. Archiving frees up expensive, high performance disk systems to support current data that is used frequently. Other parts of data management include disk and file management capabilities to provide high performance through striping, through the use of disk arrays and by providing mirrored disk file systems to protect information in case of device failure.

Reporting

Reporting is a discipline that covers many of the other management areas. Administrators need accurate and timely reports to enable them to track many of the activities of their environment as well as the management staff. Reports on failures, average outages, service availability, and quality levels should be regularly produced and distributed to those who use the information. Frequently administrators must also prepare reports for higher levels in the organization in order to track the performance of their groups. Other reports are prepared for the network users, the administrator's customers, so that they also have information about the quality of the networks and services they use.

Change Management

The dynamic environments are a challenge to administrators. If they do not keep up to date, their information becomes outdated rapidly and they are much less effective in being able to maintain services. A part of change management is the ability to plan for moves and changes such as moving a workgroup from one building to another and ensuring that all the proper resources are available. Other parts of change management include the ability to provision and position properly to make sure that resources were located within physical constraints, such as 100 meters for FDDI over unshielded twisted pair wiring. Another key aspect of change management is the automated tracking of changes through the environment so that unauthorized changes can be detected and rectified as quickly as possible.

Planning

Planning becomes more important to provide the highest value network and systems services to an organization. Capacity planning is currently used by many organizations. They use trend analysis to predict when current resources will be strained past acceptable limits and to have enough time to respond appropriately before the situation causes disruptions. Modeling and simulation are also used in planning management since alternative approaches, topologies, and traffic loading situations can be studied before the situation becomes critical.

License Management

Tracking multiple copies of software in a networked environment is a tedious task that is typically doomed to failure. License management mechanisms provide automatic means of taking an inventory of the current network applications and comparing them against the number of copies that are currently licensed to an organization. Administrators use licensing tools to protect their organizations from legal repercussions of using pirated software as well as to provide more input into planning mechanisms for the actual number of licenses that are used and needed.

Device Management

This was the starting point for network management. Device management encompasses many of the disciplines mentioned previously such as instrumentation, event, change, configuration, change, and inventory management. Each type of device also has specific requirements. Some devices such as switches and routers must cooperate with each other, which adds new challenges.

Summary

Each of these disciplines, in addition to those covered in the previous section under the standard functional areas, is challenging in its own right and there are clearly many linkages between them. For example, change management may require work in the planning management area since the topology may be changed in a way that has significant performance impacts. In this case, further alternatives and solutions must be studied. In a similar way, problem management is an area that continues to grow by encompassing more queries. For example, many help desks also provide information on company policies, network procedures, and other information that would not originally have been associated with a "problem."

4.4   STRUCTURING THE MANAGEMENT ENVIRONMENT

Choosing an overall structure for the management environment is a key first step. There are a range of options ranging from some that have been used for over twenty years to ones that have not fully taken shape yet. It is important to choose a flexible structure that can meet your needs and change as your needs will. In this section we will look at the basic choices and their relative merits. One contribution to the confusion is that the same terms are used for very different structures. The traditional structures will be examined first, followed by those that are emerging as the foundations for future solutions.

4.5   TRADITIONAL CENTRALIZED STRUCTURES

These environments evolved with the data center and supported the "glass house." The network management center was usually located within the same building and managed all the mainframe resources, the WAN links, and the attached terminals. This structure evolved to a set of centralized management sites that could back each other up while managing their own data centers. Centralized management solutions have fallen from favor with the introduction of distributed client/server environments, however, the centralized approach has some definite advantages.

Advantages

A centralized management structure offers some important advantages, especially in light of the need to leverage staff and reduce the cost of ownership.

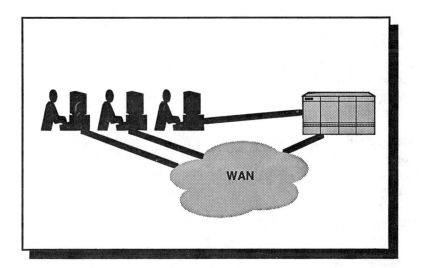

The traditional centralized structure concentrates staff at a single site, usually where the resources are located.

FIGURE 4–4   Traditional centralized structures

Staff Concentration   Centralized management allows an organization to concentrate the most expensive resources in the management environment—the staff. Concentrating staff provides a larger span of control: for example, each staff member at a centralized site can manage a larger number of nodes, servers, or other resources. Centralizing the staff also offers the advantage of being able to leverage staff members with critical expertise. These staff members now have a wider span in which to use their capabilities since they can reach every resource within the managed environment rather than a smaller subset in a local environment.

It is also easier to combine forces when several staff members are needed to resolve a difficult problem. Having all the staff members on site simplifies assembling a team, exchanging information, and coordinating activities. From a supervisory standpoint, centralization also makes it easier to oversee the entire environment, monitoring the staff, processes, and the current situation.

Concentration of Management Tools   Sophisticated, and expensive, management tools are needed to leverage staff and cope with growing complexity and ongoing change.

Centralization offers an opportunity to buy fewer copies of critical applications. This should reduce the purchase price, although vendors can be expected to respond with licensing arrangements based on the number of nodes or resources managed by the application.

Integration of network management tools may also be easier in a centralized environment since all of the management information is at least in the same physical location.

Uniformity   Organizations can use a centralized management structure to ensure greater uniformity of processes and policies across the entire enterprise. Centralized software distribution and process management ensures a higher level of consistency between different parts of the enterprise. Uniformity reduces the incidence of mismatched software versions in different parts of the company, or configuration problems due to inconsistent information in different systems.

Colocation   Traditionally, centralized management sites were colocated with many of the critical resources they were managing, such as mainframes or network switches. Although the technology allows the management site to be located in any place, many planners will still choose to place their management teams and staff as close as possible to the critical resources. This offers the advantage of quick access and minimal time to get staff on site when required.

Disadvantages

Centralized management, like any other approach, also has some drawbacks that must be considered. These disadvantages have been inherent from the earliest days of centralized management, but there are new ways to respond.

Single Point of Failure   A centralized management structure runs the risk of a single point of failure. Failures of management system hardware or the communication links that tie in the managed environment could isolate the network management staff. During this failure the environment could not be monitored or managed, and failures may go undetected with resulting service outages. The risk can be reduced through additional investments in redundant facilities. The additional costs must be considered as part of the overall solution strategy.

Scalability   A centralized management structure may have difficulties in scaling to meet new growth requirements. The centralized management site must collect increasing volumes of network management events and information, process them, and support management applications as well. The traditional centralized mainframe management solutions required expensive upgrades to keep up with management tasks, an substantial investment in the most expensive computing cycles in the organization.

4.6   TRADITIONAL DISPERSED STRUCTURES

Many organizations are still dealing with these structures, which arose in reaction to the centralized control of the data center managers. LANs were purchased by departments from their own funds and they also took on the management tasks that came with their independence. Although many organizations still talk about distributed LANs interconnected with backbones, the management is most usually **dispersed**—spread out, but in actuality isolated.

Advantages

The main advantages are offered by **local presence** and **accountability**. The workgroup administrator is part of the workgroup, is near at hand when there are problems, and further, since the administrator is paid by the workgroup, there is strong incentive to respond and keep them happy. Many workgroups were frustrated by the lack of responsiveness of a remote, corporate management center.

Local solutions typically scaled well since workgroups were relatively small and simple in the early days of Local Area Networking. Many management tools were simple desktop applications so they could easily be moved to another computer if there was a failure.

Drawbacks

Variable Quality   The drawbacks usually offset the advantages. For example, the quality of administrators could vary widely, some groups being well supported and others faring little better than they did in the days when the data center managed things. Its is common for groups to find their own "guru" within their own ranks and pester that person for help. This drains time for unofficial administration tasks and may also be expensive since these unofficial administrators may be well compensated for their usual job.

Fragmentation   More management problems surface when workgroups are interconnected into internets. The variable quality may affect a larger community, for exam-

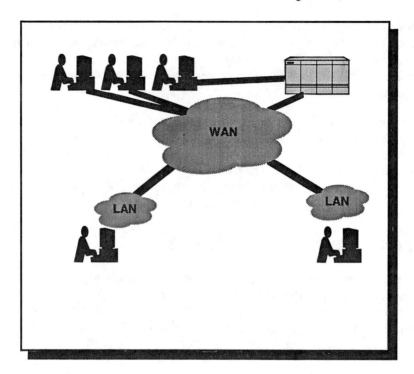

The first generation of "distributed" LAN management
created isolated management islands with little
integration with the data center.

FIGURE 4–5   Traditional dispersed structures

ple. If one workgroup needs information on a server managed by another administrator, it
is dependent without direct control (the data center revisited). Further, it is harder to manage such an environment with consistent policies and procedures.

Poor Staff Leverage   Administrators are expensive and are poorly used in a
dispersed structure. One may be expert but is not used effectively managing a small set of
resources. Other workgroups lose the support that would be available from a centralized
structure.

Poor Coordination   The toughest problems occur when several LANs, backbones, clients, and servers are involved. There may be complex interactions across an internet that cannot be solved by any single workgroup administrator. Collecting information from a dispersed structure and synchronizing actions across various fiefdoms can be
difficult.

4.7   DISTRIBUTED MANAGEMENT LEVELS

Distributed management is the long-term solution that scales while offering robustness and flexibility. Unfortunately, distributed management has existed mainly as a fantasy supported by theoretical structures and fuzzy usage in press releases. Distributed management depends on sets of autonomous management centers that cooperate, coordinate actions, and share information as necessary. Most off-the-shelf solutions do not stand up to close scrutiny. They may offer partial remedies, but lack some essential ingredient.

In fact, there are four different types of distributed management and each needs to be considered. Distributed collection, distributed information, distributed control, and distributed applications are all important elements of a distributed management structure.

Distributed Collection

Distributed collection is further along than any of the other distributed management functions. Administrators are deploying intelligent collection devices to off-load central site processing and to conserve scarce bandwidth on wide area links. This area is covered in some detail in Chapter 6.

Distributed Information

Good management solutions must incorporate information that is distributed throughout the environment in separate management platforms, isolated management tools in other corporate databases such as contracts, assets, and personnel. CORBA (Common Object Request Broker Architecture) has emerged as the means for locating and accessing information in different locations. Vendors such as Cabletron Systems and NetLabs have been using a broker for some time and SunSoft uses NetLabs technology in the recently announced Solstice Enterprise Manager.

A common data model is also needed so information can be easily shared among the management tools. High-value automation and integration of the toolset cannot occur without this level of sharing; unfortunately, the prospects for an industry-wide model are dim for the foreseeable future. The major platform vendors have opted out of the Management Integration Consortium and will work with another unspecified, official (and exceedingly slow) standards body in the future. Administrators and Independent Software Vendors will both suffer in the meantime.

Distributed Control

Distributed control is part of what the traditional distributed environment was supposed to deliver. **Domain management** also provides robustness and fault tolerance. IBM offers the enabling technology for distributed management in its next release of NetView for AIX; there will be manager-manager communication mechanisms between different plat-

forms. Hewlett-Packard offers distributed control of systems backup operations with OmniBack II and its OperationsCenter. Administrators can activate remote backup operations
and monitor them from a central site. Tivoli Systems offers distributed control and coordination through its Tivoli Management Environment framework for system management,
allowing administrators to schedule and monitor management processes across a large environment.

Distributed Management Tools

Distributing the network and systems management tools themselves is where the emerging structure departs from more traditional approaches. Most of today's platforms require
the management applications to reside on the same hardware environment as the platform
and its database. Remote access is provided through bandwidth intensive X-Windows
connections. This option also provides little local intelligence for the administrator.

The deployment of client/server architectures for management platforms gives staff
the ability to use familiar clients (a Windows client in a Windows environment, UNIX for
UNIX, and so forth) and still be able to leverage powerful management servers throughout
the enterprise. Management tools are placed on the appropriate processors with the power
to provide the most economical combination of local and remote management tools.

Management tools will be easier to use on familiar clients and also provide unprecedented portability. Technical staff can literally carry their management tools with them in
a laptop computer, plug in to any network they are servicing, and have immediate access
to all the management information they are allowed to use. Further flexibility is allowed
since a staff member can load new management tools across the network any time they
are needed. Organizations can place staff and tools where they are needed without sacrificing functionality, ease of use, or capabilities.

This type of distributed management depends on full-scale client/server rollouts
from the management platforms as well as sophisticated management tools that take advantage of such an environment. At this time, SunSoft, NetLabs, and Cabletron have the
ability to provide location-independent tools because of the distributed domain management infrastructure that they already provide. IBM will be stepping up soon with
client/server implementations for NetView for AIX. Hewlett-Packard will follow with
their own offering.

Advantages

The technology for supporting truly distributed management is beginning to appear in the
marketplace. These more sophisticated technologies will offer a greater latitude in designing the appropriate management environment.

Scalability   A truly distributed management structure offers scalability to the organization. A large, complex environment can be broken down into smaller, more manageable **domains**. Each domain manager interacts and cooperates with other domain man-

agers to provide enterprise-wide coverage. Any platform provides integrated enterprise views required by the network and systems administrators. As the network grows, new domains are created, adding only small incremental burdens to the centralized or enterprise management platforms.

Flexibility   A distributed management solution supporting full peer-to-peer management information exchanges is very flexible. Some customers can organize it hierarchically, defining particular relationships between different management sites. Other customers may choose to organize their management sites along the mesh basis, with sites communicating with each other as the situation dictates.

Flexibility in a distributed management environment is also demonstrated through its fault tolerance. Multiple management sites can monitor each other and detect a failure at another management center. At that point, another management center can provide minimal network management coverage while the domain manager is being restored.

Flexibility also allows customers to design strategies and policies that allow a hand-off from one management center to another. This is becoming especially useful in international networks where different areas of the network are busy and staffed, depending on the time of day. For example, the corporate network center might be in Europe while it is still the middle of the night in the United States. As the United States' portion of the network becomes active, network management control is transferred from Europe to the U.S. Later in the day, control may pass to the Pacific Rim and repeat the cycle on each following day.

Granularity   Each management domain can be managed with a different set of management policies. Since there is minimal interaction between domains, the internal activities can be designed to accommodate different needs. Each administrator can tailor operations to reflect their staffing, locations, and services.

Drawbacks

Distributed management solutions also have some drawbacks that must be considered. One of the drawbacks to a distributed environment is that it entails replication of network management staff and applications. Each domain will need its own staffing and a complement of network management tools. Replication also results in less effective coverage since more staff will be covering fewer resources within each domain.

Immature Technology   The technology for supporting truly distributed management environments is just beginning to appear. Distributed management support is a complex development effort, requiring the integration and coordination of activities across multiple sites, and data synchronization and protection.

It will take several years for the distributed management infrastructures to mature into an industrial-strength product. In the meantime, customers can plan and begin a transition to this style of management, but should not expect to see significant results immediately.

Investment and Integration   The distributed environment must still have some site or sites that integrate and collect information from all of the domains in order to provide an overall enterprise-wide view of the network environment. Tools that collect data for many domains, integrate it into a common data model, and provide shared access are just beginning to appear. A great deal of work is required before this level of integration is easily accomplished.

Emerging structures embody the best attributes of traditional structures while leveraging new technologies.

4.8   CLIENT/SERVER

Client/server architectures will play a significant role in emerging management structures. They provide the distributed control and information and management tools that are major components of distributed management.

A client/server architecture provides a management server (now known as the platform), separate processors for database engines, and other workstations to support the computing requirements of a large-scale management system. Workstations are connected to support Help Desk operations, user support, experts, and other management staff.

Additional processing power can be added in economical increments; the continuing cost-performance breakthroughs in processing speeds can be exploited. Redundant components can be added to decrease exposures to failures. Synchronizing data and events among a set of redundant processors is required so that all have current information in case they need to take over in case of a failure.

The components of a client/server management solution can also be geographically widespread; they are not required to be attached to a given LAN segment. In this way, portions of the management system can be placed throughout the organization. This is another factor to consider when designing a transition from a dispersed to a centralized management environment.

4.9   EMERGING MANAGEMENT STRUCTURES

The management structures of the future will be highly distributed and strongly centralized at the same time. This is not as paradoxical as it may sound at first. Distribution and centralization are selectively used to get the best from each. Some factors which must be considered are discussed first.

Investments in Remote Management Technology

A centralized solution is only viable if the staff can remain at a centralized site the majority of the time. Without a remote management capability, there will be wasted staff time

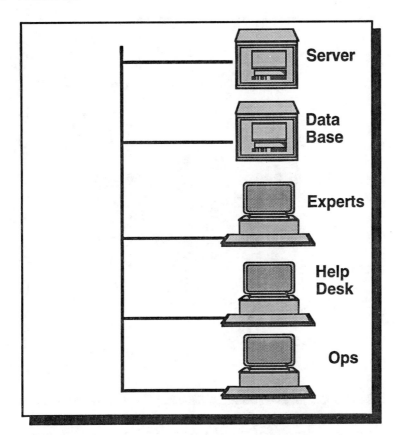

Client/server architectures offer scalability, robustness, and support for distributed control, information, and tools.

FIGURE 4–6   Client/server architecture

traveling to and from problem sites. Investing in remote management technology may be expensive since new hardware, new software, and new network products may be required.

All managed resources must be designed for remote management. If these products cannot be enhanced, then the customer has the alternative of replacing them with a remotely manageable product, living with longer service disruptions due to travel time from a central site, or maintaining local staff that can respond more quickly to failures.

The long-term economic trade-off is between an investment in remotely managed products or in staff, training, and travel time for local support. For example, remote office routers are very inexpensive and require no local support once they are operational. Send-

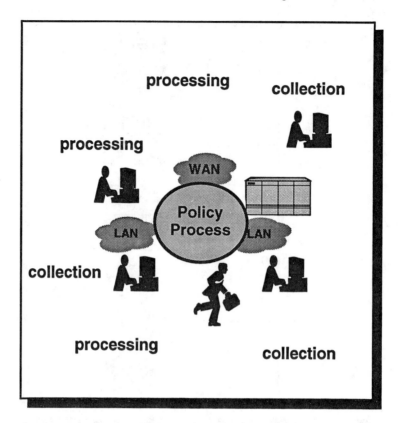

The emerging structures are centralizing the control of management policies and processes. Staff can be located where they are needed. The collection and processing functions are distributed.

FIGURE 4–7   Emerging management structures

ing a technician to repair, replace, or reconfigure the router may cost as much as the product itself.

Organizational Obstacles

Centralization may require the customer to consider the trade-offs between technical advantage and the internal political battles that usually arise with a substantial restructuring of the IT organization. Organizations that have spread management responsibility among different groups may have a harder time restructuring than those who have maintained a more centralized approach.

If there are many different groups that have partial responsibility for managing the network environment, a reorganization toward a more centralized operation may meet with strong resistance. However, I have worked with clients who were relieved to pass management tasks to another group. The flexibility of the customer organization should certainly be considered as an aspect in recommending a particular structure to be pursued.

New Centralized Structures—What is Really Centralized?

Management structures are also moving toward more centralization. Centralization of staff and management tools will continue to accelerate. The economic pressures for leveraging staff and getting the most out of expensive technology will continue to push organizations toward consolidating to fewer management centers. The most likely interim structures will be centralized domain management centers that are hooked together with the distributed management technologies. The advantages of centralization will eventually overcome many of the organizational obstacles resulting in a much flatter network management structure.

Although centralization will consolidate staff, there will not necessarily be widespread movement to central management centers. The introduction of client/server architectures and location-independent management tools allows organizations to place their management staff for maximum affect. Some management staff can be distributed where they are close to critical resources. Others will operate from central sites.

The real things that will be centralized are **policies** and **processes**. The management system spans the environment and enforces the appropriate management policies wherever management staff and their tools are located. The location of staff does not affect the policies that they follow.

Staff expertise is also centralized since any staff member can access the necessary information and tools. Experts can be brought in from any location, there is not a waste of talent in isolated workgroups. Administrators will also manage their environments from their homes or while they are traveling if they need to.

All the advantages of distributed management allow stronger centralization at the same time. In contrast, strong central policies will dictate the manner in which distributed management elements are structured.

4.10 SUMMARY

The manager-agent architecture is widely adopted by standard and proprietary products. The simplest agents require constant attention from the manager while more sophisticated agents can operate with a degree of freedom from the manager. In all cases the manager has ultimate control. The management information collected in the MIB should be hidden by quality applications that provide useful information to an administrator.

Management environments are consolidating staff and management tools to increase effectiveness and broaden the span of control. At the same time management information collection is being distributed widely. Good distributed management technology will not be widely available for several more years. Client/server implementations of management systems will ease many of the current constraints.

Chapter 6 looks at instrumentation—the ways we gather and deliver management information.

CHAPTER 5

General Widgets—A Case Study

Throughout this book, we will apply the principles and methodologies to an actual company. For obvious reasons, some specifics have been modified where necessary to maintain confidentiality, but the basic principles and outcomes reflect an actual implementation of a management solution. For illustrative purposes, we will call the company General Widgets.

5.1 THE ENVIRONMENT

The global General Widgets network supports a large SNA environment of over 50,000 Logical Units (LUs). General Widgets is in the midst of a rapid transition to a client/server environment as well as maintaining the corporate SNA network on a smaller scale. There are four major data centers that support mainframe processing as well as serving as focal points for Local Area Networks and client/server environments. One center is located in Korea; another is located in London; and two are located in the United States, one on the East Coast, the other in the Midwest. These four data centers support client/server applications through a router-based backbone of T1 links.

The client/server environment is already substantial with over 12,000 clients, almost 700 servers, and 700 Local Area Network segments. The specific complements of resources are detailed in the accompanying chart.

In addition, General Widgets has 133 remote sites containing twenty-five people or less distributed throughout the world. These sites use remote routing technology to connect to the corporate backbone with 9.6 Kbs dedicated circuits.

The management centers are located in each of the data centers and are responsible for managing the resources within that region. The wide-area backbone is managed from the East Coast site on a twenty-four-hour by seven-day basis. The East Coast center uses

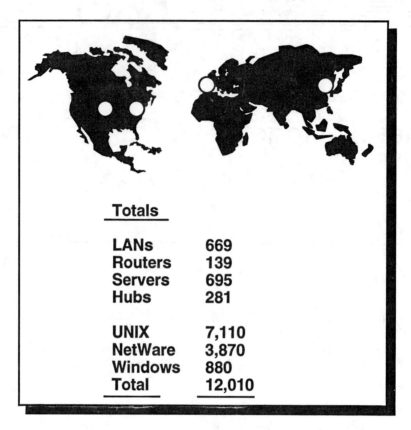

Totals	
LANs	669
Routers	139
Servers	695
Hubs	281
UNIX	7,110
NetWare	3,870
Windows	880
Total	12,010

The General Widgets global network has four regional management centers identified by the white dots.

FIGURE 5–1   The general widgets network

an SNMP management platform to control and monitor the router-based backbone. It has increasingly taken on the role of managing certain routers and intelligent hubs as requested by certain business units.

The situation with the client/server environment is much less organized at this point. Thirteen different business units share the backbone to interconnect workgroups throughout the world. Each of these groups has slightly different equipment, runs different applications, and has its own management strategies. Some business units are attempting to consolidate and centralize their management operations while others are taking a labor-intensive approach of distributing administrators where they are needed.

General Widgets has adopted a standard campus networking configuration as shown in Figure 5–4. Each floor of a building is connected to a router which may support

Center #1	US	Center #2	US
LANs	450	LANs	113
Routers	96	Routers	15
Servers	470	Servers	118
Hubs	175	Hubs	43
UNIX	6600	UNIX	435
NetWare	600	NetWare	1645
Windows	0	Windows	630
Total	*7200*	Total	*2710*

Center #3	London	Center #4	Korea
LANs	41	LANs	65
Routers	11	Routers	17
Servers	41	Servers	66
Hubs	25	Hubs	38
UNIX	100	UNIX	75
NetWare	725	NetWare	900
Windows	125	Windows	125
Total	*900*	Total	*1100*

Specific complements of resources at each regional center.

FIGURE 5–2   Center census

multiple LAN segments. Floor routers are connected to a building router whose back plane serves as a collapsed building backbone. Buildings within the campus are interconnected with an FDDI ring for high speed and redundancy. Each campus has a pair of routers that connect it to the corporate backbone. Routers are paired to provide redundancy and to ensure high availability since the configuration can survive failures of routers or links to the corporate backbone.

LANs	669	UNIX	7,210
Routers	139	NetWare	3,870
Servers	695	Windows	880
Hubs	281		
		Total	12,010

The enterprise-wide set of managed resources.

FIGURE 5–3   Total resources

5.2 GOALS

General Widgets wants to provide an enterprise-wide management solution which will have the following outcomes:

Reduction and consolidation of management staff.

Increase management staff productivity through automation and integration.

Consistent management processes and policies throughout the organization.

Reduced cost of network and systems ownership.

Increased availability and higher quality of service.

General Widgets wants to integrate the four management centers into a more cohesive management environment. One goal is to provide staffing for managing corporate resources that uses the follow-the-sun philosophy: moving from Asia to Europe to North America and back to Asia. In addition, General Widgets wants the redundancy and resilience of multiple management centers which can take over and coordinate transfers of control as necessary.

The choices that General Widgets made will be examined in the appropriate chapters that follow. We will begin by dealing with the basic disciplines that any organization must deal with.

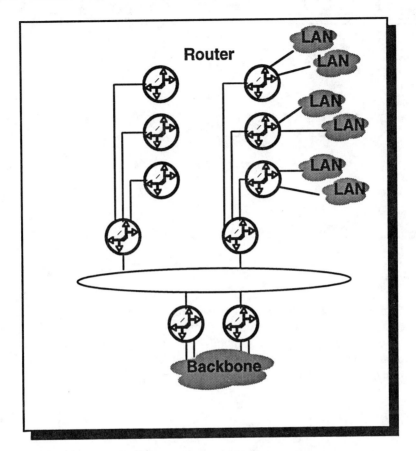

Standard campus topologies use a collapsed router
backbone to interconnect LANs within each building.
An FDDI ring interconnects buildings while two routers
attach the campus to the enterprise backbone.

FIGURE 5–4   Campus configuration

CHAPTER 6

INSTRUMENTATION

It is difficult to manage a distributed environment if all resources cannot be remotely monitored and controlled. Instrumentation is one the foundations for building effective network and systems management solutions. For our purposes, instrumentation is the generic term for all that can be known about a managed resource as well as all the ways that its behavior can be affected.

6.1 OVERVIEW

Investments in sound instrumentation pay off handsomely since good instrumentation supports so many other management functions. For that reason, we can consider instrumentation deployment and management as a distinct management discipline that spans all resources we are managing.

Monitoring Instrumentation

The dashboards of our automobiles provide instrumentation to keep us informed about the state of our vehicles. Gas gauges, speedometers, odometers, temperature gauges, and other readouts give us a lot of information at a glance. We need the same types of information about the systems and networks we manage.

Some monitoring information is generic, almost any managed resource will have indicators of operational status such as operational, down, testing, administratively removed from service, for example. Other instrumentation is resource specific. For example, an intelligent hub collects extensive information about traffic activity on each of its ports, the connectivity of its ports to back planes, and power supply status. In contrast, an operating system has information concerning the number of active processes, CPU utilization, and

disk utilization. An application may be instrumented to provide information about the remote partner, transaction rates, throughput, and errors.

Control Instrumentation

Manageable products must also be instrumented for remote control; the goal should be
that any locally performed operation can also be carried out remotely. Some types of remote operations are common to almost any resource, such as reinitializing or deactivating
them. Other remote operations are specific, such as adding a user account to a server or
setting a router table. Applications may be instructed to turn on detailed traces, to change
their demands for network resources, or to checkpoint their operations.

Remote control is critical: without these capabilities management staff will be traveling to fix minor problems. Lower network availability and poorer service quality are an
immediate result. A good example is the remote branch office routers which are remotely
configured and diagnosed. These routers are relatively inexpensive, $2,000 or less, and
even a single trip to deal with a problem can cost more than the device.

Network and systems management solutions collect information from monitoring
instrumentation and transport the packaged information to a remote management application. The management application, or an operator, can issue commands that are delivered
to remote control instrumentation where they change the behavior of managed resources.

Realizing Instrumentation

At the device level, instrumentation is usually tangible, consisting of control registers,
memory locations, and status indicators. Some of these, such as control registers, are integral parts of the hardware and control and describe operational behavior. Other registers
are volatile, containing rapidly changing information, such as the number of packets moving through an interface. Good network management instrumentation must be a basic part
of the product design in order to provide high quality information for effective remote
management. All relevant information about the device and its operation must be accessible to remote management systems.

Other instrumentation is more ephemeral, consisting of software-defined entries, for
example. Operating systems have information such as configuration files, resource lists,
access control lists, system event logs, and so forth, as part of their instrumentation.

Network applications are instrumented with embedded software. Software routines
can be activated to collect and deliver information as requested. Checkpointing and synchronizing information, logs of errors, and abnormal conditions are useful for troubleshooting and improving application design. These same instrumentation routines can
be used to change the behavior of the application.

A nice piece of instrumentation that no one has yet built would be an application
throttle, something that could be remotely controlled in order to moderate the load that the
application places on the network. Periods of congestion will occur and network or sys-

tems management applications could remotely turn the throttles of low priority applications down, reducing the flow of traffic until the condition is rectified.

Incomplete Coverage

The perfect management environment would instrument everything fully. Sometimes managed objects cannot be instrumented directly, however. For example, communication links are simply strands of optical fiber, twisted pair or coaxial cable. There are no inherent instrumentation capabilities provided. Instrumentation is collected or provided through indirect means such as the interfaces where links are attached to devices or computer systems. The statistics collected at the interface are used to infer the behavior and overall health of any communication link.

   Some devices cannot be instrumented because they were never designed for that purpose or the owners will not risk outside tampering. In these types of situations the instrumentation is indirect and inferential; the behavior of neighboring elements must be used to monitor and control these elements. It is hoped that secured management protocols will allow these uninstrumented components to be replaced with more manageable products.

Summary

Thus, instrumentation systems consist of monitoring functions, transporting the information, and control functions. The agent hides the basic instrumentation and insulates a remote management application from the specific details of each managed resource. This insulation allows a remote management tool to ask for an MIB variable such as the number of packets across an interface, for example. A remote management tool is constructed so that it remains independent of any of the details of agent-instrumentation interactions. Remote control is carried out in the same fashion: remote management tools pass commands to an agent which changes the instrumentation as needed. All the agent deployment options discussed in Chapter 4 are used.

6.2 INSTRUMENTING THE LOWER LAYERS

The transport system is a multilayer service comprising at least the four bottommost layers of the OSI model: physical, data link, network, and transport. A generic name for network instrumentation is the probe; it can be attached to a network link and collect information. There are several factors that should be evaluated when instrumenting networks.

Permanent vs. Temporary Coverage

Probes have been relatively expensive and many managers often treat the few they can afford as portable resources. Probes are moved from one location to another in response to problems.

Falling probe prices are opening new options for administrators and network planners. Probe costs are dropping rapidly from over $3,000 per LAN segment toward $1,000 or less per segment in the near future. WAN probes are still relatively expensive at $7,000 to $25,000 each. Administrators are planning for the time when it is cheap enough to leave LAN probes in place permanently. The most critical portions of the network will be instrumented first with the remaining areas receiving permanent probes as resources permit.

Full-time instrumentation of critical areas offers the administrator other advantages in addition to constant monitoring for errors. Administrators can collect information on an ongoing basis and determine the usual traffic trends and patterns. This type of information is invaluable for proactive capacity planning and resource forecasting.

Portable probes will continue to be useful where the economics do not justify permanent placement, especially on less critical segments. These probes are moved around and attached to any network as needed for troubleshooting. In addition, portable probes should be regularly rotated to carry out measurements such as baselining or general statistics collection.

Coordinating Probes

A distributed networking environment will have sets of probes in various locations. Often each probe is collecting information independently, monitoring individual LAN segments, LAN switch ports, or WAN links. The community of probes can be leveraged further if they can be coordinated when necessary.

For example, some of the most difficult problems that plague network administrators are those that involve the interactions of clients and servers across intermediate networks with unpredictable traffic flows. Permanent probes open new opportunities for coordinated monitoring for problem and performance management activities. End-to-end troubleshooting is improved with a coordinated set of probes that collect information from each network traversed by a conversation between two computer systems. The administrator can monitor traffic levels and response times across each link to pinpoint areas of congestion. Hewlett-Packard has delivered an Internet Response Manager that tracks connections across an internetwork.

More sophisticated coordination tools could simplify operations by allowing an administrator to select the conversation endpoints, possibly from a topology map or by other means. The tool could find all the probes in the path and adjust them to collect the desired information.

Another level of coordination is needed between probes and agents in the network devices. Some problems we encounter are easily understood when information from both sources can be combined and correlated. For example, a router and attached communications links may be mismatched. Consider large volumes of traffic are flowing from a high-speed link to a lower-speed link through the router. Packets will be discarded as the router's buffers fill, resulting in poor application throughput due to retransmissions. Collecting information from probes on each link and from the router agent points out the problem quickly.

6.3 INSTRUMENTING COMPUTER SYSTEMS

Quality instrumentation for the attached computer systems and their resources lags behind that of the lower layers. The ultimate stressors of any network are the applications; if there is no activity, there is little need for management. Applications load the network with traffic and sometimes behave in ways that affect network service levels. For example, an application may broadcast information indiscriminately, adding to congestion and decreasing service for other users. Poorly configured applications may time out before an internetwork can deliver a response, causing cycles of connection attempts and consistent failures to communicate.

Instrumenting computer systems and their resources offers the opportunity to bring these other areas under firmer management control. Relatively larger numbers of computer systems also represent an opportunity to leverage a management investment in systems and applications management tools. Every internetworking device such as a bridge or router, for instance, may interconnect dozens to hundreds of computer systems.

The number of resources to manage grows quickly when each computer system's internal resources are considered. Desktop systems are collections of elements such as modems, FAX boards, disc drives, network adapters, and other peripherals. Servers have network interfaces, memory, multiple disc drives, power supplies, printers, and other resources. Each system also has less tangible resources, such as operating systems, applications, file systems, databases, and user accounts. Reducing the cost of computer system ownership through centralized, remote management tools is a strong business incentive.

Instrumentation in computer systems remains largely proprietary today, unfortunately. The emergence of the DMTF (Desktop Management Task Force) offers hope for a standardized instrumentation scheme. We will examine this work in more detail in Chapter 16.

6.4 PERFORMANCE COSTS

Good instrumentation is essential; however, its advantages must be balanced against its associated costs. Instrumentation impacts the performance of networked resources, consumes network bandwidth, and adds to information processing requirements. Each of these factors must be considered when planning for the necessary instrumentation.

Instrumentation may adversely affect the performance of resources such as a network device, a computer system, or an application. Instrumentation can take a portion of local resources such as processing cycles or memory locations with a resulting performance decrease. These impacts should be evaluated when considering various instrumentation alternatives.

This problem is being mitigated with continued technology advances. Cheaper, faster silicon offers designers the options of upgrading the processor to handle more management functions or placing a separate management processor in the device. Cheaper, more dense memory chips offer more storage without requiring a form-factor change. Instrumentation will increasingly be built-in with separate processors and memory.

6.5 NETWORK BANDWIDTH COSTS

Transferring instrumentation between various management system elements consumes network bandwidth. Poor instrumentation deployment results in higher management traffic volumes and the risk of interfering with network user activities. Remote management entails some consumption of network bandwidth.

Collecting information across a wide area backbone has particularly bad implications. Wide-area links are frequently the most scarce bandwidth in the network fabric. A single Ethernet, for instance, is almost 200 times faster than the common 56 Kb/s link. Application performance can suffer across a congested low-speed backbone link, especially if polling traffic is adding to the congestion. Other wide-area backbones, such as Frame Relay services may charge for each transferred packet or for connect time.

There are several ways that the bandwidth issues can be addressed: poll/response, event-directed, intermediate agents, and distributed analysis.

Poll/Response

The poll/response approach trades network bandwidth for simple, cheap agents. As a case in point, the simple SNMP agent (remember the "S" stands for simple) were designed with a goal of minimum implementation cost and minimal performance impact on the product. Simple agents normally operate on a poll/response basis, awaiting a remote request and responding as instructed. Sometimes the simple agent accesses some instrumentation and returns it. At other times a change is made, which alters the behavior of a managed resource. Simple agents also forward TRAPs when exceptional conditions are detected.

The drawback with a simple poll/response mechanism is that it does not scale well. Each poll/response cycle consumes bandwidth: larger numbers of polled agents multiply the management traffic impact accordingly. The polling traffic can grow dramatically when computer systems are included: their larger numbers and collections of resources overtax a polling scheme. Increasing the polling interval may reduce management traffic volume, but it offers other liabilities.

Granularity must be considered. Finely detailed information is obtained by frequent polling; however, this adds the burden of increased management traffic volumes. Managers must trade between constant coverage and minimizing the impact of the management system on the networking environment that it is managing.

A low-impact strategy would poll less frequently and ask for smaller amounts of information. This reduces the management traffic load while increasing the risk of undetected failures. Longer intervals between polling operations increase the time to detect a problem and respond to it. The risk for mission critical portions may be unacceptable.

Estimating the Polling Impact

Some simple rules of thumb can be used to estimate the load that polling will place on any network link. The main trick is to keep the units consistent since there are bytes and bits and seconds and minutes to deal with. The parameters are:

> the polling interval, P, expressed as $1/$, the interval in minutes (For example, a polling interval of 5 minutes is $1/5$.)
>
> the number of agents polled, N
>
> the link speed, L (Keep the units consistent, such as bytes per minute.)
>
> the size of the SNMP poll/response in bytes, S (We have been using 650 bytes as a good metric.)

The bandwidth consumed by polling can be calculated as:

$$U = ((P*N*S)/L)*100$$

As an example, if there are 100 agents that must be polled, then the utilization for different line speeds and polling intervals are shown below. The trade-offs are clear: lower speed lines get clogged quickly and even longer polling intervals may impose too much loading.

	Poll Interval		
Line Speed	*1 minute*	*5 minutes*	*10 minutes*
9.6 Kbs	90%	18%	9%
56 Kbs	15%	3%	1.5%
T1 1.5 mbs	.6%	—	—

This simple formula can be used to evaluate trade-offs and estimate impacts before monitoring causes a problem. We can adjust granularity (the polling interval) to help control the impact of collecting the information we need. This simple model treats all agents as equally important, often that is not the case and further refinements can be used.

Tiered Polling

Administrators can adopt a tiered polling strategy to balance granularity against bandwidth. This approach assigns different polling intervals to classes of monitored resources. The few critical resources are polled more frequently while less critical resources are checked at longer intervals. This type of approach allows some adjustments between the different constraints; however, as the number of elements grows larger, the possibilities for tuning are decreased. Tiered polling is an accommodation that can extend the usefulness of a polling approach for a longer period before new options must be explored.

A tiered polling approach for the above example can show substantial reductions. For instance, there are eight critical agents such as those for routers, bridges or hubs, six of medium criticality for servers and the rest for lowest clients. An aggregate bandwidth for polling can be calculated assuming the most critical are polled every minute, the servers every five minutes and clients every ten minutes. The total bandwidth consumed is almost 7,000 bytes per minute (6,890) or about 9% of a 9.6 Kbs link. The demands for higher-speed lines are reduced proportionately. Further reductions are possible if clients are not polled at all. Users can be trusted to report a failure with their desktop systems.

Staggered Polling

Another tactic is to stagger the polling over the polling interval. If we are using a five-minute interval, for example, we should consider polling one-fifth of the agents every minute rather than using a burst of poll requests at the beginning of each interval. This minimizes the disruption of applications traffic on the links. This requires smarter polling mechanisms that can be tuned to this level of efficiency.

Event-driven Approaches

An alternative to a poll/response operation is to trade smarter agents against bandwidth impacts. A more intelligent agent compares instrumentation with threshold values and only forwards an alert when there is a need for attention. This event-based approach reduces management traffic to higher quality information. The alert already contains information about the condition and a remote application can activate the appropriate responses.

The CMIP agent is an example of a smarter agent (relative to the SNMP agent, anyway). CMIP agents are capable of performing calculations and delivering processed instrumentation rather than raw data feeds. The first level of data reduction and analysis is local, and no network bandwidth is needed at all. The trade-off is that the CMIP agent requires substantially more resources than a simpler agent risking an adverse impact on the resources it is managing.

Estimating Event-driven Impacts

We can use a simple calculation to see what the differences are between polling and event-driven collection. Many of the parameters are the same, including:

the size of an SNMP TRAP, T (We use an estimate of 320 bytes.)

the number of agents polled, N

the link speed, L

the frequency that TRAPs are issued, F (We use an estimate of one trap every forty-eight hours.)

The daily volume of TRAP traffic is:

$$T*F*N$$

For the sixty-two agents we discussed above, the daily TRAP volume is approximately 10,000 bytes. This is less than two seconds of capacity on the fifty-six Kb/s link—a substantial improvement. We need to add some occasional polling to ensure that the agents are operating.

The trade-off is between more expensive, intelligent agents and a substantial reduction in the impact of management operations. The intermediate instrumentation layer described further on can provide the same types of leverage.

Heart Beats

Event-driven approaches are clearly less bandwidth intensive. However, we can have a problem if we rely too heavily on this strategy to the extent that "No news is good news." Intermediate agents can fail without notifying any other management system element. A periodic report is needed so that the integrity of instrumentation is assured. An intelligent agent or an intermediate agent should report on a regular basis even if there is no instrumentation to pass upward. These agents should also respond to polls.

6.6 PROCESSING COSTS

Much of the available instrumentation is very raw, it must be processed further in order to provide more useful information. A simple example is determining network utilization—a common measure of operational status. Utilization is calculated as a percentage of the available capacity of a network, providing an easy measure of congestion and performance.

Converting Data into Information

To obtain a utilization value, we start with simple SNMP MIB variables that define some of the characteristics of a communications interface. The variables **IfInOctets** and **IfOutOctets** are counters that monitor the number of octets sent or received from any given interface. Counters increase monotonically, beginning at 0, and reach a maximum value where they wraparound and start at 0 again. The **IfSpeed** variable defines the interface speed in bytes per second. Although the IfSpeed variable is implemented as a gauge which can vary, most interfaces operate at constant speeds. These variables satisfy the conditions for simple cheap agents; however, they do not provide much in the way of useful information to the network or systems manager. Every time a remote management site polls the agent, it will get a new value for the IfInOctets and IfOutOctets counters. Only the new values of these counters is delivered; the useful information is still hidden. The simple IfInOctets and IfOutOctets variables must be processed in order to provide a measure of utilization.

This is a similar situation to driving a car that only has an odometer. We cannot determine our speed directly and need to perform some other calculations. To determine our actual speed we need a watch, which will enable us to measure how long it takes for the odometer to change and thereby calculate our velocity.

To obtain utilization information **the state of the measurement must be preserved** within the management system. In order to derive a utilization estimate, the current values of IfInOctets and IfOutOctets are subtracted from the previous values, adjusted for the polling interval, and divided by the interface speed to give the percentage of utilization through that interface.

At times t1 and t2 we can calculate utilization by:

traffic volume / unit time =
$[(\text{IfInOctets}_2 - \text{IfInOctets}_1) + (\text{IfOutOctets}_2 - \text{IfOutOctets}_1)]/(t_2 - t_1)$

utilization = traffic volume / IfSpeed*8 (the 8 is to keep units consistent)

then: $\text{IfInOctets}_2 \rightarrow \text{IfInOctets}_1$
$\text{IfOutOctets}_2 \quad \rightarrow \text{IfOutOctets}_1$, etc.

repeat at next polling interval

This processed instrumentation now provides information that is more directly useful to the network administrator, as well as to network management tools. Network managers and administrators are much more interested in information that defines the rate of utilization, the level of congestion, or perhaps the amount of bandwidth that is still available on the network.

It is a much simpler task to write a management tool that makes a determination if the utilization is above a predefined threshold for many types of networks and triggers automated actions to relieve the congested conditions. In contrast, writing applications that simply monitor the counters does not yield information of comparable quality.

This was a simple example of converting raw data into useful information through the instrumentation in the network management system. Although the calculations are fairly simple and straightforward, they do represent the consumption of resources. Bandwidth is consumed in order to transfer the IfInOctets, IfOutOctets, and IfSpeed variables from the agent to the remote management site. Further resources are consumed for storing the state and performing the calculation on a periodic basis to derive the utilization value.

This simple type of polling and calculation may be adequate for small-scale environments; however, it does not scale well in large environments that contain tens or hundreds of thousands of managed resources. There can be several ways of attempting to scale such simple instrumentation in a larger environment.

One way would be to provide the necessary bandwidth for larger volumes of management information. More powerful processors can also be provided to process the raw data into useful information. These approaches may not be cost-effective due to the continuing requirement to upgrade both bandwidth and processing power as the environment grows. A simpler alternative is to have the agents perform these calculations locally and send the processed results. Further savings are realized if threshold detection is also performed locally by the agents.

Correlation

Correlation becomes more important for problems that are hidden in a barrage of secondary events. For example, a server disk failure can disrupt many application connections and cause a multitude of application failure reports. Management staff can be distracted by chasing these artifacts rather than directly addressing the real problem.

Correlation is computing-intensive; many rules must be applied and alternatives must be pruned. The real-time value of correlation demands powerful processors. Fortunately, cheaper silicon helps with this problem as well.

6.7 SCALING

The overhead imposed by a fully instrumented environment must be considered when designing instrumentation that will scale with continued growth. One guiding principle is that processing is cheaper and easier to provide than bandwidth in many environments. The cost of processing continues to drop and it is relatively easy to spread processing units throughout a networked environment. Wide-area bandwidth, on the other hand, may not be available in small inexpensive increments. Local Area Networks can easily increase bandwidth through segmentation with bridges or routers or through the introduction of switching elements.

Intermediate Instrumentation Layers

The use of smarter agents can reduce the bandwidth used to move instrumentation. However, there are large numbers of devices currently installed that cannot accommodate a more sophisticated agent due to resource limitations, the inability to redesign the product, or other constraining factors. Other approaches use simple agents and retain the advantages of local processing as well.

Intermediate agents can be positioned so that management traffic across low-speed wide-area links is minimized: only reporting exceptional conditions conserves scarce bandwidth. Intermediate agents reduce communication costs while saving bandwidth for user applications.

An intermediate layer of instrumentation agents can be placed between simple agents and remote management sites for scaling to larger environments, and minimizing the impact of management traffic across critical or congested areas of the customer network. For example, intermediate instrumentation agents can be placed on a Local Area Network segment and carry out local polling and data collection for all the attached com-

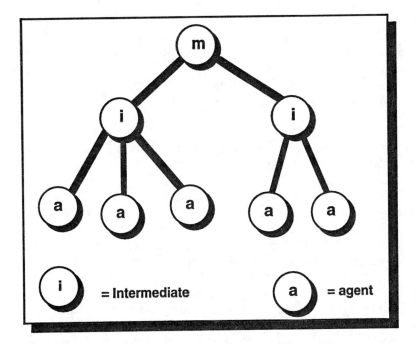

Intermediate agents collect local information and only
forward information that requires the immediate
attention of the remote manager.

FIGURE 6–1   Intermediate agents

puters and devices. These devices can use simple agents, saving money and reducing performance impacts. Local polling traffic will have a minimal impact on most high-speed
LANs. The intermediate agent can, in turn, process the collected information, comparing
it to expected baselines and performance thresholds and only forward exception information to a remote management application.

The other benefit that intermediate agents can provide is the conversion of raw instrumentation into more useful information. For example, the utilization calculation discussed above can be carried out at each intermediate agent rather than aggregated at a single management site.

Intermediate agents can also be used for more sophisticated **correlation** since they
are collecting information from multiple sources. Local correlation can extract information about complex events and only forward that which requires further attention. Intermediate agents could also be extended to carry out local diagnostic functions when problems are detected. This capability would have the agent forward a report about a specific
condition rather than a more general report that something is not "normal."

There are many examples of this approach emerging in the marketplace. For instance, Bay Networks, Inc. (Santa Clara, CA) introduced the Network Control Engine (NCE), a full Sun work station that is embedded in their intelligent hubs. The NCE collects information directly from the Local Area Network segments in the hub and the attached devices, processes it, and sends it back to a management platform. Other vendors such as Cabletron (Rochester, NH), Chipcom (Southborough, MA), UB networks (Santa Clara, CA) and 3COM (Santa Clara, CA), have followed suit with embedded processors in their intelligent hubs.

Other network management vendors are deploying intermediate agents as software modules that are placed in computer systems. Hewlett-Packard (HP) and IBM have introduced the Intelligent Agent and System Monitor/6000, respectively for the common varieties of UNIX systems.

The Systems Monitor for AIX incorporates additional functions. The Systems Monitor carries out local polling operations; it can query UNIX systems that have the appropriate agents and collects system statistics covering CPU utilization, disc activity, processes, and other behavior. Further, the Systems Monitor also polls local SNMP agents and collects information about devices such as hubs and routers.

The Systems Monitor also processes the collected information. It can test for threshold values, a common function. In addition, an administrator can define more complex algorithms that the Systems Monitor will carry out. Any collected information that satisfies the criteria is forwarded to a management platform for further attention. An administrator can also modify the testing that the Systems Monitor carries out. **Downloadable algorithms** offer the potential of evolution and extensive customization.

The Systems Monitor also collects topology information and forwards it to a management platform, it can also detect topology changes and alert the remote platform to the situation. Future information collection activities could include inventory information, configuration monitoring, performance tuning, and accounting. An element that delivers this level of information is intelligent and effective.

Other software-based agents are offered by Bridgeway Corporation (Redmond, WA), one of the pioneers. Agents can be built and distributed where they are needed. The incorporation of a powerful rules-based engine allows extensive automation and customization. Legent Corporation (Herndon, VA) has introduced AgentWorks, an architecture that allows administrators to build customized agents and distribute them throughout the environment. These agents can collect information from a variety of sources and forward it when necessary.

Intermediate processing stages offer several advantages: proximity to events, reduction of management traffic, and a future foundation for distributing intelligent management applications throughout the environment.

6.8 OUT-OF-BAND ACCESS

Out-of-band access is another consideration when planning the instrumentation solution. Out-of-band access provides another path to instrumentation such as intermediate agents or simple agents. Usually implemented through the dial telephone network, out-of-band capabilities allow the management system to obtain information even when a network failure has isolated a portion of the environment. This may be an important time to keep contact with the instrumentation on the other side of the failure. Information provided through the out-of-band link will enable some management activities to continue and may actually speed the repair of the failure.

Out-of-band access requires investing in modems and insuring that instrumentation can be connected. The low speeds of telephone circuits will also limit the amount of information that can be collected. New options with ISDN services allow higher speeds and more information to flow.

Out-of-band access may also be used to reduce management traffic by moving it across a different path, especially if ISDN can be employed. This alternative may be attractive when outsourcing is considered: the outsourcing vendor can use out-of-band access, which does not interfere with the customer's networking activities. This approach also protects the customer's privacy since the outsourcing vendor is not connected to the production network.

6.9   SEPARATE MANAGEMENT NETWORKS

Another alternative to building a robust instrumentation system that does not impact production traffic is to construct a separate network for moving management information. This is usually an expensive effort, but several clients we have consulted with are taking this path. One reason is that it reduces the interference with production traffic as their instrumentation loads increase. Another important concern is maintaining the privacy of management information and protecting the management system itself from attacks. This approach isolates all network devices from the user network; all management operations are carried out through separate interface that is not accessible to the user community.

6.10   FUTURE DIRECTIONS

Future developments will increase the intelligence of the instrumentation. **Adaptive instrumentation,** for example, will offer new opportunities for understanding complex problems and resolving them quickly.

Adaptive Instrumentation

Detecting problems with simple threshold comparisons is an everyday activity. There is a time delay between reporting a threshold condition and organizing a response to it. Frequently, a network administrator is frustrated by losing the high quality data needed to attack the detected problem. Quite often, the key information entails activities that occurred prior to the detection of the error. By the time an administrator sets up the appropriate measurements and instructs the instruments on the next steps, the key data has been lost.

An adaptive monitoring approach would allow an administrator to set a lower threshold indicating that the trend was toward a problem. When this warning threshold was exceeded, the instrumentation would automatically begin to collect different amounts of information at finer levels of detail. The probe would hold these until such time as the error condition was triggered, in which case they would be available for solving the problem.

If the measurement dropped below the warning threshold level, the probe could simply discard the collected information and return to its normal monitoring tasks. This type of an adaptive scheme would allow finer level of detail and more intelligent gathering of the required information based on the context rather than any absolute criterion.

An example of a probe that allows more flexibility is the LAN Sentry from AXON Networks (Watertown, MA). The AXON design allows for the dynamic loading of analysis applications and functions into the probe itself. These applications can be loaded ahead of time and are activated when the appropriate situations trigger them. These types of adaptive schemes will be very important for the intelligent instrumentation, which collects the information needed to solve more complex and pressing problems.

Integration with Other Tools

Analysis applications are even more powerful when they are integrated with other management tools. For example, a remote probe collects information but has no knowledge of topology or other devices. High traffic levels from a station can be detected but the probe cannot identify the location without help from other tools. A topology application can identify the physical location by matching the MAC address to the location on the network map while a hub management tool can identify the specific hub port being used. Router instrumentation can detect high loads at a router interface; integration with a LAN probe can add information about the most active nodes within the segment connected to the router.

Distributed Analysis: A New Frontier

Collecting information intelligently conserves scarce bandwidth, but does not automatically make the administrator's job easier. The volume of information from diverse sources overwhelms human capacities to understand the situation and formulate a response. Intelligent instrumentation must be complemented with better analysis.

Analysis is particularly important in the internetworked environment, where complex flows across multiple LAN segments and wide-area backbones are difficult to understand without analysis tools. The most challenging internetwork management problems arise when there are several different networks and devices involved. Each element may contribute to the problem, or a single component may be the sole cause. The same types of problems arise among a collection of clients and servers that are interacting in complex ways. Speedy problem resolution requires correlation of different types of data so that the most likely causes can be addressed first.

Some simple analysis tools are available now. Baselining follows from good monitoring; profiles of normal network behavior help administrators identify unexpected changes and respond proactively before problems develop. Trend analysis tracks changes over longer time intervals, allowing network administrators to plan for capacity increases before performance actually suffers.

Analysis Servers

Analysis servers will emerge as a foundation for an analysis subsystem supporting many types of applications. The analysis server will collect information from probes and other sources and place it in an integrated database. Analysis applications on the server deliver results to other applications as well as transfer information for processing at other locations. Hewlett-Packard has discussed this concept recently and Network Intelligence (Palo Alto, CA) is developing products that build a distributed analysis framework.

6.11 GENERAL WIDGETS

Instrumenting such a widespread and complex network requires some careful consideration. We will take Center #1 as a representative example since it has the most concentrated set of resources. One consideration with instrumentation is that information should be made available to remote sites as well as local management centers. This is especially true in this case since General Widgets wants to have a flexible change of management centers throughout the day. Any center will be monitored remotely throughout part of every day.

Center 1	Link speed	1.5 Mb
routers	96	0%
hubs	175	0%
servers	470	1%
total	741	1%
clients	7200	13%
total	8682	15%

Remotely polling Center 1 can consume up to 15% of a T1 link if all clients are included.

FIGURE 6–2   Remote polling

Local management centers will use high-speed Local Area Networks to move collected management information and should not experience any congestion. However, concern should be paid to the use of T1 backbone links when collecting information from a remote site. The relative lack of speed with T1 (1.5 Mbs) indicates that the T1 backbone links may be a potential problem, or at least more vulnerable to congestion, due to higher network management traffic loads. As shown below, the majority of the bandwidth is consumed when clients are included in the polling scheme. Polling all key, shared resources—the routers, hubs, and servers—consumes a little over 1% of a T1 link with the assumption shown—SNMP volume, 1000 bytes, and a polling interval of five minutes.

When the 7200 clients are added, the total bandwidth required to monitor at that five-minute interval approaches 15% of the total capacity. For most organizations, this would be completely unacceptable. One alternative would be to assign a level of importance to all devices. Routers, hubs, and servers are more important than individual clients since they support activities of a large community. Failure of an individual client is, of course, disconcerting to a person, but does not necessarily impact the company's ability to carry out its business tasks. A tiered polling scheme that assigns different polling intervals to resources

Figure 6-3 Tiered Polling

Center 1	Speed	1.5 Mb
routers	96	0%
hubs	175	0%
servers	470	1%
total	741	1%
clients	7,200	4%
total	8,682	6.5%
SNMP Volume		1,000 bytes
tier 1 polling		5 min.
client polling		15 min.

Tiered polling reduces the bandwidth by over 50%.
Clients can be polled at lower frequencies to reduce
management traffic further.

FIGURE 6–3   Tiered polling

based on their criticality can be chosen. As shown in Figure 6–3, most critical devices (hubs, routers, and servers) are polled on a five-minute interval while clients are polled on a fifteen-minute cycle. This reduces the bandwidth consumed by over half, approaching 5 to 6% of total capacity. This may still be high for certain organizations but it is well within acceptable limits to others. This is one area where a particular policy could be set that would place an upper bound on the amount of management traffic on constricted links.

Another alternative for instrumenting Center #1 would be to use intermediate agents to do local collection and to only forward events that require attention. Using a rule of thumb of 1/2 TRAP generated per day per device shifts the mathematics considerably. One factor is that higher local speeds indicate that an intermediate agent would probably use less than 1% of Ethernet capacity to collect the appropriate information. Further, the volume of information traveling across the T1 links would be reduced to several seconds of transmission per day, clearly within an acceptable "budget" for network management traffic utilization.

The intermediate agents are duplicated in each center so that a failure does not interrupt the flow of instrumentation for any significant period of time. The intermediate agents are remotely configurable so that the management site that is collecting the information can

Center 1		(sec)
routers	96	0.09
hubs	175	0.16
servers	470	0.44
total	741	0.69
clients	7200	6.72
total	*8682*	7.41
SNMP Volume		350
trap freq (day)		0.5

An intermediate agent that forwards Traps only uses 8 seconds of backbone capacity per day.

FIGURE 6–4   Local polling

be dynamically changed as the management centers are shifted within the organization. Intermediate agents and the remote collectors exchange periodic "heartbeat" messages in order to ensure that the instrumentation system itself is working correctly. In the event of a management system failure, each intermediate agent is configured with a backup site that will begin to receive information quickly. In the event of a failure at one of the intermediate agents, the other is activated to continue polling and data collection. A new configuration tool has been added so that local topology information is used to generate a list of all the IP-addressable resources within each center. The list of resources with associated criticality and type is loaded into the intermediate agent whenever the topology has changed. The agent uses these lists to cycle through all resources and collect the necessary information.

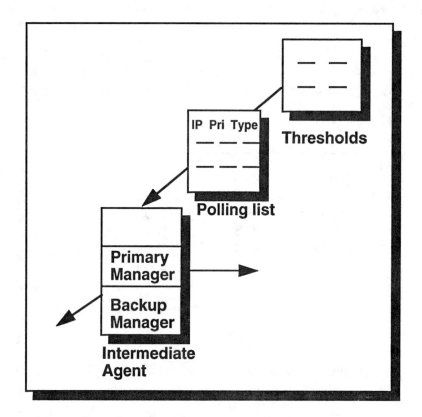

Intermediate Agents receive polling lists defining the resources to be polled by specifying the IP address, the polling priority, and the type along with any threshold criteria. Each Intermediate Agent also has remote managers addresses.

FIGURE 6–5   Intermediate agent configuration

The intermediate agents are being upgraded so that they can provide more sophisticated threshold and filtering within the local environment. Further extensions will add event correlation and rules-based processing in order to provide more accurate diagnosis and insight into the behavior of each center.

The other centers will not add as much management bandwidth since there are fewer agents. However, at any point there will be three centers that are remotely monitored. These effects must also be considered, at least to the extent that no problems are revealed. The aggregate management traffic from the other centers is approximately 10% of

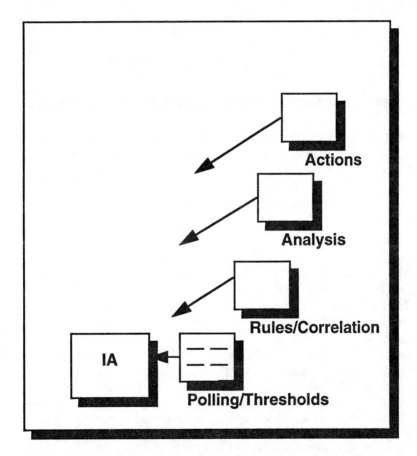

Future intermediate agent enhancements include correlation rules and simple traffic analysis. Local automated actions will be added to distribute responses to detected problems.

FIGURE 6–6   Intermediate agent enhancements

	Center 2	Center 3	Center 4
routers			
hubs	0%	0%	0%
servers	0%	0%	0%
total	0%	0%	0%
	0%	0%	0%
clients			
	2%	1%	5%
total			
	3%	2%	5%
size		1,000 Bytes	
polling interval		5 min.	

Each center contributes its part of the total remote
polling load as seen from Center #1. The aggregate
load is approximately 10% of a T1 link capacity.

FIGURE 6–7   Instrumentation traffic centers

a T1 link if Center #1 is managing the enterprise, while intermediate agents reduce the
traffic load to three seconds per day.

General Widgets has adopted a management policy of rotating the portable instrumentation throughout the Center so that periodic, baseline measurements of network activity and critical device behavior are collected. Administrators use baselining information for setting real-time dynamic thresholds as well as for collecting the historical data
needed for trending and capacity planning and forecasting.

Automated tools will be placed on the appropriate management platforms to work
with the collected baseline information. The first step will retrieve a new threshold value
every fifteen minutes and set the appropriate instrumentation so that strict profiling within
that timeframe will be highly granular and specific. This will help to filter and correlate
events, separating normal activities and indications from those that require strict and immediate attention.

6.12 SUMMARY

These considerations in designing an instrumentation system must be balanced with each
other in order to achieve an effective solution. Effective enterprise-wide instrumentation

	center 2 (sec)	center 3 (sec)	center 4 (sec)
routers	0.02	0.01	0.01
hubs	0.04	0.02	0.04
servers	0.06	0.04	0.11
total	0.11	0.07	0.16
clients	1.21	0.75	2.53
total	1.33	0.89	2.69
size	1000		
trap (day)	0.5		

Intermediate agents which carry out local polling and only forward Traps will consume only a few seconds a day of the backbone capacity. The perspective is from Center 1.

FIGURE 6–8   Impact of intermediate agents

requires distributed processing with intermediate agents in order to deliver the desired benefits.

An instrumentation system is built on a hierarchy of agent capabilities. The simplest, least intelligent agents must be incorporated, especially when there is no alternative offered by a vendor. More intelligent agents are desirable since they are close to the sources of management information. Intermediate agents must be used to aggregate a set of unintelligent agents. Intermediate agents are also useful when a wide area link separates a collection of agents from a remote management platform.

Instrumentation entails costs for network bandwidth and processing power. Poll/response mechanisms are not scalable, especially across low-speed links. The balance is toward spending for processing; silicon continues to get faster as well as cheaper. Wide Area Network bandwidth is becoming less expensive, but it must be paid for monthly and adds up quickly. Further, mission-critical applications need the bandwidth. Planners must determine their bandwidth budget and use intermediate agents to stay within their limits.

6.13 INSTRUMENTATION CHECKLIST

Take a census; collect information for building instrumentation solutions.

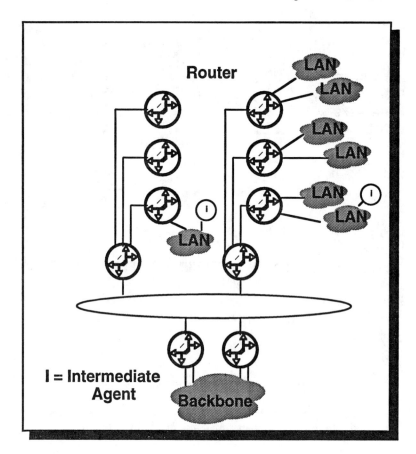

Router

I = Intermediate Agent

LAN

Backbone

Each campus has two Intermediate Agents that can monitor the campus. The redundancy insures coverage even if an agent fails.

FIGURE 6–9   Campus instrumentation

1. Identify critical applications; these are what need the most attention and the best instrumentation. Determine:
   which clients and servers are involved in these critical applications
   which segments contain these clients and servers
2. Identify critical topology elements such as:
   backbones that connect critical workgroup and server segments to the each other and to other parts of the distributed environment

LAN/WAN interfaces that interconnect critical segments to the enterprise backbone

3. Evaluate coverage of critical segments and resources:
   permanent instrumentation
   dispatched coverage
   exposure—critical segments that are not covered
   coverage of noncritical resources (Should probes be moved?)

4. Determine instrumentation: SNMP, proprietary, DMI, etc.
   determine proxy agent requirements
   for each site, determine bandwidth consumed by instrumentation
   select polling, tiered polling, event-driven requirements
   if event driven, choose intelligent agents or intermediate agents

5. Assessments
   coverage of critical servers and clients
   determine exposures
   determine metrics for systems monitoring
   determine frequency of monitoring
   determine where out-of-band access is needed

6. Results
   recommendations for covering critical resources
   permanent coverage
   portable instrumentation
   recommendations for placing intermediate agents
   supported by bandwidth utilization estimates
   recommendations for out-of-band connections

CHAPTER 7

Event Management

Building an intelligent, adaptive instrumentation system is the first challenge. Once administrators have balanced the tradeoffs between simple and intelligent agents, local collection, intermediate agents, and bandwidth, then they are ready to consider an event management system. The event management system identifies situations that require further attention and ensures that the appropriate action is initiated. The boundary between intelligent instrumentation and event management blurs since some event management functions can be embedded in intermediate or intelligent agents.

Good instrumentation can lead to information overload without good event management: there are simply too many pieces of information for humans to sift through. Event management extracts the most relevant and important events for immediate attention.

7.1 FILTERING INSTRUMENTATION STREAMS

Information streams from simple agents, intelligent agents, and intermediate agents can be filtered or correlated. Filtering is the most prevalent method today; for our purposes, we can define filters as a way of tracking a single information source serially in time. For instance, a report of increasing loading on a server may not be a problem unless the load remains high for a certain time interval. Chasing transient behaviors wastes staff time and takes them away from more pressing problems. The server load must be tracked until it is actually posing a potential problem to network users.

It is difficult to describe event filtering rules that deal with time. For instance, administrators may consider an event report to be serious only if a certain number of reports occur within a time interval, or if a condition has persisted through some number of consecutive measurement cycles.

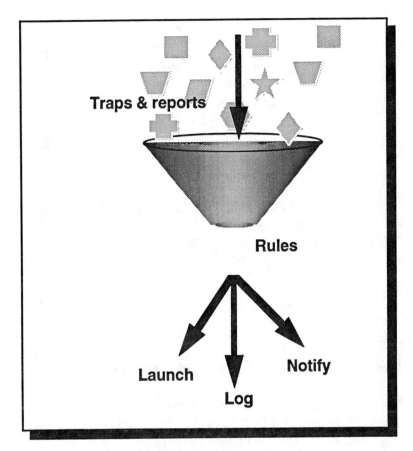

Event management systems sort through the flood of incoming information and select some for further attention.

FIGURE 7–1   Event management

Filtering Granularity   Some event management services apply the filtering rules to a class of events. For example, any event from a router is handled in exactly the same way. More sophisticated event management is more **granular,** extending the rules to specific devices, clients, or servers that are more critical to the overall operation of the organization. Finer resolution by the event management system speeds up responses since the information has been preprocessed. Finer granularity also allows administrators to apply different sets of rules for critical resources.

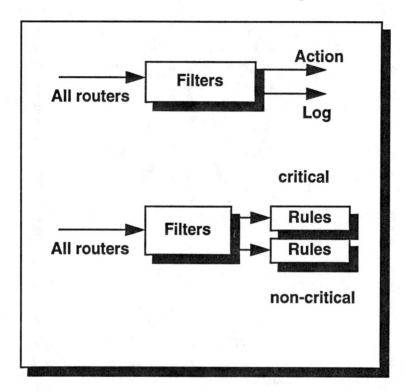

One level of filtering may not be sufficient. Identifying events from critical resources can lead to further applications of selected rules.

FIGURE 7–2   Event granularity

Filtering Rules   Good event management delivers filtered events, those that satisfy criteria for further attention. Filters are rules that the event management system uses for automatically sorting through incoming management reports and determining the next actions. An incoming report may cause different actions such as management tool activation, notification of staff, logging for later analysis, or discarding. A single incoming report may also cause more than one action to be taken.

Filtering criteria are described with the usual relational operators such as "greater than" to control the sorting of the event stream. Boolean operators such as "and" are included to describe more complex types of testing. Grouping with parentheses allows nesting to build arbitrarily complex rules. Customized operators that reflect network management comparisons, such as "unchanged" or "changed by" are appearing to make the rules more powerful. Administrators usually have pull-down menus from which they select the appropriate operators and variables. The same tools are used to review and modify rules when necessary.

Filtering automatically sorts the event stream—an invaluable feature when we consider the company mentioned previously. Only 10,000—or 1%—of the 1,000,000 monthly events actually require more immediate attention. Human beings could not perform such a sorting task in real time or with economy.

Severity Levels   All incoming events are not equally important; administrators must spend time determining their relative severity levels so that the most critical events are identified. Management staff can be instructed to heed the most important (severe) events first. Automated problem management can use severity levels to automatically assign staff to reported problems.

Sometimes severity levels are only assigned to a class of resources. Finer granularity can also be used to identify specific event sources and separate them quickly from less important ones. For example, failures in a backbone router or a key server can be identified as more severe (or critical) than a failure in a remote office router or a nonessential server. Individual elements such as critical servers or network devices can be uniquely identified, if there are enough severity levels; thereby speeding the response to the critical event.

7.2 THE NERVECENTER

NetLabs, Inc. (now Seagate Enterprise Management Software) uses a different approach to event management. The NerveCenter® uses the familiar finite-state machine state-transition diagrams as the basis for rule descriptions. A state-based event management approach allows an administrator to describe rules that span time. Each event report can cause a state transition, making it possible to count the number of events and track values over time. The power of a state-based approach is its generality and flexibility; for example, an administrator can easily draw a state-transition diagram that describes what to do if some event occurs four times consecutively.

The NerveCenter also has other capabilities. Each change of state can induce a change in the behavior of the event management system itself. As a case in point, administrators often lose critical information before they realize a critical situation has occurred. If they had collected more data just before a serious failure, they might have gained quicker insight into the source of the problem. More detailed descriptions of behavior and operational data before the crash occurred would allow quicker diagnosis and restoration of service.

The NerveCenter can alter the instrumentation management system to change polling intervals or the type of management information collected if a certain event has occurred in a certain sequence. If the event did not proceed toward a more serious level, the collected information is discarded and the instrumentation is reset to a lower level of activity.

The power of the NetLabs NerveCenter is shown by its incorporation in other leading management platforms: both Hewlett-Packard and SunSoft use it in their OpenView and Solstice Enterprise Manager products, respectively.

7.3 CORRELATING INSTRUMENTATION STREAMS

There are many other situations in which serial filtering of a single event is not helpful. A server failure, for example, may trigger reports from multiple clients that lose their connections. Management staff should address the failed server first since it is the primary problem, while the client reports are merely artifacts. Correlation deals with this dimension of event management.

Correlation engines deal with a set of events at any given time (a "parallel" event sorting). Administrators write correlation rules for sets of events that occur within a short time frame. Following the failed server example above, the correlation engine would check each client report and notice that they all named a common server. The correlation result would direct the staff toward the failed server first. These artifacts must all be

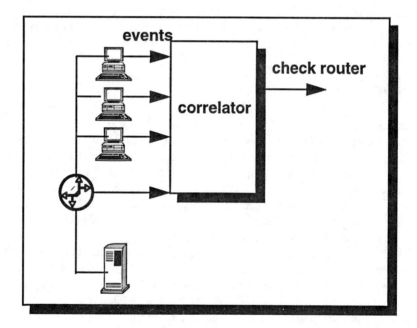

Correlation engines apply rules to a set of events in order to clarify the situation. A router failure, for example, may cause secondary reports of lost connections. Good correlation will direct staff to the route first.

FIGURE 7–2   Event correlation

checked, however, after the server is operational. This step is needed to ensure that actual client events are not disregarded with the artifacts.

Correlation, of course, brings with it the drawback of additional complexity. Administrators must have more knowledge in order to write sophisticated rules that describe relationships between events and lead to drawing the proper conclusions.

7.4 DEFAULTS

The event management system must be configured with the appropriate filters, correlation rules, and granularity before it can be utilized. Administrators may lack the detailed knowledge about devices and computers that they need for building effective rules. This is where vendors can make a difference by providing more information about their products—what variables should be monitored, what intervals give accurate perspectives, and what criteria determine when an event has occurred.

Default rules for filtering and correlation simplify event management configuration and quickly increase management control. Platform vendors and suppliers of devices and computer systems will be the major providers of these defaults. Administrators can take advantage of others' expertise and reduce their learning time. With experience, administrators will learn to adapt these default rules in ways that improve their ability to manage their own networks and systems.

7.5 TAKING ACTION

Once an event is detected, some action is required. The event management system can activate other elements of the management system, especially management tools and automated scripts.

Registration

Event management systems have registration facilities so that management tools can specify which events are to be directed to their attention. For example, a router management tool would register with the event management system to receive any events associated with that particular type of router. More than one tool can register for the same event.

Registered management tools are automatically activated when an incoming report requires prompt attention. The same report can also alert management staff through indications to a management console or by messaging with electronic mail or pagers. Other reports are logged for longer-term analysis and review. The remainder are discarded since they are not currently useful.

Coordinating Tools with Events

The event management system becomes even more powerful when other management system components can forward events like remote agents do. These internally generated events allow one management tool to activate another tool through the event manager.

Easy tool-to-tool integration through the event management system allows administrators to build sequences of management activities. As a case in point, an incoming external event can activate a diagnostic program. After completing its diagnosis, the program may use the event manager to activate a trouble ticketing or problem management tool that continues the fault resolution process. Alternatively, other tools can also be triggered by the same diagnostic program to change network configurations, reallocate bandwidth, or take other actions to keep the network running in an optimum fashion while service is being restored.

This ability to construct a sequence of management actions is key for building the foundations of automated processes. Policy constraints can also be incorporated into tool sequences in order to give the highest value solutions. (Chapter 19 contains more examples of automated management processes.)

There is a group working within the SNMP community to define a standard set of TRAPs and events that can be used for intertool communication. It is to be hoped that their effort will soon bear fruit and encourage the network and systems applications vendors to use standardized mechanisms for signaling between management tools.

7.5 EXAMPLES

Several vendors in addition to NetLabs have focused on managing events. Bridgeway Corporation (Belleview, WA) is a company that attacks the event management problem rather than specific element management issues. With the EventIX product line, Bridgeway provides a set of tools that address the organization's information management problems. Founded in 1989, Bridgeway was the first company to deliver intelligent and flexible "middleware" for the enterprise management marketplace.

Bridgeway has a sophisticated set of tools that include an extensible proxy agent and a rules-based event manager.

The Extensible Proxy Agent Builder (EPA) allows administrators to build intelligent agents that communicate with element management systems, SNMP management platforms, and legacy equipment. The ability to create intelligent agents also delivers intelligent instrumentation for resources.

A powerful, rule-based event handling system correlates and filters events and carries out specified actions. Administrators can define rules and the associated actions to be taken when the rules detect an important event. Bridgeway has also provided a testing environment to simulate events and monitor the event processing to ensure that the rules are defined properly.

Legent Corporation has followed a similar path with the AgentWorks architecture. Agents can be built to collect information intelligently and to increase the effectiveness of the instrumentation. Sophisticated agents collect the information and apply rules to extract the important information from the flood of reports. Multiple levels of agents can reduce, correlate, and filter information before passing the results upward for further filtering.

7.6 GENERAL WIDGETS

General Widgets is using several components to improve the event management systems. An evaluation of installed management platforms showed that they were not able to provide sophisticated event handling: they were limited to simple rules for filtering information from classes of objects.

Intelligent intermediate agents were used as future foundations for a distributed event handling system. Reduced management traffic and polling loads on the platform offered short-term benefits while preparing the environment. General Widgets was working with a vendor who planned to offer downloadable processing rules so each intermediate agent could be configured separately.

General Widgets identified certain routers, hubs, and servers as critical resources and wanted to apply special rules in these conditions. The issue is how to simplify and speed up the first level of screening. The first filters checked for specific IP addresses which can be time consuming as the number of critical resources grows. The critical resources were also located in many parts of the environment so screening by IP subnet address, for example, was not practical either.

Intermediate agents came to the rescue. They were used to filter for a small number of critical resources within their sphere of action. TRAPs from any critical resources were forwarded as Enterprise-specific TRAPs with identifying information included. The event management system could easily filter on the included information and invoke different rules for each resource.

Event correlation was another longer-term requirement. General Widgets wants to correlate events at several levels. Network event correlation will be used to help identify the primary source of a problem and prevent chasing after artifact events caused by secondary effects. Correlation between network and application behaviors will shorten the time to isolate application problems as network-related, system-related, or both. Correlation between failures of devices or services and the affected projects and business processes would link the management system more directly to the business processes.

The main limitation was the poor instrumentation in many servers and clients. There was little an event management system could do without any events. Adding instrumentation to computer systems was a priority task.

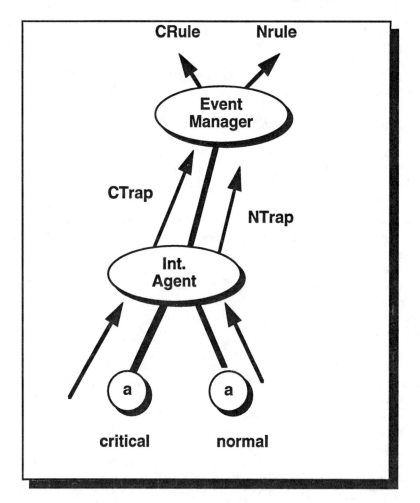

General Widgets used intermediate agents to increase
the granularity of the event management system. They
detected Traps from critical resources and relayed a
tagged report (CTrap) that was marked differently from
less critical resources (NTrap). The receiver could
apply different sets of rules.

FIGURE 7–4   Using different traps

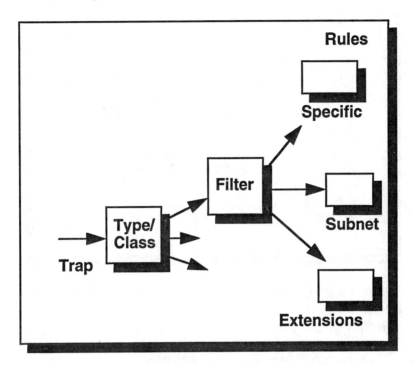

Staged event processing associates incoming Traps
with types and classes of objects. Further filtering
extracts specific elements, those associated with
designated subnets or those with specific extensions in
the Trap information.

FIGURE 7–5   Staged processing

7.7 EVENT MANAGEMENT SUMMARY

A powerful event manager acts as the "traffic cop" of the management system. It collects
incoming management events, or reports, sorts through them, and passes them to the appropriate elements for further attention. The automated sorting functions reduce the need
for humans to sift through the raw event stream and keep their focus on the important
events.

Ease and simplicity is paramount for taking advantage of the event management facilities in the platform. Administrators must be able to find rules associated with any particular event or element, and modify them quickly and easily.

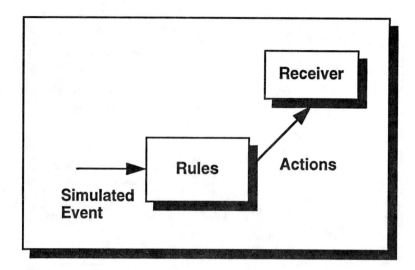

Testing rules: administrators need to simulate events
and determine if the rules they are using deliver the
intended results.

FIGURE 7–6   Rules testing

7.8 EVENT MANAGEMENT CHECKLIST

1. Event collection
     distributed, intelligent intermediate agents
     customizable filters for each agent
     ability to switch remote managers and use backup sites
2. Event processing (multilevel)
     filtering rules
     state-transition technology
     user interface
     correlation
3. Event integration
     registration by multiple tools
     activating tools
     forwarding events to other locations
     sequencing tools with internally generated events

CHAPTER 8

Automated Discovery

Discovery or autotopology is a function that is built in or supplied with every management platform. The automatic discovery of managed elements, as well as their interconnections, provides the basic means of building a representation of the managed environment. Many other management applications and functions are integrated through the information obtained by a discovery tool. A combination of techniques is used to provide varying levels of granularity and efficiency.

A network discovery tool collects information from the network, and the captured packets are analyzed for source and destination addresses to gain initial information about networks and the systems attached to them. Discovery was originally carried out at the network layer or Layer 3 of the OSI model. Networks are separated by routers that can be identified. Topology is still partly logical: the connectivity of devices cannot be directly discovered. For instance, bridges, hubs, and switches are "invisible" at the third layer since they are not addressed directly like routers.

Further refinements allow discovery at lower layers. For example, intelligent hubs can discover bridges by correlating the MAC addresses that each hub sees. Bridges forward traffic between segments, and the location of the bridge can be inferred if the same MAC address is seen on two segments. Once a bridge is inferred, it can be picked up using the ping sweeps discussed later. Layer 1 discovery lays out the individual intelligent hub port assignments and their corresponding MAC addresses. Mapping MAC addresses to LAN switch ports will also be needed as switching is introduced. This level of fine detail is very useful when understanding the actual physical connections in the LAN.

8.1 PASSIVE TECHNIQUES

Purely passive techniques are quite ineffective and inefficient in terms of time and degree of coverage. The major consideration is the placement, or attachment, of the discovery tool itself.

The placement-sensitive issue is best illustrated with a simple example of a multi-LAN campus with a backbone. Attaching the discovery tool to the backbone allows it to capture all of the internetworking traffic, increasing the likelihood of quickly discovering all the networks. However, if the discovery tool were attached to an individual LAN segment, it would only capture the majority of local LAN traffic. It would miss most of the internetwork traffic and therefore wider knowledge of networks. It usually takes a much longer time to learn about the entire complement of Local Area Networks within the campus.

8.2 ACTIVE DISCOVERY TECHNIQUES

Other tools use a more active discovery technique: leveraging information contained in internetworked connectivity devices. As a case in point, a discovery tool can read a routing table after discovering a router. The router's table provides the discovery application

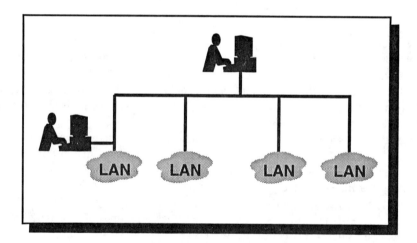

Placement has impacts on the discovery process. The discovery tool on the backbone (top) will learn about more networks than the tool attached to a single LAN. That tool, on the other hand, will have more information about the local systems and devices.

FIGURE 8–1   Discovery and placement

with all of the router's knowledge of external networks. Discovery tools can then begin probing discovered networks to find other routers, thereby obtaining further new targets for discovery. An active technique is generally much faster and more thorough than a purely passive technique. The caveat is that network discovery tools need a boundary; they can go on indefinitely trying to discover the entire Internet, for example.

3.3 DISCOVERY WITHIN A LAN

Once a new Local Area Network has been discovered, there is still the need to determine the types of computer systems and devices that are attached to it. Most discovery tools use some type of **"Ping sweep"** whereby every legal LAN address is probed. Any device or system supporting the Ping protocol responds to a Ping, indicating that is operational.

Ping sweeps are very thorough, detecting all active systems even if they are not transmitting at the moment. However, a Ping sweep is also time consuming, and uses high volumes of network bandwidth for short periods of time, possibly disrupting applications. Some tools allow administrators to specify the ranges of addresses that should be swept.

Granularity

The Ping sweep detects attached devices that support the ICMP protocol; a response indicates that an active element responds to a specific IP address. This basic discovery opens the opportunity to learn specific details. For instance, in the SNMP environment, a Ping sweep response usually initiates an attempt to communicate with an SNMP agent at the well-known port at that IP address, thereby determining if the element is manageable. Some elements may be active, but are considered unmanageable if they do not contain some type of remote management agent. Information about each discovered element is added to the database.

The discovery application can request more information from the agent to build up a detailed description. The SNMP Object Identifier is used to identify specific devices by vendor, model, and other particulars. Classes of objects, such as routers, switches, servers, and desktops, can also be discovered. Unique map icons can be used to identify the different components for the management staff.

Defaults

Discovery can be integrated with other functions so that defaults can be assigned to newly discovered elements. For instance, routers will be monitored differently than desktop computers. Detailed discovery associates each object with the proper class. Further linkage incorporates the defaults for monitoring, thresholds, icons, and associated tools. This exploitation of discovery automation saves administrators further time and effort.

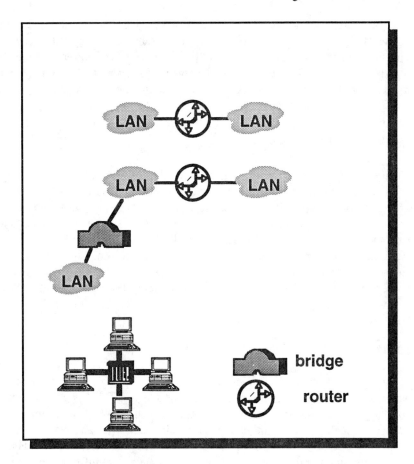

Granularity—there are levels of detail. The display at
the top shows two interconnected LANs. The next level
of detail reveals a bridge interconnecting 2 LANs. A
more refined view shows a hub and the systems on the
segment.

FIGURE 8–2   Discovery and granularity

8.4 SYSTEMS DISCOVERY

Computer systems can be discovered by the network discovery process. Those that are
transmitting packets will be noted as will those that respond to a Ping sweep. Each discovered system can be probed further to obtain specific information about the operating

system, resources, and supported software. This is the common approach for SNMP-managed computer systems.

Other approaches such as Novell NetWare and Microsoft NT use the client log-in at a server as an opportunity for updating the information about each computer system. A script at log-in collects configuration and resource information from the resident agent in each client.

There is a wealth of detail in each computer system: its hardware and software components, dynamic resource utilization, network activity, and status. This information feeds other basic tools such as inventory, software distribution, and asset management.

8.5 MULTIPROTOCOL DISCOVERY

The SNMP discovery process depends on using remote agents and tools that track network traffic and router tables to build a logical map of the managed environment. Other environments require other approaches.

Novell's NetWare operates in a similar fashion to SNMP: devices such as bridges and routers are discovered and probed. Clients are interrogated at server log-in to collect information. Digital's DECnet can also be discovered by interrogating Digital management agents. SNA however, is a different case. IBM's traditional subarea networking topologies are manually defined and stored in VTAM (Virtual Telecommunications Access Method, the basic networking software for applications) tables. Topology representations can be created by accessing this information (IBM offers a Graphic Monitor Facility for its mainframe NetView management product, for example). The drawback is there is no direct information from the "live" network. There is no means to validate the tables or to track dynamic changes caused by failures of devices or links.

The need for common data models arises quickly. Early "multiprotocol management" solutions offered separate windows for each architecture. The lack of integration forced administrators to correlate information in separate windows themselves in order to understand their entire environment. There was no simple way to determine if a server supported more than one protocol stack such as TCP/IP and IPX, for example. The administrator would need to check each window and match information. The risk is making a mistake and interrupting the services of another community of users without intending to.

An integrated view of the discovered elements is needed. IBM is among the leaders with the General Topology Manager for NetView for AIX: it incorporates multiprotocol topology information into a single database. Multiprotocol discovery and integration is still immature and further enhancements will offer higher value.

For example, integrated multiprotocol representations should offer a wide selection of views. Administrators will need the basic infrastructure views—the major devices and the interconnecting links. Multiprotocol views can be overlaid or mapped onto the basic infrastructure. Consider a set of backbone routers, for instance: there are actually independent routing domains for each routed protocol. Views of each routing domain would be extremely useful: How is the IP domain configured compared to IPX traffic? Computers supporting multiple protocols need to be identified in each specific view.

8.6 DELTA FUNCTIONS

One important use of a discovery tool would be to provide a "delta" function whereby changes in the basic topology could be easily detected when compared with the expected network configurations. Such a tool would allow a quick and easy determination when troubleshooting, since many problems are caused by what a user believes to be an innocuous change. A common example is the "intelligent building" which has been wired for networking. Users can unplug the wall jack and take their computer to another location and easily plug it in again. The problem for the administrator begins at this point. Users may have a problem that is caused by the fact they are attached to a different LAN. The administrator may also be frustrated if a technician is dispatched to the previous location and finds no user to assist. Delta functions can also be used to send alarms when unplanned changes are detected; these changes could indicate a policy violation or a breach of security.

8.7 APPLICATION DISCOVERY

Ultimately the networked applications must be discovered and incorporated into the static environment that we have discussed previously. The application discovery process is more dynamic and ephemeral. Application connections can be highly variable and last from several seconds to many hours. Web browsers, for example, can create streams of short-lived connections as users browse through pages rapidly. Sustained bulk file transfers hold connections for a longer time. File transfers can be regularly scheduled for activities such as backup, point-of-sale data delivery, or downloading new data. Other activities are highly variable. Interactive sessions and transaction-oriented applications can sustain connections for many hours.

Discovery would entail identifying application activities in many dimensions. CoroNet Systems has introduced a flexible applications probe and other tools in its CoroNet Management System. Application activity is "discovered" by capturing packets and analyzing them. The captured information reveals the type of application and the communicating partners. Further levels of detail can be extracted to track specific interactions, transaction rates, response times, application traffic volumes, and other characteristics.

The CoroNet Management System also discovers the basic topology of TCP/IP networks and can integrate the application activity information with topology. Administrators can, for instance, trace a particular application connection between server and client across the topology—through routers, link, hubs, and switches. Network device status can be correlated with applications to determine if problems are affecting mission-critical activities.

This will be the most promising area of new discovery improvements. The application focus helps evaluate management decisions based on business activities and impacts.

8.8 DISTRIBUTED DISCOVERY

Discovery tools are being distributed to keep pace with increasing growth. A single tool that is attempting to discover a large environment will take a great deal of time and also consume network bandwidth. For example, the problems with polling across a WAN link surface with Ping sweeps through a newly discovered LAN. The discovery tool may send thousands of Pings in an attempt to determine the devices on a remote LAN. Local discovery takes the load off the WAN links and a single tool. They carry out Ping sweeps and other procedures to detect bridges, hubs, computer systems, and switches. They build the descriptions of the detected resources and their relationships (connectivity and containment) and forward the topology description to a remote site. Any detected changes are also reported.

The remote site can assemble these descriptions and place them in a database. The remote site can have tools that assemble and integrate descriptions rather than polling for it. The assembled information is available for other management tools and for building the necessary topology maps.

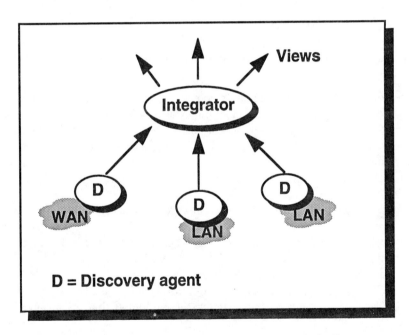

Distributed discovery uses local discovery tools to collect information and forward it to a remote integrator.

FIGURE 8–3   Distributed discovery

8.9 A PICTURE MAY NOT BE WORTH
A THOUSAND WORDS

Topology maps are built from the database populated by discovery tools. These maps give a multilevel view of the managed environment ranging from high-level enterprise maps to detailed logical and physical views of the workgroup. Color-coded icons give an instantaneous view of operational status: healthy, in trouble, out of service, etc.

However, topology maps have relatively little value at other times. Frequently, the most important information is displayed in windows such as the log of outstanding errors or problems and their status. Much of the rest of the screen "real estate" is consumed with simple meters or other recording devices that allow an administrator to see the health of the environment with a simple glance.

As switched environments continue to become more common, much of the utility of the topology map is limited. A workgroup may be spread across several switches and backbone networks; it may not even fit on the screen as a single view. Products, such as HP's OperationsCenter, have already used new visual paradigms by collecting groups of managed resources into a window for viewing rather than forcing the operator to search multiple parts of the topology to find all the elements that are grouped for management purposes.

8.10 SUMMARY

Automated discovery tools are essential for populating the database and for tracking dynamic environments. Administrators cannot track the changes that occur in large environments without more help. Active discovery techniques are preferred because of their speed and completeness. Discovery is a multilevel process that can deliver varying amounts of information. Discovery down to Layer 1 (hub and switch ports) is essential for larger environments. Linkage with other tools is needed in order to respond to unauthorized changes.

Further value is gained from automated linkage to default monitoring and threshold values for each type of discovered device. Linking proper tools by class is also effective. For example, a discovered Bay Networks router would be linked to Site Manager while a Cisco Systems router would be linked to CiscoWorks. When the administrator clicks on any icon, the appropriate tools would be offered.

Application, discovery, and integration of information are the key areas that require further improvements. Discovery is more important than simply drawing maps.

8.11 DISCOVERY CHECKLIST

1. Network discovery
2. Active techniques with boundaries (such as number of router hops from tool)

3. Ping sweeps with address restrictions
4. Granularity
    Layer 3—routers
    Layer 2—bridges and LAN switches
    Layer 1—Hub and switch ports / MAC address
5. Granularity
    device-specific details
6. Multiprotocol integration
    overlays of views
    marking multiprotocol resources
7. Systems discovery
8. Techniques
    by polling and Ping sweeps
    at server log-in
9. Delta features
10. Application discovery
    functional and service views
    identification of partners
    integration of application and topology information

CHAPTER 9

Problem Management

Problem management is an ongoing management burden. Fortunately, some problems do not always affect the users or their service. Other problems can be all too visible to the entire networked community. Problem management is also growing to incorporate more than failures. Lost productivity because a user cannot use an application correctly or a system lacks the resources for new applications are also problems.

Proactive management allows administrators to "get ahead" of some problems. One example is tracking network utilization trends in order to plan for adding capacity before problems arise. Problem management becomes more proactive as automation and integration are leveraged.

Problem management, or trouble ticketing, is an essential tool for administrators. Problem management tools collect information about problems, follow the problem resolution process, and collect information about the organization's effectiveness at solving management problems.

9.1 THE HELP DESK

Help Desks are the first line for problem management systems. Users have a single point of contact that they use to report problems, to obtain information about procedures, and to request services. The Help Desk staff answers questions, works with users to determine problems, assign problems to the appropriate staff, and tracks the open problems.

Help Desks can range from a simple operation where the tasks are carried out manually to a large-scale automated center with its own staff. Help Desks use automated procedures to speed up problem resolution, increase user satisfaction, and capture information about the problem management process itself.

130

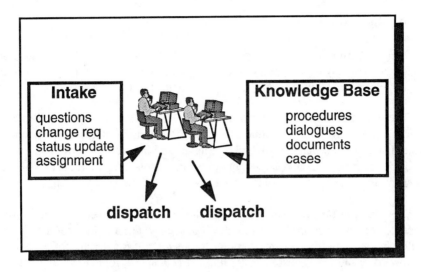

The help desk is the focal point for handling user
queries and problem reports. A knowledge base
facilitates problem determination.

FIGURE 9–1   Help Desk processes

Contacting the Help Desk

Users need flexibility: most will use telephones while others prefer using electronic mail,
especially if there is not twenty-four-hour coverage.

    Automatic Call Distribution Systems (ACD) can be used to facilitate user contact
with Help Desk staff. Recorded messages can update users by letting them know about
current situations that may affect them. The user can simply hang up if a problem has already been reported. Guidance can be given so the user can use the phone push buttons to
reach the appropriate staff person.

    ACD can also be integrated with management database information so the user's in-
formation is available to the Help Desk staff when they answer the call. Information such
as the type of desktop systems, configurations, access privileges, office location, and
other information can reduce the time taken to collect information.

    Electronic mail can also be used, and, in some cases, may actually be more effec-
tive. Users may capture information about their problem and deliver it to the staff directly
rather than trying to describe the situation.

Defining the Problem

Help Desk staff usually need to work with users to refine the problem so that it can be corrected immediately or assigned to the appropriate staff members for further attention. There are sets of tools that are being deployed to help speed the process.

Access to Management Information   It is essential for Help Desk staff to have access to management tools that allow them to determine status. A quick check may indicate that a problem has already been reported and indicate its current status. Simple tests can determine if a device, server, or application is operational. Statistics such as network or server utilization may point to the cause of a performance problem.

On-line Guidance   This can be used as a script to direct the definition phase. Answers to certain questions lead to the next questions. Staff and the user may be supplying information as needed. Many common problems are rapidly identified and moved along toward resolution. Those that are not as tractable are routed to more expert Help Desk staff who are not bogged down with simpler challenges.

Knowledge Bases   These are also appearing as another enhancement. The initial knowledge bases incorporate vendor-specific information that helps identify problems and responses more quickly. Some vendors are providing knowledge bases about their own products, leveraging their expertise and differentiating themselves from competitors. The future will see independent vendors compiling and marketing these products.

Help Desk staff can navigate the knowledge base, following the steps that narrow the problem definition. Knowledge bases will become more prevalent as the number of specific offerings reaches critical mass.

Web browsers may take over the role of scripted guides through a knowledge base. The stability and ease of use offer a familiar, dependable framework to build a wider selection of problem resolution and identification services. Once a problem has been identified, it can be dispatched or assigned.

Problem Assignment

Some problems will be resolved at the Help Desk as staff explain misunderstood procedures, offer suggestions, and verify resolution. Others are beyond the capacity of the Help Desk and are passed to the appropriate staff. Usually a trouble-ticketing tool is used to assign and track a problem through resolution.

Monitoring

Many Help Desks continue to monitor outstanding problems for the users. Staff need access to trouble-ticket reporting, network, and systems status and logs so they can answer questions about ongoing efforts. Some staff also call back users and inform them that reported problems have been cleared up.

9.2 HELP DESK EXAMPLES

There are several examples of interesting Help Desk technologies that have appeared in the management market. Remedy Corporation offers its Action Request System (ARS) as a foundation for managing such processes as problem reporting and resolution. ARS is available on a wide variety of hardware platforms and operating systems. It uses a client/server architecture that allows users direct access to many functions. For example, they can submit and track their own trouble tickets. ARS also offers easy integration to other management tools that supply information, carry out activities, or integrate data. Remedy has strengthened its usability by using Web browsers as the navigation tools for Help Desk staff as well as users.

ARS has expanded its scope as well, serving as a focus for all types of assistance for users. ARS can track policies, vacation time, and any other kind of shared, corporate information. Users appreciate the simplicity of a single source of information and support.

Legent Corporation offers Paradigm, a problem management system that uses a robust client/server architecture. Multiple Paradigm servers can exchange information, including assigning problems to different sites.

Paradigm is positioning itself as an integrated problem management framework that

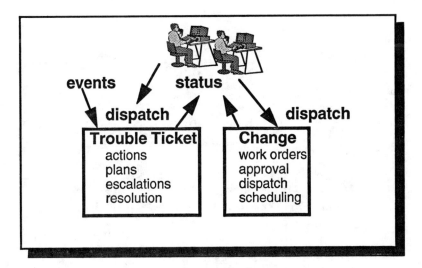

The Help Desk is being extended to incorporate other functions such as managing changes. Legent's Paradigm and Remedy's ARS are examples.

FIGURE 9–2   Help Desk integration

incorporates its original trouble-ticketing system with new modular elements. Call management can be integrated with databases so that staff can have automatic access to specific customer information.

Paradigm also offers interfaces into other systems such as change management and facilities to expand its scope beyond failure management. An integrated tracking and reporting function lets administrators monitor the overall problem management process.

Answer Systems focuses on quick recall and matching of symptom and problem with Apriori. A patented search algorithm tracks the patterns of calls and identifies common characteristics that are used to access the information needed to speed the problem definition. Knowledge base integration extends the searching strategies to product-specific databases.

The Help Desk is a process-oriented tool because many of the reports will be handled in a similar way—initial checking and screening to determine more accurately what the problem might be and issuing a trouble ticket and the assignment to the appropriate staff for ongoing attention. Help Desks are also a source of preliminary training where network users can be taken through simple procedures in order to ensure they are carrying them out correctly and that the problem is not simply one of education and understanding.

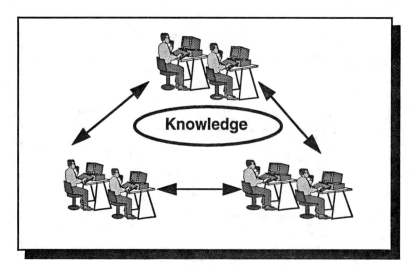

Large organizations may need several Help Desks that route reports to the appropriate staff. All Help Desks need to share a common knowledge base.

FIGURE 9–3   Distributed Help Desks

9.3 TROUBLE-TICKETING

Trouble-ticketing tools are part of an overall problem management system. Some organizations, however, treat trouble ticketing as the problem management system. There is a blurry boundary between Help Desk and trouble-ticketing. Products such as Legent Paradigm incorporate filtering and correlation for problem definition and correlation, functions that Help Desks also provide. Trouble-ticketing also provides mechanisms, often used by Help Desk staff, to monitor the outstanding problems.

Trouble-Tickets

A trouble-ticket is a report of a problem that traditionally was written and handed to a technician. Today its main use is to act as a collector of information related to a problem report and to capture all the actions taken to resolve the problem. Most tickets are electronic and are available to different management staff as needed.

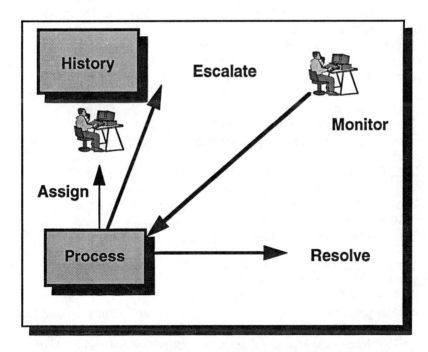

A trouble-ticketing system monitors a problem from the time a fault is received until the problem is resolved.

FIGURE 9–4   Trouble ticketing

Trouble-ticketing tools have a general set of steps and processes that they provide.

The Problem Resolution Process

The problem resolution process involves several phases and a good problem trouble-ticketing tool can produce substantial savings in staff time and improve service availability.

Problem Reports

A problem report opens, or generates, a new trouble ticket. Each new ticket enters the problem resolution phase.

Problem management systems usually have their own event management capabilities. For example, when a problem arrives or is presented to the trouble-ticketing system, a set of rules (or filters) can be applied to assign it a relative priority, select the appropriate management staff person to follow through on that problem, or activate other processes to speed resolution. Administrators must be able to define a flexible set of rules for routing problems appropriately.

Another value of a rules-driven problem management system is that it can track problems on an individual basis. For example, the failure of a key element, such as a mission-critical server or an important backbone switch, can be tracked as a different priority problem from the failure of a single desktop system (discounting the feelings of the single user, of course).

One key to effective trouble ticketing is automatic population of the ticket. Technicians need as much information as possible in order to speed their work. The most useful information is what is captured at the time the problem is recognized. Device management tools, for example, may have substantial information about status, packet volumes, error rates, and other data that point to the source of a problem.

This is an area that is still difficult for administrators today. The lack of a common data model and shared information dictates custom solutions that integrate one management tool at a time with the trouble-ticketing system.

Assignments

Problem management tools should automatically assign staff to the problem. Policies can also be incorporated into the assignment process. For example, one organization may organize its staff by areas of expertise. Incoming problems are assigned to the staff member with the appropriate training and skills. Another organization may choose to assign problems in ways that distribute the workload. A new problem is assigned to the staff person who is free to respond. The automated processing of incoming problems can also be used to guide the troubleshooting staff. A higher priority problem can be identified and staff shifted accordingly.

History

The problem resolution process can be relatively simple or quite complex: automated management of the resolution process can greatly increase the productivity of the troubleshooters. One way to facilitate easier troubleshooting is through the maintenance and collection of previous trouble tickets, which can be used to guide current actions. The troubleshooter can query the problem management system for previous problem reports for the specific element or others of the same type. The troubleshooter can scan these for information that details how similar problems were resolved in the past. This type of historical data can save much time and pinpoint the particular types of remedial actions much more quickly.

The keys to exploiting the historical data are quick matching to a specific set of symptoms. Accurate descriptions in the ticket itself are needed to complement a flexible query capability. Historical data should also detail the explicit steps and procedures that were effective.

A nice extension to these basic functions would be the automation of the steps taken once a match was found. The problem management system could carry out the tests and procedures that usually resolve the problem. The technician does not need to spend time going through repetitive steps and focuses on the problems that are not typical.

At the same time, the problem management system should be capturing all of the actions and activities of the troubleshooter, both for incorporation into the historical file and for providing accountability for each staff member's activities. This information provides much of the feedback for evaluating effectiveness.

Automation

Good problem management systems also automate as many steps of the problem resolution process as they can. Incorporating scripts and other application routines into the steps speeds up problem resolution. As an example, Paradigm, a problem management tool from Legent corporation, has action templates that coordinate troubleshooting steps.

Remedy offers easy integration with ARS so that other tools, applications, and scripts can be activated at the appropriate times. These automated operations simplify the resolution process and remove sources of potential errors associated with manually driven procedures.

Escalation

Escalation rules can also be incorporated so that other notifications are made if the problem is not resolved within a specified time interval. Automated escalation ensures that more senior members of the management team are informed of the problem and can start assembling additional resources to resolve the situation. Escalation can also be used to notify an administrator of falling service quality levels, such as an outage of a key server, offering another way of tracking the performance of vendors and their management teams.

Rules are embedded in the trouble-ticketing system so that escalation decisions are made after predefined conditions are satisfied. The granularity of the rules is also important; the escalation criteria for a critical backbone router or server will be different from those for less critical resources.

Feedback

One value of a good problem management tool is that it gives the system administrators themselves detailed feedback about their effectiveness in dealing with problems. Problem management systems provide a variety of reports, allowing system administrators to pinpoint the most frequently reported problems, those that take the longest time to solve, the relative effectiveness of various staff members for different classes of problems, and mean time between failures and mean time to repair statistics.

Administrators can use the problem management system as a valuable tool for detecting weaknesses in their problem-solving procedures, staff training, and overall effectiveness. This information can be used to assign the most effective staff member to the appropriate problem whenever possible, thereby ensuring that the appropriate help can be delivered within the accepted timeframe. For example, an organization found that the number of problems increased after new software was installed. The collected informa-

Mean Time Between Failures

Mean Time to Repair

Problem Frequency
   How often? which equipment, systems?

Problem Distribution
   Where? Random or clustered?

Staff Effectiveness
   Who are the experts, who needs training?

Problem management tools should deliver reports that facilitate improving the problem resolution process. Administrators can focus on areas that need further attention.

FIGURE 9–5   Feedback

tion was analyzed and it was found that one staff member was not following the procedures. This information was used to correct the problem very quickly.

Analysis of problems also allows administrators to identify devices, systems, or applications that have the highest incidence of problem reports. Many device problems are
solved by replacing a failed component. Information from the analysis can be used to
stock the appropriate numbers of spare components.

Calculations of mean time to repair can also be used to assess the actual availability
of services and to determine if service level agreements are actually being kept. The data
can also be used to pinpoint problems in multivendor environments. The data identifies
the problem elements and hopefully eliminates much of the finger pointing when reviews
are conducted.

9.4 GENERAL WIDGETS

General Widgets suffered from lacking a solid problem management system. The primary
problem was the dispersed, isolated collection of tools at each site. There was no sharing
of information and management staff often resorted to the telephone in an attempt to
reach a knowledgeable person at another center.

Help Desks were not used at three sites and staff accepted phone calls and manually
entered information into a trouble-ticketing tool. The historical data was sketchy and
queries were limited. The organization was finding that some problems were causing unacceptable degradation of service levels. The alternative of adding more staff was not attractive.

The trouble-ticketing tool was seriously limited since it lacked any type of rules.
Problems were assigned to staff haphazardly and sometimes a serious problem would not
be recognized for some time. A short-term solution interposed a custom filtering application between the management platform and the trouble-ticketing tool.

Administrators developed filters to improve the problem management process. For
example, backbone T1 links tended to have intermittent failures or events in Europe and
Asia. Often, these "link-down events" lasted for a few seconds, generating large numbers
of trouble tickets. Staff frequently found a working link when they were notified, and
tested it.

Filtering routines were written that "held" an event from a T1 link for a period of
time. If the outage was short-lived, the event was discarded rather than being passed to the
trouble-ticketing tool. Another filter checked for a number of these cyclic events and issued a ticket whenever those criteria were satisfied. These two simple filters reduced the
number of trouble tickets by a factor of 20. This translated into a savings of two man-
years in staff time annually that was frequently spent on chasing ephemeral problems.

General Widgets began with analysis of their needs in this area. The first requirement was for a problem management system that would eventually span the enterprise:
tools at each site could communicate and exchange information as needed. A client/server
architecture was selected as the foundation.

Help Desks were selected with the ability to incorporate scripts and knowledge bases. The initial deployments were not interconnected, but were chosen because of the vendor's future plans for client/server products.

Trouble-ticketing tools were chosen on the same basis. The selection criteria emphasized automation and analysis. The custom filters were replaced with supported products that freed development staff for other tasks. A central group builds new rules and filters, tests them and distributes them to each site as needed. Sites can also exchange filters and leverage local expertise.

9.5 SUMMARY

Problem management tools are essential for administrators, who need to understand the scope of problems and the effectiveness of procedures and staff in order to gain control of a chaotic environment. Beyond these basic needs, the problem management system can offer sophisticated rules and automation to speed problem resolution and reduce staff training requirements.

CHAPTER 10

Inventory and Asset Management

Inventory and asset management are becoming more important as environments grow larger, more dynamic, and more complex. Understanding what is being managed is the role of inventory tools while asset management deals with the business aspects of large numbers of expensive resources.

10.1 INVENTORY MANAGEMENT

Administrators need information about the numbers and types of computer systems, devices, and other resources they are responsible for.

Network devices have a complement of elements that need to be catalogued: even the simplest devices contain multiple processors, communications interfaces, and often, different modules in each chassis. Devices also have versions of microcode and other software. Administrators need to track all of these components, especially modules that can move between devices.

Desktops may literally contain thousands of objects to be inventoried. Components such as monitors, printers, fax boards, coprocessors, and modems are all found within a normal desktop. Further, dozens of applications and hundreds or thousands of files and various directories are in use. In addition, version numbers, install dates, and contract numbers are associated with each application. Other information such as modification dates and information about the files being inventoried is needed for storage management.

Detailed information about each computer system—its peripherals, components, and software—is also needed so that administrators can locate resources, check on configurations, and assist with the financial management of key assets. All of this information must be collected and organized so that it is easily searched with a combination of different criteria. Most inventory databases offer an SQL interface to allow relational structures to be created and searched regularly and on an ad-hoc basis.

Inventory systems are also a natural place to hold and obtain much of the static configuration information for each desktop and server. This configuration information can be updated and distributed just as any other type of management information would be.

Accessing Information

This inventory information must be organized in a flexible way since it will be used for many different purposes. For example, an administrator at one point may want to search for all processors of a certain type regardless of the particular operating system they may be running. At other times, an administrator may only be interested in processors of any type that support a given operating system or an application.

Good inventory tools will also provide regular reports with highly customizable information so that administrators can track inventory levels, changes in inventory, additions of new software modules, and other activities that affect the managed environment. The ability to detect inventory changes, especially those associated with configuration or adding unauthorized applications, are very useful for the systems administrator. The freedom and flexibility of the desktop allows users to make intentional or inadvertent changes to their systems, which may have a negative impact on the entire computing community.

A flexible query mechanism should also be available so that administrators can access information quickly and easily. There are times when an administrator needs specific inventory information immediately, and easy-to-use queries are essential.

Collecting Information

An important differentiator for inventory management tools is their ability to collect data from multiple sources. These types of packages collect data from different environments and proprietary tools and transform it into a common inventory format. This integration allows the creation of a flexible relational database which can then be queried in various ways to meet different information needs.

Some inventory collection will be log-in activated, in a similar way to software distribution. When a client connects to its server, local agents can provide appropriate information about configuration files, startup routines, and other information, such as the home directory for the operating system. A complementary program on the server can compare the reported configuration and inventory to that which is expected or conforms to a particular corporate or organizational policy. A further refinement restores changes configurations to those that are specified by the policies.

Other inventory functions can be discovery activated. For example, an automatic topology discovery program may report the presence of new systems to an inventory application which then carries out further queries to collect the information necessary for inventory management.

Frequently, the inventory information that is collected from resident system agents must be supplemented with information from other sources. For instance, many resident agents will not be able to report the location of the system, the personnel to contact in the event of problems, the warranty status, the name of the user, and other pertinent information. Often, this type of information is available in other organizational databases and the appropriate information should be extracted in order to provide a complete view of the systems administrator's inventory.

At other times information must be collected by hand. Some systems do not have local agents that can provide inventory information, so administrators must carry out an inventory in person. Spare parts should also be added to the inventory database. When failures occur, the inventory database can be updated to reflect the level of spares on hand. New spares can be purchased as needed to keep an acceptable level on hand.

One of the best examples of this type of an emerging architecture is the NetLabs' AssetManager, which can collect information from a variety of sources and integrate it into a single unified inventory asset view. Some of the collection points include the SynOptics' Super Agent, and collector modules for environments such as NetWare, UNIX, and NT.

Automatically scanning a system's inventory and comparing it against previous information or baseline policies allows an administrator to detect changes and act accordingly. The same server-to-client communications that are used to scan a system's inventory and configuration and report them to the server can also be used to deliver a new copy of inventory or configuration information to the client. In this way, system administrators can maintain a much more stable environment and detect those users or systems that are causing problems.

10.2 ASSET MANAGEMENT

Asset management is an extension of inventory management since it starts with the same type of information. The distinction that we can make is that asset management begins to incorporate some of the financial aspects of supporting and owning a large array of desktop systems. Asset management information can include contract information, service levels, failure rates, costs of maintenance, and other types of parameters.

Financial management also includes monitoring contracts. For example, some organizations have discovered that they are still paying for maintenance contracts on systems they no longer own. Other organizations have found that they save money by aggregating software licenses from individual departments so that they are not oversubscribed. Asset management tools can also apply depreciation schedules and other types of financial analyses that are required.

Asset management can be used to determine the actual reliability of different products, the accountability for maintaining certain service levels or uptime, and can be used to track the total value of the enterprise's assets, maintenance and service contracts, spare parts, and operations.

CHAPTER 11

Platforms

Management platforms are software environments that provide the basic foundation for building the integrated tool sets that actually deliver network and system management solutions. The management platform provides a set of basic services that support any type of management application.

Some examples of basic platform services include instrumentation control, event management, topology maps, graphing and scripting utilities, information management, and access to management tools. Instrumentation and event management were treated as separate disciplines in Chapters 6 and 7. Other functions will be covered in the rest of this chapter.

Any single platform will reach a limit of scale—the largest number of resources it can help manage without degrading the performance of the management system itself. Resource limitations such as the speed of the processor, the amount of storage, and the capacity of its database will ultimately limit the number of remote agents that a platform can successfully monitor and manage. Intermediate agents can extend a platform's capacity by offloading simple collection activities. Larger environments require multiple platforms in order to successfully manage all of the computing and communication resources. A set of cooperating platforms is the foundation for enterprise management solutions.

11.1 BASIC PLATFORM FUNCTIONS

At the most abstract level, the management platform provides the services that allow management application developers to focus on the development of their particular solutions rather than dealing with many of the ordinary details of managing data, signaling other processes, communicating with remote entities, and so forth. The management platform is analogous to an operating system: its services support other activities.

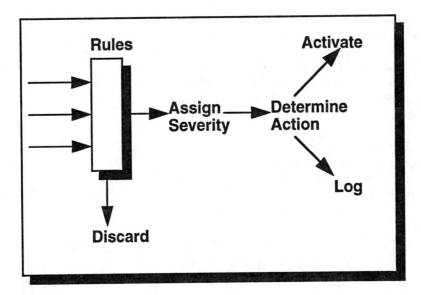

Event management services are incorporated in the platform—incoming reports are separated and those requiring further attention are passed on.

FIGURE 11–1   Platform event management

A management platform also decouples different management agents from the management applications that use their information. Many of the original network management platforms were implemented to take advantage of SNMP, the Simple Network Management Protocol; however, these original one-protocol platforms are evolving to accommodate a wide range of management protocols and architectures.

11.2 INFORMATION MANAGEMENT

Information management is a key ingredient in delivering quality management solutions. Chapter 2 covered the aspects of information management; many platforms bundle these services for the management tools they support. In fact, the effectiveness of the data management services is a major determinant in the performance of the platform and its tools. Inefficient or inadequate data management, slow, inefficient access routines, and other implementation-specific details may cause the data management services to act as a performance choke-point.

Information management services include a broad array of functions such as collecting management information, updating operational status, creating and updating topology information, and linking management tools to menus and topology maps in addition to providing an object broker, common data model, and logical repository.

Linkage   Management tools can be linked to icons on topology maps and to pull-down menu systems. Operators can launch management tools by clicking on the appropriate icon. They can also use pull-down menus for the same purpose. Configuration files are used to link tools with these launching mechanisms.

External Information Sources   Much of the information needed for successful management solutions resides in other databases within the enterprise, as well as in private data maintained by different management tools. Fragmented management information is partly caused by historical reasons such as the disjointed development of network

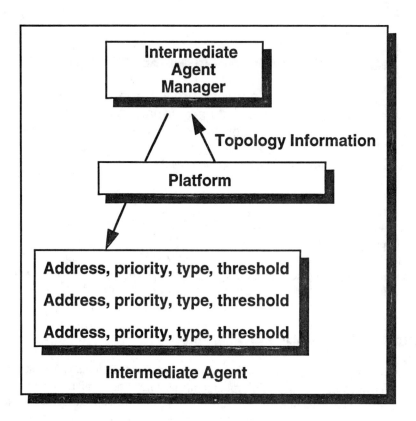

The Intermediate Agent Manager uses the platform as a source of information about associated agents. It builds polling lists and delivers them to the appropriate Intermediate Agent.

FIGURE 11–2   Managing intermediate agents

and systems management solutions. Platforms should provide the means to import and export information common to databases and spreadsheets.

The Missing Repository   A logical repository that insulates management tools from the details of finding information in different locations is key; most platforms today do not support a single, logical repository.

The Missing Data Model   Management tools can more easily share information when they use the same model for describing and accessing the information in the common repository. Increased data sharing is needed for automated management actions: each management tool must be able to find the information it needs without concern for which tool provided it. In the same way, a tool can place information in the repository without knowing which tools will use it. The data model provides a consistent way of describing all managed elements, as well as defining relationships between them. Unfortunately, we may have an emerging situation where each platform vendor is developing a proprietary data model. This will cause trouble for the Independent Software Vendors who must engineer their applications for each data model.

11.3 DOMAIN OR DISTRIBUTED MANAGEMENT

Very large environments raise scaling issues; how much can one platform manage? How are platform capacities increased as the environment grows larger?

One approach is to break an environment into smaller, more manageable portions known as domains. Each domain has a manager, and the set of domain managers cooperate and coordinate their actions as needed. Domains can be organized on geographical, functional, or skillset lines, as well as reflect policy mandates. Generally, there is an enterprise-level site that aggregates domain information to provide an overall view of the managed environment. Domain structures were originally organized along geographical perspectives in order to reduce management bandwidth, accommodate growth, and increase the management system's resilience.

The amount of information flowing within a management domain is typically much greater than that which flows between domains. Domains are often designed to minimize the flow of management traffic across expensive wide area links. Other choices for domain boundaries include different administrative policies for each domain or functional domains that encompass particular resources rather than geographical areas.

Continued growth is accommodated by adding new domains. Scaling is simple since each domain only contributes a small increase in interdomain management traffic. The enterprise-level site only takes a small additional resource increment to incorporate new management domains into an overall perspective.

Multiple domains also offer a fault-tolerant management environment. One platform can take over from another in the event of a failure or scheduled outage. During this time, management coverage may be reduced to the most essential elements, but some level of visibility, monitoring, and control remains in place at all times. One platform may also pass control to another to support scheduled changes in management operations.

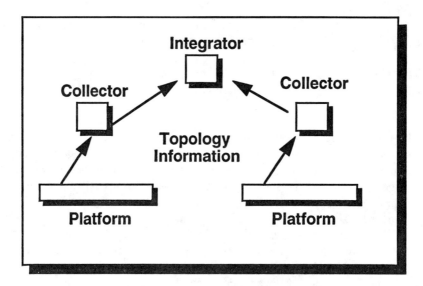

The isolation of the platforms meant that there was no single view of the enterprise networking and computing environments. Collectors extract topology information and forward it to an integrator which builds an enterprise view.

FIGURE 11–3   Topology integration

Enabling Distributed Management   Platforms must support communications between remote management tools; the ideal is that any management tool, anywhere, can use information from everywhere. Management tools must communicate to exchange information, to change the control relationships, and to synchronize information needed for "hot-standby" operation.

Platforms need the distributed information management services before they can support distributed management in the fullest sense. Distributed management tools are also required. These management tools must be designed for distributed operation. They will use services such as the request broker to locate the information they need. Distributed tools will also cooperate with each other; for example, each a tool can collect local topology information and forward it to a site where an enterprise view is created. Application designers must also develop the appropriate protocols for coordinating a set of tools on different platforms and decide on formats for exchanging information.

Host-Host MIB (RFC XX)   The SNMP Host-Host MIB provides a simple mechanism to further domain-based management. An SNMP manager uses the Host-Host

MIB to communicate with other managers. Managers can select remote MIB variables and specify thresholds. The remote SNMP manager monitors the MIB variable and forwards an event if thresholds are exceeded. Managers on "hot standby" can synchronize important data so they have the information needed to take over from a failed manager.

11.4 CLIENT/SERVER ARCHITECTURES

The SNMP management platforms are moving to a client/server architecture. The introduction of client/server architecture supplies a scalable approach where capacity can be easily added to keep pace with growth. A management platform becomes a true management server supporting clients that carry out different management tasks.

Capacity can be increased by separating functions such as database management from the management server. High performance database servers, analysis systems, and correlation tools can be placed throughout the managed environment. Fault tolerance is easily added by replicating critical elements so that single failures do not disrupt management operations.

The nature of a client/server architecture supports a different type of centralized management structure. The management team is a workgroup that shares one or more servers. The team members can be connected to any number of networks, in fact, some members will be mobile, bringing a laptop with them.

The management structure is still centralized because an administrator controls the management policies and staff throughout the environment. The administrator's privileges of configuring the management server determine which staff members can access different tools or which ones can take certain actions. Each staff member can be constrained to using a specific set of tools or managing a selected set of devices or servers. The Hewlett-Packard OperationsCenter is a good early example of this concept. Each staff member has a customized view of the managed environment with a window containing the tools he or she is allowed to use. Some staff members may only be able to monitor certain resources without being able to change their behavior. More skilled staff members will be allowed to carry out more sensitive tasks.

Administrators can determine the span of control allowed for each staff member. They can reassign tasks and areas as often as they need to in order to adapt to new situations. Further, supervisors receive reports of access control violations.

The management team members can be located wherever they are needed. They can be located at critical locations throughout the enterprise where fast access to local expertise is needed. The team members are coordinated and controlled through the management servers and the management tools and processes they support.

Client/server architectures also offer interesting possibilities for creative staffing. More enterprise networks are operating twenty-four hours a day with mission-critical applications. Around-the-clock staffing is expensive; yet the need for on-site management expertise becomes more compelling. Fewer staff can be used at the management centers while others can be on call if their experience is needed. Access with home computers or laptops gives them information and lets them activate diagnostics and offer advice.

Higher bandwidth connections will give remote users better graphics, faster interaction, and efficient bulk transfer services.

11.5 TOPOLOGY MAPS

The discovered database is used to create various levels of topology maps. These network maps show the components of the managed environment at varying levels of detail. An enterprise level view may show major sites and their wide area network interconnections, for instance. More detailed views may show the networks within a major site, a single network with attached devices, or detailed information about any connected element. Easy navigation between views is needed so the administrator can select the appropriate levels of detail. Map management allows status changes to "bubble up" to the current view. A failed server, for example, would change the color of a major site on an enterprise view, a major site view, or a single LAN segment view. Bubbling status alerts an administrator to a problem and guides him or her to the source of the alarm.

Customization options are used to build bit-mapped backgrounds for the topology maps. Administrators can use maps to show geographical, high-level views and building floor plans to show actual locations of equipment.

11.6 MEASUREMENT CONTROL

Measurement control is another basic function that most platforms support. An administrator defines polling and data collection intervals for different types of managed elements. The administrator can specify polling intervals that are dependent on the criticality and importance of the managed elements, as well as determining what types of specific information are gathered. Critical servers can be monitored more closely than those supporting less important applications, for instance. The measurements are automatically carried out after they are specified.

The discovery process can be linked to measurement control, allowing automatic setting of parameters whenever a new element is discovered. In this manner, administrators are saved from the tedious and error-prone process of specifying measurements for each element manually.

11.7 AUTOMATION

Automation is a key ingredient of effective management solutions. Platforms supply a part of the necessary automation facilities. For example, platforms allow an administrator to define and execute scripts. A scripting language allows an administrator to describe a set of rules governing actions to be taken when certain conditions occur. Scripts can be launched from the event management system whenever an event or collection of events meets the predefined criteria. The event management system can also assist automation through its ability to create sequences of tool actions into larger processes.

Basically, the platform provides simple utilities for enabling initiation of predefined procedures and actions. Scripting relieves administrators from repetitive simple tasks. Complex tasks require more complicated scripts that are difficult to create and debug. The major contributors to high value automated management will be the application providers who add automation within their own applications, as well as those who take advantage of the platform infrastructure where necessary.

11.8   INTEGRATION

Platforms are also one of the focal points for providing a more integrated management solution. Platforms help integration first by the colocation of disparate sources of management information. Platforms are the places where information is collected, although in most cases today, it is not integrated in the most useful fashion for administrators. Potential buyers need to view claims of integrated management carefully.

The platform provides lower levels of integration such as incorporating different devices into the topology maps, integrating commands and applications into the appropriate pull-down menus and other graphical user interfaces, and MIB editors or compilers. Map integration allows the different tools on the platform to add information to the map, as well as change it.

Another level gives the administrator the ability to activate tools from the icon on the topology map. Menu integration and GUI integration provide a consistent look and feel to all the platforms, tools, features, and functions, simplifying operator training and reducing the level of errors.

MIB integration provides a way for adding and removing different MIB definitions as the composition of the managed environment changes. Each new device, application, or desktop that is added to the environment will also have an associated MIB. The new MIB information must be incorporated into the standard platform schema so all the management applications can access it as necessary.

The platform also provides a level of integration through its data management and event management capabilities, as well. The highest levels of integration are not going to come from the platforms themselves. Rather, it will be systems integrators, management tool vendors, and customers who will painfully build these solutions over time.

11.9   MULTIPROTOCOL MANAGEMENT

The remaining SNMP platform vendors are actively incorporating other management environments into their platforms. This reflects the nature of real environments which are generally heterogeneous, consisting of major elements from Novell, OS/2, Microsoft's emerging NT, UNIX, SNA, and DECnet. Management tools are insulated from the basic communications mechanisms in the platform, so adding a different protocol is relatively straightforward. The key ingredient is mapping services that translate between internal data formats and that of each new protocol.

True multiprotocol management requires common data models and applications that span varying parts of the managed environment. Inventory applications can work with any managed environment while diagnostics and detailed operations will remain protocol-specific. An early leader in this area is IBM; the NetView/6000 platform has the General Topology Manager which incorporates topology information from different sources such as Novell NetWare, IBM, and SNA.

11.10 TOOLS

The value of a management platform is directly related to the available tool set. Administrators need an array of management tools and depend on the platform to support them. A few management tools such as automated discovery are usually provided with the basic management platform, most of the remaining tools are supplied by various sources.

Many tools are vendor-specific: they are supplied in order to sell other types of networking products. Vendors of network devices, computer systems, and applications offer management tools as differentiators and because most customers demand at least minimal management support today. The vendors offer additional management functions in their products through proprietary MIB extensions. This serves to make the vendor-specific product the usual choice for administrators.

There are also target-specific tools emerging in the client/server arena. Novell, for example, has the largest share of the network operating system market and there are many other vendors offering NetWare management products. Companies such as Frye Computer Systems, Central Point, Network Computing Devices, and Intel offer a suite of NetWare management products. Administrators welcome a choice of products in this area and the freedom it gives them to trade between costs and functions.

There are tools that are neutral; they are not designed for a specific vendor nor a target. A trouble-ticketing tool for problem management is a clear example. The problem management tool collects problem reports and information from sources such as device managers, operating system agents, and applications. Tracking inventory is another case of a neutral tool; it assembles information about all types of managed resources.

A large number of management tools is a strong differentiator since the tools supply the solutions. Management platform vendors continue to increase their supply of management tools. Luring the critical mass of vendors to a platform is a major goal of the marketing campaigns.

All vendors want to increase the depth, breadth, and quality of the tool sets that are available on their platforms. Some vendors such as Hewlett-Packard and IBM have formed third party groups to exchange information, help with common marketing information, and stimulate the demand for platforms and applications. These vendor groups are also defining integration levels more clearly so that potential customers have a clearer sense of what to expect.

1.11 FUTURE DIRECTIONS

The major evolutionary trends are distributed management, expanding the environments, middleware, client/server architectures, and new models. Each platform vendor is emphasizing different areas, but all of these issues must be addressed if SNMP platforms are to step up to real enterprise management capability.

Distributed Frameworks   The framework for distributed management is being attacked by all the significant platform vendors, who are defining common repository and data model strategies. Unfortunately, we are in danger of having a multitude of proprietary open common data models, basically one per platform. If this happens, it will certainly improve the quality of solutions while still making it difficult for third-party vendors porting applications between platforms. The third-party vendors and the users have the most to gain by having an industry-wide data model that would be implemented and supported on all management platforms.

Platform Middleware   A type of "middleware" is evolving, which may alter the balance and technical level of the tool sets that are available. Cabletron has done the most along this line with its Spectrum for Open Systems, an initiative that allows customers to leverage their existing platform investments. With Spectrum for Open Systems, customers using other platforms such as Hewlett-Packard's OpenView, IBM's NetView on AIX, or SunNet Manager add an additional layer of software between the basic platform and the applications available for Cabletron's Spectrum platform.

This middleware makes up, in a sense, for the (implied) lower technical level of other platforms by providing additional services to bring the infrastructure up to the level expected by the Spectrum applications. Cabletron is positioning this type of middleware to enable customers to protect their current investments while increasing the capability and functionality of their management systems. Other types of middleware are appearing without being accurately defined as such.

The Hewlett-Packard OperationCenter is another example of the type of middleware. The OperationsCenter provides a framework for systems management tools, applications, and processes. It is interposed between the basic OpenView platform functions and more sophisticated tools. The OperationsCenter contains its own message handling, multiuser access control, and automated routines for managing different types of desktops, servers, and so forth. Although not identified explicitly as a type of middleware, the OperationsCenter performs a similar function as the middleware provided by the Spectrum for Open Systems initiative.

Expanded Environments   Platform vendors are putting significant effort into moving their management platform software to as many different hardware environments as possible. Administrators want scalable solutions that match their environments. Incorporating a single UNIX system to manage a set of PCs running the Microsoft Windows Operating System is more difficult from a logistical and training perspective than having the same management capabilities on a Windows system. New operating systems like Microsoft's NT figure in everyone's plans. In the future there will be a wide range of clients that access the management server.

New Platform Models   The current crop of UNIX-based platforms are restrictive. Most still require that database and management tools reside on the same machine as the platform software. This restriction limits scalability and flexibility in platform solutions. Platform vendors have been slow to step up to the real demands of distributed man-

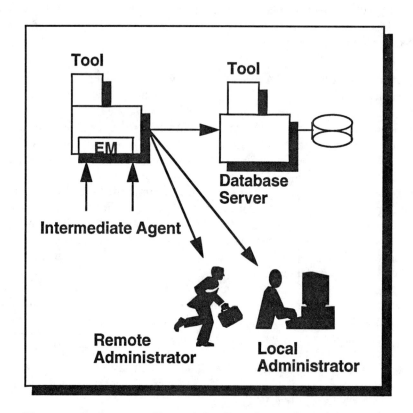

Future platforms will exploit client/server architectures.
Event managers collect information from distributed
intermediate agents and distribute it to management
tools throughout the organization.

FIGURE 11–4   Future platforms

agement. In fairness, the management tool vendors will also need to contribute better tools that exploit a distributed framework.

Future platforms will not follow the current approach. The advent of client/server architectures and distributed frameworks will make the current platform obsolete. In fact, there are several factors that could lead to a "lite" platform approach.

For example, distributed, intelligent instrumentation systems can operate without platform support; Bridgeway Corporation's EventIX and Legent Corporation's Agent-Works are two examples. Sophisticated event management is another application that can operate without significant platform resources. The NetLabs NerveCenter is being ported to the OpenView platform as an application. Much of the distributed framework can be provided by the relational database vendors who are working hard on the distributed database management problems. Client-based management tools can access information in a management server. Further, management tools can use the emerging DCE (Distributed Computing Environment from the Open Software Foundation) technology to support client/server management applications. The common model is still the sticking point, and, unfortunately, no one is stepping up to address this problem.

11.12 SUMMARY

A powerful set of management tools depends on the enabling services of a management platform. The platform services are being hidden by more sophisticated tools that offer better management solutions. The overall quality of a tool set will depend to some extent on the supporting platform and its ability to provide key services. Some platform services are actually placed there for convenience. Event management is a sophisticated management application that filters and correlates incoming management information. These services are embedded in the platform to simplify the construction of management tools and to keep leverage with third-party tool vendors.

Management platforms are still relatively immature, although all products are evolving to incorporate client/server architectures and distributed frameworks. The next chapter looks at the leading platforms and their actual capabilities.

CHAPTER 12

Real Platforms

The preceding chapter discussed the role of platforms and the types of services they provide. This chapter discusses some of the leading network management platforms, giving examples of the current state of the products, as well as some future trends and directions. We will not be comparing low-level details such as the number of event severity levels since these factors are not strategic.

Overall, the SNMP management platform market has shaken out, leaving at this point only a handful of players, Hewlett-Packard, IBM/Digital, SunSoft, and Cabletron Systems.

These few vendors have survived the tremendous competition and changes in the platform marketplace. Some got their start through licensing technology while others are combining forces for future efforts. This set of surviving SNMP platforms is complemented by legacy managers from other companies, such as Boole and Babbage, Objective Systems Integrators, and MAXM.

The SNMP platforms are evolving to multiprotocol management platforms that will eventually be able to provide an enterprise-level management solution. Most of the current crop of platforms cannot really manage a large enterprise right "out of the box" after purchase. The needed distributed frameworks are missing from most products. Platforms will also need the support of intermediate agents (see Chapter 6) and customized help to take on large numbers of managed elements.

12.1 HEWLETT-PACKARD OPENVIEW

Hewlett-Packard's OpenView is considered the leading SNMP platform in the market today. HP has exploited its early entry, solid technology, and aggressive marketing to bring OpenView to a dominant position that has captured the mind share of the market at

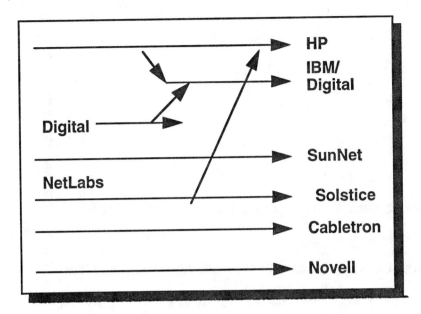

There has been considerable interchange over time. IBM
NetView for AIX was licensed from HP and Digital
subsequently licensed IBM's code. NetLabs licensed
DIMONS to SunSoft and the NerveCenter to HP.

FIGURE 12–1   Platform pedigrees

this time. Hewlett-Packard has continued to put pressure on its competitors through
steady enhancements of the basic platform, moving to other hardware environments, and
recruiting other management tool suppliers.

Hewlett-Packard was an early pioneer in building a stable of Independent Software
Vendors (ISVs) who offer well-known management tools for OpenView. This wide
choice of third-party applications was one of the major factors that accelerated the growth
and acceptance of OpenView.

The HP Vision

Hewlett-Packard is evolving its products toward a policy-oriented management solution.
As shown in the figure, there are three levels to the HP solution framework. The bottom
level contains the managed environments, such as UNIX, NetWare, and TCP/IP. Other
managed environments, such as DECnet and SNA, can be incorporated within the same
framework. The next level defines management tasks that must be carried out across all
the managed environments. Such tasks include systems operations, monitoring, and con-

> **Strong event management**
>
> **Automated tool launch**
>
> **Open APIs**
>
> **Open database**
>
> **Tool selection**
>
> **Scalability through domain management**
>
> **Client/server**

The necessary features for enterprise management are not widely available yet. Each vendor is stressing different aspects of the solution.

FIGURE 12–2   Platform features

figuration. The highest level of HP's solution strategy are the management processes themselves. These processes use individual management tasks in various combinations to carry out management activities. Examples of management processes include problem management, performance management, change management, and asset/inventory management.

A process-oriented focus provides a high level of abstraction, separating the administrator from many of the technical details of individual products, features, and functions. However, to provide this level of abstraction requires a powerful and flexible underlying infrastructure. Administrators must be able to map management processes to the appropriate management tasks and through them, to the targeted managed environments. The framework must be powerful enough for managers to be able to control the sequence of activation of various management tasks and to be able to replace point solutions in the management tasks when new products are available. A process management emphasis allows administrators to optimize their management processes rather than manage technology.

Managing at the process level hides many of the details of individual management tasks and, further, hides the particular tasks that have to be applied within each managed environment. In this way, management can be oriented toward the higher value levels.

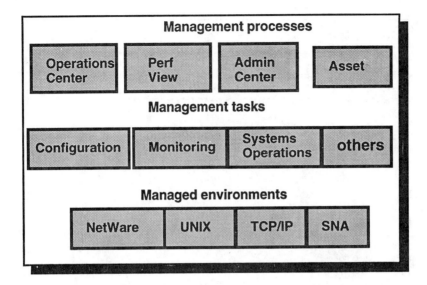

Hewlett-Packard is building process-oriented performance centers on top of the basic OpenView platform. They will be offering policy-based, distributed management through the centers.

FIGURE 12–3   HP Management vision

Basic Architecture

OpenView is available for two major environments: UNIX and Microsoft Windows. Microsoft NT will be available in the future. UNIX versions of OpenView are available on HP workstations, Sun workstations, and in the future, other UNIX platforms such as IBM's AIX. The Windows version can forward events to the UNIX platform, providing a solution from the local workgroup to the enterprise level.

Basic Platforms   The OpenView platform contains basic services, such as event management, scheduling management tools, protocol-independent communications, a topology database, and the Application Programming Interfaces. The major HP elements that are heavily integrated with the platform include the **Node Manager**, now capable of managing both TCP/IP and Novell NetWare nodes. The Node Manager provides automatic topology discovery and the ability to map events to particular symbols on the graphical representation of the networks. The Node Manager also contains basic utilities for graphing variables (the Application Builder), MIB browsers, and simple utilities to locate elements on different search criteria (MAC address, IP address, host name, and so forth).

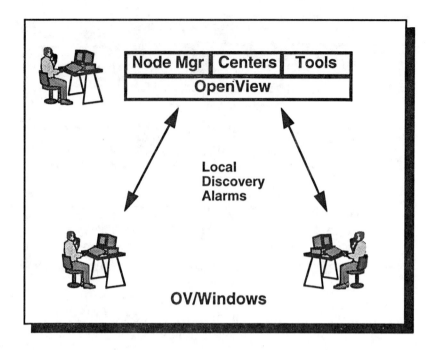

OpenView for Windows and the UNIX platform are collaborating to scale the capabilities by offloading the UNIX platform.

FIGURE 12–4   OpenView elements

Performance Centers   The **OperationsCenter** is a newer framework that supports systems management solutions. The OperationsCenter has more sophisticated message handling, allowing finer granularity and automatic parsing of events. The OperationsCenter graphical user interface organizes the system administrator's environment by grouping the managed systems in a window. For example, grouping allows administrators to monitor all critical servers in a single view: the icons change colors to indicate operational health. This is a much simpler visual organizational than trying to track critical resources which are distributed across many different LAN segments on a topology map. The WorkDesk allows multiple management applications and tasks to be assembled and coordinated by operators.

The OperationsCenter tool palette lets the administrator apply any systems management tool to any system (or group of systems with a simple drag-and-drop operation. Other windows provide automated guidance and suggestions as the administrator carries out processes. A supervisor can customize each administrator's work space so that they see only the systems they manage and the tools they are allowed to use.

The OperationsCenter assists with the automation of various steps by providing guidance as processes are carried out, offering suggestions and feedback to the administrators. The OperationsCenter is a strategic framework for Hewlett-Packard and additional applications, as well as technical enhancements, will continue into the future.

Hewlett-Packard is also providing a higher level of functional integration through the OperationsCenter. For example, a new backup product (OmniBack II) allows for central administration of multiple backup applications throughout an enterprise.

A central administrator can control the entire backup operation from a central site or can delegate any part of the backup tasks to local administrators or users. This provides a level of integration for enforcing policy and overall standards and structures, as well as providing the requisite flexibility that many locally administered environments require. The OperationsCenter provides the appropriate types of frameworks for integrating these different tools and processes and will continue to be on the leading edge of HP's continued thrusts.

HP has two other process centers—the AdminCenter and PerfView. The AdminCenter manages configuration management processes such as configuring groups of systems, testing for the effects of changes, and imposing policy control over configuration changes. PerfView uses distributed collectors to gather performance-related information from a variety of systems. It can display and compare performance data and automatically alert the management system when thresholds are exceeded.

HP offers the **Intelligent Agent** software for various flavors of UNIX systems. This intermediate agent handles local polling of SNMP devices as well as monitoring UNIX system behavior.

Future Directions

HP has announced its next two phases for OpenView. **Tornado,** the code name for the first phase, introduces a distributed framework. A central OpenView platform can monitor and coordinate a set of satellite platforms. This will be HP's first venture into a more distributed architecture for its UNIX platform. One of the goals is to offload the domain manager, OpenView, by moving more information processing to satellite sites.

The satellite sites are the key to Tornado. They are actually full Network Node Managers without the local interface. Each satellite site provides local status polling, automatic discovery, event handling and forwarding as well as long-term data collection. Powerful analysis and correlation tools can be deployed at each site to strengthen local management operations. The same tools can be used at the central site to build integrated views and overall management processes.

The Tornado approach offers considerable scalability since each Network Node Manager is capable of handling a reasonably sized management domain on its own. Multiple satellites can be deployed as needed in order to balance the processing load with the central site as well as to conserve bandwidth across WAN links.

The combination of powerful satellite sites and a central domain manager provides fault tolerance in several ways. If a satellite site fails, the domain manager can take over remote polling. This may consume more network bandwidth and provide less than optimum operation, but it maintains management coverage of at least the critical resources. If a domain manager fails, an alternate domain manager can take over control of the community of satellite sites. A new domain manager simply instructs all satellite sites to continue forwarding information to it instead of the former domain manager. Since most of the processing is carried out at the satellite sites, there is little additional load on the new domain manager. Unfortunately, a recent slippage in delivery pushes Tornado back at least a year, limiting OpenView's ability to scale with increasing growth.

The next phase, **Synergy**, adds an object-oriented framework to enable it to support distributed management operations. HP and its partners have initiated work on a common data model in order to facilitate information sharing and data integration.

HP has built alliances with other major players such as AT&T, Legent Corporation, and Microsoft. It is also developing more relationships with new vendors of management tools.

12.2 IBM NETVIEW FOR AIX

IBM entered the SNMP platform business by licensing the OpenView technology from Hewlett-Packard. IBM no longer uses the OpenView technology; it is undertaking its own development with its partner Digital Equipment Corporation. IBM is still trying to catch OpenView, although it has established itself as a serious competitor.

NetView for AIX is a UNIX-based multiprotocol management platform. Originally developed for the IBM RS/6000 processor, NetView also runs on other hardware such as Sun workstations and others such as HP are in ongoing plans.

The IBM Vision

IBM is focusing on the major issues in enterprise management: scalability, openness, distributed management, cost of ownership, and increasing management staff effectiveness. NetView for AIX is a major member of the NetView family (described later in this chapter); it manages client/server environments and can exchange information with other NetView members. NetView for AIX collects information from NetView for OS/2 and NetView for Windows and acts as the real-time manager of these environments. NetView for AIX can use the automation capabilities of Host NetView as needed.

Basic Architecture

Although IBM started with the HP core technology, NetView for AIX is far from an OpenView clone. IBM has actually taken the lead in several important technical areas. Some of its strongest features include its user interface, the General Topology Manager, and the SystemMonitor/6000.

The user interface is a key element of NetView for AIX; IBM committed substantial resources to improve the product's usability. The user interface is designed for ease of operation and effective management procedures. Some of the features that have won growing recognition for the user interface include the Navigation Tree, Control Desk, and drag-and-drop operations.

Operators use multiple windows for presenting information as they carry out management procedures. The Navigation Tree makes it easy for an operator to trace through multiple views and easily locate a specific one. Operators can move directly between views instead of traversing a series of windows to reach the screen they need. The Control Desk provides a work space for operators and was the first product that allowed an operator to control multiple management applications from a single window (the HP OperationsCenter also supports this feature now. Drag-and-drop operations simplify management tasks in the Control Desk. For example, an operator can collect information in the Control Desk window, then drag-and-drop a graphing icon on the information to produce graphical analyses of network traffic.

IBM has been first in offering topology data integration with GTM, the **General Topology Manager**. GTM incorporates information from different logical topology

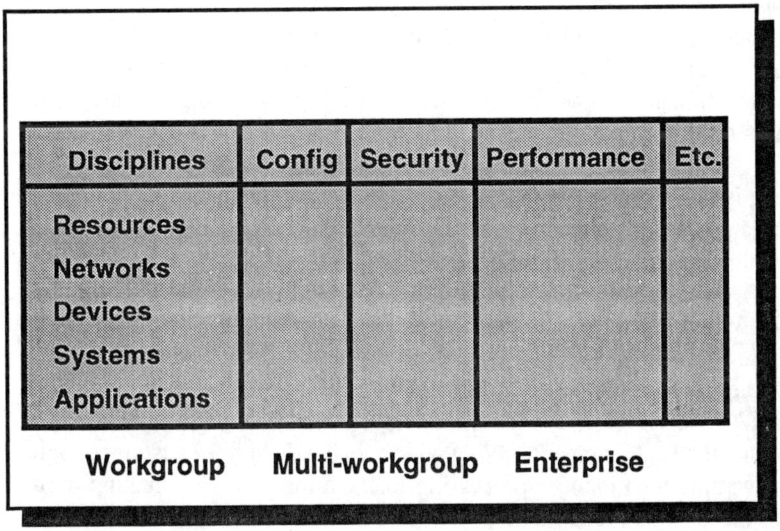

Disciplines	Config	Security	Performance	Etc.
Resources				
Networks				
Devices				
Systems				
Applications				

Workgroup   Multi-workgroup   Enterprise

IBM will use NetView for AIX as a manager of other NetView platforms such as OS/2 and Windows. Systems monitors can be used for local topology collection.

FIGURE 12–5   NetView for AIX

schemes into a single unified view of the managed environment. Topology information from the NetWare, OS/2, and the SNA environments are incorporated at this time.

Administrators can select various views depending on the management task: an asset/inventory application may look at all desktop systems while troubleshooting tools will use a specific logical view, such as TCP/IP.

GTM is an important element for integrated management, since it provides a single, consistent means of accessing and sharing information between different topologies. GTM will enable more powerful management applications. For example, an inventory application can search across multiple environments through GTM. GTM can serve as a base for incorporating more information in the future and may offer a general common data model.

IBM has also introduced **client/server** architectures for NetView for AIX. The first steps separate the database from the management platform so that the customer can choose the database server they want. This will provide increased scalability and fault tolerance in the future. The combination of domain management and client/server implementations gives IBM a strong offering for large-scale environments. NetView for AIX has also taken leadership from HP in domain management. A set of platforms can cooperate in managing a large environment. The peer-to-peer architecture allows easy transfer of control and fault tolerance since any platform can take over operations from a failing platform or one that is taken out of service for other reasons.

Client/server applications also allow administrators to deploy them on different computing platforms, offering flexibility in configuring and placing their resources for the best results. The TroubleTicket/6000 problem management application is an early example of such an application. The client-server approach provides a great deal of openness for customers since future elements can be dropped into the client-server framework as needed.

Scaling issues also arise within a single management domain; for example, managing a large number of elements may strain a single platform and consume scarce backbone bandwidth. Distributing the management processing throughout the domain offers a graceful way to accommodate growth.

SystemMonitor for AIX is the first NetView for AIX element providing distributed management processing. The SystemMonitor for AIX is attached to a LAN segment where it handles local polling. The SystemMonitor collects management information, detects thresholds, and forwards events to the NetView for AIX platform. Polling traffic is localized within the LAN segment, saving wide area bandwidth for customer applications. Problem forwarding also reduces processing loads at the platform, making more power available for management tools.

The SystemMonitor will serve as the basis for distributed management applications in the future. For instance, local discovery is now carried out and the topology is forwarded to the NetView for AIX platform.

The SystemMonitor will be joined by the Segment Manager, a product that handles local monitoring and management of attached devices and computer systems. Segment Managers will be able to deal with local problems, communicate with NetView for AIX, and take overall directions from it.

IBM and Digital: The NetView Platform

Digital licensed the NetView software as the basis for its POLYCENTER on NetView platform. Digital will provide SNMP-based management as well as supporting its own DECnet networks. One attraction is the ALPHA processor—at this time a significant price/performance breakthrough. The ALPHA provides substantial computing power to support more management tools and computing-intensive management applications.

12.3 SUNSOFT SOLSTICE

SunSoft has responded to the increased competition with its **Solstice** program. Solstice includes a core set of SunSoft products, including an object-based, distributed management platform, a set of systems management tools, and a strong third-party vendor program.

The SunSoft Vision

SunSoft is gearing its solutions toward high-level management disciplines such as capacity planning, problem management, security management, performance management, change management, and workload and data management. It is moving toward providing all four levels of distributed management: collection, information, control, and tools. SunSoft now includes core sets of management tools as part of its Solstice offerings.

Customers use a variety of hardware platforms and SunSoft offers a set of solutions. The strategy for Solstice applications is to support the leading volume platforms, the leading RISC and CISC hardware (SPARC, Power PC, and Intel processors), and the leading UNIX and Windows operating environments (Solaris, Windows, and Windows NT) and to manage all objects in a network environment. Customers can choose the environment that is comfortable and familiar without sacrificing functionality.

Management Platforms

SunSoft is building a family of management platforms and infrastructure products that addresses management needs, ranging from a single workgroup to a multinational enterprise. Some of the products such as the Solstice SunNet Manager are established market leaders while new platform technology for the high-end enterprise solution is introduced.

The **Solstice SunNet Manager** (formerly the SunNet Manager) has been a proven product for many years and remains a leader in terms of installed units. SunNet Manager is a powerful SNMP manager that is targeted for the workgroup or departmental environment. It supports a single user at a management console and has a wide selection of third-party management tools. The Solstice SunNet Manager protects current investments in management tools while providing a path to more advanced technology. Future plans, discussed later, will enhance this product substantially.

The recent introduction of **Cooperative Consoles** provides another level of man-

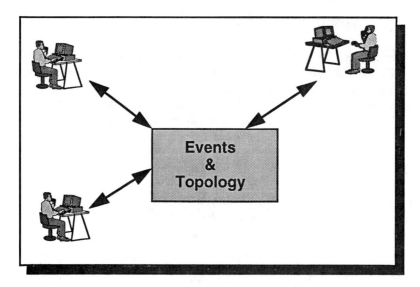

SunSoft is focusing on the set of management
disciplines that must be applied to resources in
managed environments of differing sizes.

FIGURE 12–6   SunSoft management vision

agement coverage and represents a significant technology leap for the Solstice SunNet
Manager platforms. Multiple SunNet Manager consoles can share topology and events
through Cooperative Consoles interconnections. Security and access control mechanisms
filter information as it flows between different consoles.

The **Solstice Enterprise Manager** (SEM) is SunSoft's new enterprise management
platform. Based on the NetLabs DIMONS/3G technology, the Solstice Enterprise Manager is an advanced multiuser, multiprotocol management platform. Further, it is designed
from a truly distributed management perspective: network management staff can manage
anything in the network from anywhere on the network. The major element is known as
the **MIS**—Management Information Server.

The SEM has a powerful set of capabilities for enterprise management. A **distributed framework** supports multiple MIS throughout the enterprise. Each MIS exchanges
information, forwards alarms, and ensures that management coverage extends throughout
the enterprise.

Multiuser support allows customized views as well as access controls for each
staff member. An administrator determines exactly what each management staff member
sees, the tools that can be used, and privileges that are allowed.

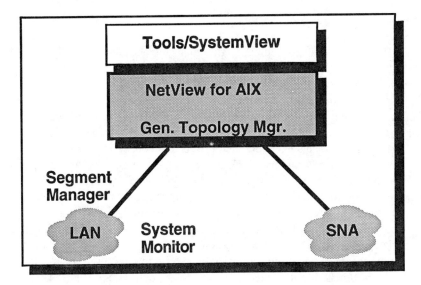

Cooperative Consoles acts as a switch for event and topology information between SunNet Manager consoles.

FIGURE 12–7   SunSoft cooperative consoles

The Solstice Enterprise Manager operates with a distributed **object-based** management repository. An object request broker locates objects on any MIS. Object technology is also used for automating discovery, for example. When a new object of a certain class, such as a router, is discovered, default monitoring and thresholds are applied. This allows an administrator to create policies that can be applied to any managed object of the appropriate class.

An important consideration: the SEM was initially designed for an object-based framework. This is a distinct advantage since SunSoft will not have to reengineer its products to scale up to new demands in the future. Both HP and IBM will require substantial development efforts to reach this level, and HP's Tornado has already experienced significant delays.

The SEM also supports **remote application execution.** The use of the **Portable Management Interface** separates management tools from the management platform. This is a powerful feature since it places the tools where the staff are located. It also supports highly mobile staff since the tools can be moved through the network if necessary. Management staff can use any appropriate tool from any location and have the power and the flexibility of the Solstice Enterprise Manager at their fingertips.

Solstice Core Management Tools

Advanced platforms are useless without quality management tools. SunSoft is building a set of tools that are tightly integrated with their platforms.

SunSoft characterizes superior tools as those that deliver automation, replication, and simplification. **Automation** can be used to automatically configure a new system with the same profile that applies to the other systems in that group. **Replication** leverages management tasks against as many resources as possible, freeing management staff for more important efforts. Systems managers apply their efforts to a collection of systems rather than one at a time. **Simplification** eases network administrators' burdens by providing powerful graphical user interfaces, effective screen navigation, and other productivity aids.

SunSoft is building a set of systems management applications with solutions targeted for the end-user, workgroup, and enterprise. The end-user products are designed to minimize local management labor through pre-defined profiles, automatic application registry, serial port management, user account management, and software distribution methods. Much of this configuration information can be set up before the machine actually arrives and is attached to the network. As much as possible, the new Solaris systems are self-installing.

Workgroup and enterprise management solutions address larger environments. Sets of clients and servers are managed through the network. Process management is essential; administrators need embedded intelligence to help them oversee complex management activities. Further, the use of smart defaults simplifies initial configuration and gives administrators a base from which to customize their own management operations.

The Core Product tools give administrators the capabilities needed for solid, productive enterprise management. The **Solstice Firewall-1**, for example, is a sophisticated IP firewall that protects an enterprise network from external attacks. Violations are signaled to one of the SunSoft management platforms. **Solstice AutoClient** is an innovative approach to software management since no software, including the operating system is distributed to the client. **Solstice JumpStart** uses predefined profiles to automate configuration and installation of software on desktops. Configuration management for Solaris and PC environments is available with **Solstice Admintools** and **PC Admin**, respectively. Administrators can configure resources and apply profiles to groups of systems.

Data Management is a critical area and SunSoft provides a set of tools. **Solstice Backup** supports backup and restore services for twenty-two types of heterogeneous clients. **Solstice DiskSuite** offers disk mirroring and striping for high performance. Journaling allows quick file system restart and recovery. The **Solstice High Availability Suite** adds failovers and RAID capabilities to the DiskSuite product.

Future Developments

This initial introduction of the Solstice program is only the first step of an ongoing process that will continue to strengthen SunSoft's entire enterprise management offering. The line of Solstice products will be unified to provide the best solution across the entire line. For example, application portability is already provided so that applications written for SunNet Manager, Version 2.2.2 or later, will also run on the SEM without modifications. SunSoft has moved to protect customers' investments and allow them to move to a more sophisticated management platform.

In addition, SunSoft will retrofit the SunNet Manager with some of the advanced technology that is being interdicted in the Solstice Enterprise Manager. Future directions include incorporation of object technology and the ability to communicate and exchange information between the two platforms.

12.4   CABLETRON SPECTRUM

Cabletron Systems introduced Spectrum, another technical leader, several years ago. Spectrum was one of the first commercially available platforms to differentiate itself through the incorporation of inference technology. The initial Spectrum rollout was expensive and complex, although very powerful. Many end-users found the product to be very difficult to configure, and some of the initial acceptance was through systems integrators, who had the technical expertise to build a turnkey solution. Spectrum has a growing following of users who appreciate its innovations and expert technology.

Cabletron's Vision

Cabletron is attacking the enterprise management problem with "artificial intelligence" in Spectrum as well as embedded management processing in its own products. Spectrum incorporates the "network model" into its inference technology. This model describes each element and its relationships such as connectivity or the area of responsibility or control.

Any event is passed through the network model and the appropriate rules are applied. These rules should yield a diagnosis or suggestion for corrective action. Other management tools can be activated after the network model delivers its findings.

There are some barriers to using the network model effectively. The primary one is understanding a complex piece of technology and learning how to exploit its capabilities. Administrators need to be able to create new rules and modify them as necessary. Another issue is testing new rules: How are they verified without creating problems in the network? Finally, each new device, system, or application that is added must be accompanied by a set of rules that can be incorporated into Spectrum. Cabletron has made strong progress in simplifying Spectrum and making it easier to use.

Basic Architecture

Spectrum was initially built with a client/server architecture, allowing for scaled solutions and for distributed management. Spectrum has two major components: the SpectroServer and SpectroGraph. Typically two workstations are needed to handle the heavy computing

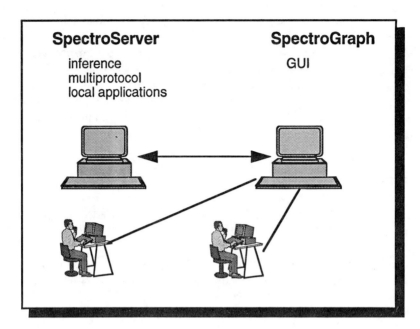

Spectrum has two major elements: the server and the presentation manager. The client/server architecture allows staff to access information from any location.

FIGURE 12–8   Cabletron spectrum

demands that both elements make. The **SpectroServer** contains the **Network Virtual Machine**, the model of the managed environment along with the appropriate rules for each managed resource. Tools allow managers to build new rules and apply them to the model as needed. The basic connectivity information is supplied by an automatic discovery tool.

The **SpectroGraph** contains the graphical user interface, maps, and other management tools that use the model in the SpectroServer. Cabletron also provides a database isolation layer so that administrators can use a variety of database managers with Spectrum.

A distributed data management facility is already available. Any application running on any SpectroServer can access information stored in any other SpectroServer.

Cabletron has also embarked on the Spectrum for Open Systems program; it offers management middleware that enhances the technology of other platforms such as Open-

View or SunNet Manager. Spectrum applications can take full advantage of these other platforms as well as provide superior solutions that depend on the middleware.

Tools

Spectrum suffers most from a smaller selection of management tools relative to the other players. Part of this is due to competitive realities: Bay Networks is understandably reluctant to port its management tools for SynOptics Hubs to a competitor's management platform, for example. Other third-party vendors have not ported their tools to Spectrum because it offered a smaller market than HP OpenView.

Cabletron responds that its easy modeling technologies allow customers to incorporate any device easily and build the appropriate event management rules to manage it without needing additional specific tools.

Future Directions

Spectrum will become more distributed as pieces are embedded in Cabletron's networking products. The Network Virtual Machine can be extracted and embedded into other management tools, increasing their intelligence and functionality. Spectrum has very powerful features and it should do well in complex environments. Cabletron is also working to add more functionality for managing the emerging switched environments.

12.5 NOVELL MANAGEWISE

Novell and Intel have combined to offer ManageWise, an integrated product combining Novell's NetWare Management System and Intel's LANDesk Manager. ManageWise offers SNMP management as well as management of Novell NetWare clients, servers, routers, and other network devices.

Basic Architecture

The NetWare Management System is based on management services that are distributed on NetWare servers throughout the enterprise. The set of management services includes device management, software management (distribution, licensing, and metering), server administration, inventory management, traffic analysis, and storage management. The management services are applications that can access local server information and the collected inventory and topology information as needed.

LANDesk is an integrated set of Novell management utilities that include printer management, virus scanning, and desktop management. LANDesk includes scripts for many common problems. If users report that they cannot access the printer, for example, an administrator can execute the "I can't print," which automatically runs through a set of diagnostic steps to identify the cause of the problem.

Future Directions

Novell is continuing to strengthen its management solutions for its NetWare customers, especially with Microsoft's aggressive entry into systems management with the Systems Management Server (Hermes). Novell still has to establish that it has a multivendor enterprise management solution. The incorporation of leading SNMP management tools is a key factor that will determine Novell's success. Novell is under pressure from the enterprise platform vendors such as HP and IBM. They are improving their Novell management capabilities and offering deeper integration with other tools.

12.6 NETLABS DIMONS/3G

The DIMONS/3G platform from Seagate Enterprise Management Software (formerly NetLabs, Inc.), is one of the leading pieces of platform technology available today. Seagate has pioneered the development of a distributed management framework, integrated applications running on many platforms, and the implementation of high quality network management solutions, such as their AssetManager.

NetLabs Vision

NetLabs attacked the enterprise management problem by building a technically advanced framework for scalable, distributed management. The framework supported objects from the outset: a translator took SNMP MIB variables and mapped them into OSI management objects using the Guidelines For the Definition of Managed Objects. The goal was to provide high levels of integration and automation to attack enterprise management problems.

Basic Architecture

One of the key DIMONS elements is the Management Information Tree (MIT) manager. The MIT is a hierarchically structured tree that contains all the managed objects. All objects are mapped into the tree and their positions define containment relationships; for example, an add-on board is contained within a computer system.

Management tools request information from the MIT manager, which traverses the tree to find the appropriate information. NetLabs uses the idea of a "shadow node" which contains a pointer to an object that is actually located in a remote DIMONS platform. The MIT manager then directs a request to the remote node and retrieves the information. Thus, DIMONS offers a distributed, logical repository for all management information.

The NerveCenter was mentioned in the previous chapter. This event management system is based on state-transition descriptions rather than simpler relational operators. The NerveCenter is an integral component; administrators use the NerveCenter to control measurements, sort events, and activate other DIMONs services and management tools. This unique integration allows administrators to adjust their information collection activities as events occur (see the Chapter 6 on instrumentation as well). The rules for filtering and correlating events can be adapted as new situations arise.

The DIMONS discovery tool also offers a unique capability: it can automatically compare a discovered topology to a previous version and detect any changes. This feature allows administrators to detect unexpected or unauthorized changes to the managed environment. It can also build a topology description from scratch as all other platforms do.

NetLabs has suffered from a scarcity of management tools for its platform. It has provided its own applications including the AssetManager, the Service Desk (a help desk application), Assist (a problem routing tool), and Vision desktop (a graphical desktop management tool).

Future Directions

The new thrust at NetLabs will be in management applications. NetLabs has announced Co-Pilot, a management applications framework that will integrate their tools with those from other sources. Co-Pilot will be integrated with other management platforms. Net-Labs will continue to support DIMONS for its current customers.

NetLabs is also working to make the NerveCenter a stand-alone event management application that will be available on HP's OpenView platform in the future. It is expected that the NerveCenter will eventually be incorporated into HP's Operation Center.

12.7 LEGACY MANAGERS

There are other management platforms that were not initially targeted to the SNMP environment. They are called "legacy" platforms, implying that they manage equipment that is not standard (SNMP); however, the reality is that most managed equipment is not SNMP-compatible today. Therefore, legacy management platforms will be important as long as nonstandard products must be managed.

Legacy platforms share some common characteristics. One of the most important is that they offer a level of data integration that is not yet found in SNMP platforms. Legacy platforms accept management information from a large variety of sources. This information is, of course, in different formats.

A **parser** is used to deal with the variety of formats and information. It is instructed to extract information from different fields in an incoming management message. The extracted information is translated into a common format and placed in the legacy manager's database. Thus, management messages from different sources may contain similar information in different formats; the parser extracts it and transforms it into a common form that can be dealt with consistently. The parser also performs the reverse function, using common information to build a specific management message format; outgoing messages can be used to control element managers. One advantage that legacy platforms offer is that the parsing rules for most legacy equipment have already been developed and new users can take advantage of pre-packaged parsing rules for their equipment.

Legacy platforms use **event management** to sort the incoming event stream and to trigger automatic actions when criteria are satisfied. Automated actions include notifying staff, sending directives to element managers and activating other applications on the legacy platform.

OSI NetExpert

Objective Systems Integrators has a background in managing large telecommunications networks and working with carriers. They have extended NetExpert into other environments with SNMP interfaces. The NetExpert parses all incoming management messages into a CMIP format. After transformation, messages are forwarded to IDEAS (Intelligent

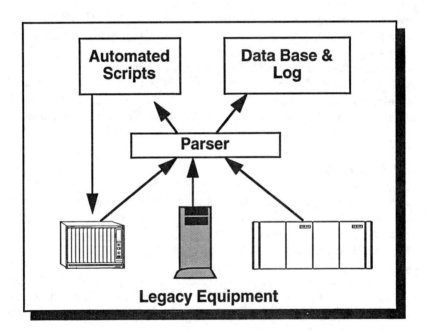

Legacy managers accept input from nonstandard equipment, translate it and capture it in logs. Scripts can be triggered to take corrective actions.

FIGURE 12–9   Legacy managers

Dynamic Event Analysis Subsystem), an expert rule-based module that analyzes each message. Messages can be correlated and trigger automated actions.

The Authorization Agent takes processed messages and assigns them to individual staff members for further attention. Rules can be used to assign problems by areas of expertise, severity, workload, or other criteria.

OSI provides a full set of editing tools so administrators can create and modify rules for IDEAS, the Authorization Agent, and other elements of NetExpert.

MAXM and Boole & Babbage

MAXM Systems Corporation offers similar services, stressing the automation capabilities of their platform. Parsing rules for many standard products are available as well as the rules for acting on different management messages. Extensive libraries of automated actions are used to eliminate staff involvement with most management tasks. The goal of the MAXM product is to deliver the "lights out" management that reduces costs and improves network service.

The Boole & Babbage COMMAND POST platform also stresses integration of legacy equipment and automation. Boole & Babbage have been aggressively collecting third party management tools for COMMAND POST, including storage management and backup tools.

Both products emerged from mainframe management environments and are being extended to the distributed networked environment.

IBM Host NetView

IBM is addressing management issues with a family of NetView management platforms. IBM wants to offer scalable, integrated management solutions for a wide range of environments. The NetView family will work together and each can be used to best advantage. The family includes Host NetView, NetView for AIX, NetView on OS/2 and NetView for Windows.

Host NetView is the original mainframe-based NetView product. It was originally intended for managing IBM's proprietary SNA networks and it is being extended as the enterprise management platform for SNA, TCP/IP, and other environments. Host NetView has suffered from the fact that it was never designed as an initial product. It began as a collection of individual tools that were lumped together under the NetView umbrella. IBM is still improving and integrating the product.

Host NetView also offers message parsing and automated actions. Parsing is more important now that Host NetView is taking on a bigger management role. Some degree of automation was provided through scripting and linkage to user written applications.

The early NetView product lacked a common logical management repository for sharing data among management tools. IBM is offering a two-level data management scheme using RODM and INFOMAN.

INFOMAN (Information Manager) manages configuration information in an SQL database. INFOMAN offers reports and search functions for administrators. Management applications can use INFOMAN for topology management, asset management, and software version control. Additionally, a single trouble-ticketing application can track faults from a variety of sources and manage them in a uniform way.

The **Resource Object Data Manager** (RODM) is an object-oriented data cache; implemented in virtual memory for fast access to real-time management information. Fast access is provided by explicit search keys for each specific instance in the virtual store. RODM only contains real-time management data which is periodically transferred to permanent media. Changes in a particular object can cause RODM to activate other applications. For instance, a server failure launches the appropriate tools for the type of server: OS/2, TCP/IP, NetWare, etc.

IBM has published the RODM specifications, opening the way for NetView for AIX and other management platforms to transfer their topology and status information to Host NetView. RODM will be used to integrate the information from any type of network that can be described with the RODM data models. RODM and INFOMAN will serve as a future data integration points, providing a consistent set of services to describe and access all types of management information.

One issue that continues to plague Host NetView is that it is a mainframe-based product that consumes expensive computing resources for management tasks. The performance has been improved, but it is still a difficult proposition to justify using mainframe resources for simple management tasks. Tighter integration with other products in the NetView family should ease this problem since they will handle more detailed management activities.

12.8 WITHER THE PLATFORM?

Network administrators haven't gotten what they expect from SNMP management platforms yet. The essential common data model and integrated repository are not available from all the vendors. Differences in platform interfaces and functions restricts third-party tool suppliers to porting to only the most popular platforms creating a self-fulfilling trend. The necessary functionality is still in the elusive future.

A new question is arising in organizations that are trying to divine emerging trends and possibilities. The question is the future of the SNMP platform as we know it now. The majority of platform products are still single-system solutions with the database and all management tools coresident with the platform software. Evolution to a distributed framework will take several years.

Many of the current platform functions can be outsourced to intelligent agents and tools located throughout the networked environment. We have already seen that most data collection will be carried out by intelligent, intermediate agents that require minimal supervision and interaction with a remote manager. Event management will be increasingly distributed as well. Higher level event management tools will correlate incoming events and initiate automated local responses.

In the future, simple management tools will control the distributed intelligent instrumentation system. Most management tasks consist of configuring intermediate agents and monitoring their status. In a similar way, distributed event management will be controlled by simple management tools. The major task is configuring each element with the appropriate rules. Monitoring the behavior of the elements is another simple task. Most management platforms spend most of their time on these activities today. How will their role change?

Platforms will become management servers that collect, organize, and distribute information to management tools. Client/server designs will place some management tools with the management servers, while other tools will reside on many different types of computers, including portable laptops.

How likely is this transformation? The emerging Distributed Computing Environment (DCE) offers some interesting possibilities: many of the missing platform functions such as distributed information access and client/server infrastructures will be available. Perhaps a common infrastructure may shift the platform functions into something more tractable.

12.9 SUMMARY

Network administrators have a polarized set of platform choices. They can choose SNMP platforms that are still trying to make the transition from workgroup to enterprise management or they can consider a legacy management platform that is substantially more expensive and lacks the SNMP tools for dynamic management.

SNMP platforms are converging on the same functionality: multiprotocol management, distributed infrastructures and object frameworks. Some vendors such as Cabletron have offered these capabilities for some time. Others like SunSoft have acquired strong technology while other players such as IBM have begun the transition to the new platform.

Maturation of most platforms is several years away. Administrators need to continue searching for the best management tools and then pressure the vendors to port them to the platforms they use. Universal tool availability depends on standard data models and repository mechanisms that will not appear in any reasonable time. The platform vendors have minimal interest in standards for this type of openness.

Legacy managers have some elements that the SNMP platforms are missing, such as integrated information, client/server architectures, and sophisticated automation. However, they are also substantially more expensive than SNMP platforms. There is a wide gulf with no products; perhaps the legacy managers will see an opportunity for a platform that outperforms the current SNMP products and is less expensive than the current legacy management platforms.

Focusing on distributed instrumentation and event management is a good alternative. Intermediate agents, event managers, and other elements will be important to future management solutions regardless of how quickly better platforms appear. Distributed data collection and processing offloads current platforms, allowing them to oversee larger environments. Distributed event management will also enhance current platforms. The transition to client/server platforms and tools can be delayed with these strategies.

The next chapter examines the types of management tools that can be used with platforms.

PART III

SPECIFIC
MANAGEMENT AREAS

Building on the foundation in Part II, specific management areas are discussed in this part. Managing network devices is the subject of Chapter 13. LAN management is covered in Chapters 14 and 15. General LAN management issues are covered in Chapter 14 while Virtual LANs, a new technology, representing new management challenges and opportunities are the topic of Chapter 15. The next two chapters address systems management frameworks and tools, respectively.

CHAPTER 13

Managing Network Devices

There are a range of network devices that administrators encounter: routers, bridges, LAN switches, hubs, multiplexors and, WAN switches. Device management applications are a common example of vendor-specific management tools. Some device functions are generic—common to almost any device—while other functions are specific to each type of device.

13.1 ENGINEERING FOR MANAGEABILITY

Fortunately, engineers have improved some aspects of device management. Administrators can choose, for example, to buy devices that have redundant power supplies so that a power supply failure does not bring the device down. Administrators can replace the power supply while the device continues operation. Most redundant power supply designs use a sharing principle. All the power supplies provide part of the necessary power at any given time; a failure of any given power supply causes the remaining supplies to increase their output and keep everything running.

A further refinement allows an administrator to specify power budgets or priorities for all of the modules contained in a device chassis. Chipcom Corporation has offered this type of capability with their intelligent hubs. An administrator can specify which modules are to be shut down if the amount of power falls below the minimum necessary to keep all modules operating correctly. This type of refinement allows for a gradual device shut-down while maintaining the most critical operations.

Incorporating an uninterruptable power supply (UPS) offers further help with power-related problems. The UPS is basically a battery storage mechanism that allows the device to continue operating for some period of time after external power is lost. In the best case, the UPS will keep the device operating through transient outages or, in the worst case, will at least allow a graceful shutdown and termination of services, as opposed to a catastrophic, unexpected stop in operation.

Most chassis-based network devices are designed to support hot swappable modules. Hot swapping allows an administrator to replace a failed module without turning off the power supply and interrupting the rest of the device's operation. Swapping a module involves a very simple operation of disconnecting any external connections, replacing the module, and then reconnecting external connections if needed. This type of design allows the replacement of a failed component in a few minutes while minimizing the impact on the rest of the users depending on that network device.

For example, in a large intelligent hub there may be twelve, twenty-four, or more ports on a module supporting individual computer systems, servers, and other types of systems. A very large intelligent hub may actually support several hundred individual ports. A failure of a given module may impact twelve or twenty-four users while allowing the remainder to continue their networking activities.

Many devices are also offering environmental monitoring, allowing a remote administrator to keep tabs on such factors as the temperature, operation of the fans, power supply levels, and even intrusion. These monitors track particular variables and are capable of triggering unsolicited reports to a remote management site to report, for example, that someone has intruded and opened a device cover.

Most network devices have flash memory for configuration information. This flash memory can be loaded through the network, allowing administrators to change configurations from a remote management site. Flash memory is also exploited in some devices that offer dual memories. Administrators can load a new configuration without disturbing the current configuration memory. If the new configuration information is not accurate, the old configuration is easy to restore. Another advantage of flash memory is persistence, the contents are stable even when the device is powered down.

All of these engineering advances have made devices much simpler relative to failure management. Administrators should certainly consider paying the extra money for these manageability features, especially as consolidation and centralization of management staffs continue to accelerate. With more robust devices, a skilled management person need not be located at every location that supports network devices. A minimal amount of training would allow a designated person, or persons, at each site to perform simple functions, such as replacing failed device modules. However, there are many other aspects to device management that simple engineering at the hardware level cannot help.

13.2 LIMITED CHOICES

Most administrators do not have the luxury of choosing from a wide array of device management tools. The harsh reality is that in most cases there is no choice at all. Most device management applications must be purchased from the device vendor because of the proprietary MIB extensions that most vendors utilize. The proprietary MIB extensions provide each vendor with a means for differentiating its product by adding more management value. While this is to be welcomed by administrators for improving the quality of products through competition, it is also difficult to have a choice once the products have been selected.

The alternative is to use a more generic management application that uses only standardized MIB variables. While this is feasible, it also represents a lowest common denominator solution, leaving the administrator without access to many valuable extensions and features. The difficulties in building a general purpose device manager that understands all of the various proprietary extensions are significant. Not only are all the extensions hard to understand, but frequently more complex operations require setting or changing variables in certain sequences in order to get appropriate behavior. Without a thorough understanding of the semantics of the proprietary MIB, as well as the syntax, it would be impossible to provide equivalent management capability.

13.3   OTHER DEVICE MANAGEMENT MECHANISMS

Although we talk about SNMP management for devices today, there are other mechanisms that are also complementary or, in some cases, supplementary to the SNMP capabilities. Before the introduction of SNMP, there were many other mechanisms that were already developed for remotely managing network devices. These mechanisms were necessary for dynamically loading new configuration information, as well as for troubleshooting and monitoring purposes. SNMP is not sufficient because many vendors have implemented additional mechanisms and protocols to provide a more complete management solution. At the same time, some of these other mechanisms can be thought of as artifacts from an earlier time before a standard framework for network management.

These other mechanisms provide the ability to move information in bulk, which the first version of SNMP does not support. For example, many devices use the **Trivial File Transfer Protocol** (TFTP) as a means of loading basic configuration information into the device after it is initialized. In fact, many vendors take advantage of TFTP by having a configuration or a boot server available for devices to transfer basic configuration information every time they are initialized.

The **Boot Protocol** (BOOTP) is also used by device management tools as an initial means to obtain the necessary configuration parameters for a complete reboot. BOOTP transfers basic network configuration parameters, such as IP addresses and subnetwork masks, which allow the device to communicate effectively over the network to obtain the remaining configuration information it requires.

The newly emerging Dynamic Host Configuration Protocol (DHCP) will allow more complete and generalized extensions from these initial configuration protocols. This will allow a more generalized mechanism, such as dynamic IP address assignments or other types of extended configurations for the emerging circuit-based environment, such as ATM.

Many device management tools still use **Telnet**, a protocol for interactive access. Many device vendors supply Telnet as a means of connecting to management software in their devices and extracting or changing management information as necessary. The lack of security or authentication in Version 1 of SNMP led many vendors to continue supporting their Telnet management options. Telnet could use a password or other types of mechanisms in order to authenticate the identity of the remote manager. However, Telnet transfers a password in the clear, just as SNMP Version 1 does. The real differences were more likely the result of vendors delaying building more sophisticated SNMP applications. Security and authentication for device management has been pushed forward by some vendors. For example, Wellfleet Communications uses a set of encrypted counters that managers and agents exchange. Both parties decrypt the received counter and compare it to the expected value before carrying out any management activities.

SNMP Version 2 offers possibilities of consolidating device management functions while at the same time increasing the security level of the management system itself. The bulk transfer operation for SNMP allows a more efficient means to transfer the large volume of information required to configure a device. Complex network devices, such as multiprotocol routers, may have many dozens or hundreds of configuration parameters that must be set before the device can operate. A bulk transfer of these configuration parameters is more efficient than using the simple SNMP mechanism of changing one variable with each manager-agent interchange.

The various authentication and security mechanisms also provide the administrator with new options for protecting the management system and its operations. There are varying levels of authentication mechanisms that can be used to establish the identity of the remote manager, as well as encryption options to protect the privacy of the management information.

13.4 DEVICE MONITORING

SNMP is well suited for monitoring the status of various device MIB variables. They can be collected with a simple poll-response operation from a remote management site, or an intermediate agent can collect the information before passing it to a remote site. The trend is toward embedding more intelligence in the device agent. Newer agents perform local testing against thresholds and forward TRAPs to a collector. Agents should still exchange heat-beat messages with a collector periodically. The collector needs to know that a silent agent is operating, but has nothing to report. The agent, on the other hand, can have an alternative collection site configured. The backup collector is used if communication is lost with the primary collector. This keeps critical devices visible to the management system.

Most monitoring today involves tracking a few simple MIB variables in order to track a device's status and operational effectiveness. These variables can be collected on a periodic basis through simple poll-response mechanisms. As discussed in the instrumentation section, a few devices can be polled from a central site without significant impact on network traffic levels or processing requirements. Large numbers of devices, such as all devices within a domain, may require intermediate agents to perform local polling, data collection, and consolidation before the appropriate information is forwarded to the next level.

More complex monitoring operations are best done locally within the device itself. Embedded agents in the device can monitor multiple variables and perform basic correlation, threshold testing, and other calculations within the device itself. This would allow devices to be managed on an exception-only basis; they would only forward events and higher-level analysis to a remote site whenever conditions warranted. Adding more so-phisticated monitoring and management processing capabilities to devices will have to be done carefully in order not to degrade device performance and throughput by consuming too many resource for management tasks.

More sophisticated devices will incorporate separate management processors that perform more sophisticated functions while minimizing interference with the common de-vice operations.

Integrated Monitoring Functions

New levels of device monitoring are possible with the integration of various monitoring functions. Frontier Software and Concord Communications, for example, have added an SNMP collector to their RMON probes (Chapter 6). The Resource Manager (Frontier) and Universal Poller (Concord) have an intermediate agent which does local polling and data collection from SNMP devices. The intermediate agent can apply simple threshold and correlation tests to determine when this information requires attention.

The real value of the integration of polling and monitoring is that it provides an ad-ministrator with two concurrent views: the RMON probe showing the behavior at the de-vice network interfaces while the resource manager provides an internal view based on the different MIB variables for the device. These tools were used in one case to detect a resource problem with a router. Application performance dropped sharply when traffic volume reached a certain level. The RMON probe measured a utilization level that should have been comfortable, not approaching the LAN's saturation level. Information from the SNMP collector showed that the router started discarding packets, the cause of the slow-down. Further investigation determined that the router had been configured incorrectly, leaving it without sufficient buffering for higher loads.

This problem could have been detected more easily with a traffic generator that al-lows an administrator to deliver traffic to the network in a controlled, repeatable fashion. Stress testing, replays of problem sequences, or steady volumes can be used to explore real device behavior under controlled circumstances rather than waiting for operational conditions to trigger a problem.

This kind of tool also allows an administrator to correlate throughput, for example, with the amount of free buffer space contained inside a router. In this way, information from both sources can be integrated and used to facilitate a better understanding of device behavior and performance under a variety of conditions. Tools that integrate both views and facilitate troubleshooting will be the next step.

13.5 FAULT MANAGEMENT

Simple monitoring will keep an eye on the device's normal activities. Problems are detected by checking collected information against threshold values or by changes in monitored vari-ables. When these conditions are satisfied, events or alarms can be forwarded to the appro-priate device management tool for further investigation and action. Embedded agents in the device also send unsolicited management events in the case of sudden changes in state.

The key to good fault management is quick isolation: determining the cause of the problem and its location in the device. Once the problem is isolated, replacement of the failed module is straightforward, and with hot swappable design, the impact on the network community as a whole is minimized.

Most device managers can provide a graphical view of the device, showing in detail the modules, interfaces, status, and other indicators that the device may have. Periodic polling updates the dynamic information, changing the color of status lights to reflect the actual device. Most of the fault isolation involves alerting the operator, indicating exactly which module has failed and activating other tools such as trouble ticketing.

Faults must also be collected and logged for longer-term analysis. Administrators need to know the relative failure rates of different devices or modules within them. This information can also be used in order to effect future purchase decisions based on the relative reliability of devices from competing vendors. This information is also key for managing spare parts inventories. Administrators need to maintain the appropriate levels of replacement modules for each type of device.

There are other device management challenges, unfortunately. Although fault management has become tractable, other areas, such as configuration and performance management, security, and accounting require further work. These areas are becoming the center of increasing attention as the fault management and day-to-day operational issues for device management are addressed. Getting the most out of the device and securing its operation are the new areas for development and innovation.

13.6 CONFIGURATION MANAGEMENT

Configuring a complex device can be a labor-intensive and error-prone process. Many devices such as WAN switches or routers have multiple network interfaces. Each interface may have its own set of specific configuration parameters. Multiprotocol devices such as routers may have additional sets of parameters for each protocol on each interface. Configuration tools are improving, but this task is still too difficult.

Many devices are configured by editing a text file that describes the parameters and their values. The file is translated either before it is sent to a device or locally by the device after it is received. Text files are "administrator-friendly" since they do not require detailed knowledge of the device's internal architecture and operations.

Other device vendors provide fairly good configuration tools for single devices. The majority of those work on a visual paradigm providing accurate graphical representations of the device's panels, chassis slots, and other functions and features. Most configuration can be done by simple point and click operations on the visual representation, allowing an administrator to enable or disable ports or assign privileges and protocols on a very granular basis.

An administrator can click on any port, for example, enabling or disabling it. Other configuration operations can be based on using pull-down menus that represent other configuration information for the selected port, allowing the administrator a quick and simple way of configuring devices. Other representations allow the administrator to determine

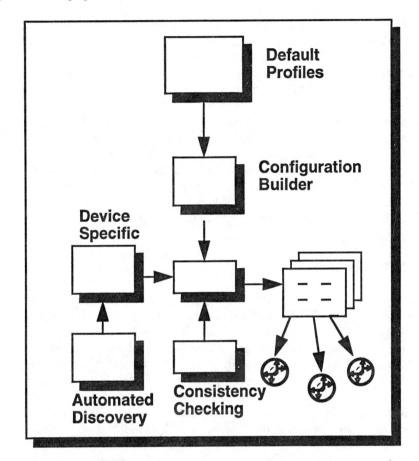

Device configuration can use default profiles to incorporate configuration policies. Automated discovery provides device-specific information automatically.

FIGURE 13–1   Configuration

how many slots in the chassis are filled, the types of modules in each chassis, and other detailed information, such as serial numbers, software versions, and other information.

Device configuration tools should also provide for the creation and maintenance of a configuration library. If a configuration error is discovered, earlier versions can be found and used to restore operation quickly.

Configuration management libraries can also keep sets of **configuration templates** for a collection of routers or devices, allowing a single remote management site to distribute and update a collection of devices. There should also be the capability to retrieve all the configuration information in a remote device so it can be analyzed.

Configuring devices also involves setting limitations on their networking behaviors. One challenge with routers, for example, is combining variable delay internet traffic with SNA traffic that is time-sensitive. Proteon, Inc. responded with Proteon Internetworking Traffic Management (PITM) for its routers. PITM allows administrators to allocate bandwidth on the serial links between routers. Administrators can reserve a percentage of the link bandwidth for a specific category of traffic, creating a dedicated channel for time-sensitive applications. Internet traffic can be limited, preventing it from consuming all the bandwidth. Finally, the administrator can assign priority levels for each type of protocol traffic for finer granularity of control. PITM provides a general bandwidth management solution, although SNA management is the most important concern.

Domain Configuration Challenges

The real issues in device configuration management relate to management of a **domain** or **collection of devices**. All devices of the same type in a domain must cooperate and collaborate in order to provide effective overall performance and behavior. For example, multiple Ethernet bridges use the Spanning Tree Protocol in order to avoid routing loops and other types of instabilities caused by complex topologies. All of the bridges must have the same understanding of the topology, expressed through weights and port costs, in order to work cooperatively and adjust to any topology changes created by failures or additions of links or bridges. Configuring a spanning tree environment requires the consistent setting of configuration information in each bridge so that they all behave in a consistent and expected fashion.

Routers in a domain use a routing protocol in order to coordinate their routing decisions. Some routing protocols, such as the traditional distance-vector models, require periodic communication between neighboring routers in order to adjust their routing metrics for changes in the topology. The emerging link-state routing protocols use flooding of information to all routers in a domain whenever there is a change in topology. Link-state protocols, in particular, depend on the appropriate assignment of weights or costs to every communication link and for every protocol. A change in topology requires a recalculation of available routes based on the assigned weights to provide paths with the least cost or the minimum delay.

Router vendors have begun to respond with better domain configuration tools. Cisco Systems uses a Global Commands feature that allows an administrator to configure a variable, such as a password, for a group of routers with a single command. The newly announced Configuration Builder has taken functionality much further, replacing a command line interface with a graphical configuration tool. Point-and-shoot operation with context-sensitive help enables administrators to configure a domain with minimal training.

Configuration Builder has features to speed the configuration process. For example, routers can be queried and information about their interface cards loaded into a configuration window, saving the time to enter the information manually. Administrators can also apply access lists and priority lists with configuration **snap-ins** in a single command. Configuration Builder is also introducing automated configuration checking to reduce errors by checking for valid parameters such as protocol addresses, routing metrics, and WAN parameters. Further checking ensures that each router in a domain has unique addresses and network numbers.

Hewlett-Packard offers the Network Configuration Manager for its AdvanceStack routers. Administrators use this tool to configure a set of routers. The configurations of each router are verified and then consistency checks are applied to the domain. Duplicate addresses, out-of-range parameters, and inappropriate combinations are detected. The administrators can then initiate loading the verified configurations to each router.

Administrators require tools that allow them to view and configure a domain of devices in an integrated fashion. For example, consistency checks should be applied to ensure that the appropriate addresses, filters, and other parameters are compatible across a set of devices. Such things as checking for duplicate IP addresses and other types of information are beginning to be incorporated into domain-level device management products. These functions can be thought of as proactive in the sense that they prevent configuration errors from causing operational problems. They can also simplify troubleshooting tasks.

Administrators also need ways of viewing the results of a domain—wide configuration. For example, in the spanning tree bridging environment, administrators need a quick and simple graphical representation to determine if the assigned port costs have actually created the spanning tree topology they intended. In a similar way, administrators that are configuring a routing domain need simple tools to allow them to evaluate the consistency and accuracy of the metrics they've assigned to each communication link and router interface. Administrators need to be able to determine if the routing behavior will meet their intended goals in terms of bandwidth, consumption, load balancing, prioritized connections, and routes through the domains.

These configuration issues are becoming even more difficult as more sophisticated time-sensitive applications are carried across traditional router backbones. For example, moving SNA traffic across a traditional internet requires detailed assignments of priorities, or bandwidth reservations, in order to ensure that connections are not timed out due to excessive delays. The incorporation of video conferencing, the transmission of real-time graphical data for visualization, and other emerging applications will also make the appropriate configuration of a router domain increasingly difficult.

Configuration Changes

Another key element for good device management is the ability to detect **unexpected changes** in the device configuration. Although in the best of worlds, those types of things never happen, they are still possible due to inadvertent modifications by a user at a remote site or malicious tampering with the device. Periodic comparison of the retrieved configuration file against the file held in the configuration library can alert the administrator to any changes. Any detected changes can trigger activation of tools that automatically restore the

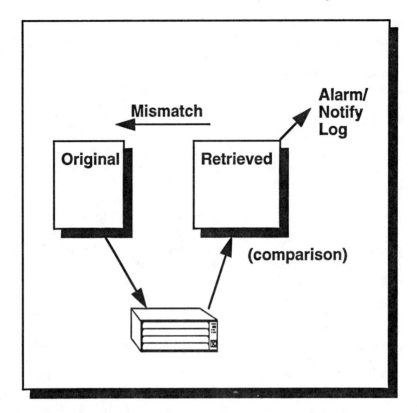

Configurations can be tested periodically and
discrepancies can be noted. Automated procedures
can also be invoked to restore the desired
configuration.

FIGURE 13–2   Enforcing configuration policy

configuration. Embedded device agents can also be improved to report any configuration
changes; this would help identify the circumstances or people causing the problem.

13.7 SECURITY

Securing the network also requires securing the devices. This is particularly important in
devices that interconnect large parts of an enterprise, such as the backbone or campus
routers. A malicious intruder can thoroughly disrupt networking activities by tampering
with networking devices, causing potentially large losses to the compromised enterprise.

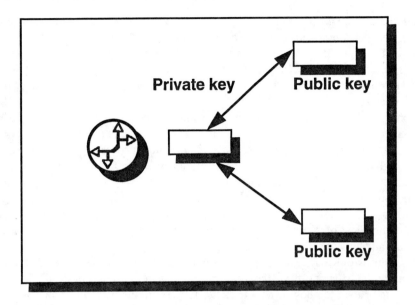

Private key   **Public key**

Public key

Devices can be secured with encrypted exchanges. Any privileged manager can have a public key to communicate with the agent. The private key is closely held to protect the parties. Authentication procedures can also be added to identify each party.

FIGURE 13–3   Securing devices

Other types of interference could allow unauthorized access to important information flowing on the network, possibly compromising proprietary information and business processes. There are many aspects to secure device management, including mechanisms that must be used to enhance the integrity of the management system itself.

The physical security of network devices must be considered as a first line of defense. The evolution to the server center on many campuses provides performance enhancements by placing all servers on high-speed backbones. A server center also allows administrators to collect these critical resources into a localized area where they can also be more easily protected. Rooms that contain sensitive networking equipment are designed so that network management alarms are forwarded in the event that the room is entered. This can inform a management site that a potential security problem needs investigation.

The devices themselves can be engineered in the same fashion so that they can forward management events if the device enclosure is opened, a module is removed, or anything is changed. The extra expense for this type of instrumentation must be balanced against the potential damages from local tampering.

Remote management offers security problems even while it is supporting the centralization and consolidation of staff. There is a danger of "spoofing," whereby an intruder system masquerades as a remote manager, seducing the local agents into providing information or changing behavior in unauthorized ways. Authentication mechanisms are required between the parts of a distributed management system so that the identity of the parties can be confirmed before any actions are taken. There are various **authentication** mechanisms requiring the exchange of keys, cycling numbers in a predetermined fashion, or using encrypted passwords. All these mechanisms are feasible and provide higher levels of security. However, they frequently also require more processing resources in order to encode and decode the appropriate authentication markers.

Authentication levels should be granular so that simple types of information that are not confidential can be retrieved in the shortest amount of time without incurring the overhead for authentication. Other types of operations, particularly those that provide confidential information or change the behavior of network devices, should be protected by full-scale authentication and verification procedures.

Other levels of security are provided through filters, screens, and rules that are created to control the behavior of interconnection devices at a finer level of detail. For example, filters may be set to allow certain traffic to flow from one network to another, to exclude traffic entirely between different networks, or to allow selected addresses within each network to communicate. Further refinements would allow these same types of restrictions to be placed on particular types of applications activities. These filters can be used to partition traffic in the network in ways that keep high priority traffic from being interfered with or to compartmentalize confidential traffic onto certain parts of the enterprise network. Administrators need tools that allow them to review settings of a collection of filters in different devices in order to ensure that the intended operation meets their goals.

At a different level, security can also be a consideration when selecting network devices. For example, hubs, which are basically repeaters, have traditionally maintained the broadcast nature of Local Area Network activities. There are hubs on the market today, however, that allow selective repeating. Only the targeted destination port receives the actual traffic. All other hub ports either receive nothing or a jammed transmission of nonsense information. In this way, privacy constraints can be applied so that all systems do not eavesdrop on network conversations.

This selective repeating mechanism is configured through access controls which define the target systems that any attached computer can reach. This type of mechanism allows a fine level of control over interactions and protects sensitive resources. The appropriate management tools allow the system administrator to configure all the appropriate communication paths in such a way that fewer compromises are possible.

13.8 ACCOUNTING

Accounting is becoming more important to many organizations as their traffic volumes and networking costs continue to accelerate. Accounting is also important for other functions besides the charge back for using networking resources. Planners can use the detailed accounting information to look at trends in protocol usage, different applications, and to determine where the heaviest network users are located. This information is very helpful for future planning activities, as well as for determining that capacities are matched appropriately to needs.

Large volumes of information must be collected and processed before the perspectives and insights into the networked behavior are available. The resource drains for individual devices may be too expensive; instead, a separate device may be employed. RMON probes and other types of stand-alone analyzers or monitors can collect all the necessary information from the broadcast LAN traffic. In this way, no performance penalties are imposed on the devices. The probe can break down this information or send it to a remote site for more specific analysis.

Accounting for switched networks will be an increasingly difficult problem since port-to-port dedicated communications will replace the broadcast operation of traditional LANs. More accounting resources will be required in the switches where many streams of traffic converge. It is most likely that switches will collect basic statistics and deliver them to a site where they will be correlated.

13.9 PERFORMANCE MANAGEMENT

Monitoring is also needed for performance management. Most device performance problems are usually caused by faults or configuration problems. Fault management is the easiest to solve, especially when failed elements are easily replaced.

Configuration-related problems cover a variety of possible causes. Individual devices may be improperly configured in ways that cause their performance to suffer. For example, a router may have insufficient memory for the number of communications interfaces it supports. Under heavy loads the router will discard packets and end-to-end performance suffers. Integrated monitoring of network and device behavior helps to identify these problems.

Domain-level configuration problems can also make any device perform poorly. The interactions of devices must be considered, and the same tools used for configuring a domain can be used to advantage in this situation as well. Path tracing and monitoring tools may also be needed to evaluate the possible causes of performance degradation.

The actual network topology may also contribute to performance problems. A change in topology may shift traffic to devices that could handle previous loads without any problems. The increment in loading may push the device into poorer performance. Device profiles are helpful in detecting when the normal operational limits are no longer in effect. Changes in device loading can be a clue to a possible problem.

Systems configuration problems can also cause devices to appear as poor performers. For example, a system that is configured with a small packet size will not use bandwidth effectively; its behavior may cause the device to perform poorly. Response time and end-end measurement are quick ways to determine if the network is contributing to low throughput or if the problem is more likely inside one of the communicating systems.

13.10 HUBS

Hubs are key devices in most LANs: they support shared media workgroups and LAN interconnection devices as well frame and cell switching. The modularity of the chassis-based hubs offers mix and match deployment of various LANs and WANs.

The hubs have large volumes of configuration information since there are several modules. Each module has information that describes its type: Ethernet, FDDI, CDDI, etc. Other configuration information includes the serial number, any firmware version numbers, and other related information. Each module may contain twelve or more ports and each port has further information. Port configuration information includes: operational status (up/failed/disabled) and assignment to a hub backplane. The chassis also has configuration information that describes power supplies and the module in each occupied slot. Configuration information must be persistent, saved in Read-Only Memory or on a boot server.

The hub must be instrumented to provide real-time and static information to a device manager. For example, hub management tools should be able to discover the hub configuration, chassis slots, and port settings. Serial numbers on each module facilitate tracking as they are moved from one hub to another.

Real-time information includes the MAC address of attached devices. Well-managed hubs provide the **MAC address-hub port mappings** to management tools. This feature allows a simple lookup when a TRAP is received from a MAC address. The administrator immediately has the associated hub port and can proceed to act quickly by disabling the port or physically disconnecting the device, for example.

Hub vendors are adding substantial management processing power to their hubs. Cabletron Systems has one or more processors on each hub module. These processors also manage the module operations such as routing, switching, or repeating. 3COM Corporation has an embedded SmartAgent which collects information intelligently and forwards events to a remote management site. The SmartAgent can also take actions as instructed. For instance, it may reconfigure the hub ports in off-business hours to isolate certain parts of the network and detect unusual activities.

UB Network uses embedded intelligence in its Access/EMpower architecture to respond to a common management problem—broadcast storms. These storms can quickly degrade performance and take a while to track down the cause. The **Netstorm Terminator** is configured to check for a certain level of broadcast traffic on a LAN segment. If the broadcast traffic exceeds that threshold, the Netstorm Terminator analyzes the traffic, determines the source of the broadcasts, and deactivates the appropriate hub port.

13.11 ROUTERS

Router management can be further categorized as tools for LAN interconnect routers and those for remote offices.

Remote Routers

Usage of remote routers is growing rapidly as organizations interconnect their remote offices into their enterprise network. The remote router uses a simple procedure; it forwards all packets for other sites to a central backbone router which handles the usual routing tasks.

Simple installation at a remote site is a key. 3COM (Santa Clara, CA) offers its Remote Office router line with centralized installation features. Remote site personnel need only connect cables and turn the power on. The remote router loads its configuration from a central router. An administrator builds the remote configurations on a central router before they are distributed to the remote routers.

The Remote Office routers contain the 3COM SmartAgent, an intelligent agent, which performs local monitoring from the router, thereby consuming minimal management bandwidth and central site processing. The local SNMP agent is configured to monitor specific variables and check for threshold values. Data is collected by local polling and alerts are only sent to a central site whenever thresholds are exceeded. Wellfleet provides a similar feature called SNMP Statistics Thresholds, for both remote and conventional routing products.

QuickStep software installation for its DNX 300m remote router is offered by Proteon, Inc. Proteon configures the router before it is delivered and QuickStep guides the operator when changes are necessary. Also, all cabling is checked for proper connection. Flash memory makes it easy to load new software from a remote management site once the DNX 300m is powered. Users at the remote site can change parameters with guidance and error checking, reducing the time and risk of errors.

Conventional Routers

Regular routers interconnect small workgroups, act as collapsed campus backbones, and interconnect campuses across Wide Area Networking services. These routers are considerably more complex than remote office routers. Each routed protocol has different configuration parameters and another routing protocol to support.

Poor routing behavior leads to aggravated users and overworked management staff; the entire organization also suffers when internetworks behave poorly. Effective router management becomes even more essential as more organizations use their internetworks for mission-critical applications. Good router management solutions must be simpler and require less staff time and training.

Routers can determine routes dynamically and they can readjust to topology changes. The link-state routing protocols such as OSPF (Open Shortest Path First) and IS-IS (OSI Intermediate System-Intermediate System) use "weights", or metrics, for each link or router interface. Routers use these metrics to find paths that minimize the cost, delay, errors, or other factors. For example, a slower 9.6 Kbs link may have a (desirable) low value for cost and a high value for delay, while a T1 link will be weighted the opposite way. A router would choose the slower link for a minimum cost path and the T1 link for applications requesting minimum delay. Tools that help select the appropriate weights are not yet mature; there is still an art to configuring a router domain.

Cisco Systems (Menlo Park, CA) uses a Global Commands feature that allows an administrator to perform configuration operations, such as setting a password, on a group of routers with a single command. Global Commands reduce the chance of entry errors and saves substantial staff time as well.

The Cisco Configuration Builder has features to speed the configuration process by automatically discovering as much information about each router as possible. Information about the interface cards is loaded into a configuration window, saving the time to enter the information manually. Administrators can construct Configuration snap-ins for access lists and priority lists and apply them to any router with a single command.

RETIX (Santa Monica, CA) has introduced RETIXVision for its routers. RETIX-Vision offers some of the same functions as Configuration Builder, but has placed more emphasis on a graphical management tool. Administrators see a complete representation of a remote router including interface cards and status indicators. Ports can be reconfigured by point-and-click operations and pull-down menus. RETIXVision can also be integrated with the leading SNMP platforms—SunNet Manager, OpenView, NetView/6000, and NetLabs DIMONS. An additional software package adds more alarm management and icons to the platform services.

13.12 GENERAL WIDGETS

Device management policies were difficult to formulate because there was an array of disparate tools. A preliminary audit indicated that a large percentage of problems were configuration-related rather than direct failures. Improved configuration management was expected to increase performance as well as reduce the number of problems.

Configuration management was instituted by defining configurations for each device and identifying the common information that could be set by defaults. The remaining device-specific part was catalogued for each device. Programs were developed which periodically read device configurations and compare them to the expected information. Differences were brought to an operator's attention and logged. Manual restoration was needed for those devices that offered stand-alone device management tools. There was no means to activate those tools when an event was generated.

General Widgets adopted a policy of testing new devices to determine their behavior under differing conditions. Traffic generators and scenarios were used to drive devices with various traffic loads and mixtures of packet sizes. Testing was designed to determine **realistic** values for setting the instrumentation. Vendor performance tests are usually conducted with favorable parameters; real-world results often varied. Many vendors use an independent testing organization to provide more objective data—Scott Bradner of Harvard University is a pioneer in offering objective testing methodologies for routers and switches.

Automated scripts were added to management platforms and device management

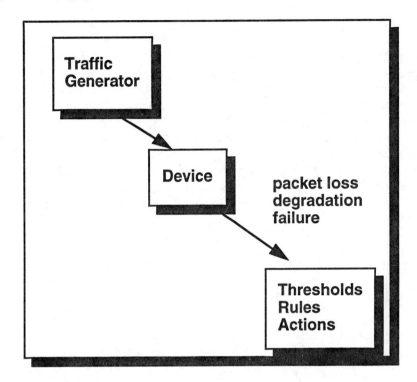

A traffic generator is used to test new devices, the
results are used to define realistic thresholds, rules,
and automated actions.

FIGURE 13–4   Testing device parameters

tools to simplify some management processes. The biggest difficulty in automating some
tasks was encountered with building the scripts themselves. Some technicians were
skilled diagnosticians, and poor script writers. Each script needed checking and refinement to ensure it actually satisfied the requirements.

Securing key devices such as access and backbone routers is an important need that
has been difficult to satisfy. Strong cryptography cannot be legally exported, making it
impossible to build a secured global network. General Widgets depends on Telnet connections with encoded passwords and messages for changing important information. The
plan is to adopt SNMP Version 2 if the export restrictions are ever resolved. Another option is pushing vendors to adopt PGP (Pretty Good Privacy) as a secure exchange mechanism. Critical devices are monitored closely since they cannot yet be protected adequately. Physical access is also restricted as another measure.

13.13 SUMMARY

Device management is the most mature area in the management environment. One factor is experience; some device vendors have had quite a few years to develop their management tools and engineer their devices for more manageability. Device markets tend to become crowded, and competition forces prices toward commodity levels. For example, hub prices were originally on the order of $500 or more per port; now hubs with more functionality are available at $75 per port. Vendors have used better management as a value-added differentiator.

The tough management challenges are dealing with collections of devices when troubleshooting or configuring them. More automation is needed so that administrators can focus on detected problems and leave the remainder of the tasks to the device management tools.

CHAPTER 14

LAN Management

LAN management is becoming simpler at one level and more complex at another. For example, device engineering and structured wiring eliminate many management problems associated with failures. On the other hand, internetwork management is a much tougher challenge.

Instrumentation is the place to begin. LAN instrumentation covers several areas such as remote monitoring probes, protocol analyzers, and even network adapters. Traditional LANs operate in broadcast mode, simplifying monitoring since instrumentation can be attached without interfering with traffic.

14.1 RMON

The trend toward increasing centralization of management, staffs, and tools depends on remotely monitoring the dispersed set of LAN segments found in most organizations. The RMON (Remote Monitoring) standard was developed to allow sophisticated remote monitoring.

A centralized management operation can be severely impacted by failures or problems at remote sites. It can be expensive and time consuming to find the appropriate staff member, collect the needed tools and equipment, and dispatch them to a remote site. If extensive travel is required, such as an airplane trip or overnight stay, the expense of sending a troubleshooter may exceed the cost of the device that is causing the problem. Besides the staff time wasted in travel, other liabilities include much longer times to resolve the problem, resulting in higher revenue and productivity losses.

There is also the problem of providing adequate staff coverage in this type of environment, since many of the staff may be unavailable to respond to problems while they are in transit. If this occurs, the only alternative may be to increase staffing levels, resulting in higher operational costs and less effectiveness for the management solution. The alternative is using a remote monitoring tool to bring the data to the staff rather than vice versa, saving travel time, expenses, and minimizing the time to resolve the problem and restore service.

RMON is an SNMP MIB standard for controlling a remote monitoring probe. MIB variables control the operation of the probe and specify what types of information are to be collected and returned to a central management location. The RMON probe is actually designed as a remote monitoring server capable of supporting multiple concurrent monitoring operations for one or more remote sites.

The RMON standard assumes a probe with storage, enough processing speed to keep up with LAN segment transmission rates, and enough intelligence so that it can be controlled and instructed to carry out a wide variety of monitoring tasks. The remote probe is assumed to be self-contained and capable of operating independently even if a continuous connection is not maintained with a remote management center. The remote probe collects information and stores it for later transfer to the appropriate locations. It is important to keep in mind that the MIB represents an abstract means for accessing remotely monitored information and controlling its collection; actual implementations will vary depending on the product, the type of packaging, and application requirements.

The **RMON MIB for Ethernet** is divided into nine functional groups, each providing a different part of a remote management solution. RMON probes also support the standard MIB-II definitions, as well. The MIB-II definitions for interfaces and systems are included in the information provided by the probe.

Monitoring Groups

Three of the nine groups are used to control different types of monitoring activities. The **statistics** group provides information on the LAN activities seen at the RMON interface. The RMON probe returns information on segment activity such as the number of packet or octets that have been transmitted or the number of broadcast or multicast packets seen on the LAN segment. Information is also collected on the occurrences of runts (packets that are too small) or jabbers (packets that are too large). The RMON probe can also provide information on packet size distributions, basically providing a histogram of all the packets, 65 bytes to 127 bytes, 128 to 255, and so forth, up to a maximum of 4,096 bytes.

A **history** group provides for periodic collection of information that can be used for trending and capacity planning activities. The history group parameters control the polling interval and the number of samples that are saved. Sets of statistics are saved, with the exception of the packet size distribution histograms. The historical information is captured and saved at the remote probe until a remote management application requests that it be transferred.

There are two thresholding triggers for the **alarms** group. The first threshold triggers an event when a monitored value increases above the threshold value. The second threshold value is triggered when the monitored variable value falls below the threshold, thus signaling a return to a more equilibrium condition. The monitored variable must fall

Statistics	**History**
Host	**Ring Station**
Matrix	**Ring station config**
TopN	**Source Routing**
Filter	**Capture**
Events	**Alarms**

Standard MIB groups for Ethernet and Token Ring
Remote Monitoring probes. The Ring Station and Source
Routing groups are only used for monitoring Token
Rings.

FIGURE 14–1 RMON groups

below the falling threshold value before another rising event is triggered. The falling
threshold is added to provide a hysterisis control mechanism for thresholding. Without
that, an event that crossed the threshold and remained above could then trigger a steady
series of alarms—generally not a desirable feature.

The remote application that receives these two events will always understand on
which side of the threshold value the monitored variable is lying, as well as the time intervals between the two events for more sophisticated types of analysis.

Analysis Groups

The remote monitoring probe has sufficient processing capacity for some simple types of
analysis. Local analysis saves network bandwidth and the processing load for the raw information at a remote site.

The **host** group is used to control an automated discovery process carried out by the probe. The probe compares source and destination addresses of every packet that it receives and can detect activities of a previously unknown (or inactive) host. Each host is then tracked and the information is kept on a per-host basis. The RMON probe captures the time of discovery of each new host, as well as packet error rates, multicast packets, packet volumes, and other information about host activity. These are the same statistics captured at the interface, but they now provide a more granular view by looking at individual host behavior on that LAN segment.

The **TopN** group provides a means of preparing different reports covering host activities. The TopN group-control parameters select a beginning and ending time for collecting a set of samples. The statistics to be monitored are defined, as well as the number of hosts.

At a later time, the remote management application can retrieve a TopN group, such as the top ten clients in terms of total traffic, or the top three hosts that are causing the most transmissions errors and so forth. These simple reports are used to narrow down potential sources of problems as quickly as possible.

The **matrix** group, the last of the analysis groups, traces conversations between pairs of systems on the LAN. In actual practice, most of the conversations are between clients and shared resources such as servers. The matrix group builds two tables to measure traffic flows in each direction so that asymmetric activity can be easily detected. The same sets of statistics are used on an even more granular basis now, providing packet counts, error counts, and octet counts, as necessary.

Filtering

Remote monitoring probes can be instructed to **filter** the traffic they monitor and select certain specific packets for further levels of analysis. Packet-matching criteria are specified, beginning with a byte offset from the beginning of the packet. This offset parameter allows the selection of multiple layers of information contained within the packet. Various protocol layers can be examined to monitor higher-layer protocol flows and exchanges.

For example, information pertaining to the network layer could be extracted by filtering for IP addresses, IPX addresses, or other types of Local Area Network addressing structures. The OSI NSAP can also be captured in the third protocol layer.

Specific application connections can be filtered from either the transport layer (filtering on well-known sockets), or higher levels, depending on the particular protocol suite. Filtering on offsets is only viable when filtering through the fixed-length portions of the packet. Once variable-length fields are introduced, the offsets are no longer guaranteed to be accurate for fields that follow a variable length area. The filtering criteria include bit masking on an equal or unequal basis, as well as searching for any particular status on packets, such as the runts, jabbers, or transmission errors.

The RMON MIB uses the abstract concept of a channel on which captured packets are transferred. Packets meeting the specified criteria are delivered to a channel, which can also simultaneously trigger an event. The event can be used to notify a remote application that the packets of interest have begun to arrive. A **packet capture** group represents a buffer where the packets from a particular channel are stored for retrieval.

The rate of channel events can be controlled by a similar mechanism to that used for alarms. After the first event is triggered, the channel remains in a state where it continues to accept packets, but generates no further events. The remote management application can reset the channel to trigger on the arrival of the next packet that meets the filtering criteria. This mechanism is used to reduce the flow of management events when many packets may be accepted into the channel.

The packet capture group can be configured to accept variable numbers of packets, depending on the probe's memory resources. Buffer control mechanisms determine the actions taken when the capture buffer is filled. The probe can continue capturing packets by overwriting the oldest packets in the buffer, or it stops collecting further packets at that point.

Frequently only the packet header information is valuable for further analysis. Extra packet storage is saved, keeping only the part of interest and discarding the rest. The remote manager may also configure the size of the packet slice that is transmitted back to the remote management station, optimizing large transfers to preserve bandwidth and mitigate the probe's interference with user activities.

Events

Events are generated internally by the remote probe and are used to control activities, such as sending a TRAP to a remote site or the activation or deactivation of one of the channels accepting captured packets. Different criteria and conditions can be used to trigger events based on changes in other RMON MIB variables. This allows a level of monitoring and control, such as timed activation or deactivation of captured channels.

The **Token-Ring RMON MIB** has several different groups that control monitoring of Token-Rings. These new groups are needed to address the differences between Ethernets and Token-Rings. The Token-Ring depends on physical order on the ring and has rules to cover adding and removing stations and monitoring the activities of the token. Token-Ring probes can be configured to capture information in two modes. Information in the Token-Ring management packets can be used to monitor activities. Promiscuous mode, on the other hand, captures all the packets on the ring, operating in a broadcast mode that is similar to Ethernet monitoring.

Token-Ring Statistics

This group contains current utilization and error statistics. The token-ring MAC-Layer Statistics Group collects MAC-layer reports about utilization and errors. The promiscuous statistics group collects utilization from promiscuous capture of all passing packets. Information about packet size distributions, multicasts, and broadcasts is also collected.

Token-Ring History

The token-ring history groups are analogous to the same Ethernet group. Historical statistics for ring utilization and errors are kept. Both MAC-layer and promiscuous history are collected.

Ring Station

This group contains the statistics for each attached station's status and errors. This group offers increased granularity of monitoring. This group keeps track of the last station to send a beacon, nearest upstream neighbor addresses, the current active monitor address, and the adds and deletes that have occurred.

Ring Station Config

This group actually controls attached stations by active means. Any station can be removed from the ring. Station configuration information can also be collected. The ring station order group provides information on the actual ring topology. It tracks each station and determines the upstream neighbors.

The source routing group collects source routing information from passing packets and provides statistics.

RMON Groups Summary

The various groups contain control parameters which must be set appropriately before monitoring begins. Each group provides information at a different level of granularity. The statistics and history groups for both Ethernet and token-ring give an overview of activity at the LAN segment level. Adding the host matrix and station status groups provides more details about the behavior of attached stations. The filtering groups offer even finer levels of detail, allowing a remote administrator to examine the contents of individual packets.

A caveat: The Internet Engineering Task Forces accepts RMON compliance with the implementation of **any** group. Make your vendor define the groups that are actually available for the probe. Actual probes are implemented in a variety of ways, as the next part discusses.

Packaging RMON Probes

RMON probes are packaged with different options. The initial RMON probes were **stand-alone** devices with a LAN interface. The probe was connected to the LAN it was to monitor, and controlled remotely through the network. RMON probes are also being embedded in other types of products. Stand-alone probes are losing favor with many administrators who prefer their probes embedded in other products.

For example, many of the hub vendors, such as Bay Networks, Chipcom Corp., and UB Networks, among others, provide an RMON probe module which can be incorporated into the chassis. Cabletron Systems does not take a module, and its chassis slot for an RMON probe. Instead Cabletron uses high-performance RISC processors on each hub module; they can be loaded with the software to carry out RMON functions.

Embedding the probe in a hub is a cost-effective strategy, especially with intelligent hubs containing multiple backplanes. The RMON probe can be easily switched between different backplanes, enabling the probe to be shared among a set of segments. This provides a cost-effective deployment for remote monitoring rather than using multiple stand-alone probes for each particular segment.

One of the drawbacks to a hub-based probe is the difficulty of obtaining information from multiple segments at the same time. This is especially needed for tracking down and understanding problems that occur because of the interaction of traffic and activities on different LAN segments. Hewlett-Packard and Hughes LAN systems have addressed this problem by embedding a multiport probe in the Hughes' enterprise hub. A multiport probe allows simultaneous collection of information from multiple LAN segments contained within the hub.

Stand-alone multiport probes are being offered, as well by vendors such as ARMON Networking, and AXON Networks. Multiple LAN interfaces are used to monitor a set of segments. The price point of a multiport probe is lower than an equivalent number of stand-alone probes. Another potential advantage is that shared resources such as memory can be better utilized for capturing traffic and performing detailed breakdowns.

CrossComm Corp., an innovative router vendor, has embedded an RMON probe into its line of routers. Cisco Systems, the major router vendor has announced plans for incorporating a probe into future routing products.

Frontier Software, an RMON probe vendor, has carried out a reverse process. It has embedded other functions in its stand-alone RMON probe. An SNMP management agent is embedded capability within its probe, allowing local polling and data collection from SNMP agents that share the same LAN as the probe. This offers opportunities to consolidate information from both sources.

AXON Networks uses another variation; it can download management applications to its LANServant probe. The administrator selects applications and moves them to the probe as needed. Local processing reduces management traffic and provides higher value information to a remote management site.

Hewlett-Packard NetMetrix probes also process information at the probe before sending it back. An option uses an X-Windows connection to update information displays with real-time probe information.

Software Probes

A series of software-only probes is being introduced for different environments, such as NetWare, OS/2, and Unix. Software-only probes offer significant price reductions, compared to a stand-alone product. Software probes are also highly portable, since they can be shipped through the network to any given location in a matter of seconds. Software probes can also be left in place, and activated when conditions warrant.

Software probes may not be able to keep up with full wire speed capture and data collection, especially under heavy traffic conditions when the software probe is placed on a busy host. Software probes are best suited for situations with many low-traffic level LAN segments dispersed throughout an organization. They are also better suited for collecting operational statistics as opposed to very sophisticated packet filtering and capturing schemes. Placement of software-only probes must be carefully considered and balanced against the intended usage.

Probes that are embedded in other products, such as hubs or routers, also have potential performance drawbacks if they are sharing the same processor with the device. In this case, heavy traffic loads or increasing functional demands may require more expensive engineering, or entail a loss of monitoring capability or device throughput. If the RMON probe consumes enough processing power to degrade the device performance, it will be an unacceptable addition to an administrator's tool set.

Another development is the incorporation of a stand-alone probe on an add-on board for PCs or other computers. The add-on board contains a processor, memory, and a LAN interface, taking only chassis power. This packaging option provides a high-performance embedded probe that does not impact the host.

Packaging Summary

Probes range from stand-alone devices to software modules in a server or other computer system. The market is moving toward embedded probes since they reduce the number of separate elements in the environment. Embedded probes may degrade the host performance unless they are restricted to their own add-on board. Next-generation devices will have sufficient processing power and storage so that full monitoring will not impact performance.

Other probes have local applications to improve data collection and analysis. Another advantage with local processing is that it reduces the traffic between a probe and a remote management application.

14.2 USING RMON PROBES

The real value of remote monitoring probes cannot be realized without robust applications. The first things these applications must do is hide the complexities of the RMON MIB from administrators. Easy configuration is a must, especially when administrators need to change monitoring activities frequently. Default filters for various protocol layers and applications are a big help in getting started with more sophisticated monitoring activities.

RMON applications should also offer a variety of information presentation formats, permitting the administrator to organize the collected information in ways that are concise and easy to understand. The next level of functionality requires analysis of the collected information in order to provide a variety of solutions. This next section describes some of the applications that remote monitoring probes support.

Tactical and Strategic Perspectives

RMON probes are valuable tools for tactical management, detecting a problem and responding to restore service as quickly as possible. Current RMON probe users are making a transition from tactical to strategic uses. Our research shows that administrators mainly collect tactical information such as utilization, errors, packet size distributions, and TopN measurements.

Probes are also valuable for longer-term strategic functions. Profiling is one example of a strategic function: data is collected over a period of time in order to understand normal operational behavior rather to fix an immediate problem.

The probe's discovery function can be used to alert a security management system whenever a new system is detected. The security management tools can determine if the system is authorized to use network resources, if it has been moved without permission, or if it is a legitimate network user.

Administrators are starting to use probes for accounting purposes, management tools collect usage data and organize it for billing purposes. These reports break down activity by node, by LAN segment, or other criteria and use the data to determine charges for network usage.

Probes can also be used to collect real information for modeling tools. Some modeling tools use libraries that describe devices and networks from a statistical basis. These models are usually easier to work with, but the results may not be directly applicable for complex environments. Probes can capture real traffic and provide it to modeling tools. Make Systems, for example, already collects information from several RMON probe vendors.

Troubleshooting

RMON probes increase troubleshooting effectiveness for certain types of problems. They can report excessive utilization or error rates as indicators of problems on a LAN segment. Management tools can respond to the report and automatically select new monitoring operations to narrow the possibilities; for instance, a report of excessive errors can trigger TopN measurements which identify the elements that generate the most errors.

These actions can narrow the possibilities or identify the problem within a small time period. Frequently the time to isolate the problem is less than the time it would take a management staff member to travel to the site and start collecting information. This translates into shorter resolution time and therefore higher network availability. RMON probes also save staff travel time, increasing productivity. Several organizations we have worked with estimated travel time savings of over $50,000 annually.

Profiling

The history group is used to collect data over periods of time. The information can be used for profiling. Profiles of LAN activity can be used to determine loading and granular behavior over a period of time. Most networks have rhythmic and regular periods of heavy usage, as well as periods of lower network utilization. Building normal activity profiles allows administrators to adjust their measurement operations appropriately.

Collecting profiles over a longer time interval allows the detection and projection of trends in networking usage. Although the peaks and valleys of network utilization may retain a similar shape and pattern over time, the absolute values may shift to reflect higher application traffic volumes or larger number of users being connected to the network. By having this type of information, administrators can prevent catastrophic collapse of resources by having lead time to plan for ways of accommodating the upcoming shortage of resources.

Finer granularity can be used to increase understanding of behavior. Filters can be used to build profiles of protocol or application activity within the overall usage patterns. Administrators can exploit this information to discover that growth may be driven by particular applications or protocols. More precise information allows an administrator to plan more effectively to head off potential problems.

Reporting

Reporting is another valuable RMON application. Management tools can extract information from the probes and prepare regular reports on utilization, errors, busiest nodes, and protocol activity. More detailed reports can break down activities by applications.

Accounting

Other probe data can be used for accounting, giving the administrator a detailed view of the activities within a LAN segment. This information can be used for charge backs, to monitor appropriate resource usage, and, in certain cases, has also been used to detect unauthorized usage of network and computing resources. Many desktop systems do not have appropriate accounting software and the probe collects accounting information without consuming desktop resources.

When to Use the RMON Groups

There are nine basic groups for Ethernet probes and several additional groups that are used for the Token-Ring version. What we will do in this section is look briefly at the types of measurements that can be collected and where they might be useful.

Utilization of the LAN segment is a basic metric that provides a quick and reliable indication of the overall activity and potential problems. Utilization is calculated as the

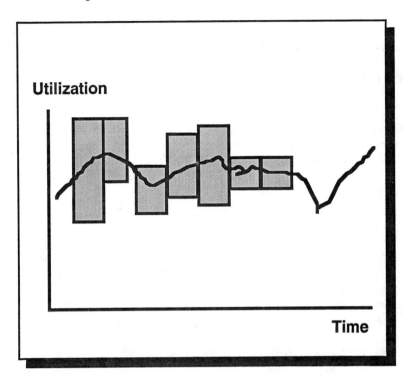

Activity baselines use average (line) and standard deviations (shaded rectangles). Standard deviation indicates variability over time—for example, there is more variability on the left than later in the day.

FIGURE 14–2   Baselining a managed resource

percentage of capacity consumed by network user activities. It is generally calculated by finding the number of octets that are transferred. The maximum Ethernet utilization is approximately 14,000 packets assuming minimal packet size (64 octets).

Packet size distributions are useful for understanding certain types of performance problems. For example, a system transferring large files with the minimum size (64 bytes) packet will not only experience slow application performance but it will also add to the congestion and contention on a shared LAN segment. Sometimes bulk file transfers, which use very large packets, may cause excessive delays and interference with transaction-based applications, which typically use small packet sizes. Insight into the mixture of packet sizes may give clues to competing application requirements that cannot be mutually satisfied.

Administrators may choose to segment activities so that bulk transfers are separated from transaction processing activities or they may try to schedule certain types of application activities at different times to avoid interference.

The RMON probe collects information about certain **errors** such as packets that are too short (runts), packets that exceed the maximum length (jabbers), and transmission errors, CRC errors. These can be used as an overall metric to indicate the general health of the LAN segment itself as well as point toward problems in network adapter cards installed in clients, servers, or network devices.

TopN measurements can be used to find the next level of detail needed to determine the cause of particular problems. For example, an indication of increasing numbers of runts can lead an administrator to use a TopN measurement to find which systems are generating the majority of the runts. Typically, it will be a single system whose network adapter can be tested or replaced to eliminate the problem.

The **Hosts** measurements are used to collect information about newly discovered hosts. The probe time stamps this discovery and begins collecting individual statistics about the Hosts, such as its transmission activity and volumes. Administrators can use the Host group as part of a security mechanism since newly added systems are detected as soon as they become active. This allows the administrator to begin a procedure to identify unexpected traffic or activities on the LAN segment.

However, it does not protect a segment from a system that simply is attached and listens to all the traffic flowing past. To protect from these activities requires a hub or switch with the appropriate security and access control mechanisms on a port basis. This restricts traffic to the communicating parties and reduces the possibility of eavesdropping on private or sensitive communications.

The **matrix** measurements are supported by the Hosts group. Each conversation between systems on the segment can be tracked in each direction. Administrators can use the traffic matrix to achieve a finer level of detail in observing the LAN behavior since they can now determine the relative volumes of traffic between any pair of Hosts connected to the segment. The matrix is useful for determining the exact volumes of traffic between the TopN Hosts, for example.

Frequently, a client/server interaction may have very high volumes in one direction and very small volumes in the other. These types of measurements allow an administrator to understand more fully the types of behaviors and the potential problems they may be causing.

Filters are very useful for administrators who need finer levels of detail. Filters are set to extract the required information from individual packets that are captured on any probe interface. Filters extract information about protocol activity, particular application behavior, or specific client/server interactions. All the packets must have a consistent offset from the beginning of the packet so that fields can be extracted in a uniform and consistent way. Filters are typically set up to provide certain common measurements and views for administrators, as well as for very specific and detailed troubleshooting operations, when the simpler measurements have not sufficed.

The **capture** group is used to transmit filtered packets to a remote monitoring site where they can be analyzed further with other tools or by an administrator. The captured information can be broken down, decoded, and categorized to provide a fine level of detail. Frequently, problems that are initially reported as "network" problems turn out to be application level problems whereby a client and server are not using the appropriate protocol sequences that make their conversation successful. Detailed decoding of the captured conversation provides the administrator with the insight to understand the exact interaction and why it went wrong.

Alarms and **events** conserve precious network bandwidth since the remote probe is not continually polled to determine when these conditions occur. The operation is "management by exception" since the probe will continue to monitor and only signal a remote site when a condition has been detected that requires further attention.

Alarms and events can also be used to trigger application programs that can reconfigure the probe and begin collecting the appropriate information automatically. This allows a management system to be much more proactive since it does not require a human being to receive the alert, make a decision on the next appropriate steps, and then initiate action. Information can be collected and logged for later analysis if nobody is available at the time. Other management tools such as trouble tickets can also be activated by a probe TRAP.

Token-Ring Statistics

This group provides the overall view of aggregate ring behavior. The traffic levels for the ring, the packet size distributions, and broadcast and multicast traffic are monitored. Token-Ring-specific statistics such as the number of beacons, claim token packets, ring purges, and other information can be used to gauge the overall "health" of the ring.

Token-Ring History

This group operates with the same pattern as the Ethernet probe. Statistics are collected periodically and stored for later access. History measurements build the foundation for trend analysis.

Token-Ring Station Group

Administrators use this group for more granular views of the ring and the stations attached to it. The ring status is available along with the current active monitor and token holder. The detailed status information about each station can be retrieved.

Station Order Group

The physical connectivity of Token-Ring nodes is important for maintaining the integrity of the token-passing operations. Administrators can determine the "distance" of each attached station from the RMON probe. They can use this information to locate problem areas and to associate specific nodes with hub ports.

Station Config

Can be used to remove a troublesome node from the ring and to collect that node's configuration information. Reading configuration information from a remote node can help an administrator determine the accuracy of the configuration or if it has been modified.

Source Routing

The operations of the Token Ring source routing mechanism must be monitored to track interring traffic flows and to assure correct operation. Each source routing bridge must be configured properly. Different types of interring traffic can be monitored and alarms can be sent when the traffic is excessive.

14.3 FUTURE RMON DIRECTIONS

Future RMON enhancements will take several directions. First, the major improvements will not involve the probes themselves; the standard probe will be an essential, but minor, component. Probe prices will continue to drop as the market matures. Probes will become commodities that will be economical to deploy across critical segments.

Probe Integration

Remote monitoring depends on probe management tools, extensions in functions, and tighter integration with the rest of the management system. Most probe management tools are available for the leading SNMP management platforms; however, tighter integration offers more powerful solutions. The probe can be leveraged more easily when it is integrated. For example, probes collect information at the MAC-layer, which is not easy for humans to use. Integration with platform services can provide translation between a MAC address and a node name address or a specific location of the equipment.

Information collected by a probe can also be incorporated into the platform's database. Administrators can use other report-generating tools to increase their insight into problems and LAN behavior. Once the probe information is in the database, administrators can use other tools for baselining, trend analysis, and integrating trouble-ticketing data.

Probe information can also be incorporated into topology maps. Visual representations can help pinpoint problems quickly. For example, a report of network congestion causes the probe on that LAN segment to carry out a TopN measurement to find the nodes that generate the most traffic. Those systems can be highlighted on the map and the probe information is much more valuable, since an administrator can quickly determine that some busy nodes are external to a specific LAN segment, for example.

Integration with the platform's event management system takes advantage of the platform's ability to filter events and activate various management tools such as problem management, diagnostics, or notification routines that speed the resolution of problems.

Embedded probes can also be used to advantage. For example, a router may find that a LAN interface has an unacceptably high utilization level. Routers, unfortunately, only detect overall traffic levels. An embedded probe can be activated to find the nodes that are causing the congestion. Probes can also be integrated with device managers. A probe may detect an overloaded server and cause a server management tool to be activated. The server management tool can examine server parameters such as memory usage, disk activity, and the number of active users in order to understand the potential problem.

RMON-II

The next generation of RMON is being finalized. In contrast to the current MIB, RMON-II focuses on monitoring the internetwork layer. Collecting information at the IP level (IPX later) allows management tools to construct an end-end view of internetwork activity while the current RMON provides information about a single segment. The matrix groups can be extended through the application layer to offer the needed understanding. Armon Networking has already introduced Eye-Node, a proprietary implementation of RMON-II capabilities.

RMON Extensions

Probes can also be extended to offer additional functions. Concord Communications and Network General, among others, incorporate response time measurements in their probes. These probes can determine round trip times between different systems. Administrators can use this measurement to eliminate possibilities when poor response is reported. The response time measurement can determine if the network is loaded or if the problem is within the client or server.

RMON Summary

RMON probes have proven their value by reducing problem resolution time, allowing organizations to consolidate staff, and providing information to other management tools. The probe applications are the key to exploiting the RMON probes for strategic management tasks as well as fire fighting.

14.4 PROTOCOL ANALYZERS

The RMON probes are the standardized versions of network monitors that collect different statistics. Protocol analyzers also collect some of the same basic statistics, such as utilization, packet levels, transmission error rates, and so forth, as the monitoring probes. Protocol analyzers, however, provide more detailed information than monitors. Analyzers provide higher level, more refined breakdowns of the captured traffic on the LAN segment or WAN link.

Analyzers break the LAN or WAN packets apart, decoding each protocol layer and presenting information to the troubleshooter. Protocol analyzers were first used to provide a user-friendly environment for troubleshooting and understanding behavior. Captured strings of binary 1's and 0's are decoded into formats that are easier to understand. The descriptions of the packet headers, significant fields and flags, and other variables speed interpretation of network and device behavior. This type of translation enabled human troubleshooters to more quickly understand the protocol interactions and use them for determining the cause of problems.

Detailed protocol interactions between clients and servers can be captured and analyzed. Troubleshooters can watch systems attempt to establish connections with each other, recover from transmission errors, control the flow of traffic between them, terminate connections, and carry out other types of protocol-based activities.

Today, protocol analyzers are frequently used for determining interoperability problems. By having detailed breakdowns of the interchanges between communicating parties, it is much easier to determine when one party has broken the "rules" of the protocol.

Analyzers have also been used in limited fashion for tracking down application-related problems. They have been very useful, especially when systems lacked the instrumentation to deliver the information directly. Troubleshooters use analyzers to infer the state of systems. Analyzers watching a slow file-transfer process may find that the LAN packets are very small—an inefficient way to move bulk data. The administrator may check the appropriate system to see if there is a configuration error.

Early analyzers had a major drawback: administrators still needed detailed knowledge and experience with the protocols before they could use the analyzer effectively. Those who did not understand the protocol or did not have in-depth experience with the variations of behavior would not find the protocol analyzer to be a significant help.

Automated assistance lowers the skill level required to make effective use of the analyzer. New analyzers, such as those by Network General, Hewlett-Packard, Spyder, Wandel & Goltermann, and others, take the analyzer to its next stage by providing automated analysis of the captured traffic. Once the traffic has been analyzed, suggestions are offered to the administrator in order to help speed up and clarify the troubleshooting process.

Most of these newer analyzers work on several different principles. The Network General Expert Sniffer matches captured traffic to pattern profiles in order to determine the source of a problem. It offers an analysis of a problem and offers suggestions to the administrator. It can actually find some problems before users are aware of them. One example is a duplicate IP address—a source of headaches for administrators.

The Hewlett-Packard Network Advisor, on the other hand, operates from a symptom-oriented basis. The administrator describes a problem such as a failure to connect to a remote server. The Advisor runs through various sets of tests and measurements as it narrows down the alternatives and reaches a conclusion. It reports its conclusion, identifying a cause or a small set of possible causes of the reported problem. These examples of intelligent analyzers will become more powerful and will not require as much human interaction in order to deliver results.

Another possibility is using analyzers and RMON probes together. Expensive, sophisticated analyzers can be centralized and driven by information collected and delivered by RMON probes. Administrators configure the appropriate filters and the probes collect the information. This strategy also brings information from multiple segments to a single location where it can be correlated and analyzed in detail. The introduction of switching will also encourage this monitoring and analysis approach.

14.5   SAMPLING WITH HEWLETT-PACKARD'S EASE

Another instrumentation alternative is to use sampling techniques. Hewlett-Packard has introduced EASE (Embedded Analysis Sampling Environment). EASE employs a sampling technique collecting a small percentage of the total packets in order to provide characterizations of network behavior. At this time, the EASE probe samples approximately one in four hundred packets. Each captured packet is only processed to the extent that the protocol headers for the first four layers are preserved. This allows application analysis programs to determine finer levels of detail. For example, an analysis program could scan the TCP header and ascertain application activity by checking the port numbers used for the connection. The captured packets, as well as certain counters for total packet traffic, observed errors, and so forth, are shipped to a remote analysis site. The EASE server collects the samples and provides different characterizations depending on the time interval. For each minute, the server determines the busiest nodes (similar to the TOPopN statistic from the RMON probes). On an hourly basis, it calculates site-wide matrices across all segments. These provide the administrator with information concerning traffic flows between different segments and provides varying levels of granularity. For example, an administrator can look at total flows, or can select flows by protocol family, such as DECnet and AppleTalk. This information can be used to find potential bottlenecks across complex Internets and to provide for capacity planning, the optimum placement of switches, and other types of long-term management functions.

The EASE technology offers several advantages. One is that its power and effectiveness do not depend upon capturing every packet on the network. Sampling provides a different level of detail. Another advantage is performance; since the EASE probe is capturing such a low volume of traffic, it can keep up with much higher-speed networks than those currently available. For example, the EASE probe already works with the 100 VG-ANY LAN at 100 MB/s per second without any problems. Higher-speed networks, such as ATM, can also be sampled and characterized, although the captured information will change to match the ATM network.

Another attractive aspect of EASE is its relatively low price. EASE can be embedded in workstations or other types of processors at a very reasonable price, providing an economical incentive to cover a large collection of network segments.

EASE is intended to be a complement to RMON, working cooperatively to reduce outages. The sampling techniques that EASE uses can be used to point to problems, and then the RMON probe can be applied for detailed analysis and troubleshooting.

One drawback with EASE, however, is that it is proprietary at this time. Hewlett-

Packard is in the process of negotiating agreements with vendors of routers, switches, and other networking products, which would incorporate EASE into a variety of offered products. Widespread availability would mitigate the drawbacks of choosing a proprietary technology. In any case, EASE fulfills a definite hole in the instrumentation puzzle.

14.6 NETWORK CARDS

Network adapters are a fine source of instrumentation for the system and network administrator. Providing silicon-based SNMP agents and extended MIB support, the network cards become simple information repositories, as well as control points for the system in which they are embedded. The new generation of network cards can be configured and checked through the network itself. Advances in hardware allow the administrator to download new ROM images to update driver and configuration information directly into the card. Remote access also allows an administrator to check the card's configuration remotely. This remote access capability shortens the time for a problem resolution cycle since travel time is eliminated. It further provides consistency and integrity checks so that if cards are changed, the configuration can be restored from the remote site.

Further extensions allow the SNMP agent to take minimal control of the processor. For instance, the UB Networks Master LAN Adapter can cause the system to reboot under remote control, giving the administrator ultimate control. Further refinements allow selective disabling of the transmit port, effectively detaching the computer system from the network if it is behaving in a way that has an adverse effect on the entire networked community. This detachment is only logical since the SNMP agent is still in communication with the remote management site and can be instructed to resume communication at a later time.

14.7 LAN MANAGEMENT TOOLS

Effective LAN management depends on an array of tools. Administrators need tools to manage their physical wiring plant, tune performance, manage security, control devices, track inventory, and carry out other tasks.

Physical Management

Many organizations require physical management tools that help them track their basic physical infrastructure. Many elements such as connectors, cross-patch panels, cables, wall jacks, and the other physical paraphernalia in a networked environment do not report to any manager.

These tools provide graphical representations of network paths from wall jack to connections, termination boxes, punchdown blocks, hub ports, cable trays, and other elements. The relationships of all these elements are also maintained so that easy tracing of paths simplifies troubleshooting.

These physical management tools use relational databases in order to describe and track all of the elements they are managing. Many can import this type of information from other sources, such as building plans and so forth, where it is available. In many other cases, it is a time-consuming and labor-intensive effort to document all of the physical plant and enter all of the information into the database. Once the data has been collected, different types of views—by resource, by floor, by area of the building, by types of connection, and so forth—can be created and used to simplify the manager's activities.

However, simply keeping track of all the physical components is only one of the possible benefits these tools provide. This type of information can also assist in capacity planning, since the actual number of physical connections, cables in the building, and so forth are always known. They can also be used to assist in planning for moves of groups or users, since the available resources can be tracked and allocated as necessary.

Moves, adds, and changes are also simplified, since an administrator can determine if there are enough facilities in the new area and can obtain lists of equipment to disconnect and locations where it should be reconnected.

Integrating plant management with other tools is necessary to exploit all the information that the plant management tools have available. For example, logical connections are displayed on platform topology maps when SNMP TRAPs report failures. The plant management tool can display the complementary view of the physical infrastructure, finding the elements related to those connections to assist in troubleshooting and locating failed elements.

The physical management tools are evolving rapidly and taking on new functions. For example, the Command 5000 System from ISICAD began as a physical management tool. The ISICAD WAN Manager module allows description of virtual circuits using the same techniques as the description of physical connections. In this way, virtual circuits can be managed and traced through all of the switches. Quality of service measurements can be applied for service-level management.

Further extensions could apply the same types of mapping techniques to applications. For instance, an electronic messaging system could be described as a set of connections between message transfer agents, user agents, gateways, and other elements. In this fashion, mail paths could be traced and monitored, and the same types of troubleshooting and tracing techniques could be applied to applications as are now being applied to virtual circuits, as well as the physical "plumbing."

Path Tracing

Path tracing can be used to resolve connectivity and performance problems. Detailed topology data provides the framework for path-tracing tools by showing the linkages between the intervening networks. Detailed discovery of devices, such as intelligent hubs, can be used to determine the actual hub ports being used while the same type of probing with bridges and routers determines the exact communication interfaces that the path uses.

Administrators can quickly determine if a path exists between two communicating nodes and also its overall characteristics. This simple test may identify the connectivity problem at this point. The path-tracing tool may find quickly that a connectivity problem is caused by a failed link, a failed interface, hub port, or device. The administrator has the information to address the problem at this point. If an intact path exists, the problem may be caused by an improperly configured end node or device. The administrator need not waste additional time chasing a problem in the physical path.

Path tracing can also be used to tackle performance problems. The tracing tool may indicate that the path uses poor routing, a low speed link, or a congested LAN segment. Path monitoring is a further refinement: devices and links in a path can be monitored and tested for thresholds so that any bottlenecks are quickly identified. Congested LAN segments and overloaded devices can be associated with a particular performance problem involving a pair of computers.

Some examples of path-tracing tools can be found in basic platform services from HP's OpenView and IBM's NetView for AIX. The administrator selects the two endpoints (the pair of computer systems having the problem), and all possible paths between them are highlighted on the topology map. This feature allows for a quick inspection, but it doesn't offer detailed information about the actual path that is used.

Digital Equipment Corporation has the Path Doctor management tool. The Path Doctor can trace a path in great detail, including hub ports and router interfaces. Rules can be applied to collected measurements in order to determine if the path is suitable for the supported application. Bay Networks also has PathMan, a component of Optivity, which offers the same types of functionality.

Hewlett-Packard introduced the Response Time Manager, which traces a path and measures the delays in each stage. The Response Time Manager exploits HP RMON probes to determine the delays across each part of the path. Simple graphical displays allow an administrator to determine where congestion is occurring. Other management tools can be brought to bear on the proper area. Quickly focusing on the most likely trouble source restores service more rapidly than time-consuming measurements.

Profiling

RMON probes can profile the activity on a LAN segment. LAN administrators also need to profile important devices such as routers, bridges, hubs, or switches. Device profiles can be correlated with LAN segment profiles to offer a more complete picture. Traffic generators can be used to stress network devices and determine their actual behavior and the conditions that cause performance degradation. Appropriate warning thresholds can be selected rather than using vendor-supplied data.

Baselining individual LAN segments is an important start, but does not provide the thorough coverage that is really necessary. Intersegment profiling will become increasingly important since the flows between different parts of the internetwork are the next problem area. Intersegment baselines would provide basic metrics on the volumes and amounts of traffic between different segments as a function of time. This type of profiling would allow administrators to make more accurate decisions on the placement of switching services and shared resources, such as servers and other systems.

Graphing Tools

LAN administrators need simple yet powerful graphing tools that allow them to look at the values of different variables across time. Sometimes graphing tools can be used on an ongoing basis to provide snapshots or at-a-glance indicators of activities and status. Other times, graphing tools will be called into play quickly to help troubleshoot certain problems by looking at behavior in finer detail.

Graphing tools must allow easy selection of the graphing variables, the time intervals, and other parameters. A choice of formats, such as strip charts, bar charts, pie charts, and other types of presentations, must be easily selected so that the administrator can move between different views as necessary.

Metering

Many network management tools provide simple metering presentations, allowing a quick, at-a-glance review of the status of LANs or other key elements. Meters follow the graphical paradigm by showing swings of highest to lowest activities, typically monitoring gauge variables. The easiest displays to follow shade the background of the dial to show the maximum and minimum values while a needle shows the current gauge value.

Threshold conditions can be indicated by changes of color. Most meters measure simple types of variables and do very simple comparisons. However, more sophisticated meters will allow the incorporation of complex algorithms to develop the appropriate metrics for display. Quite often, an administrator may have multiple meters on the screen as a way of providing an overall snapshot of the state of the environment being monitored and managed.

Modeling and Simulation

Modeling and simulation tools are becoming more important to administrators. These tools can be used for optimizing performance by modeling traffic flows and alternative configurations to find the best configuration to support the normal traffic flows. Modeling can also be used to help with optimal placement of elements. For example, LAN administrators will improve bandwidth for LAN users through segmentation, splitting a loaded LAN segment into interconnected segments with smaller numbers of systems attached to them. Information is needed to ensure that segmentation is optimal—that those systems which communicate most with each other are on the same segmented LAN segment.

Switching offers similar challenges. Administrators want to put the most active clients and servers on switches so they can take advantage of the dedicated bandwidth that switching offers. SynOptics offers DesignMan, which accepts information and produces automated suggestions for optimal switch placement.

The Traffic Expert from Hewlett-Packard uses their EASE sampling technology to characterize Ethernet operational behavior. It offers indications of problems through a "radar" screen which points to areas that may require attention. The areas include CRC errors, runts, jabbers, utilization, and collisions. The Traffic Expert also analyzes traffic patterns and offers suggestions that improve performance.

Make Systems offers the XA modeling system, which incorporates operational information from actual networks into its functions. XA system can offer alternatives for topology and for reducing costs across connecting wide area links. Make Systems supplies libraries of device descriptions and parameters that are the basis for modeling operations. These device models are developed in cooperation with the specific device vendors.

CACI offers a simpler alternative: prepackaged device models that can be graphically connected to build a description of a modeled network. The modeling relies on assumptions about behavior such as traffic loads, time distributions, and errors. The model is simpler to create and use, but it suffers from its inability to accept real-world data.

Optimal Networks focuses on defining optimum solutions. Optimal Performance builds a model of the network from information captured by monitors (the Network General Sniffer, initially). The model includes topologies, devices, protocol, and application activity. An administrator can select a goal, such as reducing congestion or improving response time between a client and server, and Optimal Performance then produces recommendations for achieving that goal.

Modeling tools are increasingly important as the managed environment grows more complex. Any modeling tool offers trade-offs between complexity, accuracy, level of detail, scalability, and time for solutions. Continuing improvements in user interface capabilities and the introduction of object-oriented technology may make modeling tools more sophisticated and much easier to use in the future.

Modeling tools should be calibrated before being used extensively. Choose an environment that is well understood, especially a small one for which there is good historical data. Build simple models and check their results against actual behavior. Use the historical data to compare changes to the model and the environment. Use a few iterations to learn how long it takes to build or modify a model. Use the experience to get a sense of the results produced by the modeling tools.

Up the ante by tackling more complex, but well understood, environments, until you have confidence in the tool's accuracy and knowledge of its limitations. More experience refines the usefulness of any modeling tool. It is not uncommon for organizations to have several modeling tools. Simple tools may be used for quick, high-level modeling tasks. The results may not be as refined as needed for making decisions, but quick results can narrow the possibilities relatively quickly. Once the focus is sharpened, more refined tools can provide more detailed information and recommendations.

Security Management

Firewalls are becoming more common as the stories of intruders and the damage they wreak spread. Firewalls are mainly used to isolate an organization from the larger world of the Internet. Firewalls are dedicated computer systems and Internet hosts that are interposed at the boundary between private and public network environments. Traffic flowing across the boundary passes through the firewall and can be controlled. These firewall systems are placed in a physically protected area where they are not subject to modification or disruption. These systems are also configured to refuse all offers of direct log-in so that outsiders cannot easily compromise them.

Traffic from outside the organization is delivered to the firewall, outsiders cannot directly access any systems on the other side of the firewall. The firewall is usually constrained to an incoming messaging receiver. It accepts mail for designated users and disconnects. The mail is relayed to the designated user inside the organization. The firewall should have the capacity to modify user addresses so that internal addressing structures, site locations, and other information are not available through the firewall.

Outgoing traffic can be monitored in the same way: the firewall checks the user, the specified destination, and the application or service. If no access violations are detected, the firewall makes the Internet connection and relays traffic. Administrators can set the appropriate rules that the firewall enforces.

Firewalls can be fooled, unfortunately. One trick that has been effective is to modify the IP source address of an intruder's packet so that it appears as if it was transmitted from a valid node within the organization. The firewall relays the packet to the target and an attempt to compromise the system commences. Firewall filters can screen for this situation.

Some firewalls support directory or naming services for locating users or information. Attackers have masqueraded as other name servers and obtained information that can be used for attacking the firewall. The example above holds true, the legal address of a user can be obtained and then used to "spoof" the firewall.

RMON probes are being used as another line of defense. A probe can be interposed between the firewall and the private networking environment. It can filter packets looking for suspicious incoming addresses. Another level of protection is offered for the receive-mail-only firewall. Incoming traffic is filtered to detect any nonmessaging traffic. The RMON probe can send an alert that indicates a possible attack on the firewall. Automated tools can turn off all firewall network interfaces while other responses are marshaled.

Device configuration is another aspect of securing the LAN. Bridges and routers have filters that screen traffic before passing it to the next network. These devices can compartmentalize traffic and, in theory, repel attackers from reaching targets. Probes are useful for testing the filters; make sure they work or that they are set accurately. Using a traffic generator usually allows modification of addresses as needed.

14.8 SUMMARY

Instrumentation is the place to begin. RMON probes are becoming more important for long-term strategic monitoring as well as for tactical troubleshooting. Nonstandard monitors and protocol analyzers are also used. Protocol analyzers break captured traffic into multiple-layer presentations so that administrators can quickly understand problems in protocol interactions. Protocol analyzers will become fixed, remote probes deliver the information for detailed decoding and breakdown.

The newest types of network cards also provide instrumentation through built-in

SNMP agents that provide information about configuration and activity of individual interfaces.

Sound LAN management depends on profiling, path tracing, and modeling tools in order to track behavior and get the most out of the LAN. The challenges are moving to intersegment monitoring and analysis, performance optimization of complex internets, and incorporating switching and shared media.

14.9   GENERAL WIDGETS

General Widgets had several challenges as it organized its LAN management strategies. LAN management is being organized for each campus in as uniform a way as possible. Future plans call for more centralized campus management when the underlying technologies are ready to support it. LAN management is focused on transport services—providing connectivity and bandwidth throughout the campus.

General Widgets is pushing its device vendors for better authentication in their device agents. The company wants to secure all manager-agent interchanges in order to protect its networks from attackers posing as members of the management team. The global span of the corporate network makes the problem more difficult since encryption technologies cannot be exported. This leaves device vendors and customers without any tools that legally work across national boundaries.

The campuses are being transitioned to a standard topology with FDDI rings acting as backbones. One campus in the U.S. was selected as the pilot for testing the new approaches. The experience gained with the first campus site will be leveraged for those that follow. The topology also provides a strong foundation to introduce switching in the future.

One main issue is the instrumentation of each campus environment; the use of high-speed FDDI and multiple backbones poses some challenges. At this time, there is no standard RMON probe, although a standard for an FDDI probe MIB is forthcoming from the Internet Engineering Task Force. The routers that connect the buildings to the FDDI rings provide basic interface statistics. This basic information identifies the most active buildings on the campus backbone, but it lacks granularity. For example, the explicit flows between different ring-attached routers cannot be derived from the bulk perspective supplied by raw interface statistics. Further, there was no information about protocols or applications that were using the backbone. An overall view of the rings could be provided, but the information needed for troubleshooting and capacity planning was not easily available. New agents for the routers will collect some specific higher-level information that will be useful to the campus administrators.

Probes for FDDI rings are already offered by Frontier Software, and other vendors will follow suit as the standards effort nears completion. Other analyzers are available, but they are designed for interoperability testing and are still expensive. General Widgets is evaluating an early RMON probe to see if it can deliver the necessary information.

RMON probes can be used within buildings: the issue is the number that should be deployed permanently and those that should be portable. Some probes are being placed in

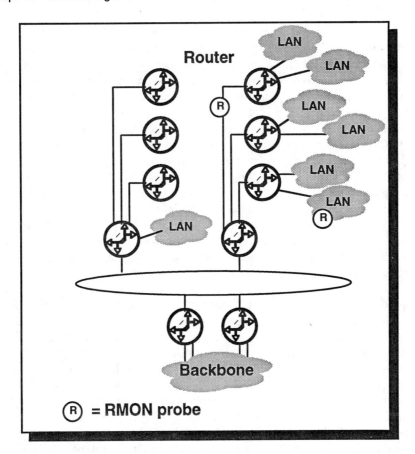

General Widgets can place probes on workgroup
segments or backbones that interconnect floors. The FDDI
ring cannot be monitored with a standard product at this
time. Higher speed LANs will demand more bandwidth in
building and campus backbones.

FIGURE 14–3   RMON in general widgets networks

intelligent hubs, thereby gaining the advantage of being able to monitor several segments
with a single probe. Multiport probes are necessary for monitoring several LAN segments
simultaneously, and General Widgets will use portable probes when a multisegment problem arises. Permanent probes will be placed in those segments that contain critical
servers. A future option of consolidating servers will change the placement of probes.
Servers will be placed on FDDI rings or high-speed switches. Higher-speed probes will be
needed. Switches will contain embedded probes when they are acquired.

The building backbones were originally designed as point-to-point links between the floor routers and those connected to the FDDI rings. However, this left no place for attaching an RMON probe. Modifications were made that incorporated a small hub in each building where the floor links were joined to the FDDI-attached router. An RMON probe can be attached to the hub and switched to any desired floor link. This approach served for handling permanently placed probes as well portable monitors. Monitoring critical building backbones provides information about intra- and interbuilding traffic. There are too many backbones to consider permanent probes at present prices. However, a set of portable probes are used for regular baselining activities.

Baselines of all LAN segments, floor links, and FDDI backbones are taken on a regular basis. The baseline information is integrated with a simple time-activated process that sets the traffic thresholds according to the baseline information. The adjusted thresholds are used to identify events that indicate a significant change in operational behavior.

The baseline information is also used for ongoing trending and capacity planning. Each collection of baseline activity is added to the historical log and the trends are projected for administrators. Administrators want to collect more detailed information about application usage and patterns rather than link-level information. RMON filters will be used to collect some of the information in the short term; General Widgets is also evaluating specific tools for monitoring application activity. The application data will be used to understand the communication patterns that are in effect, and will help administrators understand the impacts of each application. If more users of an application are added, administrators will be better able to predict the changes in service levels that may result.

Modeling tools are being evaluated for the campus. Administrators want to be familiar with these tools in a relatively stable setting before using them to help reorganize the campuses for server farms and the introduction of switching. Information collected by the probes is the desired input for the modeling tools. Several varieties are being evaluated before a selection is made. The information from these tools will be used to evaluate changes and optimize behavior.

Information management also entails collecting information about failures, intermittent disruptions, and other problems. The trouble-ticketing system is being upgraded to provide reports on the most frequent problems, the duration of outages, and other factors that can be addressed such as relative staff effectiveness. Administrators will use this information to evaluate their processes, their staff training, their spare parts inventory, and the robustness of their devices. A Help Desk is being introduced as a point of contact for network users. The Help Desk will be integrated with the problem-management tools to assign staff, track resolution, and evaluate the problem-management process itself.

Integration of information is still a struggle, the different point tools for managing LANs do not offer the needed levels of integration. For example, it is still difficult to get an end-to-end trace of the physical path between any pair of computer systems. Each device manager has information about its own device, while the topology maps offer a logical view. Administrators want detailed path-tracing tools that follow a client/server conversation wherever it actually goes.

CHAPTER 15

The Virtual LAN—New Management Challenges

Switching is the future networking fabric—stretching from the desktop to the enterprise backbone. Switching offers more than high speeds, however. New possibilities for structuring and configuring networks are raising new issues. Future LANs will be created with management software rather than physical attachments.

Several levels of switching are used to build these new networking environments. Each adds its own features and capabilities to the whole. Traditional shared-media LANs will, of course, remain part of any new environment.

15.1 SWITCHING HIERARCHIES

Switching solutions arose in part because more bandwidth is needed to keep pace with more powerful desktop systems. Growing numbers of network users also strain shared-access LANs. Past a certain limit, shared LANs cannot accommodate more growth since each user's bandwidth is provided at the expense of another user on the LAN. **Segmentation** is a stopgap approach that breaks a heavily used LAN into a set of LAN segments with fewer users on each segment. It is an expensive proposition to consider interconnecting each segment with bridges and routers. Placement becomes essential: if clients and servers are separated by several bridges of routers, they will simply congest the intervening segments and defeat the purpose of segmentation. Adding more users starts the problem cycle again since the limitations of shared media remain. Various types of switching deliver more bandwidth while accommodating growth.

Port Switching

Intelligent hubs have multiple backplanes, each supporting a LAN segment (the LAN in a box as it is commonly known). Administrators use port or module switching to move network nodes between LAN segments on an individual or group basis, respectively.

Port switching is useful for load balancing or fault isolation. Quick segmentation is available when bandwidth is needed. However, port switching only allows an administrator to juggle the available bandwidth in the backplanes among all the network nodes. Port switching scales poorly as the total number of network nodes grows, delivering a lower effective bandwidth for each node.

Port Switching Issues

Traditional LANs will remain major elements of the virtual infrastructure for at least another decade. Moves between traditional LANs will still be carried out through port and module switching within intelligent hubs.

Traditional LAN segments that are interconnected by bridges pose no problems for simple port and module switching within the hub. Since bridges relay on MAC addresses, a change is easily accommodated through an update of the bridge's learning scheme. Bridges can quickly adjust their relay table to reflect a new port for a particular MAC address.

Crossing a router boundary is not such a simple operation. Attaching a workstation to a different LAN segment is not as straightforward at the network layer as it is with bridging. For example, moving a workstation from one segment to another might require a change in its IP address. The move may also require a change in the IP subnetwork mask. Updates to the Domain Name Server will also be required so that other systems can reach the appropriate destination through the routing infrastructure.

LAN or Frame Switching

LAN switching adds bandwidth along with network nodes. Ethernet switches were introduced by companies such as Kalpana and Grand Junction. LAN switching delivers full LAN speed to each switch port. A single system has the luxury of full Ethernet speeds; a shared segment must still allocate the bandwidth among the competing systems.

Switches allow **multiple communications** at the same time: if a switch as n ports, then a maximum of n/2 interactions could occur simultaneously. This also increases the available bandwidth for a workgroup since bandwidth on each switch port does not depend on the number of nodes attached to the switch. Switches can be interconnected to accommodate more ports, although latency is increased when traffic travels through more switches.

First generation LAN switches are actually **multiport bridges**; the switch learns where other systems are located. Frames arriving at each port contain a source and destination address; the switch learns the home port of a system by associating source addresses with ports. LAN frames arriving at a port are switched to the appropriate home port or broadcast to all ports if the destination has not yet been learned.

LAN switches operate on traditional variable-length LAN frames. A variable latency is introduced since each variable length packet takes a different time to move through the switch.

Symmetrical and Asymmetric LAN Switches

The first generation LAN switches were **symmetrical;** all switch ports operated at the same basic LAN speed. A limitation arises at some point since the workgroup communications patterns do not change. Workgroups usually communicate in a star pattern; servers are the center of most workgroup activities. Individual workstations may have dedicated LAN speed connections, but server congestion may reduce the actual performance.

Asymmetric switches are being introduced to address this problem. The Catalyst from Cisco Systems, the 28000 from Bay Networks, the MME-6 from Cabletron Systems, and the Ridge from Newbridge Networks are some examples. Each has a high-speed port (100 Mbls or higher) for attaching servers or higher-speed links for interconnection.

LAN switches can be provided as stand-alone devices or placed in intelligent hubs. Systems attached to the same hub-switching module communicate through local switching. The hub backplane interconnects hub switching modules or traditional segments.

Switched ATM Services

The fixed-length ATM cells offer predictable latency since the delays are constant. Thus, ATM can also support time-sensitive applications such as videoconferencing, multimedia, or image processing.

ATM offers scalable, higher-speed switching services for interconnecting traditional and switched LANs across a campus or through wide area links. ATM is being introduced initially as a high-speed campus backbone and will migrate toward the desktop and the wide area.

ATM switching is different from LAN frame switching since it uses a **virtual circuit service** to route fixed-length cells from switch to switch. Virtual circuits are either permanent or switched. Permanent virtual circuits are administratively designed and last for indefinite periods. Switched virtual circuits are established when they are needed and usually last for shorter time periods. A system must signal the ATM network and request a circuit setup.

Connection Management Systems

ATM requires a routing, or Connection Management, System (CMS) to find a path through a set of switches. The CMS gives each switch specific instructions once the path is selected. Switches need only look at an incoming cell, check the virtual circuit number, and forward it to an output switch port. Separating path selection from switching gives ATM its high performance. There is no routing calculation with each cell as in the traditional router.

The CMS can be located anywhere in the network; it receives a connection request and sets up the switches between two parties. A distributed CMS in multiple sites will be needed in the future.

15.2 TYING THE PIECES TOGETHER: EDGE ADAPTERS AND ROUTERS

LAN frame switching and ATM are complementary; LAN switches deliver higher bandwidth to the desktop without requiring new network adapters or other infrastructure changes, while ATM provides high-speed campus interconnections. However, the two environments operate with different principles. LAN frame switching works with the traditional TCP/IP paradigm of variable length frames and connectionless operation. ATM is based on fixed-length cells and virtual connections.

Edge Adapters

Edge adapters are the place where the two environments are integrated. An edge switch is a further elaboration of the asymmetric switch. The high-speed port connects the edge adapter to the ATM environment. Additional functions are embedded to provide frame-to-cell conversions—breaking variable length frames into fixed length cells or vice versa.

The edge adapter also communicates with the Connection Management System so that it has a virtual circuit for traversing the ATM environment. Translations between virtual circuit identifiers and destination IP addresses are also maintained.

The Role of the Router

Routing must also change in this emerging environment. Routers process each packet before making a relay decision. The intensive processing places an unacceptable limit on performance. Router vendors are also separating the route determination and packet switching functions in separate processors. This improves routing performance, but leaves other issues to be resolved.

Traditional LANs will be connected into the switching environment by routers with the edge adapter functions. The add-on modules will segment variable-length frames into cells and reassemble them as well. The edge adapter also communicates with the CMS to get virtual circuit assignments as needed.

15.3 LAN EMULATION—CROSSING THE ATM BACKBONE

The devices described above can all be fitted together. However, the two operational paradigms must be interconnected. How does an IP datagram cross a cell-switched virtual circuit backbone? LAN Emulation is the answer. The LAN Emulation strategy is a way to carry variable-length datagrams inside a series of ATM cells, in effect tunneling through the ATM network.

The major elements of the LAN Emulation approach include LAN Emulation Servers and Clients, a BUS Server, and address translation information.

LAN Emulation Client

The LAN Emulation Client is placed in an edge adapter or a router with an edge adapter. The client is responsible for **segmentation and reassembly**—breaking IP datagrams into fixed-length cells and reassembling them as they arrive from the ATM network. However, the remainder of the work requires the cooperation of the other LAN Emulation elements.

The LAN Emulation Client needs an ATM virtual circuit identifier so it can reach another edge adapter (or native ATM device) across the backbone. The client can issue an ARP (Address Resolution Protocol) request to the LAN Emulation Server. The server maintains a list of ATM/IP Address mappings and determines the appropriate ATM network address. The Connection Management System can be activated to select a path between the LAN Emulation Client and the target ATM node.

The virtual circuit identifier is returned to the client. Once the virtual circuit is activated, the client can send IP datagrams to the specified destination. Once the cells arrive, they are reassembled and the IP address is used for further forwarding through traditional routers or by LAN frame switches.

The BUS (Broadcast and Unknown Server) handles the broadcast, multicast, and discovery functions. Broadcasts are forwarded to the BUS, which maintains a list of all recipients of the broadcast/multicast transmission. It fans the broadcast across the ATM backbone to the appropriate IP destinations. Packets to unknown destinations initiate a discovery process whereby the BUS floods an ARP request to all parties. The edge adapter that services that IP address responds and a new node is added to the address mapping tables.

Switching hierarchies offer a scalable solution that provides bandwidth and flexibility. Better technology must deliver better business outcomes, however. These values are discussed next.

15.4 VIRTUAL LANS

Another value that a switched environment offers is **reduced cost of ownership**. The emerging management solutions simplify one of the most pressing problems—the cost of moves, adds, and changes. Administrators will be able to reconfigure their networks from a management console and will have the technology to introduce **policy-based management**.

Organizations want more fluid networking structures that can be adapted to constantly changing business requirements, challenges, and opportunities. Workers are assembled in project teams that cross traditional business unit lines. Team members may have different skills, such as marketing, product design, research, advertising, software, engineering, and so forth. These teams are assembled for varying periods of time, ranging from days to months or years. Some teams have a planned lifetime to achieve a short-term goal. Other teams will last for extended periods of time—for example, taking their products from inception through design, marketing, development, and sales. Some stable teams last for extended periods, although their membership may change as different project phases demand.

Workers may often be members of more than one project team, depending on their particular skills, time commitments, and ability to juggle multiple tasks. Whenever a project team is disbanded, members will be redeployed and reassembled into new teams to meet the next challenge.

Network designers and administrators are using a different paradigm to create new types of networks. Workgroups will be defined and connected based on **functions** rather than having membership determined by **attachment** to a specific LAN segment. The **virtual workgroup** is constructed with management software rather than moving attachments. Being able to group by function, as well as team membership, will be an important attribute of the emerging information-intensive enterprise.

The interconnection provided by Connection Management Systems allows project teams to collaborate electronically from many different locations. Project team members can exchange information, cooperate on designs, keep each other informed of progress through messaging, and share other data and software needed to complete their task.

The same type of flexibility that provides for cross-disciplinary teams can also be used to provide more consistency among the traditional business units. For example, financial services groups may be distributed throughout a corporation, but can be viewed as a single collective subnetwork within the enterprise.

Virtual LAN Characteristics

The **virtual infrastructure** has a different set of characteristics from what most of us recognize as an internetwork today. These characteristics offer new advantages and challenges for network designers and administrators. There are more degrees of independence that must be addressed.

Technology Independence   Workgroup definition and connectivity is independent of the underlying networking technologies. Virtual workgroup membership includes network nodes attached to traditional shared LANs, to switched LANs, and to ATM-switched services. Connectivity services among workgroup members accommodates any combination of these technologies. Membership is defined by the needs of the organization rather than by any physical connectivity constraints.

Dynamic Topologies   Administrators will also be able to reconfigure networks quickly from a management console: changing topology, connectivity, and bandwidth al-

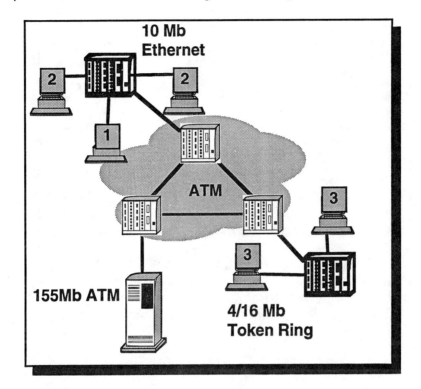

10 Mb Ethernet

ATM

155Mb ATM

4/16 Mb Token Ring

Virtual workgroups are created without restrictions associated with location, speeds, or local technologies.

FIGURE 15–1   VLAN properties

location in a matter of moments. Users can be moved to another workgroup with management software rather than by changing physical connections to hub or switch ports.

Location Independence   Virtual networks provide connectivity independent of location. Virtual workgroup members may be located on different floors or in different buildings within a campus, across wide-area network links, and ultimately in entirely different organizations collaborating on projects. Seamless connectivity will be provided to all group members regardless of location.

Bandwidth Allocation   Another important characteristic is that full LAN speeds can be delivered to any network nodes that require maximum speeds. Users requiring low or bursty bandwidth may be served effectively by shared LAN segments, while other LAN users can use a dedicated connection to a LAN switch port. Higher performance elements, such as servers or powerful workstations, can use even higher speeds by direct attachment to ATM switch ports.

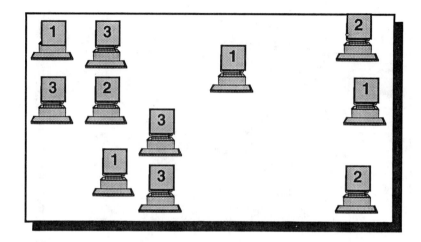

Virtual workgroups are defined by function rather than connectivity. Systems may be clustered physically but belong to different communities of interest. All systems with the same numbers are members of the same virtual workgroup.

FIGURE 15–2   Virtual LANs and workgroups

Policy-based Management   Virtual environments offer administrators the beginnings of policy-based management for network administration and operation. The CMS will be the nucleus for introducing policy-based management. The Connection Management System needs a global view of the networked environment in order to provide optimal route selections. This global perspective also allows constraints (or policies) to be incorporated. For example, routes can be selected based on user profiles, bandwidth limitations, time of day, application needs, and other criteria.

Management policies are embedded in the Connection Management System and are carried out by the switching elements in the virtual network. The manner in which switches are instructed, in effect, creates a policy decision. Some routes will be based on metrics such as minimal cost or delay, while others will receive bandwidth assignments to support given application needs.

Functions such as connection management, bandwidth allocation, security, and topology changes can be defined and implemented from a policy perspective rather than simply as a set of management tools. For example, integrity policies prevent an administrator from inadvertently adding a user to a secured workgroup or from changing topologies during critical times of the day.

For example, Cabletron Systems has the ACMS (Automated Connection Management System), which allows an administrator to fill in options about each user such as the

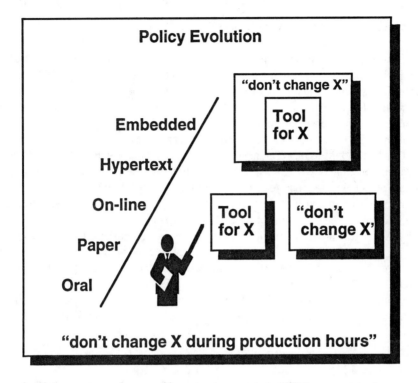

Policy evolution—policies can be described orally or they can be embedded as constraints for management tools. Automatic enforcement offers a new opportunity for managing complexity.

FIGURE 15–3   Policy-based management

number of allowed connections, the amount of bandwidth to be allocated, time of day, routing metrics, and other constraints. ACMS incorporates these policies and applies them each time a user requests a virtual connection.

The CMS will carry the policies out once the administrator specifies them. This automatic policy incorporation and enforcement offers a new level of control. The CMS functions must be extended into the traditional routers and the LAN frame switches. Access control on switch ports replaces the learning behavior of the first generation LAN switches. Administrators will control virtual workgroup membership; users on the same switch will not communicate unless the CMS allows them to. The CMS also updates router filters to provide some isolation between traditional LANs.

15.5 BUILDING THE VIRTUAL WORKGROUP

A brief aside about the physical topology: **structured wiring** and **intelligent hubs** make the transition to switching much easier. We still talk about Token-Rings, FDDI rings, and Ethernet buses, but the reality is that all new LANs are based on a star topology. Structured wiring leads all connections to the intelligent hub. It is the choice of network adapters in the end nodes and hubs that determines whether a token is passed for (FDDI and Token-Rings) or stations contend (Ethernet) for access.

This leads to a stable, permanent physical infrastructure that is changed at other levels, such as selecting network adapters to determine the access rules. Switching leverages the stable physical infrastructure to make the topology more flexible.

Membership in a virtual workgroup will be defined in multiple ways: the traditional shared LAN attachment or connection to a LAN or ATM switch port. Those systems on a shared LAN segment will be members of the same virtual workgroup since access control cannot be more granular than an entire segment. Systems attached to LAN ports will be members of a virtual workgroup as determined by the access control policies. Systems attached to an ATM switch will be controlled by the CMS as well.

Membership will also be defined by IP (Layer 3) addresses. Switches such as those from Agile Networks and Newbridge Networks recognize IP addresses when systems

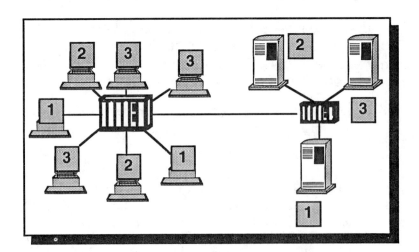

Virtual workgroups can be defined on a port basis.
Each port is associated with one or more virtual
LANs.

FIGURE 15–4   VLAN definition by port

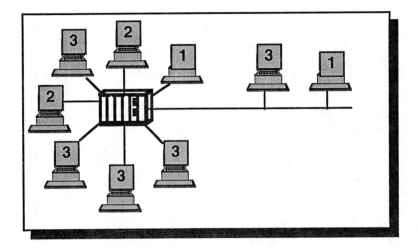

Port definition raises the issue of granularity when
shared segments are attached to the switch. Assigning
all systems on a segment to a single VLAN is easy.
Assigning systems to different VLANs will be allowed
in the future.

FIGURE 15–5   Port granularity

are connected. The connection Management System sets access controls to incorporate that system with others sharing the same subnet address. Changing the system's IP address can affect a change in membership, it will automatically belong to a different community.

More sophisticated rules can constrain membership to applications users. Sophisticated silicon collects information from each packet and assigns target virtual workgroups based on rules. Thus, a single system can be a member of multiple virtual workgroups. Each packet can be routed to the appropriate destination through local LAN switching or crossing the ATM backbone with LAN Emulation. XYLAN has pushed this area more aggressively at this point.

Interconnecting different switched virtual workgroups is a different matter, however. Different workgroups may be interconnected through a router that serves as an adjunct to an ATM switch. The ATM switch forwards cells to the router which translates the virtual circuit identifiers before sending the cells back to the switch for relay to the other workgroup. Future ATM switches will incorporate the routing functions internally.

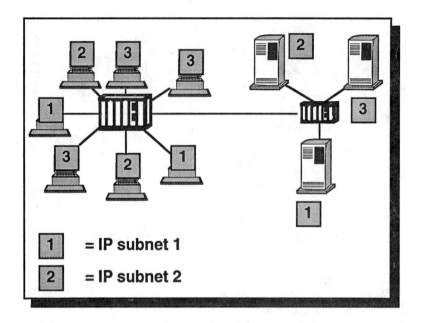

VLANs can also be defined by addresses—either IP or MAC (others such as IPX will be available). Definition by address increases mobility—the management system recognizes the address when a system is moved and re-configures automatically.

FIGURE 15–6　　VLANs by address

15.6 MANAGING THE VIRTUAL INFRASTRUCTURE

The stability of the physical infrastructure allows a highly dynamic virtual infrastructure to be created. Administrators will not be able to take advantage of switching and exploit it to the fullest possible extent without the appropriate tools to manage large and complex sets of relationships. Evolving the appropriate monitoring tools, selecting useful and informative virtual management metrics, and integrating other management tools are ongoing issues that must be solved over a period of time.

Operator Interfaces

Virtual topology management requires a new level of sophistication and simplicity in the operator interfaces. Network maps of physical connectivity and logical topology must be

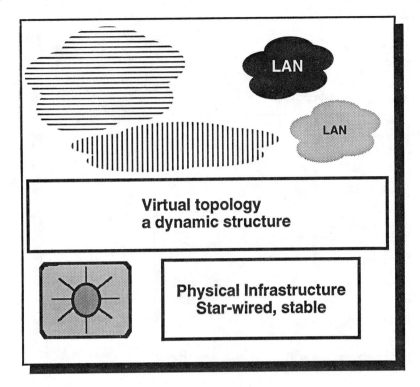

The basic physical infrastructure remains in place while the actual topologies are varied as needed to create a set of Virtual LANs.

FIGURE 15–7 Physical and virtual topologies

provided. Operators must be able to see at a glance which systems are members of various virtual workgroups. Multilevel views will be required so that operators can selectively view virtual workgroups, physical topology, or other types of information.

The topology maps we use today will be less valuable in the virtual environment since virtual workgroups are not localized. Windows that contain the members of a virtual workgroup and provide status, statistics, and other information inside are emerging as the early choice for presentations. Grouping will be more useful than topology views since administrators can view the set of elements in a particular window, monitor their status, and so forth, without having to search through physical maps to locate the elements they manage. Hewlett-Packard's Operation Center and the Control Desk for IBM's NetView for AIX are current examples of logical grouping. Icons can also be used to access the windows when they are closed.

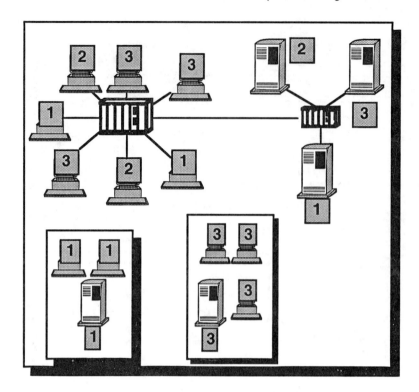

Topology maps are not effective for viewing VLANs. Grouping members in windows will make it easier to view the various VLANs.

FIGURE 15–8   VLAN views

Moves, Adds, and Changes

Administrators will use drag-and-drop operations to move individuals or groups of users between different virtual workgroups. This process seems easy on the screen, but it can be potentially complicated and more automation is needed.

Logical moves also entail other functions. For example, moving a computer from one virtual workgroup to another also entails a change in access control policies and a possible assignment to a new workgroup server. The Connection Management System can adjust the access control information in the appropriate switch ports. However, the assignment to a new server and other functions are not part of the CMS functions. Without automation the administrators will have to supplement the simple drag-and-drop operation with manual procedures.

All of the flexibility that comes with switching and virtual LANs must be constrained in most cases: just because something can be done is no reason that it should be done. Policy considerations must be incorporated so that critical networks are not changed during operational hours or secured networks may not be changed without special authorization. Global configurations of logical topology may be required so that the entire networking fabric can be easily switched between testing and operational configurations. Other policies may be incorporated that place constraints on the size of virtual workgroups, geographic membership, or other factors unique to each management organization.

Traffic Analysis

Traffic analysis is also essential for making effective moves. For example, moving a set of systems between segments may do nothing to improve the performance situation if the server remains on the original segment. Instead, the interconnecting bridge or router becomes more congested. Traffic modeling offers administrators predictive help before making substantial topology changes. The modeling tools collect real information about traffic flows between elements and make projections of the impacts of changes. Administrators may need to use several alternatives until they find the best solution.

Physical Moves

Automatically detecting physical moves is also important. Cabletron Systems and Newbridge Networks are adopting a strategy of proactive registration to help with physical moves. Both vendors use automatic discovery and registration to simplify physical moves. The Connection Management System is notified when a new computer system is connected to a switch port. The MAC address is used to determine the next actions. If the system is already a member of a virtual workgroup, then all appropriate access control information in the CMS is adjusted to reflect the new location. The privileges move with the user automatically. Virtual workgroups built with IP addresses can also adapt to movement of the members. Attaching to a new switch port causes a report to the CMS, which adjusts the access control information as needed.

If the computer system is not a member of a virtual workgroup, the switch port is disabled and the administrator is notified. Further administrative actions will be needed to determine the next steps.

Monitoring

Monitoring tools are another important consideration as the virtual infrastructure matures. Monitoring traditional LANs is quite straightforward, since a monitoring device like an

RMON probe can be attached to the shared media and collect information from the broadcast traffic. The monitor doesn't interfere with the performance of the network or disturb it in any way. The new virtual environment, however, poses a new set of challenges. For instance, there is no broadcast traffic in the traditional sense. Individual members of a virtual workgroup may be distributed across multiple switch ports and traditional LAN segments.

Future monitors will be embedded into the switching fabric itself. The forerunners of this approach are already visible in products such as the embedded RMON probes in intelligent hubs. The RMON probes can be programmatically switched to monitor any hub port. In this way, a network administrator can selectively monitor the appropriate ports for troubleshooting or traffic analysis. However, this approach may have some limitations if multiple ports on the same hub must be simultaneously monitored in order to track down complex interactive problems.

Switch monitoring offers several alternatives. Probes can be embedded in the switch and monitor different ports as instructed by a remote management center. This makes switches more complex and expensive. Another alternative is to add an additional switch port where an external probe is attached. The switch can be directed to copy traffic from any other port to the attached probe. A further elaboration has the switch sending the port's traffic to a remote site for further analysis. Several switch vendors, such as Newbridge Networks and Cisco Systems, are already pursuing this option. The concerns with steering conversations arise if switches do not forward badly formed packets; that would certainly defeat the idea.

Embedded probes may not be as effective in delivering the needed information. If a virtual workgroup spans multiple switches, then there is no place to aggregate the information needed to provide the TopN measurements provided by current RMON probes. Monitoring will likely involve simple port statistics collected by the switch and other traffic delivered to external monitors and analyzers.

Another challenging area at this time is the definition of the appropriate **metrics** for monitoring a virtual workgroup. In a traditional LAN, metrics such as packets per second, error rates, packet-size distributions, utilization, and throughput had well understood meanings and could be used for many simple characterizations of the LAN. Metrics such as utilization offer a simple rule of thumb to indicate overall health and functioning.

The virtual workgroup does not lend itself so easily to characterization with simple metrics. Members of a workgroup may be using different speeds; for example, high performance servers may operate at 155 Mb/s while individual workstations are still operating at 10 Mb/s speeds. This variety of speeds, as well as geographic distribution, makes it difficult to determine what an appropriate metric would be for a virtual workgroup load, utilization, or throughput.

Another key consideration will be the ability to relate measurements made on the virtual workgroup to the underlying physical infrastructure. For example, network administrators must be able to understand and evaluate the impacts of moving groups of users to different workgroups. If servers are distributed, then the traffic patterns may change dramatically. More organizations are grouping their servers in high-speed LANs, which also mitigates these problems. Network administrators must be able to see the results of changes in the virtual topology and their effect on the underlying physical structure.

Integration with Management Applications

Other management tools need access to logical and physical information. The virtual management environment must make both types of information available. Some management applications will continue to work with physically oriented data, whereas others will be targeted toward virtual resource groupings. For example, an administrator delivering new software to members of an engineering team will want to specify the target in that way. The software distribution tool starts by accessing the logical description of the members of the engineering team. At some point, that description must be translated into physical addresses in order to actually deliver the software.

At other times, physical information may be all that is needed. An administrator scanning for assets of a particular type, such as desktop systems with a specific type of processor, video board, fax attachment, and so forth, might need to scan the descriptions of all the computer systems regardless of their virtual workgroup membership.

Functional integration will be needed at a higher level, as well. For instance, inventory and asset management information must be automatically updated when users are moved from one logical workgroup to another. Other tools may need to update licensing information since licenses still move with systems.

15.7 VIRTUAL LAN SUMMARY

The virtual infrastructure offers unprecedented flexibility in building workgroups and re-configuring the network environment as often as necessary. Execution of policies in the switching elements enables more optimum levels of control over such a dynamic environment. Examples of emerging virtual LAN management products indicates the range of approaches.

15.8 EMERGING ARCHITECTURES

Vendors are beginning to deliver elements of the virtual infrastructure today. Hub, router, and switch vendors are converging on the same general approach, although specific architectural details will vary. The common visions define an ATM backbone with edge switches connecting LAN frame switches and traditional LAN segments.

Cabletron Systems

Cabletron has a very thorough virtualization story, although all of their elements have yet not been assembled and brought to market. They are likely to have a strong leadership in this particular area, based on the recent introduction of their MMAC-Plus, as well as new modules and alliances.

The SFPS (Secure Fast Packet Switching) architecture offers high-speed switching between connected systems. Each hub module contains one or more high-performance RISC processors which control switching operations.

The introduction of the MMAC-Plus hub provides Cabletron with a high-capacity hub able to interconnect switching modules, traditional LANs, and external ATM switches. Cabletron depends upon Fore Systems to provide ATM switching to complement the MMAC-Plus hub. ATM switches are connected externally to MMAC-Plus through 155 Mb/s links. MMAC-Plus modules such as the ESX-MIM and EMME-6 provide onboard switching, as well as access to the high-speed backplane for intermodule or module-to-switch connectivity. The SFPS modules perform header translation and normalization which eliminates the need for routers to interconnect Ethernet, Token-Ring, and FDDI segments within the SFPS environment.

The MMAC-Plus modules provide the basis for the Secure Fast Packet Switching architecture (SFPS). Today, Cabletron provides a segment switching option with its EMME modules, and its ESX-MIM modules provide dedicated per port Ethernet switching. In addition, the SFPS provides embedded routing services for interconnecting Ethernet, Token-Ring, FDDI, and ATM networks. This interconnection is achieved by LAN header modifications within the MMAC modules, translating Ethernet to Token-Ring headers, etc., as appropriate.

Cabletron will exploit the high bandwidth of the MMAC-Plus backplane, as well as the local switching elements that comprise SFPS. Modules already in use, such as the EMME-6, the ESX-MIM, and the TPX-MIM, are all bridged or port-switched devices today. Cabletron has positioned its modules for flexibility using the INTEL i960 processors with flash memory. New software can be loaded which, in time, will convert these bridging products to asymmetric LAN frame switches. High-speed ports from these switching elements will connect to the MMAC-Plus backplane, providing intermodule connectivity, as well as connectivity to outboard ATM switches from FORE Systems. The MMAC-Plus also interconnects with ATM switches from Cisco Systems, Light-Stream, and the i960 ATM switch from FORE Systems.

Cabletron will initially leverage its investment in its Spectrum management platform, particularly emphasizing the power of its Virtual Network machine, a rules-based system for determining faults and diagnosing symptoms. In the future, Cisco Systems may also place its virtual management applications on top of the Cabletron middleware that is supplied for the Spectrum for Open Systems program.

Cabletron leverages Spectrum's graphical user interface in order to develop multi-level views of the virtual environment. Some of its strategies include specific color-coding when viewing the physical topology, as well as iconized representations of logical workgroups. Icons allow a set of systems to be manipulated as a group. Future views allow the incorporation of additional pull-down menu items for viewing such things as virtual circuit identifiers and other statistics related to the virtual environment.

Cabletron uses the common drag-and-drop operations: moving the icons for particular workstations into windows or other icons representing a particular virtual workgroup.

Cabletron also has an autoregistration capability within its management system, allowing a network administrator to attach a system to a new switch port without any further manual management actions. The hub modules recognize the new connection, extract the MAC address, and forward this information to the Connection Management System. The CMS determines if this system is already a member of a virtual workgroup, and if so, simply moves all the assignments of paths, access privileges, and other resources to the new switch port. However, if the newly attached system is not a member of a predefined workgroup, it is assigned a default workgroup and the administrator is notified that an unknown system has been attached to a particular port.

Cabletron has the ACMS (Automated Connection Management Services) initially implemented on a SPARC station. ACMS uses the automated discovery facilities of Spectrum to discover the topology and connectivity between switching elements in the environment. ACMS incorporates access control policies, allowing administrators to define the rules for connecting workgroup members or interconnecting workgroups. Some of the initial path selection criteria are the bandwidth required, time of day, the type of connection, the number of active connections, and the holding time for each connection.

Cabletron also provides a Preferred Route Application, which allow users to define particular criteria for path selection. Administrators may define different paths in order to keep traffic flows of different workgroups separated from each other or to ensure that particular types of traffic flow across a more secure fiber link, for example.

ACMS is centralized at this time. It will be distributed into the embedded i960 processors when scalable connection management systems are needed.

Cabletron provides screens that allow administrators to view, modify, and create rules. Cabletron provides a set of default policies and rules to help administrators get started. Initial rules are constrained to determining access control and connections between communicating nodes. Administrators will also have menus of relational operators to combine with particular variables when they build or modify rules.

Cabletron provides an embedded i960 processor, supporting the RMON MIB for each module. The RMON probe is connected to the backplane, capturing the traffic flowing between modules. Programmable filters can be used to extract higher-level details, such as particular source and destination address pairs, embedded protocols, or application-level information. Individual ports on each switching module also collect the standard MAC-layer statistics, such as packet counts, runts, dropped packets, and other defined information.

Cabletron is positioned to exploit its embedded i960 as a base for future management applications that will be distributed throughout the virtual fabric. They will offer local diagnosis, event correlation, and automated responses. Cabletron is embedding i960 processors on every MMAC module it delivers, providing a scalable management processing capability. The i960 processors will be used for RMON, as previously mentioned, as well as for other management functions. Eventually, much of the ACMS will be migrated to the i960 processors to provide a robust distributed connection management service.

In addition to building a distributed Connection Management System, Cabletron is also providing a LAN emulation server. Cisco Systems will be helping with further refinements of the ACMS, partly to incorporate the Cisco ATM switching that will be interoperable with the MMAC-Plus. Cabletron plans to have its MMAC-Plus hub interoperate with a variety of ATM switches, including those from LightStream, Cisco Systems, and Fore Systems (the ASX-100, as well as an i960-based product). Cabletron provides the necessary engineering support, such as SNMP management, TELNET connections, or other mechanisms, to seamlessly integrate this range of ATM switches with its products.

Cabletron is aggressively positioning itself as a premiere management provider for the emerging switching environments. Cabletron's message is that Spectrum is a high-technology platform that has already developed the technology required for managing these complex new environments. Cabletron already has client-server architecture for its management platforms, a distributed database, and object-oriented modeling, coupled with artificial intelligence, in the Spectrum platform. Cabletron believes that it already has the base technology necessary for controlling a virtual infrastructure.

Cabletron is aggressively pursuing sophisticated applications such as traffic modeling, optimization, and granular monitoring that leverage its technology. Cabletron believes that superior management will be one of the key differentiators for continued growth and success as switching becomes a dominant technology in the next decade.

Cabletron will also push some of the Spectrum applications into the i960 processors within the MMAC-Plus and will emphasize local response and distributed intelligence for delivering more effective management.

Cisco Systems

Cisco has announced its CiscoFusion strategy which calls for the integration of LAN frame switching, cell-based switching, and the eventual integration of router-based functions. Cisco is positioning itself to become a major provider of the enterprise network. Its increasing focus on SNA connectivity, virtualization, and management differentiation are parts of its strategy to capture this strategic market.

NEC is supplying its ATM switching expertise to Cisco for campus and wide-area-network connectivity. This alliance complements the Crescendo and Kalpana acquisitions for LAN switching. Both levels of switching capabilities are necessary if Cisco is to have a complete enterprise-networking solution. Collaboration with Cabletron will also give Cisco access to virtual management tools and approaches.

CiscoFusion outlines a phased approach for the introduction of ATM and LAN switching in a cohesive environment. Cisco is already leveraging its acquisition of Crescendo with the introduction of its Catalyst switch, the first of a series of switching elements with a high-speed backbone connection. The Catalyst is an asymmetric switch providing Ethernet switching, as well as a high-speed port that interfaces to a dual FDDI ring for high-speed backbone connections. The second generation asymmetric LAN switches will incorporate a direct interface to an ATM backbone. This asymmetric switch will perform segmentation and reassembly functions, communicate with the Connection Management System when new virtual circuits are needed, and provide switching between the LANs and the ATM backbone.

Cisco is also positioning its 7000 series of routers as forerunners of the new environment. Many public statements have stressed the separation of the path selection and the switching functions within its router. This, of course, is an evolutionary step to prepare for eventual transition to ATM-switched services. Cisco has also been showing its muscle with the testing results from its Silicon Switch Processor. The improved performance allows Cisco to start staking a claim to providing high-performance silicon switching.

Cisco proposes attaching high-performance routers with ATM interfaces as adjunct devices to the ATM switches. Routers will provide switching between virtual workgroups by receiving the packets, translating the virtual circuit identifiers, and sending the cells back into the switching fabric.

Cisco will evolve CiscoFusion to incorporate a Connection Management System that controls Cisco's ATM switches, the intelligent Kalpana and Crescendo-based switches, and its routers. The Connection Management System will control switching between virtual workgroups, as well as switching within each logical domain.

The Cisco ATM switch will attach to the Cabletron MMAC-Plus, offering potential customers a complete solution. This move also strengthens Cabletron's Open Systems positioning since Cabletron will have access to multiple ATM switches.

The overall strategy is the development of stand-alone virtual applications which are integrated at a later time into the CiscoWorks management product. This is consistent with the company's past approach with modules such as the Configuration Builder and the Software Manager.

Cisco plans to provide a range of views with VLANView, including physical topology, logical views of workgroups, logical views of resource groups, virtual workgroup membership on topologies, and the ability to build and view hierarchical virtual workgroup relationships. Hierarchical workgroups are needed to approximate the actual environment more closely. For example, a large department may have common resources such as mail servers while each workgroup has its private set of resources. Users are actually members of both workgroups—the department workgroup with shared resources and individual workgroups with private resources. The number of levels must be adequate to deal with corporate-level, regional, national, or other types of aggregations.

Cisco is investigating different tactics based on the customer culture. For example, it provides centralized control of workgroup membership. With this method, an authorized administrator makes assignments or changes in virtual workgroup membership. The appropriate information is conveyed to the Connection Management System, which applies the appropriate access control policies, bandwidth allocations, and new workgroup membership lists.

Cisco plans to allow a move toward hierarchical workgroup structures wherein nodes can be members of more than one workgroup. Users will initially contact a server that assigns the appropriate memberships and privileges.

There will also be internal mechanisms to define containment memberships of hierarchical workgroups. Cisco's initial effort will deliver a common zone: a domain with shared resources for the entire enterprise, such as E-Mail servers, file servers, FAX servers, and so forth. These resources will be reached by all members of the organization, although other virtual workgroup traffic will be isolated.

Cisco appears to be putting its initial effort into more developed access control policies. Administrators will be able to set up access control privileges by virtual workgroup membership, as well as by defined application profiles. These application profiles will identify the priorities and bandwidth assignments for electronic messaging, video conferencing, file transfer, or other services. Cisco believes that it will be the only vendor able to offer service-oriented route selection at an early date.

Cisco appears to be looking very hard at policy management issues. It will provide tools for administrators to define the rules for various types of management policies. For example, it provides graphical-user interfaces with the appropriate menus and tool selections. In addition, it uses macros and input lists to simplify the construction of new policies. In addition, Cisco also allows the application of rules and policies to systems spanning single or multiple virtual workgroups. Some of these features are already available with the Global Command feature as well as in some of the new elements being added to CiscoWorks, such as the Configuration Builder.

Cisco allows several levels of policy gradation; for example, it will provide go or no-go with policy implementation, prioritization for finer granularity, or preemption policies, actions to be taken when capacity decreases occur due to failures. Cisco will be using proprietary MIB extensions for managing its switching elements until the accepted IETF MIB standards are adopted in the future.

Cisco is introducing RMON probes into its LAN switches. Future routers and those for branch offices may also have RMON probes. These probes will be programmable, allowing administrators to drill down to specific packets or data streams, as necessary. Switch ports deliver the basic interface statistics collected and condensed for delivery to a remote management site.

Cisco will also use a copy port on its switches, which duplicates traffic on any of their regular ports. This copied traffic can be fed to connected analysis tools to provide deeper levels of detailed analysis when needed. Cisco is also considering shipping selected port traffic to a remote center for detailed analysis—similar to the Newbridge approach.

Cisco plans on using simple RMON-type metrics, providing interhost traffic displays and presentations for its initial characterizations of workgroup behavior.

Optimizing these complex environments requires automated assistance from tools such as those provided by MAKE Systems. Cisco is actively seeking other partners that complement its basic management products with more sophisticated applications. Higher levels of integration are required between these tools in order to provide the value and seamless functionality required by administrators.

Cisco is using MIPS processors inside its products. At this point the processors collect management information in addition to performing other functions. This approach will not scale well as higher speeds and virtual workgroups are introduced. Cisco will likely switch to dedicated processors with specialized ASICs to collect and reduce low-level information such as packet counts, utilization, etc.

Cisco is providing an API to its Sybase database. The API will allow third-party vendors, such as MAKE Systems, to access information collected from the virtual environment and use it for other functions such as traffic modeling, capacity planning, building activity profiles, and so forth. Cisco will depend on the OpenView, NetView for AIX, and SunNet Manager SNMP management platforms for other integration services.

Cisco is positioning itself as the enterprise network supplier. Its management strategy will focus on the same area SynOptics has exploited—managing the entire transport system rather than devices. Cisco will enhance CiscoWorks as a key element, adding more functions and integrating with other tools as needed. Cisco will also stress manageability solutions over time—building policies and handling processes such as configuration, inventory, and access control.

Newbridge/VIVID Networks

Newbridge is taking the tack of building the virtual environment with its own technology rather than through partnerships. The major pieces are the Ridges that provide asymmetric LAN switching, as well as connectivity to the cell-based backbone supported by the Newbridge VIVID (Video Voice Image and Data) ATM hubs. Ridges will cache routing and switching information to minimize latency.

The Ridges are asymmetric LAN switches that connect switched LAN users being supported by (yellow) Ethernet, (blue) Token-Ring, and (red) FDDI. The Ridges support a maximum of twelve ports. The ATM hub is a twelve-port device with a total capacity of 1.6 Gb/s, supporting twelve ports running at 155 Mb/s each. Newbridge also supplies ATM adapters for the SBUS, EISA, and GEO buses at 155 Mb/s.

Traditional LANs are connected through the LAN Service Unit, interconnecting with routers and providing segmentation and reassembly capabilities, as well as interaction with the Route Server, the Newbridge name for the Connection Management System.

Newbridge will supply the VIVID Network Manager as its leading virtual management application. The virtual network manager will be available on standard SNMP platforms, such as HP's OpenView, SunNet Manager, and the Newbridge 4602 Network Manager. Newbridge is obviously stressing the 4602 Network Manager, particularly for its ability to integrate LAN and campus ATM backbone management.

Initial management offerings focus on moves, adds and changes, and workgroup definition. Newbridge believes that it has a strong position supporting workgroups across multiple switches.

Newbridge provides a set of views ranging from simple physical topologies to groups of elements collected into "communities of interest." Different color schemes and icons will be used in order to clarify the information for the administrator.

Newbridge provides the usual complement of drag-and-drop operations for administrators. Newbridge counts on the Route Server to apply access control policies when connections are established. A graphical matrix is used by administrators to define access policies between pairs of workgroups. Administrators can fill in each intersection to determine if access is allowed. One-way access is possible between groups.

Newbridge also provides an auto registration function for elements that move within the campus. When a system is connected to a Newbridge Ridge port, it is interrogated and the information is passed on to the Route Server, which updates its topology and access control databases appropriately.

The Route Server applies access control policies when call setup requests are received. Other policies to accommodate latency (time-sensitive), bandwidth allocation, security, and other factors will be included in future releases.

The Route Server operates on Sun workstations. Newbridge has the capability for multiple Route Servers, although at this time they are only used in a "hot standby" mode. The active Route Server updates those on standby with any changes made during its connection management functions. Newbridge may, in the future, provide multiple Route Servers that act in a distributed fashion to allow them to scale for larger campus environments.

Newbridge provides standard port statistics on each of its Ridge ports. These are captured through the use of special ASICs and an embedded RISC processor within each Ridge. In addition, further analysis is provided by copying any Ridge port traffic across the campus to a management site where more detailed analysis can be carried out. Newbridge will provide simple path tracing and monitoring in its initial release, with the ability to capture information about traffic flows across any given connection. Future plans would allow this same information to be captured for quality of service monitoring, as well as billing.

Newbridge is leveraging its extensive experience in wide-area-switching environments. Its management experience brings high value to the switched campus environment. Another factor that Newbridge is stressing is that it manufactures and builds all of its own products and they are all tailored to fit together for ease of operation. For example, twelve Ethernet ports on the yellow Ridge fit comfortably within the 155 Mb/s links that connect the Ridge to the VIVID hub. This ensures that there is no congestion by oversubscribing or having too many ports served by a particular link speed. Newbridge's message is that it provides a scalable, compatible product set all the way from the end node through the ATM switch.

Chipcom Corporation

Chipcom has continued to emphasize its positioning relative to life-cycle costs and manageability. It has designed its chassis, modules, and management system to address these issues.

Chipcom plans to exploit the technology in the Galatica switch from Artel, moving from bridging to true LAN frame switching. The same technology will be used to introduce a full-scale asymmetric LAN frame switch. IBM is supplying the ATM switching technology for Chipcom. Chipcom will be able to exploit IBM's ATM technology to provide the other ingredient for a full-scale campus virtual infrastructure.

Chipcom customers have a very solid satisfaction level with Chipcom's ONdemand management product. Chipcom will leverage ONdemand and enhance it to incorporate new functions for virtual management. Chipcom has always had a strong management story in terms of the integration of applications, the amount of local management processing, and the high quality of the ONdemand application.

Chipcom will leverage a lot of the work that Artel has done in the switching environment in terms of defining closed user groups for public networks. Much of these tools and applications can be used in the description and creation of virtual workgroups within the switched hub environment. Chipcom also intends to provide multiple memberships, allowing a node to be a member of more than one virtual workgroup concurrently.

The Connection Management System is being built in conjunction with IBM. At this point, it appears to be fairly immature and there was not much information that could be collected about its operation, granularity, policy definitions, or expected timeframe.

At this time, Chipcom plans on implementing policies that can be triggered to apply constraints to such things as applications, time of day, detected problems, and other criteria. However, this is expected to be a phased project with very little policy management available in the initial release of a virtual management application.

Chipcom uses embedded 68K family processors and will provide the normal port interface statistics for all switched modules. In addition, RMON probes will be available within the ARTEL switching modules. Chipcom intends to continue differentiating itself by providing substantial processing power to provide local management information processing, reduction, and preliminary analysis. In future enhancements, Chipcom will also enable these applications to act locally, responding to errors and reporting outcomes to a remote management site.

High performance 68K processors are being used today. These processors handle many other tasks and dedicated management processors may be needed. Chipcom will continue to place more management functions outboard—in the hubs and switches.

Chipcom is letting the platform vendors build the tools for integrating other applications with ONdemand. Chipcom will continue to focus on driving more management processing close to the events. Automated responses can be embedded within the ONcore switching hubs management processors to increase the ease of management.

Chipcom will continue to focus on driving more management processing close to the events. Automated responses can be embedded within the ONcore switching hubs management processors to increase the ease of management.

Chipcom has a phased strategy that is based on intelligent agents in its devices and a domain manager. The intelligent agents collect information on configuration, performance, RMON probe data, and environmental parameters such as fans. The domain manager is also resident in the device; it collects information from the agents, filters it, and forwards alarms to a management workstation. The domain manager has automated procedures for responding to errors, allocating bandwidth and reconfiguration. Customers can add customized scripts.

The next phase introduces advanced device management, more sophisticated applications that automate more management functions with intelligent and flexible options. Advanced modeling is the next successor; this level incorporates sophisticated modeling tools to provide planning, simulation, and optimization. The final stage introduces full-scale virtual management.

3COM

3COM is basing its virtualization strategy on its High Performance Scalable Networking (HPSN) architecture. The acquisition of Synernetics gives 3COM access to switching. ATM switching technology is provided by FORE systems. The NETBuilder II router will be enhanced for ATM LAN Emulation and as a base for its Connection Management System.

3COM is introducing its Transcend line of management products, which will eventually provide a virtual management solution. Transcend is an umbrella name for a range of management products for hubs, routers, and adapter cards. Transcend runs on the three major platforms: OpenView, SunNet Manager, and NetView/6000.

3COM uses a connectivity system as a basic unit. At this point, enterprise, campus, and workgroup connectivity systems have been defined. The connectivity groups have containment relations; i.e., workgroup systems are contained in campus connectivity systems that are in turn contained within the enterprise system.

The initial virtual management application is Transcend for Workgroups, an application that will initially run on a Windows platform. Transcend for Workgroups will manage adapters and FMS hubs.

The usual complement of logical and physical views are provided. Iconized virtual workgroups are used with windows to show the individual members of any group. The early product will be simple since it focuses on workgroup management. The campus manager will incorporate router management and WAN interfaces.

3COM is not providing any type of autoregistration with the initial release, although it will incorporate this feature in a later release. The introduction of the Transcend campus connectivity systems manager will add integrity constraints that affect the membership rules.

There is no Connection Management System to manage with the initial Transcend for Workgroups product. The FMS stackable hub does not support switching. Workgroups can span multiple FMS hubs. Future plans include adding path selection policies based on criteria such as security, application type, priority, and time of day. The introduction of the CMS coincided with the Transcend campus connectivity manager release.

The initial CMS will be centralized; the next enhancement would be hot standby with a distributed CMS considered after that based on scaling issues.

There are few policies that have been discussed. There is a scheduled access control policy as part of the workgroup product that can be applied to individual nodes or a virtual workgroup. An administrator can set times when nodes or workgroups are allowed to use the network. If access is attempted at other times, the transmit port of the adapter card is disabled.

Monitoring is provided through the 3COM SmartAgent in the hub. RMON probes will not be available until the October release. The SmartAgent has several varieties: hubs and routers have built-in SmartAgents while adapters are monitored through a proxy in a server. 3COM suggests an upper limit of 1,000 nodes for the proxy.

The SmartAgent is the foundation for building more sophisticated management functions. SmartAgents will keep getting smarter; they will move beyond data collection and reduction. Local analysis and response to predefined conditions will be incorporated in the next releases.

3COM has a breadth of products: hubs, routers, switches and adapters which allows them to provide complete management coverage.

The Connectivity System Model provides the appropriate architecture and approach for a sound management solution.

Transcend will use object-oriented technology to provide the most sophisticated tools for administrators.

LANNET

LANNET stresses that it has built its own switching technology with ASICs it developed internally. The MultiNet intelligent hubs claim to have a cell-based switching backplane at this point. The LANNET approach is similar to that of Cabletron, providing a high-speed 1.28 Gb/s backplane which, in the present, has low enough latency to behave as if it were a switched environment. LANNET offers local switching for its LANswitch modules, as well as access to the high-speed backplane.

LANNET is building its LANswitch, a dynamic Ethernet switch, as well as the ASICs needed for interconnecting to the cell-based backplane. The LANswitches are asymmetric, providing Ethernet rates today; switching is on a dedicated, one address per port basis. LANNET also provides a segment switch supporting up to 64K MAC addresses.

The recently announced agreement with General DataComm has given LANNET access to ATM switching technology. GDC and LANNET will work to take the ATEX ATM technology and incorporate it into bridging/routing modules for the MultiNet hub. The two companies are also developing interface modules for the 1.28 Gb/s cell backplane and ATM. LANNET is offering switched 100 Mb/s Ethernet, with switched FDDI for high-speed servers following soon.

LANNET also has access to high-performance routing technology through its partnership with Wellfleet Communications. Wellfleet has provided LANNET with embedded routing modules for the MultiNet hub.

Multiple hubs can be interconnected with the new LHB module that is just beginning to ship. This provides a high-speed fiber connection initially supporting FDDI. LANNET plans to incorporate the ATM technology from General DataComm into its products in the third quarter of 1995.

LANNET has a base management application product called MultiMan that is available on OpenView, the SunNet Manager, and NetView/6000 SNMP platforms. LANNET is offering a new application called the VirtualMaster, which will initially be bundled free with the base MultiMan product.

LANNET has the usual complement of views, ranging from physical topology through logical topology. Iconized representations of virtual workgroups, and common workgroup windows are provided. Color coding is used extensively, particularly in the physical topology views to define membership of nodes.

The VirtualMaster allows administrators to create virtual workgroups within one hub, or, with the addition of the LHB module, workgroups can be defined across multiple hubs. At this time, the tool is limited in concept to setting up workgroups on a hub-by-hub basis in a strict canonical order. Workgroup administrators have a palette representing all the virtual workgroups associated with a given hub. They use drag-and-drop operations to move particular nodes between different virtual workgroups. This will be extended to multiple hubs when the LHB module is used.

LANNET plans to allow the definition of hierarchical workgroups in the future, although the containment rules and descriptions are not clearly defined at this time.

Policy management at this time is relatively immature, based on the lack of a Connection Management System to use as the framework and implementor. Policy in terms of access controls can be maintained today through the setting of access ports on the LAN-switch modules. Access control across an ATM backbone will depend upon the partnership with General DataComm whose wide area experience will be needed.

LANNET uses embedded i960 processors to act as RMON probes collecting information on the backplanes. At this time, RMON probes only monitor the traditional backplanes within the MultiNet hub. A high-speed probe that can match the 1.28 Gb/s cell-based backplane will not be available for nine months to a year. Lack of a high-speed probe will seriously limit LANNET's ability to monitor and profile traffic within its hubs, as well as between its hubs.

Bay Networks

Bat Networks has announced BAYSIS (Bay Networks Switched Internet Services). SynOptics communications contributed intelligent hubs, LAN switching with CelliFrame technologies, and ATM switches. Wellfleet contributed routing capability.

The key philosophy is route where necessary, switch everywhere else. The Virtual Node router interconnects different workgroups. BAYSIS will use a distributed connection management system that offers scalability and fault tolerance.

BAYSIS segments the environments as desktop, LAN backbone, WAN backbone, and Remote Site. Integration of all segments is the long-term goal. Evolution to switched environments with ATM as the ultimate stage is planned for all segments of the enterprise network.

BAYSIS applies three major disciplines to each of these segments. Transport Services address connectivity through shared and switched technologies and the supporting distributed routing services. Policy Services deal with security, traffic management, and virtual networking. The remaining discipline is Operation Services, which use the Optivity platform for configuration, fault management, accounting, asset management, and analysis tools.

BAYSIS will introduce virtual LAN capabilities to its workgroup products and extend its scope across the enterprise. Workgroups will be defined at the network layer, defining membership by the subnet address. Further membership distinctions can be made through the protocol used. This leads to multiple memberships that can be sorted by these criteria.

Optivity provides capabilities for defining and changing membership in virtual workgroups. Operators can select various views of physical topologies, virtual workgroups, and network resources. Windows contain the members of workgroups and offer simple ways of organizing the information. Policy-based management is being introduced with integrity constraints and connection management operations.

Likely future trends are to add more analysis tools to complement the DesignMan and TrendMan tools. DesignMan, another Optivity tool, collects traffic information and offers suggestions to improve performance and place switches and routers effectively. DesignMan uses RMON data and can play back the captured traffic to test new configurations.

Bay Networks is stressing the breadth and depth of its BAYSIS approach to the delivery of multilevel switching for new enterprise networks. Coexistence of shared and switched media is preserved at all stages. The strength of Optivity will be another area that is emphasized with the addition of more modeling tools and deeper integration with other management elements.

Digital

Digital Equipment Corporation has launched enVISN, the architecture that delivers switched, virtual networking. Digital has a set of strong technology products with its DEChub and switching elements for FDDI, ATM, and LANs. One of the early distinctions of enVISN is its distributed policy capability. Policy agents are placed in each switching element to oversee the operations of the rest of the virtual networking system.

Each switching element contains routing, access control, and connection management functions. Centralized control points can deliver the necessary information for initial configuration, and then the switches communicate as needed to keep the virtual LAN running smoothly.

End nodes can be members of multiple virtual LANs if desired. The virtual networking elements detect membership by destination address and set up the appropriate routing and resource allocation for each connection.

15.9 SUMMARY

Virtual LANs offer some interesting possibilities for improving management through embedded policies, simplifying moves, adds, and changes, and automating configuration tasks. There are still important issues such as interoperability: various architectures mentioned here will not necessarily interoperate, although all use LAN and ATM switching. The issues arise with Connection Management Systems; each vendor can use its own proprietary approach when setting access controls on its LAN switches.

ATM switches are more interoperable due to efforts of the ATM Forum. End nodes can signal the ATM network when they need a switched connection to another destination. There are no open standards that define the interactions between a Connection Management System and any LAN switch at this point.

The virtual LAN is built with management software rather than changing wiring. Virtual LANs, or workgroups, can be defined with different criteria: by switch port, by IP address, or application activity. A simple user interface that organizes and presents information in a variety of formats and levels of detail will be needed.

There are many places where policy constraints can be embedded. For example, the Connection Management System is the logical place to incorporate bandwidth management policies. Administrators can assign bandwidth based on the identity of the communicating parties, the type of application, time of day, available bandwidth, and the class of service. On the other hand, the tools that control the definition of virtual LANs are the place to add restrictions that govern changes to membership. The administrator may limit the types of changes that can be made depending on the time of day, level of staff, or other criteria.

CHAPTER 16

Managing Computer Systems

Managing distributed computing systems has so far been an unrewarding, demanding task. Introducing distributed computing systems intensifies systems management problems. The staffing demands and complications arising from a geographically distributed environment can overwhelm most management teams. The management problems are made more difficult by the fact that many organizations have different types of network operating systems, such as NetWare, NT, OS/2, UNIX, BANYAN, and others. This diversity of operating systems ensures that many current systems management tools can only be applied to a small portion of the managed environment. Most of the systems management tools in use today use proprietary data structures, protocols, and agents to carry out their limited systems management functions.

Many of the available products are also highly fragmented: for example, one software distribution package may also incorporate inventory management, while another package distributes software and does virus checking, while yet a third does asset and inventory management exclusively. Poor modularity and lack of interoperability have led to a multitude of tools that makes the administrator's job quite difficult in the heterogeneous environment we must manage.

Another contributing factor is the relative immaturity of systems management tools compared to LAN or WAN network management solutions. Network management has been addressed for a longer period of time and, consequently, more sophisticated approaches have been developed. However, the systems management area need not take as long to reach the same level of maturity since many of the technologies may be transferable from network management. For example, network traffic analysis applications analyze the flows between networked segments and recommend actions to optimize performance. This same type of pattern recognition and analysis can be applied to interactions between sets of clients and servers.

Managing a distributed client/server environment today is often accomplished through the local management staff. Unfortunately, hiring more staff for each new work-group is a luxury few organizations can afford and a major reason why so many client/server applications have yet to escape from the development lab into the real world.

A further pressure on systems administrators is caused by the introduction of mission-critical applications. Systems failures have much more impact as business activities depend on high availability and high-quality service levels. In fact, the low quality of systems management solutions is another inhibitor to many organizations which cannot yet risk their business on distributed systems.

Systems management requires some of the same basic elements as LAN management: instrumentation, platforms, and tools. Instrumentation, with embedded agents in systems and intermediate agents for aggregation, will be the foundation for remote monitoring and management. Platforms are the focus for collecting and integrating the appropriate management tools.

16.1 MIX AND MATCH

Most administrators deal with a heterogeneous environment with different hardware platforms and operating systems. The advantages of client/server capabilities are exploited by separating the client used by the administrator from the server containing the information and management tools. Systems management tools are evolving to a mix and match approach: administrators select the client they are familiar with and use the most appropriate server. A Windows client may be familiar, while a UNIX server on a RISC workstation provides the backend power.

Mix-and-match capabilities are also needed for management operations. Administrators can use tools across environments—for example, backing up an OS/2 client on a UNIX server. Administrators can use one client to monitor activities on dissimilar systems. The key is a common agent and data structure that is used in all systems.

Some tools for systems management also overlap with tools for other management areas, especially for functions such as problem management, asset management, and accounting. Other tools will deal with specific computer systems, operating systems, and applications.

16.2 INSTRUMENTING COMPUTER SYSTEMS

Current instrumentation for clients and servers lacks features that are really needed for effective systems management. Much of today's instrumentation depends on "hooks" that allow access to such things as system logs, files, or configuration information. The systems were never designed with remote instrumentation in mind; instead, the hooks are an attempt to make some of the system-specific information available.

Daemons are used in many UNIX-based environments to check system logs, configuration files, and other information periodically. In the DOS world, small Terminate and Stay Resident programs (TSRs) can capture some information. These types of approaches provide some simple instrumentation, but they have serious drawbacks. The main drawback is that they are easy for users to wipe out or disable, intentionally or otherwise. Loss of instrumentation renders the system invisible to the management system and often requires some type of local access in order to reestablish the management instrumentation. Most of these instrumentation approaches are also proprietary, forcing administrators to use a set of different tools for each type of computer they manage.

Standardized, embedded instrumentation is not yet available, but the emerging DMTF (Desktop Management Task Force) specifications may deliver a solution in the future. Systems must be provided with standardized instrumentation that is built in and immune to user actions. Open instrumentation standards allow management tools to be applied across a variety of computer systems.

The Internet Engineering Task Force is developing an SNMP MIB standard that is complementary to the emerging DMTF efforts.

16.3 THE HOST RESOURCES MIB

The SNMP community has reacted to the need for better instrumentation and standardization of systems management formats with the definition of the Host Resources MIB. As detailed in RFC 1514, the Host Resources MIB describes the resources contained within a particular system. The host resources MIB also depends upon the standard MIB-II, particularly the system and interfaces group, to support host resource monitoring. The host resources MIB is composed of five basic groups: system, storage, devices, running software, and installed software.

The **systems group** from MIB-II provides basic information that uniquely identifies the system, such as the system name, the vendor, location, contacts, and operational status. The **interfaces group** defines the types of communication interfaces used by the system. Interface characteristics such their speeds, access mechanisms, and counters that provide information on the flow of packets in both directions are available. The systems group provides basic information about the length of time the system has been running and the system's understanding of date and time. Other information is provided in order to monitor system startup parameters. For example, the bootstrap device, the path name, and any other startup parameters are specified as variables in this group. The remaining information in the systems group comprises the number of current users and active processes, as well as the maximum allowed values for each.

The **storage group** contains information describing different types of storage resources that a system contains. The storage group provides fine granularity so that storage can be described for compact disks, RAM disks, removable disks, fixed disks, virtual memory, and other categories. For each class of storage there is an indicator describing its type, the size of units allocated for that particular category of storage, the maximum storage size, the amount of storage in use currently, and a counter describing the number of allocation failures.

Each type of storage is represented as a table to accommodate multiple instances—

for example, several floppy disk drives. An index is used to access any particular instance in the table.

The **devices group** describes the devices contained within each system. Many types of devices, such as processors, network interface cards, printers, disk storage, video, audio, coprocessors, keyboards, modems, pointing devices (a mouse), parallel and serial ports, tape units, and volatile memory, are all defined as specific categories. Each type of device is described with a textual string, as well as a unique product identifier. A set of status indicators is also available so that particular conditions, such as down, warning, testing, or operational, can be determined. Errors for each type of device are also defined so that conditions for each type of device, as well as general status, can be monitored.

The optional **software group** describes each piece of software executing at the current polling time. Each piece of running software is described by its type: identifying the product, version number, and vendor. The amount of storage used and its operational status are also available to a remote management application.

The **installed software group** describes each piece of software that is on long-term storage, each software module has the same information as the running software group. In addition, the actual location of each file is available for monitoring purposes.

The host resources MIB is a first step toward monitoring remote systems. However, there are not yet capabilities for controlling behavior in these remote systems. Other mechanisms must be provided. This is a weakness in the MIB specifications since administrators must have remote control in addition to monitoring.

16.4 DMTF—A VENDOR-NEUTRAL APPROACH

The DMTF (Desktop Management Task Force) was formed in May 1992 by an influential group of eight leading vendors—IBM, Hewlett-Packard, Digital, Intel, SynOptics Communications, Microsoft, and Novell. New members of the steering group include computer manufacturers Dell, AST, Apple Computer, and Compaq. Symantec, a leading vendor of desktop management utilities, has also joined the steering committee. There are over 100 other vendors that are developing products using the DMTF specifications.

DMTF Design Goals

The DMTF was formed to deliver open desktop management interfaces. The open interfaces offer access to a simple infrastructure which supports managed elements and the applications that manage them. Vendors and application providers can focus their resources on delivering more manageable components and better management applications.

The DMTF outlined several practical design goals including:

➡ **independence** from any specific computer or operating system
➡ **easy vendor adoption** through development of Beta code, software developer kits, implementers workshops, and joint marketing efforts

➡ **independence** of any network or systems management protocols

➡ **mapping** of information from DMTF to current management protocols such as SNMP and CMIP.

DMTF was also designed for **local use** so that unattached users would also have better desktop management. The real power of DMTF is the possibility of a standard, open framework for managing diverse systems through the attached networks, however.

Basic DMI Architecture

The DMI **(Desktop Management Interface)** architecture is simple in order to meet the goal of easy implementation and vendor adoption. The DMI contains three major elements: the Management Interface (MI), the Service Layer (SL), and the Component Interface (CI). The two interfaces insulate manageable components and management applications from the specific details of the operating system or hardware environment in which they run.

The **Service Layer** is the real-time manager of DMI functions. The Service Layer uses operating systems-specific services as necessary to support desktop or server management. A fourth component, the **MIF database**, is an implementation-specific collection of component descriptions. The MIF database represents all the components that are manageable at any given time.

Components are manageable elements within a system, including processors, add-on boards, memory, storage, and applications. The **Component Instrumentation** is the software that carries out component management functions. The Component Instrumentation provides information about a component, changes the component's behavior as directed, or signals an asynchronous event when unexpected conditions occur. The CI provides access to component instrumentation for management applications.

The MIF—Describing Managed Components

The **Management Information Format** (MIF) describes managed components in the computer system. The MIF descriptions are text-based for simple parsing. Each component is defined with a unique name and identifier. The DMTF has developed a standard component identifier group, which includes the manufacturer, the version number, the serial number, a product identifier, the time and date of the last installation, and a verification level, which is used to check proper component operation. This identifier group is used in all definitions. Each component definition also contains a path identifier to locate the files where the actual Component Instrumentation code can be accessed by the Service Layer.

Components can be composed of groups, which are collections of attributes. **Groups** are an easy way of organizing attributes by categories such as configuration, performance, faults, and other functional areas. Each **attribute** is represented by one data type, such as integer, counter, gauge, dates, strings, and octets. Attributes may also exist independently of a group.

Tables of attributes can also be created when there are multiple instances of a component in a system—for example, when there are multiple communications interfaces on a server.

The MIF definitions provide unique identifiers for each component, each attribute group within a component, and for individual attributes. In this way, a simple hierarchical naming structure identifies any particular piece of information that the management application wishes to access or change. Attributes are addressed by a triple of integers representing the {component identifier, group identifier, and attribute identifier}. Tables are accessed by supplying a key or index instead of an attribute identifier.

MIF database

The MIF database contains all the component descriptions that have been registered with the Service Layer. Registration makes a component visible through the Management Interface to all management applications. Components can also be unregistered, which removes them from the MIF database and therefore from any further DMI management activities. The MIF database is a logical management information store that is implemented in a system-dependent way. The only requirement is that it preserve information across system failures or reboots.

The Management Interface

The MI provides a way for management applications to register for events, discover the types of components in the system, and access Component Instrumentation in order to carry out systems management tasks. A management application uses the Management Interface to transfer a structured block which contains commands, parameters, and return codes. The interface is not based on procedural functions, but simply passes data asynchronously. Each management application is allowed to make multiple management requests.

The Service Layer

The Service Layer provides run time management: controlling the flow of data blocks and events between Component Instrumentation and management applications. It handles buffering, error checking, integrity, and synchronization of all activities.

Data Blocks

All interactions for normal management operations are carried out through the exchange of structured data blocks. These blocks contain parameters and pointers to other memory areas, which are used to describe structures and to receive information from the Component Instrumentation. A standard set of commands has been defined by the DMTF and the command set will grow richer as new functions are incorporated into the DMTF definitions.

Management Protocols—Staying Neutral

The DMTF has chosen to remain protocol-neutral, endorsing neither SNMP or CMIP. Network management protocols can be used to manage DMI-compliant systems across a network, with a proxy agent or translator at the Management Interface. The proxy agent translates network management protocol traffic into the appropriate DMI commands and attribute identifiers. In a similar way, it translates information from the Component Instrumentation into the appropriate SNMP MIB variables before transferring them to a remote management application.

Actually, the use of Remote Procedure Call (RPC) protocols is likely to be common for DMI applications. Distributed computing applications generally use a type of Remote Procedure Call mechanism, and the introduction of the Distributed Computing Environment will employ RPCs. It will be more economical to use the same protocol mechanisms for management rather then adding SNMP protocol stacks.

An Example

Installing components on desktop systems often requires complex procedures that involve setting switches on add-on boards and entering esoteric information into a mysterious installation program. The usual process is prone to errors as well as introducing new problems by creating conflicts with other components that use interrupts, DMA channels, and other shared resources.

DMI-compliant components will come equipped with an MIF description, management applications, and an installation program. For example, suppose an administrator is installing a DMI-compliant device in a desktop.

The administrator runs the installation program after physically installing the appropriate add-on boards. The installation program registers with the Management Interface and uses information from the MIF database to determine if other needed resources are available in the system. Versions are checked to ensure that all elements will work together.

The MIF database makes installation programs much more intelligent; for example, the installer can find an unassigned interrupt or DMA channel and assign it to eliminate conflicts with other components. The installation program uses this information to update the appropriate system configuration files and component software.

The component MIF is registered through the Service Layer and added to the set of manageable components in the MIF database. Users will be freed from the tedious details of installation and all the problems associated with resolving interrupt assignments, memory allocations, and so forth.

Another scenario addresses simplifying manageability. A component diagnostic program can be run as needed by the user or on a periodic basis. This program can run tests and make decisions about the ongoing viability of any component. Regular diagnosis spots trends, indicating potential problems before anything catastrophic actually occurs. The management application notifies the user or a remote administrator that the component is showing signs of imminent failure. Other information, such as warranty information and vendor contacts is also supplied from the MIF database in order to facilitate the problem resolution or component replacement process.

Current Status

MIF definitions for printers, network adapters, and PC systems are completed. New groups are building MIF definitions for servers, mass storage, modems, and applications. Bringing applications under a common framework will improve the administrator's situation. Managing and monitoring applications provides the means for delivering guaranteed service levels. Managed applications will also make network management simpler since abusive applications can be turned off.

Specifications, by themselves, do not offer tangible benefits. Early commitments from vendors are shaping up. Operating systems vendors that have agreed to a DMI interface in the future include IBM (OS/2), Microsoft (Chicago and Hermes), Novell (NetWare and UNIXWare), Sun (Solaris), and Intel (DOS and Windows 3.X).

Intel and Microsoft have engineered the LANDesk Manager and Hermes management applications for the DMI. SNMP agents are being provided by FTP, NetManage, and SNMP Research. These agents will provide the DMI/MIB mapping, allowing remote management from an SNMP console.

Hewlett-Packard has equipped its next line of workstations with DMI-compliant management interfaces. Intel, SMC, and 3COM are delivering DMI-compliant network adapters, while Dell, AST, Apple, and Compaq are expected to bring DMI-based computers.

Future Prospects

There is already substantial interest in DMI; a recent study we conducted indicated that over one-third of the system administrators are already planning to investigate and invest in DMI. This is a very strong indication of interest, considering that products are not yet available. The long-term prospects for DMI look bright. Major vendors, such as Novell and Microsoft, have committed to implementing DMI in future product releases. Many third-party management application vendors are attracted to a consistent interface across a wide number of systems supplied by Intel, IBM, Digital, Hewlett-Packard, Dell, AST, Compaq, and Sun.

There are several factors that can influence the viability of DMI in the marketplace. Administrators do not yet know the resource demands that DMI will impose on their systems. DMI will be less attractive if it requires large amounts of resident memory, local storage, and processing.

Probably the strongest factor that will influence DMI's eventual acceptance is the quality of the management applications and the manageable components that will be provided. Many vendors will have to cooperate in order to provide a wide array of DMI-compliant products; a partial solution will not be acceptable. Component vendors must commit resources to designing Component Instrumentation and better management applications that fully exploit the possibilities of DMI.

Another factor that should be considered is the quality of integration for desktop management solutions. The set of tools and functions for systems management is extensive. It would be disappointing to find an array of DMI-compliant point tools that do not share information with each other. Administrators need a packaged solution rather than a set of unconnected desktop management tools.

Third-party management application vendors also have a challenge: to take their top-quality solutions and extend them across a wide spectrum of hardware and software environments. DMTF has attracted many vendors because good management is one of the key differentiators in an increasingly competitive marketplace. The next year will give potential buyers a good indication of whether the DMTF consortium can deliver on their promise.

16.5   SYSTEMS MANAGEMENT FRAMEWORKS

Systems management vendors are offering their own management frameworks—infrastructures that support a set of systems management tools. This idea has already been discussed in Chapter 11 on management platforms; these frameworks are emerging as platforms using SNMP management platform services. The same idea is being proposed: individual systems management tools are integrated into the frameworks so that their individual capabilities can be leveraged. The frameworks are a layer of middleware that insulate tools from the platforms. Frameworks are also, not surprisingly, a way for vendors to ensure their influence on customers by raising the barriers for competitors. Vendors will attempt to collect systems management tools within their frameworks rather than have customers buy tools for direct attachment to the platforms.

This may not be a bad idea since the platform vendors haven't completed the necessary work to develop their products and quite a few harried administrators prefer a nicely integrated toolset rather than taking the time, money, and energy to select individual tools and integrate them themselves. Further, the best-of-breed tools change rapidly; there is a steady deployment of enhancements. Instead, there may be a higher value in a suite of tools that are integrated in ways that are more useful than a collection of point solutions that may compare favorably on a feature-by-feature basis. Systems management vendors seized the opportunity to offer a packaged solution for administrators.

Some frameworks vendors such as Computer Associates, Inc. and Legent, Inc. began with a suite of products for managing data centers of mainframe and minicomputers. They are migrating their products into a distributed client/server environment. Others such as Tivoli have built a distributed management framework themselves. OpenVision has built a business through acquisitions while Hewlett-Packard, Digital, and IBM are expanding beyond their traditional customer bases.

Systems management processes involve a set of tools and staff members; they are more powerful when they are automated as much as possible. The frameworks offer opportunities to integrate individual tools. Systems management tools can communicate with each other through the framework's messaging and event services. However, the framework providers do not offer an integrated database for their tools at this point. This missing element means that individual tools still manage their own data and sharing requires special arrangements between tools.

A framework can also be used for controlling and managing the systems management applications themselves, wherever they may be located within the environment. Systems administrators must be able to activate applications at any management site. Some examples of systems management frameworks will illustrate the variety of choices.

XPE by Legent

Legent Corporation has introduced XPE, its Cross Platform Environment, as a systems management framework for distributed computing. Legent first offered IBM mainframe management tools for data centers. It has taken its tools, knowledge, and processes and is moving them into the client/server world.

The XPE framework ties systems management applications together, even though they are geographically separated. The framework services are actually provided by a product known as XPertware. XPertware provide three basic functions: API services, APIs, and the management services themselves.

API Services   The API services allow different XPE applications to communicate with each other. These capabilities include messaging, which supports the exchange of information across different systems. Management tools can exchange information and coordinate their activities through XPertware. XPertware also performs **protocol conversions** when applications are on different networks. The key communication protocols supported include TCP/IP, SNA, IPX, and OSI.

The **directory services** provide a way of mapping between different operating system conventions for naming and addressing. For example, Windows NT file-naming conventions are quite different from those used by MVS. The directory services provide all the information required to understand each XPE application, the platform upon which it runs, the protocols being used, and other resources associated with it. The directory services provide another hidden translation mechanism that allows an XPE application on a OS/2 platform to communicate with a UNIX-based XPE application, for instance.

The third part of the API services are **data translation** services that provide the appropriate mappings and translations between data formatted for specific environments. In this way, XPE applications in different environments can understand the messages and can actually share and use information generated in different environments.

Open APIs   Legent also provides a set of software development kits that allow developers or customers to interface other applications to the XPE framework. By using the software development kits, new applications can be interfaced into the API services and take advantage of messaging, directory services, and data translation. The open APIs allow the extensibility of the XPE framework to incorporate legacy applications, as well as enable customers to move forward and deal with future requirements.

Management Services   Systems administrators use the Management Station as a software component for managing the framework itself. The Management Station in effect is a central point of control where the XPE framework can be viewed, monitored, configured, and maintained. Using the management station, an administrator can manage communication links between XPE applications on different platforms using different protocols. This perspective creates a system-oriented view of the systems management environment itself: various components can be configured and tuned in order to provide optimum management coverage.

Management Applications   Management applications in the XPE framework allow system administrators to place their tools anywhere in the network to provide the coverage, economy, and scalability required of new solutions. The XPE framework allows all of these applications to behave as if they were located in a central site, although their distribution can be altered to meet changing requirements.

Some of the individual solutions supplied by Legent include tools for managing problems, software distribution, resources, backup and recovery, automated operations, and distributed database management.

Legent provides its Paradigm trouble-ticketing application as the basic problem management tool. Software distribution is also a key concern. With the XPE framework, Legent supplies a set of applications for transferring files, or software, between sets of different computers. The XPE framework allows software to be stored on nonnative platforms and then distributed to any type of target system.

Resource management allows a system administrator to monitor activities in varying types of system environments, such as UNIX or OS/2. By collecting resource utilization from many different types of systems and integrating the views, administrators have an overall perspective on the behavior, service levels, and problems occurring in any part of their environment.

Recovery and backup management are, of course, essential requirements. The XPE framework allows system administrators to activate backup activities in varying parts of their environment under automatic control. Administrators also have capabilities and flexibility in controlling backup activities, such as controlling the amount of information flowing across wide area links versus on-site backup and archiving.

Operations management, or console management, is another important feature and function of a widespread environment. Console management collects messages from many different types of systems and presents them in a single unified view. Automated processing of these messages selects those that have higher priority or require more immediate attention.

Distributed database tools allow managers to replicate databases from one site to another. Translation from mainframe database formats to common client/server databases is also provided.

Tivoli Systems

Tivoli Systems has been a leader in building systems management frameworks. The major element is the Tivoli Management Platform (TMP) which operates in a distributed fashion, allowing administrators to create different TMRs (Tivoli Management Regions). Each management region has a server that supports a set of systems management applications. Tivoli supports a wide range of server environments including all the common UNIX environments. Any server can support a heterogeneous set of clients.

Tivoli was a leader in developing an object-oriented approach to systems management. Tivoli employs CORBA (Common Object Request Broker Architecture) to provide a mechanism for location-independent access. Each agent in a managed system, as well as the servers, supports the mechanisms for issuing object requests and finding and retrieving information from any location. In addition, Tivoli provides a name registry so that different managed resources can be registered and made known to the entire management environment.

The distributed framework allows TMRs to be constructed in a variety of relationships. Hierarchical relationships are possible as well as flat, mesh-based relationships between servers in the different management regions. Servers in each region can communicate with each other in order to pass information about the resources they are managing. In this way an application on any server can find resources in any other management region if necessary.

Tivoli has supplied a set of management services as part of its basic infrastructure. It also focused on managing the management system itself. These services allow systems management applications developers to focus on their applications rather than on creating fundamental services to support them.

Using data that is distributed across multiple management regions introduces the risk of synchronization problems. A **two-phase commit** service provides coordination of operations across a set of servers. Important management information is changed in a way that prevents unsynchronized information in different parts of the managed environment. For example, without a two-phase commit some servers might update management information while another server would be unable to do so. This would result in different servers in the managed environment having different information and understanding about the state of the resources for which they are responsible.

Two-phase commit begins with a **prepare** phase that asks all servers to determine if the update can actually proceed to a successful conclusion. Once all the servers have agreed that they can make the update, the second phase, a **commit** message, which actually instructs them to carry out the transaction, is sent. If any server reports a problem with the prepare phase, an abort is sent instead of a commit, which causes all servers to disregard the intended operation. In this way the abort erases all state or memory of the proposed transaction and all servers remain in a synchronized state.

Tivoli also provides **locking** and **concurrency** services so that systems management applications can concurrently access databases. Common databases are fundamental for building integrated systems management applications; however, concurrent access also leaves the possibility of modifying key information in inconsistent ways. Locking services allow one application uninterrupted access to a particular set of data so that no other application can modify it at the same time. The locking services, therefore, provide a coordinated way of modifying information that is shared between a set of management applications and tools.

Management applications can also be written to operate in a secured environment by use of the **Kerberos security services**. The Kerberos server acts as a mediating agent between the client and the servers they wish to access.

The Tivoli framework also supports management applications **scheduling** so that administrators can control the activation of management applications. Regular management tasks are executed without further administrator intervention, freeing the administrator for other tasks. The scheduling algorithms are robust, allowing scheduling across different regions. For example, a management application in one TMR can be scheduled by an administrator at a server in a different region. This type of function and feature is very helpful especially in large environments where there are many tasks that need to be carried out on an ongoing, regular basis.

The object-oriented approach that Tivoli uses provides administrators with several other capabilities. The first of these is the capability of defining a **collection** of resources. A collection is a logical grouping of managed resources such as all members of the marketing team, all desktops within a particular building, or other types of groupings that are useful to the administrator. Once objects have been grouped into a collection, the administrator can apply operations to the collection as a whole rather than to individual members repetitively. These collections will also be quite helpful when they are integrated with the virtual LAN management tools discussed in the new switched environments. (See Chapter 15.) In addition to the logical grouping, there are several other basic services that take advantage of the object-oriented framework.

Policy services are provided so that administrators can apply policies to collections of objects. Policy services are enforced within a defined policy region. The regions define the boundaries and the constraints of a particular policy being applied. As an example, a policy may be applied to a collection of all users in the marketing department. This policy may restrict access to certain types of activities or data based on time of day or other types of criteria.

A sophisticated **change and configuration management** service also takes advantage of the object-oriented framework. Administrators can define configuration profiles that contain requirements for setting of certain systems configuration parameters, access control lists, operating system privileges, and other types of configuration information. These profiles are modeled as objects and therefore allow inheritance. This means a corporate profile can be determined and each sub department can start with that as a basic profile. Administrators can further leverage the object framework by implementing or specifying subsets of policies to be applied in certain areas. Further, certain parts of the policy may be overridden at lower levels so that system administrators have more freedom and flexibility to tailor policies to their unique needs.

The control of what can be modified, extended, or overridden rests with the "parent" or the corporate-level configuration profile. Various resources, either individual resources or collections, can subscribe to particular policies. The act of subscription defines default configurations which are applied to every member of the collection. These types of operations also simplify the system administrator's task since a change to the policy profile is automatically applied to all resources that are subscribers. In this way a system administrator can quickly and consistently change the way policies are applied to large sets of resources.

Microsoft System Management Server (Hermes)

Microsoft has stepped forward with an aggressive system management architecture with its Systems Management Server. Originally code-named Hermes, the Systems Management Server has ambitious design goals which include:

Collecting detailed software and hardware inventory. This includes the ability to group resources into domains, thereby simplifying the administrator's management and view of all the systems environments.

Scheduling management activities in servers and clients. This is the same type of function seen in the Tivoli framework and provides administrators the ability to ensure that many repetitive management tasks are executed when appropriate.

Access control from desktops to servers. Desktops can be constrained to use a server or set of servers and certain applications that they contain. Further, administrators can group servers so that load-balancing is possible.

Remote control and operation of desktops and servers from a central administrative site.

Embedded intelligent agents in managed clients and servers so that event-driven management is possible.

A key part of the Microsoft strategy is that systems management is built into all NT products. Microsoft has provided extensive instrumentation for all clients and servers providing access to system configuration files, system event logs, performance parameters, and other types of management information. Further, Microsoft has worked to make SMS an open client/server management solution by supporting the DMI (Desktop Management Interface defined by Desktop Management Task Force). In addition, Microsoft is publishing the schema for their SQL server database.

The Site Server provides all the SMS management applications as well as connection with a SQL Server which contains all the SMS management information. The SQL Server provides information on the client/server environment including performance statistics, configuration information, and asset and inventory data. The SQL Server also acts as a management repository that is available to third-party systems management applications. Microsoft uses the MIF (Management Information Format) to describe all of its managed components. Further, it can incorporate MIFs provided by other vendors into its SQL Server, thereby extending the scope and range of management information that SMS encompasses. SMS will be the first significant application that will accelerate the adoption of DMI-compliant products by many users.

Microsoft carries out most of its client management activities when clients log into their designated servers. At this point, inventory information is collected from the intelligent agent in each client and compared to previous configurations. Management applications can compare the collected configuration information to established baselines or previous versions to detect unauthorized changes. If this is the case, a new configuration can be established before the log-in procedure is completed and the client proceeds with its activities. Software distribution also takes place at this time.

The Microsoft software distribution function provides the administrator with a choice of "push" or "pull" delivery options. If the pull option is selected, the client is notified at log-in that software is available. The client then makes a choice whether to download the software or continue with other activities. The administrator, however, can also select a time interval after which the software is pushed to the client whether convenient or not. A further option allows for the installation of a TSR in the client which will periodically poll for new software and download it when it is available.

The systems management server is a significant development for Microsoft since it leverages the built-in management instrumentation and agents provided in Microsoft systems as well as extends to other environments such as LAN Manager and NetWare. The open solution is further extended through the support of DMI.

SMS also has SNMP capabilities so that it can link with common management platforms such as OpenView, NetView, or other platforms. SMS can forward SNMP TRAPs to these platforms where they can be used to activate other management applications and integrate SMS with network management solutions. Further, management applications can use TCP/IP connections to directly access the SQL Server when they need to access the collected management information.

Legent AgentWorks

The Legent Corporation has introduced AgentWorks, a framework for managing large numbers of intelligent agents throughout a managed environment. AgentWorks extends Legent's management scope from systems management into network and applications management. AgentWorks is comprised of several components including Agent Factory, DB Manager, Enterprise View, Domain Manager, and System Manager.

The **Domain Manager** acts as an intermediate agent collecting information from other agents. The Domain Manager carries out local polling as well as correlation of information from other agents embedded in computer systems, network devices, servers, or applications. The Domain Manager can test information for specified thresholds as well as correlate information from a set of agents. It forwards any management event reports to the appropriate management center. The domain manager is a state-based event manager that offers power and flexibility. Rules for transitions include actions that allow the Domain Manager to adapt its activities as the managed environment changes.

The **DB Manager** is used for instrumenting databases. It monitors database performance, tracks table fragmentation and table usage, transaction rates, disk and input/output activity, as well as trace and log files. Administrators can set thresholds and other criteria for triggering management events that are reported to a remote management site.

The **Agent Factory** is a tool kit that allows administrators to build new agents or increase the intelligence of agents they have already created. The tool kit provides the basic communications mechanisms for SNMP and CMIP as well as a kernel agent. These agents can be constructed for a variety of target systems.

The **System Manager** is used for monitoring UNIX and other types of servers. Intelligent agents in the servers provide information on system resources such as CPU, memory utilization, swapping activity, and file systems capacity. Additional information on processes, logged events, security violations, as well as the standard SNMP space MIB-II are also available. Intelligent agents can also apply predefined thresholds to determine when events should be forwarded to a management site.

Enterprise View is the central repository for the AgentWorks framework. One important function that Enterprise View carries out is the automatic discovery and configuration of intelligent agents created by the Agent Factory or from other vendors. Very large environments require these types of mechanisms in order to ensure that all the resources have agents and are actually under management control. Enterprise View also collects information from all the managed agents and stores it in a common data repository. Management events from the intelligent agents, the Domain Manager, the DB Manager, or the System Manager are forwarded to the Enterprise View where they are filtered and correlated.

The SNMP capability of Enterprise View allows it to forward events to other management platforms. In a similar way, Enterprise View can receive management events from other platforms and respond appropriately.

AgentWorks will be integrated with Legent's XPE. A connection through XPertware will be used to link XPE applications with the AgentWorks framework. In this way, any XPE application will be able to access information stored in Enterprise View. In this way, Legent's applications for software distribution, problem management, storage and backup, and so forth will be able to use information collected by the intelligent agents.

Digital's Polycenter

Polycenter is a system management framework that depends on the Polycenter Manager on NetView, the core technology of IBM NetView for AIX. In this sense, Polycenter Manager on NetView is the third generation of the HP OpenView technology. Digital leveraged its experience in managing its own corporate network supporting over 80,000 employees in eight hundred worldwide locations. The lack of a common framework that allows all of the Polycenter applications to work easily with each other may turn out to be a problem for Digital when comparing its offering with those from Legent or Tivoli, for example.

Digital has spent considerable time in the security management area providing the Polycenter Security Manager, Security Intrusion Detector, and the Security Report Manager as well as DECathena.

The Digital Polycenter Security Manager searches managed systems and compares settings of different variables against an established security policy or security profile. The areas that the Security Manager investigates are accounts, passwords, networks, systems, and auditing.

When the Security Manager is investigating accounts, it is looking for account privileges as well as indicators of potential problems such as lengthy inactivity. Quite often accounts are left active when employees leave the business, go on extended trips, or take sabbatical leave. These active but unused accounts offer opportunities for attackers since they are still valid although not closely watched.

The Security Manager also investigates password files, checking to make sure that easily guessed words are not used and that passwords are changed on a frequent basis and do not provide length violations. Many organizations have further rules including the alternation of vowels and consonants, minimum length, and requirements to change passwords on a regular basis. Network activities are examined for NFS, TCP/IP services, network access parameters, and dial-in or dial-out parameters and privileges.

The system itself is checked for configuration parameters whose settings might offer a weakened security environment. Finally, auditing is investigated. Event files are checked to determine the number of failed log-ins, failed access attempts at files, and other information that may indicate that a system is being probed or is under attack.

The Polycenter Security Report Manager can query all of the individual agents and collect and consolidate security information into a set of reports for an administrator. These reports can detail particular activities, variations from security profiles and policies, or other potential problems that require attention.

The Security Intrusion Detector is used to actively fight attacks to distributed clients or servers. Alarm thresholds which trigger automatic notification of a potential intrusion or attack, can be set by the administrator. Further, when attacks are detected, automatic countermeasures can be initiated within the system. Some possible responses could include stopping the process that is the cause of the attacks, disabling the user account that was used to access the system, or in the worst case, isolating the system from the network until further measures can be undertaken.

The Polycenter FullSail product is a systems management framework similar in concept to the Hewlett-Packard OperationsCenter. It provides a task-oriented approach to managing groups of distributed systems. The Navigator is the central control point whereby the environment is monitored and managed. Sets of systems can be collected into a logical group, which would provide easier means of managing large numbers of systems. Administrators can control the membership of groups by simple moving and exchanging systems between different collections. The Navigator also provides access control for the management staff, restricting their access to particular management tools as defined by the administrator. Finally, the Navigator provides the ability to automatically launch other FullSail applications and indirectly access the full suite of Polycenter systems management tools.

The account manager is a simple application that provides the administrators easy ways to do user account management on remote servers. Administrators can create new accounts, modify account parameters, and delete old accounts. Account management can also be applied by default through group memberships. For example, adding a user to a group can also provide a set of default parameters used for account setup. The file system application provides a means for managing NFS file servers. Administrators can cause autoconfiguration and automatic startup of file servers on remote systems. The performance monitor, finally, provides a set of monitoring capabilities for the systems' storage resources and NFS activities. Administrators can use thresholds in the usual way to trigger event reports and potential problems.

The Polycenter Scheduler provides a production scheduling tool that works in the mixed environments, including different varieties of UNIX, NT, OS/2, and NetWare. Further, the Scheduler works across a heterogeneous set of networks including LANs as well as wide area links. The Scheduler supports multiple custom calendars so that scheduling can be optimized to fit any particular enterprise's work process. Automatic error recovery and notification are used to provide job integrity. Administrators have the ability to restrict jobs to nodes and to send jobs to particular areas where load balancing can be achieved through the use of VAX clusters. Dependencies are defined so that jobs can be scheduled across multiple nodes anywhere in the enterprise and execute in a proper sequence.

16.6 SUMMARY

The overview of these frameworks shows the value and the power they offer for systems management, particularly in the absence of the appropriate types of infrastructure services embedded in management platforms. The frameworks themselves are being incorporated into management platforms to provide tighter integration with network management functions and other types of activities. The ability to share information between the different types of management areas, such as network and systems management, will continue to be a key requirement in the future.

The drawback with frameworks, of course, is that they are still proprietary. Applications can be added to a framework through the appropriate development to a proprietary API, sometimes an effort that may be too expensive or complex for independent vendors or customers. Just as we have had a tremendous amount of activity between ISVs and platform vendors, we will have the same type of churning as different framework providers try to capture the leading edge of systems management applications for their frameworks. Frameworks may also negate the advantages of higher-quality point tools since they will not be as easily integrated into the overall infrastructure.

16.7 GENERAL WIDGETS

The systems management teams were focused on the computer systems, the applications, and the information they used. There are several environments with the most common being divided between Windows, NetWare, and varieties of UNIX. Some business units of General Widgets used centralized management approaches while others left the management decisions to each group. There was also significant overlap within the entire organization; some groups used some of the same management tools, and in other cases they used different tools to manage the same types of systems. The initial goal was to consolidate management of each environment and then to build an enterprise-wide systems management capability. One campus was chosen as the initial trial of new approaches. The experience would be transferred to other sites as the lessons were learned.

The first stage was aimed at physically consolidating the various management consoles and gaining an accurate overview of all the available tools and resources. Some management tools were stand-alone products and others were used on different management platforms. The physical consolidation allowed the administrators to identify the most useful tools and assess the capabilities of the staff members.

There were clear differences in skill levels and breadth; some staff were adequate with a given system, but lost with new systems or tasks; others had deep expertise in broad areas. The outcome of the first phase was to upgrade training where it was needed and to have a clear picture of the available tools. Administrators evaluated cases where there were multiple tools for the same task or system and chose one to proceed with. This tool pruning ensured higher levels of consistency and allowed staff to cover each other more effectively after they were trained. Needless to say, these changes caused some discontent with the management staff.

CHAPTER 17

Systems Management Tools

Client/server management requires a large set of management tools supporting real-time, as well as longer-term operations. The current environment makes it difficult to apply a single management tool across a set of diverse systems, such as NetWare, UNIX, or NT. However, the complement of tools for an adequate management solution is emerging, as well as recognition of the most important characteristics. Systems management tools can be grouped by function.

17.1 REMOTE CONTROL

Remote operation, or control, is the necessary first step for centralizing the administration of a distributed system environment. A remote administrator must be able to control and operate any networked system in order to manage it. Remote control minimizes the need for local management staff and eliminates user involvement in management processes.

Remote operations today involve the capture of a remote computer's keyboard, screen, and pointing devices, such as a mouse. Administrators can see what a remote user is actually doing, or can enter commands and scan files as if they were sitting at the keyboard and screen themselves.

One important use for remote control is faster troubleshooting when users report problems. The staff person at the Help Desk can take remote control of the user's computer system after a call to the Help Desk. Help Desk staff can watch a user demonstrate the problem and correct simple errors in procedure or parameters quite quickly. Many problems are caused by a simple lack of information and knowledge on the user's part.

Looking over the user's shoulder, so to speak, saves management staff time and resolves simple problems quickly.

Another option, at that point, is that the administrator carries out the process or demonstrates the appropriate and proper way to access networking services and resources while the user simply gets to watch and learn.

Some remote control products provide a "chat" window whereby the user and the remote administrator can carry on a conversation without activating any operations. While this appears useful in theory, in practice it tends to be quite cumbersome if the dialogue is complex or lasts over a long period of time. Frequently, it is much simpler to use a telephone and have a regular conversation while both parties are working on the screens.

Administrators also use remote operations to support other management activities. For example, a remote administrator can check configuration files, execute commands, and transfer files to resolve a problem without visiting the user's office. Remote operation also allows administrators to change a desktop configuration without involving the local user.

Remote control is also needed so that remote management operations can be carried out when the computer systems are not normally used. Other applications in the desktop can be activated to transfer and install software or to collect inventory data. These tools can be used for software distribution and inventory functions during evenings and weekends. Minimal interference with ongoing activities is a goal: most users should be insulated from management operations.

Remote control depends upon resident agent software that provides the linkage to a remote management site. The agent must be protected from accidental or intentional modifications. Incorporating agent functions on network adapter cards is one way to build a protected agent with more robust remote control functions.

While remote operation is a key for centralized management, other factors must be considered as well. Many workgroups that value their "independence" from corporate or centralized IS operations are resisting a big brother presence where external or unknown administrators can change things in their systems. These users, unfortunately, have taken the idea of a "personal" computer literally; desktop computers are still corporate assets and they must be managed in a more consistent and uniform way. Remote managers must be constrained, however, through access control mechanisms so that they cannot violate the privacy of the users.

Remote control also allows an administrator to restart, or reboot, a remote system. This function is a basic way to control system behavior and force appropriate configuration changes from a central site.

Remote control is used in two ways: over telephone links and through networks. Telephone linkage depends upon a modem at each end. This type of support will continue to be important for supporting telecommuters at home or mobile users on the road. Products such as KopyKat from Hilgraeve and ReachOut from Ocean Isle Software are good examples of these programs. Key-View from Fox Networks takes remote control even further. Special hardware is interposed between the controlled system and the controlling system so that a remote administrator can force the system to reboot itself.

17.2 MONITORING

Monitoring remote clients and servers is a basic foundation for many other management tasks. Unlike RMON probes, systems monitors consume some amount of processing power, storage, and network bandwidth from the monitored system. Monitoring tools must provide adjustable granularity: the ability to collect operational information at varying levels of detail. Administrators need to adjust granularity in order to balance the bandwidth used to transfer information, the resources needed to collect it, and the level of detail they need for different tasks.

In some cases administrators need high-level macro information, such as the number of active processes on a server. In other situations, detailed information about each active user process may be required. Administrators usually monitor a small set of important variables on a frequent basis and then select more detail when a variable indicates that systems operations has shifted.

Agents in each managed computer system need enhanced intelligence so they offer a scalable management approach. Administrators define the appropriate thresholds so that the remote systems agents can trigger events under specified conditions. More sophisticated monitoring will also incorporate rules or filters within the remote agents so that more complex criteria can be used to define when an event or management report is forwarded to the systems management site.

An intermediate agent may be necessary if the managed systems have only simple agents. The intermediate agent aggregates the information from the simple systems agents and applies filters and rules to the incoming management event stream. Only a small number of event reports are forwarded to the remote management site. Intermediate agents will also serve as the foundation for more sophisticated processing tasks.

For example, IBM offers the Systems Monitor for AIX as an intermediate agent. The Systems Monitor carries out local polling of other systems and processes the responses. The Systems Monitor for AIX can monitor resource usage such as available memory or disk queue lengths to keep tabs of important systems. It forwards selected reports to an SNMP management platform such as NetView for AIX. The latest version also incorporates a local discovery application.

17.3 CONSOLE MANAGEMENT

Another form of systems monitoring captures existing system messages and does not depend on a local, resident agent for monitoring. Sophisticated servers and workstations usually have system consoles—local screens that display messages, error reports, and other information about system behavior. The console information stream can be routed to a remote management site where a console management tool can be used to oversee a set of systems.

Some console management products operate with multiple RS-232 interfaces (one for each monitored system) while others transport the console streams across the networks. The RS-232 interfaces are simple to implement, but large numbers of systems consume large numbers of modems and telephone circuits. This may not be a problem if the systems are located within a small area where direct connections eliminate the need for modems. Systems that are spread across a wide geographic area are monitored more effectively through the networks they are attached to.

Console management collects the system console streams and parses them by simple text matching. Events can be logged for auditing purposes or for later analysis. Critical messages are extracted and used to trigger other actions to respond to a problem.

17.4   EVENT MANAGEMENT

Incoming systems management events must be filtered, correlated, and passed to the appropriate systems management tools. Centralized collection and final analysis will be done at the remote systems management centers. Event management is an important linkage between the real-time behavior of clients and servers and the appropriate tools to deal with reported problems.

The network management platform's event management system may be adequate for managing incoming systems events and alarms. However, it is not crucial for systems management. Frameworks such as Bridgeway's EventIX and Legent AgentWorks allow a distributed set of intelligent intermediate agents to collect information and extract significant events.

The platform is useful for processing network management events and making them available for correlation with systems events. This level of event management allows administrators to see the interactions between network and systems events.

17.5   SOFTWARE DISTRIBUTION

Software Distribution is one of the most labor-intensive and tedious tasks that system administrators confront. Manually distributing and installing complex applications on hundreds of clients can consume tremendous amounts of staff time and money. Manually repeating complicated processes also introduces the possibility that some installations will be performed incorrectly—causing further problems, staff expenses, wasted time, and lost productivity.

Distributing software in this way consumes tremendous amounts of staff time and is very costly. One client found it took two hours per system to install and upgrade three applications. For 150 systems the cost was $22,500 at $75 per hour for staff time alone. If uniformity is needed, then a rollback is required if the installation fails with any system, adding to the expense and disruption. Many groups fail to take advantage of software enhancements because of the expense involved in distributing and installing them.

Our experience with network administrators shows that version control consumes administrator's time. For example, users usually report a problem to the Help Desk with low-quality information, such as "it's broken," or "the network is too slow." Administrators often find that the connectivity problem is a result of version incompatibilities rather than any fundamental problem with the physical network between client and server. Eliminating these types of problems saves management staff time and increases the productivity of the desktop users.

The problem is further exacerbated by the increasing complexity of desktop applications that demand more configuration options and choices. Certainly the software developers can improve the situation by using more intelligent installation programs that minimize the number of decisions required for a successful installation. More intelligent installation procedures will certainly reduce the problem; however, it will not eliminate some of the burdens.

Interconnecting all users through the enterprise network intensifies the problems with version control. A local administrator may be able to keep the versions consistent for a small workgroup; but cannot dictate what versions other workgroups are using. As sharing increases, the problems with incompatible versions grows apace.

Distributing software through the network allows administrators to ensure a much higher degree of consistency between different groups throughout the organization. Maintaining version consistency and delivering software in a timely manner ensures that desktop users can take advantage of new enhancements and upgrades to their software. Some of the most important characteristics of software distribution systems can be described beginning with staging.

Staging

Staging allows an administrator to create a hierarchically controlled distribution scheme that minimizes impacts on Wide Area Network bandwidth. Software can be distributed from a central repository to regional staging servers (called "depots" by some vendors) and the software can be further distributed to local sites where it is available to clients across high-speed Local Area Networks. A staged scheme minimizes the "fan out" of multiple copies of the software until the latest or closest stage to clients on a Local Area Network.

Delivery Options

Software distribution can be done in either a **push** or a **pull** fashion. Pushing drives the software toward the targeted node and forces delivery and acceptance at the earliest possible opportunity. A pull operation, on the other hand, gives the client the option for accepting and installing new software. Other software distribution schemes are adopting a combination to allow the maximum flexibility. After a certain amount of time has elapsed, the operation makes a transition to push mode and delivers the software without the client's permission.

Many software distribution packages deliver new software to the client when it logs into its normal server. Simple routines on the server activate local client agents, which then scan the appropriate directories and report the presence of certain software applications and their versions.

Missing software or software that still remains to be delivered can then be transferred to a client before it resumes its normal network computing activities. Other software distribution schemes allow the software distribution tools to contact local agents and initiate the transfer and installation at any time selected by the administrator.

Defining the Distribution Process

Good software distribution tools allow an administrator to **group** sets of **target systems**. For example, an administrator should be able to select the engineering group and have software delivered to all members without manually entering the name or the address of each targeted node. Administrators must also have the ability to set up deferred **delivery schedules**. These allow unattended software distribution during periods of low network utilization in order to minimize interference with ongoing networking activities.

Reporting and tracking functions must also be available so that the administrator can follow the distribution process. Event notifications of failed installations should be routed to the software distribution tools. Ongoing reports allow the administrator to track progress by defining which systems have received the new software and which ones are still using the older version. Good tools should provide automatic reports for the administrator.

Packaging and Installation

Many software distribution tools use the concept of a **package**—a collection that includes the software to be delivered, installation scripts, and other types of supporting information. The package is ultimately delivered to the target system and a resident agent takes over for the last step—installation. Installation can be automated through the delivery of scripts; these pre-packaged sets of instructions guide the resident agent in creating new directories and path names, initializing the appropriate configuration parameters, and placing the delivered software in the appropriate directories. More sophisticated scripts test for a variety of parameters and conditions in order to perform a more customized installation or check for unexpected errors and problems. The outcome of the installation process is reported to the depot or staging server where the information is aggregated into reports for the system administrator.

Automated scripts can also be provided for removing old versions of software or for rolling back the installation process. Many software distribution operations will only be successful if all the intended targets actually receive and correctly install the new software. A partial delivery may result in a flurry of troubleshooting activities caused by incompatible versions between clients and servers. In any case, rollback is a function that restores the state of the software before any attempted replacement was initiated. A rollback operation will make the attempted delivery of a new version of software completely invisible, as if it never had occurred.

An unsuccessful software delivery or installation consumes staff time and network resources even if it fails. Other features of software distribution tools can be exploited to increase the probability of successful delivery. For example, many software applications have certain **dependencies**, such as needing a certain version of the operating system, a certain amount of memory or disk storage, or possibly a specific type of video board or other type of add-on module. Information about dependencies can be used by installation scripts to verify quickly that the delivered software can be successfully installed. The same type of information can also be integrated with other tools, such as the inventory database, to check on available resources before initiating any software delivery attempts.

Software distribution packages can be judged by the power, flexibility, and ease of use of their package building functions. Administrators should be able to define installation scripts that encompass a wide range of conditions and flexible behavior based upon the state of the installation process. The ability to describe dependencies and test for them will be another important differentiator. Good software distribution tools must also be as platform-independent as possible. For example, a UNIX server should be able to store and transfer software for another type of systems, such as NT or NetWare.

17.6 LICENSING

License management is an ongoing issue that is of concern to both software vendors and system administrators. The easy distribution of information across a network enables a user or an organization to buy a single copy of an application and distribute it to an unlimited number of users. This situation causes the software vendor to lose revenue and may also increase its support burden since many "owners" of the product may call for help. Some organizations are also quite nervous about this situation since they can be held liable for the unauthorized distribution of a vendor's product across their company networks. One response to this issue has been the creation of a site or corporate license that allows a customer to use either an unlimited number or some other specified number of copies concurrently. This type of licensing does not typically restrict the users of the application, only the number that can be used concurrently.

Metering

Metering is a primitive form of license management that uses simple monitoring to track application usage. Simple data collection functions in each server monitor the number of applications in systems or the number of copies of an application being used. These reports are provided to an administrator who can determine if an unauthorized number of copies exists and can then take the appropriate steps to remedy the situation. Metering gives a gross view of application usage and provides a way of maintaining compliance for short periods of time. However, the lack of enforceability limits the control that system administrators actually have.

Enforcement

An enforced licensing system interposes itself between the user and the application in such a way that the licensing policy is enforced. For example, several solutions, such as those offered by Gradient Technologies, provides a license server with a set of tokens.

The tokens are used to activate a licensed application. When the server is out of tokens, no further copies of that application can be used. Typically, clients are given the option to wait for a token to become available or to try at a later time.

An important aspect of licensing will be the ability to apply policies with fine granularity. For example, software vendors could provide temporary licenses for demonstration copies of their products. These licenses could be set to expire three days after the first use of the program, for example. Other granularity could restrict specific users to certain applications, change the quota of applications based on the time of day or other types of networking activity, constrain users to certain servers, or provide the ability to define other constraints as required.

The real barrier to more effective license management is the lack of a defined licensing standard, interface, and protocol. Many software vendors also need to engineer their products so that they can be activated through a licensing system rather than directly by the user.

17.7 CONFIGURATION MANAGEMENT

Configuration management is an ongoing challenge to most administrators. The amount of configuration information is large and incorrect configuration causes many problems for administrators. Configuration errors, such as an improper network address assignment, can cause problems that appear to be failures. Other configuration problems may degrade performance.

For example, poor configuration at the network level for high-volume applications can result in systems transferring megabytes of information in extremely small packets—an ineffective use of bandwidth. Other nodes may cause performance problems because of improper setting of configuration parameters, such as application time-outs. A setting that is not appropriate for the networked environment can cause unexpected termination of application activity with a subsequent loss of performance and productivity. Further, both client and server must be configured and tuned to work effectively with each other so configuration also has a global aspect in addition to configuring each system individually.

Configuration information includes such things as systems configuration files, the path names and directories of the appropriate system files, user accounts on servers, access control privileges for a community of users, network parameters, and so forth. Configuration management is basically a subset of the inventory management function previously discussed. An inventory database can incorporate configuration information with other inventory data.

In any case, configuration databases should be considered to ease the challenges of managing large volumes of information. Configurations have versions, just as software does. Databases can be used to link versions of configuration information so that an old version can be retrieved and restored if an error occurs.

Administrators need templates of common information that can be applied to a collection of components in a single, simple operation. Graphical configuration tools with drag-and-drop operations simplify many configuration tasks. Network Computing for example, offers this function for its LANAlert management console. Administrators can define an icon for a configuration profile and drag all systems to it when configurations are modified.

Organizations are turning toward configuration policies in order to provide a more uniform and consistent environment for management activities. An important part of configuration management is the ability to check configuration information in individual systems against the policy baselines. Unauthorized changes can be reported to a system administrator, and automatic actions can be taken to reestablish the appropriate configuration.

17.8 PERFORMANCE MANAGEMENT

Performance management will become increasingly important as administrators try to squeeze the most from expensive client and server applications. The remote monitoring capabilities discussed earlier will be used to collect performance-related information, such as CPU utilization, memory usage, the number of users, disk activity, and other parameters that provide insight into the operation and behavior of computer systems.

Monitoring tools provide the basic information which can be used for performance management at several levels. The basic information can be used by administrators who evaluate it and make decisions without further support. Unfortunately, only a few administrators can exploit raw information and make good performance improvements. Increasing complexity makes it even less likely that humans will be able to analyze information and use it directly.

Real-time Performance Management

Profiles are used as one of the early warning signs for potential problems. More sophisticated monitoring tools will be able to provide alarms that are not based on absolute activity levels, but relative difference between current activity and the normal profile.

One aspect of performance management is real-time responses to situations that cause performance levels to drop below acceptable standards. This implies frequent monitoring of critical information. Gross measures such as server loading can give a simple check that operations are satisfactory from that perspective. Refined monitoring is needed to track response times, transaction rates, or throughput delivered to applications. When performance levels suffer, further steps are necessary.

Administrators must quickly determine how much of the problem is related to network problems like congestion, poor routing, or network device failures, or how much delay is associated in a particular client or server's processing tasks. System administrators need access to network performance information, especially path tracing and monitoring data. This initial determination allows the administrator to focus more quickly on the most likely cause of the performance problem.

If there are no apparent network problems, then the focus shifts to the client and server. Quick checks of the current client configuration against the expected configuration eliminated the possibility of a modification. Comparison of server and client software versions can also eliminate a common cause of difficulties. These simple tests should be automated so they can be completed quickly and move the focus to better opportunities.

Administrators need monitoring tools that focus on system activities. They can use RMON probes to trace connections by filtering for specific packets. They must also depend on network management services for tracing the connection and measuring congestion and delay in the different parts of the path.

Tools that extract information from clients and servers are also needed to determine if internal problems are affecting performance. Error logs and application traces may be useful. Server monitoring is more critical since many users are affected. Detailed breakdowns are needed to indicate the number of active users, application mix, and disk and network activity.

Other steps can also be considered such as server disk **striping** options. Spreading files across multiple disks can increase the access speeds and transfer rates of information. Other information may lead to multiprocessor servers that deliver more computing power.

CoroNet Systems offers the CoroNet Management System, which includes a sophisticated probe, modeling tools, and information presentations. The CoroNet probe collects more information than an RMON probe. It discovers topology information and also analyzes the traffic to determine the applications that are being used. Administrators can understand how the mix of applications actually behaves. Response time and throughput measurements can be used to determine performance levels. Some administrators have already reported catching internal users abusing the network; in one case several users were congesting expensive wide area links with an interactive game in the middle of the day.

Modeling tools can be used to explore changes. The real information collected by the probe is used to determine the impacts of moves or changes. The modeling tool, Quick Model, also automatically checks for performance and configuration problems. For example, it can report servers that it considers to be placed improperly. Application deployment and distribution questions can be addressed with QuickModel. This is the level of examination that systems administrators need: applications and services need to receive the attention. Too many of our tools are bottom-up, feeding on low-level information and offering relatively less value. Understanding the impacts on applications allows administrators to make better planning decisions.

Long-term Performance Management

Baselining is needed for systems management as well. Server loads and application profiles are needed for long-term planning as well as for detecting strange real-time behaviors. The same forecasting and projection tools will work for trends with network volume, server loads, and application volumes, fortunately.

Optimization

Another important aspect of performance management is finding optimal performance ranges for workgroups, or at least for the key servers. Modeling or simulation of client/server activities can give insights into behavior under different loading assumptions. The usual facility of modeling changes before they occur is also valuable with systems management once the modeling tools are calibrated and trusted.

Optimal Networks has focused on application flows as a target for optimization. Solutions then dictate the appropriate changes to the network infrastructure. This is an effective weapon to use; it is often more likely that frustrated administrators start modifying the infrastructure, hoping that the change will have the desired effect. Monitoring tools come into play again so that the changes can be measured and evaluated.

17.9 SCHEDULING / WORKLOAD BALANCING

Many environments run regular processing-intensive applications in their client/server environments. Job-scheduling tools are a helpful way to ensure that jobs are executed on a regular basis and that the appropriate resources are available. The most critical jobs are identified and assigned the required resources, and automatic actions are taken to ensure a smooth flow of these jobs through the organization's servers.

Functions

Scheduling tools allow the administrator to assign jobs to particular servers and to define sets of rules for the conditions under which those jobs are actually executed. Many large applications may actually run on multiple servers within the organization. Quite often, these large computing jobs are carried out in several phases which have dependencies among them. For example, one phase of the application that requires data from a previous step should not be automatically executed if the previous step failed. At other times, the applications may depend upon data availability. Retail organizations update their inventories and target popular products on a frequent basis. However, the application depends on new point of sale data being collected and ready for processing at a certain time; if the data is not ready then execution should be deferred and the administrator should be notified.

Rules for dependencies should be extended across multiple servers to provide the greatest flexibility. Dependencies within a single server are not sufficient for large, complex systems environments. The specification of rules and dependencies requires an easy-to-use interface.

The Polycenter Scheduler provides a production scheduling tool that works in the mixed environments, including different varieties of UNIX, NT, OS/2, and NetWare. Further, the Scheduler works across a heterogeneous set of networks including LANs as well as wide area links. The Scheduler supports multiple custom calendars so that scheduling can be optimized to fit any particular enterprise's work process. Automatic error recovery and notification are used to provide job integrity. Administrators have the ability to restrict jobs to nodes, to send jobs to particular areas where load balancing can be achieved through the use of VAX clusters. Dependencies are defined so that jobs can be scheduled across multiple nodes anywhere in the enterprise and executed in a proper sequence.

Other types of rules determine the automatic reassignment of high-priority jobs in case of a server failure. Application checkpointing and restart capabilities can be used to minimize the disruptions of a failure. Robustness is strengthened by copying the checkpointing information to the backup server. Checkpointing information may be very large and the bandwidth demands must be considered when building a redundant scheduling environment. The trend toward consolidating servers on high-speed LANs mitigates this concern.

Scheduling tools must also provide easily understood reports that allow the administrator to follow the behavior of these applications in real time or over some longer time interval. Certain types of failures in the scheduling system should provide immediate alerts and reports so that the administrator is notified as quickly as possible when problems affect overall production schedules.

17.10 BACKUP

Data backup is another labor-intensive and frustrating process for the ordinary user. At the same time, it is a critical element for systems management; a failure that loses important data can interrupt important business processes and cause significant monetary losses. Although users understand the importance of backing up their data, the sad reality is that they often neglect to follow through. Most users routinely ignore necessary backups because of the effort and frustration with manual procedures.

Backup Mechanisms

Backup tools provide automated mechanisms for saving client information on a backup server. Scheduling is an important part of a successful backup management system. Administrators must be able to specify when designated systems are backed up. Generally, backup schedules will be designed for off-peak network periods. High volumes of backed-up data can adversely impact normal networking activities. Further, users need some control too; they must be able to back up key files on an as-needed basis.

Scheduling may also be organized for various categories of files. For example, important files may be backed up much more frequently than files that are of relatively little importance. The backup system must also be selective so that only those files that have been modified since the last backup are saved.

Uninterrupted operation is another important feature for computing environments that require high availability. Backup operations can be initiated while the systems remain in operation and provides services. This is a preferred option compared to the penalty of taking systems out of service for periods of time while their files are backed up.

Backup is being extended beyond data files. Products from OpenVision and BMC Software, for example, can also back up database tables. This protects critical transaction processing and other database applications from failures. The tables can be recovered and the application can resume from that point. Audit logs can be used to restore incremental changes since the last table backup.

Retrieval—A Key Function

The major problem with early backup systems was the difficulty of retrieving backed-up information. Files were usually written on magnetic tape and retrieval could be a time-consuming process. System administrators were reluctant to take long periods of time to locate the appropriate backup tape and then scan through the entire tape sequentially to find the desired file. This led to backups that were never used for retrieval except under the most urgent situations when there was no alternative.

Backup systems today emphasize direct user recovery of the necessary files. Tape indexes and user directories are stored on high-speed disk so they can be searched quickly without waiting for a serial search of tape media. When the appropriate file is located, the system administrator simply has to mount the designated tape, and the file will be recovered and restored automatically from that point. More sophisticated retrieval indexes also provide explicit positioning information so the file can be directly located and recovered.

Another important aspect for user retrieval is file directory integration. Backed-up files are still shown in the users' local directory structures. Users simply access the backed-up files as they would any file on their own computer. Backup retrieval software then takes over to find the appropriate file and restore it to the client's local desktop. The only affect seen by users is slower access times while the file is being restored to a local file system.

Media Management

Media management is an important aspect and feature of backup tools. Media management includes such functions as labeling and tracking all of the backup tape volumes. Labeling is important for managing the appropriate rotation of groups of tapes. Media management checks the labels and prevents a tape being inadvertently overwritten before its expiration date because of an operator error.

Some media management features also include keeping a life cycle count of all tapes and retiring them from the backup set after they've been used a predetermined number of times. This type of function ensures that physical or mechanical tape failures will be avoided or at least minimized.

Other aspects of media management include **automatic verification** of all tapes after data has been saved to ensure that backed-up files can actually be retrieved at a later time.

Media management must also support multiple volumes. Many backed-up files for Computer Aided Design, graphics, and image processing applications are very large. The backup management tools allow transparent storage and retrieval on multiple media volumes. Administrators cannot afford the time to find a tape with the appropriate space before continuing with the backup. Backup services should be able to transparently span multiple volumes, reels of tape, optical platters, and so forth, so that the system administrator and the user are not concerned with the physical limitations of a particular medium.

Most backup systems today also support multiple media types. The system administrator can choose or combine different types of backup storage media, including different types of magnetic tape, as well as optical storage. The media management functions insulate the system administrator from most of the details of managing specific media.

Large amounts of data entail large numbers of tapes or optical platters. Media management should also incorporate the use of jukeboxes for tape or optical storage. These devices can automatically find the appropriate volume and mount it for access as needed. They can also track tape reels as they are mounted, dismounted, and remounted over time. Jukeboxes can save significant time for administrators as well as reduce operator errors.

Compression and Encryption

Encryption is an important concern for both backup and longer-term storage management tools. Private or proprietary information will be backed up on tapes that can be removed from a site or copied by unauthorized people. Encrypting information before it is backed up maintains privacy, since only the user retains the appropriate key for decoding the data. Encryption and decryption should be carried out on the user's desktop before backup and after retrieval, respectively.

Some backup systems provide a choice of encryption systems of varying complexity and computing requirements. Others, such as that provided by OpenVision, also provide a means for users to attach customized encryption applications to the backup and archiving tools.

Backed-up data can consume a great deal of storage. Much of the backed-up data usually consists of empty file space or repetitious data patterns. Compression algorithms can reduce data volumes by as much as 60% in some cases. The actual reduction depends upon the data itself. Compression also reduces backup and retrieval time since less data is actually transferred between the backup media and the file system.

Other Backup Features and Functions

An interesting extension to the automated control of backup has been offered by Hewlett-Packard in its new OmniBack II backup management product. OmniBack allows centralized control and delegation of backup activities throughout the enterprise. In this way, a single administrator delegates certain types of privileges and controls to local management areas while retaining overall control and oversight of the distributed backup process. This allows the incorporation of policies to determine when backups occur and what types of activities should be initiated as a result of problems. This type of centralized control of distributed operations is welcomed by many administrators who are trying to coordinate previously isolated environments into a cohesive operation.

More sophisticated schemes can go beyond the local backup server to back up data at a central data site where the mainframe storage capacities and I/O volumes can be used to maximum effect. Backing-up data beyond the single site also provides a level of disaster recovery in the sense that copies of the data will be saved in more than one location. The trade-off, of course, is the network bandwidth consumed by these transfers.

17.11 STORAGE MANAGEMENT

Storage management is a natural extension to the backup services. The goal of storage management is to allow system administrators to use relatively expensive disk storage as effectively as possible. One form of storage management is carried out by administrators once the disk is full. Files are manually selected and removed in order to provide more storage space. This takes time and delays user activities.

Automated storage management identifies data that is not used frequently or has not been accessed for some period of time for migration from disks to magnetic or optical long-term storage. This type of **archiving** is managed by allowing the administrator to set particular thresholds for remaining disk space. The archiving routines are activated to scan user files for migration candidates when these thresholds are exceeded. The LAN-Desk from INTEL Corp. is a good example of an automated storage management tool. When free disk space reaches a certain dangerous level, LANDesk automatically searches for the oldest files to migrate. This is an on-demand strategy as opposed to a time-expired approach.

OpenVision provides an option that also manages client storage. Client data is archived to a server when thresholds are triggered. Users still see all archived files in their file system directories; Users retrieve archived files automatically and see only a longer delay.

Another variation is Digital's AdvFS (Advanced File System). AdvFS allows an administrator to reconfigure and resize the file system while the particular client or server continues operation. The file system storage capacity can be increased when more space is needed. Other interesting features include a quick reboot feature and full auditing trails to recover from crashes. The major drawback at this point to the AdvFS solution is that it is still restricted to Digital's OFS/1 operating system.

Mirroring critical disk systems is another aspect of storage management; the expense is traded off against the impacts of data loss or delayed availability. Mirrored systems increase the availability of the information. Adding redundant power supplies and dual controllers also increases the availability.

17.12 SERVER MANAGEMENT

Server management entails the maintenance, creation, and modification of user accounts and the proper configuration of a set of resources. New users must be assigned accounts, file space, access privileges to certain applications, accounting limitations, and access rights to devices such as printers. User account maintenance is an ongoing activity because users are moved between workgroups, moved to new servers, require more resources, and use new applications. The growth in networked computing users also demands ongoing account management.

Much of this tedious and possibly error-prone work can be automated by the creation of profiles of access privileges, resource allocations, and application access. Administrators can apply these profiles to new users or change them when users move between workgroups having different profiles. Much of the access control and assignment to applications are being simplified through drag-and-drop graphical interfaces that automate much of the process. Symantec's LANLord was an early innovator in simpler server management features.

Server configuration is also a timely and error-prone process. Good server performance depends on a balanced mixture of resources, such as CPU speed, memory size, buffers, and caches for the disk system, appropriate network buffering for the user load, and so forth. Adding profiles or templates has simplified server management since an administrator can easily define and use a template from another server and then modify it based on experience to get an optimum balance of resources.

Server management tools are available from several vendors, fortunately. There are a large group of NetWare server management products as well as another group that tackles UNIX server management. The keys are ease of use, application of profiles to users or groups, and tuning tools.

17.13   VIRUS PROTECTION

Organizations have suffered greatly from the damage that viruses cause, ranging from lost productivity while the virus is eradicated through more serious consequences, such as the loss of critical information caused by a destructive virus. Virus protection tools are constantly undergoing modification to deal with the continued introduction of new types of viruses. More potent viruses are being discovered; some modify themselves as they move to new systems. Virus detection that depends on recognizing a particular virus "signature" will fail to detect the new mutations.

Static virus protection tools check system and application files for characteristic bit patterns for known viruses. These scanners can be very fast because they are looking for predicted patterns that are often in specific places in a file. However, static virus protection tools are easily defeated by a virus that mutates or changes its characteristic pattern or by the incorporation of viruses that are unknown to the scanner.

Dynamic virus scanners that look for particular types of patterns representing anomalies are being introduced. Quite often, they are more capable of picking up new strains of a virus. Other virus detection schemes are quite simple; they compare any particular file to a clean, uncontaminated copy of an application. Any discrepancies are noted and the file is replaced.

Virus scans of client and server files can be activated on a periodic basis, such as in off hours. Administrators also need the capability of activating a virus scan for any system whenever the need arises. Other virus scans are conducted when a client logs in to a server. Files are checked before the client proceeds with normal activities. Users tend to grow impatient if the scans delay them for too long, making unattended scans the preferred approach.

Virus checking tools must be integrated with the rest of the management system. A detected virus should trigger an event report to the event management service. Rules and filters can be applied and other management tools can be automatically activated. Administrators want to respond as quickly as possible to an introduced virus to contain the problem as much as possible. Some responses include disconnecting the computer system with the virus from the network until all files have been checked.

Other automated responses include searching activity logs to determine other systems that may have been exposed through network connections. Shared applications on servers may also be quarantined while further checking is carried out.

17.14 SECURITY MANAGEMENT

Increasing the security of client/server environments is a concern of most administrators. A range of security approaches that allow a combination of tools to offer a larger degree of protection is being offered.

Compliance

Compliance tools are used to check the configurations and settings of security-related parameters in any client or server. In this sense, a compliance tool has similar functions to configuration and inventory management that have been discussed previously. On a periodic basis, an agent can be activated to scan the appropriate security-related information and report to a security server. The scanned information can be compared with the acceptable security baseline and deviations can be reported to a system administrator. RAXCO supplies a set of security management tools that have been incorporated into other vendor's products.

Other aspects of compliance management can include password checkers, which check password lists to ensure that commonly used words, abbreviations, and other easily guessed passwords are not used. Administrators can use these deviations to strengthen their compliance procedures, as well as identify users who are not cooperating with the given policies.

The Digital POLYCENTER Security Manager searches managed systems and compares settings of different variables against an established security policy or security profile. The areas that the Security Manager investigates are accounts, passwords, networks, systems, and auditing.

When the Security Manager is investigating accounts, it is looking for account privileges as well as indicators of potential problems such as lengthy inactivity. Quite often accounts are left active when employees leave the business, go on extended trips, or take sabbatical leave. These active but unused accounts offer opportunities for attackers since they are still valid, although not closely watched.

The Security Manager also investigates password files, checking to make sure that easily guessed words are not used, that passwords are changed on a frequent basis, and do not provide length violations. Many organizations have further rules including the alternation of vowels and consonants, minimum length, and requirements to change passwords on a regular basis. Network activities are examined for NFS, TCP/IP services, network access parameters, and dial-in or dial-out parameters and privileges.

The system itself is checked for configuration parameters whose settings might offer a weakened security environment. Finally, auditing is investigated. Event files are checked to determine the number of failed log-ins, failed access attempts at files, and other information that may indicate that a system is being probed or is under attack.

Intrusion Detection

Other security tools provide intrusion detection, alerting the administrator when unauthorized attempts are made to access protected resources. Intrusion detection tools have automatic actions so that the appropriate account, network port, or other access mechanisms are disabled until more information is collected about the situation.

The POLYCENTER Security Intrusion Detector is used to actively fight attacks to distributed clients or servers. The administrator can set alarm thresholds that will trigger automatic notification of a potential intrusion or attack. Further, when attacks are detected, automatic countermeasures can be initiated within the system. Some possible responses could include stopping the process that is the cause of the attacks, disabling the user account that was used to access the system, or in the worst case, isolating the system from the network until further measures can be undertaken.

Session Monitoring

Session monitoring tools can also be used as part of a security enforcement mechanism. These tools allow system administrators to monitor designated sessions in order to observe suspicious activities. Monitoring can be triggered by attempts to access critical applications or protected resources. Some monitoring tools, such as the Session Watchdog by Digital Equipment or OpenV Star Monitor from OpenVision, allow the administrator to monitor sessions covertly or provide an option for informing the user that a session is being monitored.

Kerberos

Kerberos was developed at MIT as part of Project Athena. There are several companies, such as Digital, offering this functionality today. Kerberos is also part of the emerging DCE infrastructure. Kerberos is designed to secure client/server interchanges by authenticating the client.

As a first step in a secured operation, the client presents encrypted credentials to the

Kerberos server. An encrypted description of the server and the services or data required is included as well. The Kerberos server decrypts the presented credentials to authenticate the identity of the client. Once the client is authenticated, the Kerberos server checks access-control information to determine if the client is allowed to access the server and the particular services or data requested. If the client is not authenticated or there is an access control violation, Kerberos will send a management event notification to the appropriate administrator.

After Kerberos has determined that the access is allowed, it returns an encrypted "ticket" to the client. At the same time, Kerberos sends a complementary ticket to the targeted server. Once the client receives the ticket, it presents the ticket with its request to the targeted server. The server compares the incoming ticket with information supplied by the Kerberos server to verify that the client has indeed been authenticated and allowed to access these services. To prevent capture of encrypted messages on a Local Area Network, Kerberos also supplies an encrypted time stamp with the tickets. This time stamp provides a lifetime for this operation, and the client must supply its ticket to the server before the time has elapsed or the request will be rejected.

17.15 TOOL ARCHITECTURES

System administrators need tools that allow them to manage their clients and servers with a higher level of abstraction than is possible in most cases today. For example, administrators would like to invoke or activate backup procedures in a general way and apply them to Novell clients, OS/2 clients, UNIX workstations, or other types of systems. The particular details that must be considered for each type of system should be as hidden, if possible, from the normal operational staff. Legato Systems NetWorker has enjoyed success in the backup market because it supports over twenty different clients.

Tools that will provide this capability generally are not yet here and are evolving in stages. The first stage that is becoming available includes tools that deal with the monitoring or collection aspect of management rather than control.

These collection tools are evolving with a set of "collectors," which are targeted for specific environments. These collectors obtain information from different types of computers or operating systems and deliver it to a central collection point. The information from various systems is transformed into a common format so that the administrator can view the collected information in a consistent fashion independent of its source. The interface to this tool allows the system administrator, for example, to see the type of software stored in each client and server in a way that does not depend on intimate knowledge of file systems, naming conventions, and other ways of obtaining the information. Of course, the drawback with a common format is the risk of lowest common denominator factors— the exclusion of particularly useful information because it is not incorporated into other types of schemes.

In any case, collector-based tools are beginning to appear on the market. One example is Hewlett-Packard's new release of PerfRx. This product uses a series of collectors that can read system files, application logs, ASCII character streams, and other information sources. These collectors deliver this information to an analysis program that can track performance and behavior of systems and applications and alert the administrator to problems. NetLabs has a similar product, the AssetManager, which collects information from a variety of sources, such as network device managers, intermediate agents, and resident agents in clients and servers. This information is incorporated into a single relational database, which provides a uniform and consistent way of tracking and monitoring the inventory information.

Control is a slightly more complex problem since individual vendor and operating-specific tools must be activated to carry out the activity. For example, it would be very simple for an administrator to drag and drop a backup icon on a particular client or server in order to activate that process. However, the vendor-specific details of file systems, operating system interfaces, and other particular information demand that targeted tools be used for each environment. The means of activating each individual backup tool, the kind of information it needs, and the types of reports that it generates must be built into the overall systems management tools so that it can be selected. Integration with other elements of the management system, such as the topology map, would be useful so that administrators could simply point to the targeted system. Information about its specific type and so forth then could be used to select the proper tool to actually carry out the operation.

17.17 GENERAL WIDGETS

The organizational groundwork was described in the previous chapter. General Widgets desires an integrated set of systems management tools and is evaluating the offerings of the framework vendors such as Hewlett-Packard, Computer Associates, Legent, Tivoli, and IBM. This is an ongoing effort since no vendor can deliver the packaged solution wanted by General Widgets. While the company waits for the industry, it is filling out the tools it currently uses with the best tools it can find. General Widgets hopes to take advantage of an emerging trend: many framework vendors obtain, or partner with the best point tools they can find, and integrate them into their own frameworks. Thus, a quality tool taken today offers value while remaining a candidate for inclusion in one or more frameworks.

General Widgets will have a basic set of management tools for each environment. The basic set includes remote operation, configuration, backup, and software distribution. Remote operations tools allow an administrator to query any computer, execute a subset of the commands, change key files, and transfer small files. This allows an administrator to observe a user's actions when providing assistance. Remote operations are also necessary when users are not present, especially as a basis for activating other management processes such as software distribution.

Configuration management is a policy-level concern. The company has defined several standard configurations for each type of computer and operating system. Standard configurations include resources such as memory and video cards, for instance. Other aspects of the standard cover systems configuration parameters, operating system configurations, and standard directories for certain software. Users, of course, have their private files space that they organize however they wish. Users cannot change the standard configurations on their systems. This policy is mandated by the large amount of management staff time that was consumed in tracking problems in a large variety of configurations. Further, users can change configurations and degrade network and application performance.

This policy is enforced by an automated process that is activated when a client logs into a server. The system configuration is compared to the expected configuration and any differences are logged. Administrators learn which users change their system configurations in violation of the policy and can take the appropriate actions. The specified configuration is restored before the log-in sequence is completed. Other systems are polled periodically and their configurations are compared. The initial results are promising: the time to troubleshoot desktop problems has dropped significantly since many alternatives are eliminated. Users who changed their configurations are identified and follow-up actions include training, discussions, and possible loss of network privileges. High-level management backing allows the administrators to build policies with consequences.

A further benefit of configuration consolidation is increased automation. It is easier to write better scripts since they work for larger numbers of systems. Earlier scripts needed to account for differences in configuration and were limited as a result. Now scripts understand the configuration and focus on automating more tasks, further leveraging the staff for more important tasks.

Backup and recovery of desktop data was another high-priority tool. Requirements included minimal user involvement in identifying critical files. Defaults allowed no user involvement; all were backed up on a regular basis. All data could be saved without any involvement. However, there was a higher risk of losing key information between scheduled backup operations; that was a choice the user had. The default ensures minimal data integrity with minimal user participation.

Most backup activities are driven from the backup server which schedules activities for off-peak hours. Client-initiated saves are necessary to protect key files each time they are changed by the user. Compression is performed by the desktop agent and optional encryption can be selected.

The backup servers support an array of computers and operating systems. The heterogeneity of General Widgets systems led to a choice of a single backup system that supported as many of their environments as possible. Backup servers have media management features that help operators manage the off-line library, check media, rotate media, and keep track of the information.

Server storage management is also important and General Widgets is installing its first system. The storage management system automatically migrates information that is "stale" (has not been accessed for some period of time) from high-speed disks to other media such as digital tape or optical discs. Media management features track information, cycling for tapes, and multivolume operations reducing retrieval time and operator effort.

Software distribution is also a mandatory management tool. There is a variety of software distribution tools for the heterogeneous systems within General Widgets, and administrators are forced to use different tools as they await tools that span various systems. Installation is a mandatory requirement; delivered software must be automatically installed. Recovery is difficult in some cases since there is no automated rollback; the earlier version can be delivered and installed.

Configuration standardization comes into play here as well. Stable configurations make for more successful software deliveries; the wrinkles with a configuration can be worked out once for thousands of systems while individually selected configurations can introduce hundreds of unique glitches to be dealt with. The installation routines can be very thorough because they have deep knowledge of the target system.

The future software distribution wishlist includes the ability to specify dependencies such as operating system versions, specific add-on boards, and other software, memory or disc space. An integrated scheduling and reporting system that encompasses all the General Widgets systems is also a key requirement.

Security management has gained a higher priority because of increased media attention and the introduction of a virus into one of the General Widget campuses. The virus was relatively harmless; the company lost some productive time while the virus was isolated and eliminated from all infected systems. General Widgets is taking multiple steps to address this concern.

Internet firewalls are being installed at one campus. They will filter all incoming call requests and only allow those to identified servers. These servers are used for receiving electronic mail and other information from the outside world. Any other target is blocked and invisible to the exterior world. In a similar way, outgoing calls can be filtered. Specified users are allowed to go to approved external sites and the firewall prevents all other outgoing traffic. The rapid introduction of World Wide Web Browsers has changed this part of the equation. Users are "surfing" the Internet as they find information in many places, and the firewall cannot keep pace with these activities.

The servers for accepting external traffic will also be isolated from the rest of the General Widgets network with another firewall. This firewall will block all incoming connection requests. If the server is attacked and breached it cannot be used as a stage for further penetration into the General Widgets network. In fact, attempted connections will serve as an alarm for a potential security violation.

Further security management is focused on auditing, checking every system for potential security violations. Another advantage of selected configuration standards is increased security; obvious holes are plugged, and the automatic checking helps keep security tighter. Any potential problems can be corrected and monitored. Intrusion detection tools are being evaluated, they can detect some types of breaches, alert an administrator, and activate automatic responses.

General Widgets is also working with its server vendors to build authentication mechanisms for users and for network administrators. An authenticated connection between an administrator with server tools and a server adds another layer of protection to critical resources.

The next members of the tool set are inventory/asset management and license management. Inventory collection is the most difficult part of the inventory problem today; tools that collect information from an array of sources are not yet mature. Proxy agents are being used as well as SNMP agents. The company has been using a database it developed a few years back and would like to make the transition to a commercial product that exploits relational databases. The decision is to wait and see; when viable products reach the marketplace the company will select several for evaluation and testing.

Licensing is actually a facet of asset management as well. The company found that its business units had collectively licensed copies of some software that far exceeded the number of employees. Each manager had picked a large number of licenses in order to be safe, in aggregate they were three times the employees in General Widgets. License management will track and monitor the appropriate numbers of copies and give administrators accurate usage data. The company will reduce its liability with easily copied software while reducing its licensing costs as well.

Longer-term plans include tracking the development of the DMI-compliant products and evaluating them as soon as they are available. This complements the tracking of different systems management frameworks and looking for convergence with DMI. Another goal is obtaining application monitoring and management tools that allow administrators to watch the real activity of the client/server environment.

PART IV

SOLUTION ELEMENTS

This concluding part ties the preceding material together and introduces guidelines for building an effective management solution from the disciplines, platforms, and tools that have been discussed. Chapter 18 discusses management processes and their characteristics. Chapter 19 offers suggestions on formulating a solution strategy. The final chapter offers ideas on future management directions and an example of integrating business process management into the management environment.

CHAPTER 18

Processes

Management processes are often neglected in the struggle and rush to accumulate the critical mass of point solutions for fire fighting. A large portion of management activities and operations are processes, as well as more specific activities. We will define a process as a set of actions and procedures that to some extent are independent of the particular cause of their activation. For example, a Help Desk has certain processes that are followed irrespective of the particular type of problem that is reported. The Help Desk staff goes through certain steps to refine information about the reported problem, assign the problem to the particular or appropriate management staff member, and then track it until it is resolved. This process is followed whether the user reports a problem with the server, a piece of software, or network connectivity.

Focusing management solutions on the appropriate policies allows an administrator several advantages. A major one is providing a certain level of abstraction and distance from individual point solutions so that a more global perspective can be brought to bear when designing and implementing management solutions. Effective and well-conceived management processes will be the major determinant in the overall effectiveness of any management architecture or solution for any enterprise. An effective management process coordinates the appropriate people, management tools and applications, and procedures into an effective and cohesive series of steps to resolve a problem or achieve some other management goal. Using the right mix of skills and experience with the proper combinations of tools and procedures provides an optimum strategy for attacking large classes of management tasks and requirements.

18.1 CHARACTERISTICS

Some of the characteristics of well-conceived management processes include documentation, testing points, escalation points, branching points, and exit points. All management processes must be well documented so that management staff have access to all the information needed to understand and carry out any particular steps. The documentation is generally written, but can also include on-line access. Context-sensitive access simplifies the operator's task of finding the appropriate information as it is needed. Many organizations have expended considerable design and implementation resources in order to make these processes and their documentation easily available to management staff as needed.

Branching points allow for the specification of various paths that a process can take toward completion. Quite often, further steps of a process depend upon the outcomes or information collected in earlier steps. Design of a good process specifies very clearly the criteria required for choosing a branching point, as well as a list of the possible alternatives. Careful design and layout can optimize a process by minimizing the condition points and smoothing the flow of the process, ensuring that the minimum numbers of steps are carried out to achieve the goal.

Each process must have a clearly defined goal and an easily recognized and identified outcome. Each staff member must be able to ascertain quickly and easily the criteria and means for determining when a process has been completed successfully. These places will be the exit points of a well-designed process whereby the process set of steps has been brought to a successful conclusion.

Every well-designed process must also have an escalation point whereby the process has been deemed to have failed. The escalation point specifies what actions are to be taken when every step of a process has been successfully completed and yet the outcome has not been attained. Escalation points will generally require access of more highly skilled management staff with deeper expertise or the activation of more sophisticated and complicated processes to address the issue. Without an escalation point, management staff have no recourse for those times when even the best of designs will not be effective.

18.2 AUTOMATION

Automating as many management processes as possible will provide the highest-value solution and provide the most effective approach to bringing complex client/server environments under control. Automatic activation and carrying out of process steps will improve management effectiveness by reducing the time to carry out repetitive and complex tasks. At the same time, it will ensure a much more rigorous approach to process-oriented management since it will be possible to constrain and document the actual steps carried out to complete one. Management staff will be guided by reminders and cues, and many parts or steps will be activated and completed without human intervention.

A further value to an automated management process is that it is basically enforceable. Many of the steps will be sequenced automatically, ensuring that they are followed in the proper order with the proper steps. It is unrealistic to expect overworked management staff dealing with many fires to remember all the steps required, or to take the time to access hard-to-read documentation or other sources of information. If that information is embedded in the proper context, staff can follow processes with minimal disruption and reduce errors. As long as the automated processes have well-defined escalation points, even failed processes can be handled and reported in the appropriate fashion.

18.3 FEEDBACK

Another value of an automated management process is that it can collect information as it is being carried out. Administrators can use this information to gauge the effectiveness of the process in terms of its ability to achieve the desired goals. Information collected provides an objective means of assessing the process design relative to the time and resources required. Good process design can also be used to detect poor procedures, inadequate training, or places where the inappropriate staff member has been assigned. Administrators may also be able to collect information determining and defining which processes are actually activated and used most frequently, thereby being able to focus their designs for optimization and increased efficiency.

Without these types of automated tools for activating and collecting information about management processes, we will never be able to bring such complex environments under control with a minimal use of resources. As networks grow more complicated, the processes required to manage them will also grow more complex. Without the ability to bring the appropriate tools, the appropriate staff, and the appropriate actions together in the correct sequence, we will never be able to control things at the appropriate level. A process-oriented perspective is independent of the particular point solutions that may comprise it, allowing a level of extraction and independence from any given management application.

Administrators will be required to spend increasing amounts of time designing and evaluating their processes to determine and ensure that they have effective and adequate solutions to meet the increasing demands of complex environments.

18.4 PROCESS DESIGN

Administrators will need the appropriate types of tools to enable them to design their own management processes. The way this can be expected to develop is already shown by some prototypical approaches that are becoming available. Most of these, such as Cabletron's Automatic Connection Management System (ACMS) begin by allowing managers to fill in the blanks. Administrators can choose from multiple options in pull-down menus and specify different aspects of the process steps and sequences. These types of pull-down menus and selection of operators and variables and criteria for each aspect and step of the process will allow easy specification, inspection, and modification of policies.

Stored policy templates can also be used and easily modified for similar classes of operations that require customization.

More sophisticated policy design tools are not yet available, but they will be necessary in order to allow administrators to specify the tools and other resources required to create and implement efficient processes. The most likely path for developing these tools will require a graphical interface whereby individual process steps can be linked, calibration and branching points can be specified, along with the appropriate exit and escalation points. A good model that could be used for designing such processes can be found in the NetLab's Nerve Center, which has a state transition graphical interface. This could be used to specify various steps in a process, as well as the conditions for leaving one step and initiating the next.

Such descriptive tools must have enough intelligence to allow the particular steps to be linked at a lower level to the appropriate tools or staff that will be required for each designed process.

Point Processes

Many management processes can be classified as point processes, being focused on a very specific and constrained area.

Examples of point processes include asset/inventory management, software distribution, problem management, and license management. This level of process is easier to automate since all activity takes place within the scope of a single management tool. Further examples in details of point processes will be discussed later in this section.

Integrated Processes

Higher-value solutions will provide integrated processes that combine point processes and other management tools to handle the more complex and critical management processes.

Building integrated processes will require the ability to concatenate individual point solutions and point processes into the appropriate sequences. The major mechanisms that will support this will be event and data integration.

Event integration, as discussed in the platform section, allows one application to generate an event that can be used to trigger or activate another process or point application. In this way, a system administrator can define the sequence by chaining them together through an event management tool. Some of these tools are embedded in platforms, while others may be more sophisticated applications that use the basic platform infrastructure for their own purposes.

Data integration complements the event management by allowing different tools and processes to share information as necessary as more complex processes are constructed. Each individual tool or process must be able to access information from any source, as well as place it in common repositories so that it is available to even higher-level processes. Without a solid means of integrating and sharing data, it will be very difficult to construct the types of complex processes that will be required.

18.5   POLICY

Once automated processes have been constructed, we are well on the way to laying a foundation for policy-based management. Policies will allow us to control the behaviors of management processes in order to achieve overall business and organizational goals. Policies will allow administrators to constrain or select the appropriate management processes based on a more coherent and cohesive view of the overall business processes and requirements of any particular organization.

There will be many situations where policy can be applied. For example, the administrator may specify a choice from a set of processes dealing with the same issue constrained by time of day, the type of problem, who is available to respond, or the types of business processes that have been affected. This type of specific and targeted policy constraint will allow the appropriate selection of a policy that achieves an overall outcome with minimal disruption of the activities that are most critical to the enterprise. As a case in point, a different process may be employed to deal with a problem that occurs in the middle of the day when heavy production activity is undertaken than if the same issue arose during a late night on a weekend when traffic levels were low and the impact to the organization would be much different.

Policy decisions will also be embedded in more sophisticated processes, probably in the conditional branch points, so that different actions will be taken, depending on the particular operational context specified.

The incorporation of policy descriptions and constraints will allow the management of these complex technologies in order to achieve particular goals for the organizations rather than simply managing the technology in its own right.

18.6   EXAMPLES OF PROCESS TASKS

There is a group of tasks that fit the definitions of being process oriented, although they are also assigned to other particular categories. This section looks at these tasks from a process-oriented viewpoint, trying to identify those steps that are independent of particular devices or other types of constraints.

Problem Management

Problem management, or trouble-ticketing, tools have been used in the past and are growing more sophisticated. The problem management itself is a process with many steps that are followed independently of the type of problem encountered. Problem management systems begin their activities with the report or detection of a given problem, either reported by a user, detected by management staff in their ongoing activities, or through an alarm or trap.

The detected problem is entered into a ticket describing the source of the problem and as much information as can be initially collected. More sophisticated problem management systems, such as Legent's Paradigm, are able to correlate problems when multiple reports are made concurrently. This type of correlation mechanism allows the management staff to be focused on the most likely cause of the problem or the most critical or important problem at any given time, reducing problem resolution time and using staff resources effectively.

Problem management systems follow the reported problem through all the different steps necessary to bring a complete resolution. One of the initial steps is assigning the ticket to the appropriate staff member for ongoing attention.

Assignments themselves can be automated, allowing the administrator to use rules to select the most appropriate staff member to handle any reported incident. Staff members have access to historical information about each element, as well as classes of elements, and are able to access the types of actions and remedial steps that were taken in the past. Once the device or problem has been resolved, the trouble ticket is cleared and all of the actions taken to clear the problem are captured in the historical database for use in the future.

This a great example of a process-oriented tool. Many different types of problems, staff, and actions can be accommodated and organized within this type of framework.

The Help Desk

Help Desks are more generalized user-support services that may use a problem management tool as part of their repertoire. Help Desks are available for users to call with questions and problem reports; the staff is the first line of taking care of user needs.

The Help Desk may have other tools, such as access to management platforms, to determine network status, utilization levels, and error logs. Help Desks may also have automatic call answering devices so that known problems are reported to customers when they call in, obviating the requirement of chasing multiple reports of the same incident. The Help Desk framework allows a user support person to field inquiries, to answer many first-line types of problems, to offer advice and oversee an attempt to repeat the action or activity that is causing a problem, and to access to the information to help the network user.

The Help Desk is a process-oriented tool because many of the reports will be handled in a similar way—through initial checking and screening to determine more accurately what the problem might be, and issuing a trouble ticket and the assignment to the appropriate staff for ongoing attention. Help Desks are also a source of preliminary training where network users can be taken through simple steps of procedures in order to ensure they are carrying them out correctly and that the problem is not simply one of education and understanding.

Asset and Inventory Management

This is a process-oriented task that involves the collection of information about every managed element. This information is collected and organized so that those responsible for managing technical or financial assets are able to search the information to obtain the data they need. Asset and inventory information must be collected from many sources. Remote management agents can supply a subset of the required information when the elements they manage are discovered on the network. Remote agents can supply basic information about the type of resource, version numbers, amount of memory, number of interfaces, operational status, and so forth. However, accurate and thorough asset and inventory information requires the incorporation of information from other sources, as well. For instance, it is important to know the locations of the managed assets, the vendors responsible for the products, and any warranty or vendor support contact information that would be applicable. This information is often in one or more other databases within the enterprise and must be accessed and integrated to provide an asset manager's view. Much of this work is independent of the particular type of resource being managed, whether it is a router, intelligent hub, or a sophisticated server.

Accounting

Accounting is becoming increasingly important for network management solutions. The ability to collect information on resource usage and then use this information for appropriate charging, as well as planning information, is key. Accounting mechanisms require the collection of information about resource usage from many different levels of granularity: basic network usage, usage on a protocol basis, and application-specific usage. This information can be correlated for specific workgroups, as well as individual users, as necessary.

Profiling

Profiling will become increasingly important as a basic means of understanding the usual behavior of networks, workgroups, and individual components. Profiling is used to detect problems, as well as to provide foundation data for more sophisticated and longer-term planning processes. Profiling involves the collection of information that can characterize the behavior of an entire network, a subnetwork, a single LAN segment, or other network components. Profiling will soon move to monitoring the normal behaviors of critical servers, workgroups as a whole, and the particular types of application activities that are carried out over time. Profiling will also be important in order to detect periodic and normal changes from normal behaviors, such as end-of-week traffic or end-of-month closing traffic volumes, and so forth. Profiling must be carried out on a regular basis and the captured data must be organized so that it can be compared over time and significant changes noted.

Capacity Planning

Capacity planning is a process-oriented task that takes information from varying sources, such as profiling and other types of accounting data, and is used to build forecasts and trends to enable system administrators to predict situations where resources will not be sufficient to keep up with projected growth rates.

Reporting

Network administrators, as well as their superiors, need sets of reports produced on a regular basis in order to calibrate the effectiveness of their activities. Reports will be generated on many different topics, such as overall network and systems availability, utilization levels, mean times between failures, mean time to repair, and other standard statistics. These reports can be of varying levels from high-level overviews to very detailed breakdowns of specific problems and processes. Reporting should be carried out on a regular basis so that reports from different periods can be evaluated and compared as accurately as possible to detect trends. Much of the reporting will involve periodic collection of the appropriate information, either directly from remote agents or from information collected from other management tools and processes. This information is organized and then presented in the appropriate way with tabular information, charts, and other types of graphics to assist in understanding.

These examples of process-oriented tasks span many different areas that are required to be managed, such as networks, systems, and applications. The process-oriented nature allows one level of abstraction and generality so that these processes can be applied in many new places as opportunities arise. A high-level, high-value opportunity, for instance, exists as networked applications are instrumented so that more appropriate information can be collected.

CHAPTER 19

Building a Solution

All of the material in this book is intended to give you a practical perspective on the issues, challenges, and possible solutions for managing a distributed computing environment. Putting all the pieces together is a challenging task. This chapter discusses a process for building management solutions.

I once had the good fortune to speak with Buckminster Fuller, the inventor of the geodesic dome, among other things. When I asked him how he made his creative leaps, he replied, "I simply spend 90% of my time understanding exactly where I am and where I want to go. The other 10% is finding the obvious path between those two points." It sounds simpler than it is, but its a good strategy.

We'll start with where the customer (the organization you are helping solve network and distributed systems management problems) wants to go and then return to finding the starting place. Keep in mind that the description of the process is linear, the way books work; however, it is much more interactive in practice. Finding out certain information may open up possible alternatives for solutions. Finding out what the customer wants to do may direct you to get better information about certain aspects of the environment.

19.1 DESIRED OUTCOMES—WHERE YOU WANT TO GO

Now the task is to get a clear picture of where the customer wants to go. Most customers know that managing distributed computing environments is a challenging job.

There are many ways to specify the desired outcome. Some typical goals include availability, service levels, staff productivity, and reduced costs of ownership. However, make sure that outcomes are described in ways that make them attainable. Get specific metrics whenever possible; a goal of 99% availability can be reached, and you can make recommendations that realize it. On the other hand, a goal of increasing availability doesn't offer enough information for you to make a specific recommendation regarding the equipment, staffing, and resources that are needed.

Determine if the customer wants to have a policy-based approach and what policies are needed. This is an area worth spending time on even if the customer is not accustomed to thinking about management in this way. Policies may not all be automated, but they need to be explicit so that they can guide other details of a proposed solution.

Some policy examples can illustrate the possibilities. For example, does the customer want data collection policies that determine the maximum load that the instrumentation imposes on networks and systems? Does the customer want to have intelligent instrumentation that processes data locally? Selecting a management structure is also a policy decision: Will management be centralized or distributed?

Does the customer want to identify critical applications and ensure that they get the attention and priority they require? If the customer needs to support key applications, then other requirements will surface for granular monitoring, application control, and reallocating resources. Configuration policies are important to consider; many organizations want to establish standard configurations and monitor them. The management systems detect configuration changes and restores them to the standard profile.

Policies that constrain the actions of the management staff are also important. Better management technology offers opportunities to make substantial changes in the environment with a few simple mouse clicks. Time-of-day restraints may be useful in order to minimize disruptions during peak productivity hours. Access control mechanisms may also help restrict staff to specific tools and resources that they can monitor and manage.

Policies that aid proactive management tasks should also be considered. Capacity planning requires periodic collection of data that can be used to identify usage trends. A policy determines the frequency of data collection and the amount of collected information.

There are many periodic management tasks such as data backup that are also policy based. Scheduling management tasks brings us to policy issues again. Management operations may conflict with other activities or with each other. For instance, a backup operation may consume substantial bandwidth for an indefinite period of time. A management policy would restrict the bandwidth that can be used in order to mitigate the impacts on other network activities. Software distribution may also use substantial bandwidth, and similar policies are needed to constrain their activities.

A scheduling tool can be used to prioritize these management tasks. The administrator can apply rules that determine which activities have precedence and when they should be preempted. The same tools can schedule production jobs at the same time to minimize interference between management and production activities.

Other customer goals include reducing the cost of ownership, managing distributed assets, increasing competitive advantage, and increasing management staff productivity.

Where You Are

Finding the starting place can be a revealing process in itself. Some customers have reliable information about their current technologies and management strategies while others are so enmeshed in fire fighting that they haven't given much thought to a strategic direction.

The information you collect is used in several ways. Some information is background and context that helps you understand and learn about constraints and possibilities; it helps guide your solution and identify potential problems in accepting a solution. Other information is used for **calibration points**—data you use to check the direction of your solution. For example, knowing what tasks consume the most time will help you prioritize the deployment of management tools. Other information is used as **data points**—to calculate estimated impacts and benefits.

High-level Views

A primary task is to understand the environment that you are dealing with. Take a perspective of a high-level corporate manager for a few hours to understand some of the business opportunities and constraints that your customer confronts. Any significant investments in network and distributed systems management solutions will eventually come to the attention of the business managers in these days of thinner resources. It helps to present some of the solution benefits in terms that make it clear that the target is increasing the capacity for competitive advantage and effective action.

Determine the major lines of business and the market structures of each. The overall structure of the customer market should be understood; for instance, is the market volatile and how is the customer share changing? Understanding the competitive strengths and weaknesses are important so that a proposed solution will be shown to strengthen competitive advantage and mitigate weaknesses. For example, a business that differentiates with customer service can appreciate higher availability, proactive management that shifts traffic before customer response suffers, and better capacity planning.

The culture is also an important factor: Is it collaborative or competitive? Are there strong rivalries between groups that have to collaborate on a management solution? These factors should also be considered as early as possible since they may, in fact, determine what an acceptable solution's parameters actually are. For example, an organization may benefit from centralizing more management functions, but the struggle among units for control (the smart ones will be trying to get out of it and do something more rewarding) may be too exhausting and difficult. It might be better to work on centralizing each region, which demonstrates the value of the approach and may lay a foundation for further consolidation. The ultimate goals shouldn't be compromised, but the stages to reach them will be different for each organization. Good relationships with the customer are key so that you can get some insight into the organization itself.

The Environment

You need a lot of information about the customer environment. A good place to start is the Information Technology, Management Information Systems, and other groups that are responsible for the networks and distributed systems. Determine the spans of control; for instance, are distributed systems managed by a single group, locally by each group, or a mixture of groups? This indicates the type of fragmentation and degree of overlap that can be addressed as part of a proposed solution.

An Overall Census   Get an overall census: the networks, systems, servers, data centers, remote offices, mobile users, and telecommuting workers. This is what needs to be addressed in a management solution. It is also good to know that your customer cannot easily provide this information. It is a calibration point; other information and estimates may be suspect, and it may take a little more digging to determine that you have the best possible information (it is often woefully inadequate in the best of cases).

Obtain the customer client and server inventory. The numbers and distributions of clients and servers are important in designing a properly scaled solution for the customer. The information yields calibration points for building a solution. Some calibration points such as projected growth rates are used to check the solution for future scalability. Information is also gathered for assessing management impacts on the bottom line. The critical servers and clients are identified so they receive appropriate attention in the formulation of a solution.

Information about the LANs, WANs, and remote access is also important to collect. Critical LAN segments are identified for future reference in building a solution. Projected growth rates are needed to check for scaling problems. Information on Wide Area Networks is also collected for the purpose of identifying critical LAN-WAN interfaces and to understand the future directions of WAN backbones for the customer.

Critical applications are defined as those that have an adverse impact on the organization if they are not available. Critical applications need to be identified as calibration points; often critical applications end up on servers without redundant power, for example. Other information concerning the impacts of these applications is collected for later analysis. Be wary of incomplete information or answers that appear to be guesses; incomplete information may affect the quality of the management solution.

Its also helpful to identify critical activities in addition to applications. For example, some organizations only think of financial, order entry, or customer service applications as critical without considering the fact that many activities depend upon electronic messaging or work-flow processes. Interruption of critical activities should also be brought to light.

Revenues   Revenue impacts are difficult to estimate in some organizations. Others have specific networks, users, and applications that generate most or all of their revenues. Even if the customer has weak information, try to get as much of it as you can. If possible, identify revenue producing applications and the revenue they produce for the organization. Whenever possible, identify specific clients and servers that produce revenue and attempt to get specific metrics such as revenue produced on a per hour basis. Some networks may also carry revenue producing traffic while others may carry internal traffic.

Other metrics are useful. The employees and revenues are collected for later impact calculations. Also, determine the proportions of network users who are clerical, professional, and management.

19.2   THE CURRENT MANAGEMENT ENVIRONMENT

Understanding how the customer is managing today gives you an idea of what will need to be added, modified, or replaced. Review any overall strategy directions and future plans that are documented. Find out how these plans have been executed: Have previous goals been met on time? Is there a single management team, or teams that are compartmentalized and separated?

There are three basic environments that must be covered: LAN and WAN management as well as systems management. Collecting data for each follows a similar pattern. We will cover the common areas first to avoid repetition.

A word about granularity. Some customers will have detailed information and others will offer educated guesses. The following discussions can be applied to any scale—individual workgroups to an enterprise. Better granularity gives a more accurate picture; for example, details for each LAN workgroup allow specific calculations that show differences in management effectiveness. If there is poor granularity, then overall estimates can be applied across a set of diverse environments with a loss of insight. The customer, the information, and your time to collect and analyze data determine the level of detail you can handle.

Management Structures

Determine what type of management structure, or structures, is used for each environment. WAN management is usually centralized while LAN and systems management environments are put together in a variety of ways. You need this information in order to recommend any changes to the basic management structures. Generally, organizations need to centralize more of their management operations as the technologies and political barriers allow.

Widely dispersed management environments offer significant opportunities to leverage a centralized approach. Reducing management staff or reallocating them to other tasks can deliver substantial savings while improving the quality of the management team.

Staffing and Budget

This information can be combined with the census to determine appropriate calibration points that define current effectiveness. You need a view of the current management resources and how the customer allocates them. This information is useful for justifying your proposals by showing impacts on the management budgets and staffing levels. These early calibration points can be compared over time to evaluate improvements.

This information may be distributed throughout the organization; collect as much as you can. Some customers may have separate budgets for various activities while others have a single budget and do not look at specific allocations. Break budgets down into salaries, training, management tools, management hardware, and platforms.

Salaries are often a major component of management budgets, especially in organizations that have not invested in the management technology infrastructure. Some organizations must also spend more for training, or cross-training when there are multiple tools.

Management tools include those that operate as stand-alone products as well as those that are part of a management platform. Management hardware can include stand-alone probes, analyzers, and monitors as well as cable testers. Management platforms include SNMP and proprietary products.

Staffing is important to understand and evaluate. Determine the number of skill levels in the operations groups, and especially, the number of staff who have specialized, irreplaceable skills. These staff represent a serious exposure for the customer.

The actual staffing levels may vary by business hours, twenty-four-hour by seven-day coverage on-site, 24×7 coverage with a smaller staff with others on call, or other possibilities. Attempt to determine what the average coverage is. In particular, focus on the critical elements that were identified in the census.

Staffing estimates may be tricky since some departments may have part-time LAN administrators. Make sure to obtain an accurate count in terms of equivalent staff; i.e., two half-time staff should be counted as a single full-time staff position. The assignments to areas such as operations may be loose estimates in many cases. If groups claim they have no administrator, add a half person in your estimate; it's probably someone down the hall who is recognized as knowledgeable, rather than an official member of the management and administration team.

Metrics

Determining the current management metrics will yield information for estimating the impacts of failures. If the customer does not have documented metrics, then the implication is that they lack detailed knowledge of their own environment and it will make any calculations more difficult to validate. The lack of metrics will make some calculations difficult; at the same time, lack of information should be used as another problem that a management solution will solve. There is a wide range of metrics to collect as well as calculate.

Health Metrics   Most customers will use some type of metric to determine if their networks and systems are operating satisfactorily. Find out what metrics are used and if they are applied differently for critical networks or systems. Determine the frequency of collecting these metrics and the granularity used for critical resources. For example, all servers may not be equally important and those that are critical should be monitored more closely.

Find out if the health metrics measure up/down status, availability, service levels, throughput, response time, or other parameters. Metrics that reflect service levels and application performance are as important as simple measurements of errors or link utilization. The network and systems users will have a service-level perspective since that is how they are affected.

Measurement Metrics   A set of metrics can help you understand what is actually happening in the customer environment (or to establish that no one really knows what actually occurs). These metrics may be captured in detailed trouble-ticketing tools, written down on forms, or conveyed by electronic messages or even conversations.

Failure metrics are important: find out how often failures occur and how long it takes to restore service. The frequent/duration product defines the impact as a cumulative value over a week, month, or year. Even a series of small interruptions that total fifteen minutes a day add up to more than a week and a half of lost time per worker annually. Find out what levels of staff are assigned. Highly skilled staff are often dispatched to deal with problems that can be addressed by other staff. If not, these are opportunities to add automation or better analysis tools.

Determine if the customer has detailed information about failures: Can the customer identify the components with the highest failure rates? Often it is easier to replace elements that fail consistently with more reliable products. There may also be a shortage of replacement modules on hand that aggravates the problem.

It is important to get more detailed information about failures of critical LANs, WANs, and systems. Find out if the critical elements have the needed features: Are there redundant power supplies and hot-swappable modules installed? Detailed logs help; otherwise, gather estimates of averages. If the management staff has poor-quality information, try talking discreetly with users; they probably have a good estimate to offer as well.

Failure reports must be associated with the number of users affected. For example, a hub failure may isolate several dozen users while a backbone router outage can affect hundreds.

Another way of determining the customer's actual capabilities is by examining the management reports the customer uses. Are reports produced on a regular basis? Determine if anyone uses the current reports, evaluate what information should be added, modified, or deleted.

The volume of user complaints may also help with understanding and checking the metrics. For example, if the customer says that servers rarely fail, but there are substantial problem calls about poor performance, then more probing may be required to understand the actual situation.

Calculated Metrics   There are sets of metrics that can be computed to focus your solution and to provide supporting data for your recommendations. Use the staffing and census data to calculate how many resources are managed by the staff today. A metric of distributed systems per staff member or the number of LAN segments managed by a staff member gives an estimate of current staff productivity.

A weighted average cost for network user costs is useful as another calibration point. Average employee expenses can be obtained from the customer, from Department of Labor statistics, or by comparing salaries and benefits from comparable organizations. Be sure to include benefits plus salary to get accurate cost estimates. The proportion of clerical, professional, and executive users is used with these costs to determine the cost per hour for an average user. This metric is used to estimate impacts of downtime.

Task Breakdowns

Look at current management tasks in some detail. Find out where time is spent and where the challenges are. This is another place where you have an opportunity to revisit this question at a later time and to learn if progress is actually occurring. For example, one organization reported that over 60% of staff time was taken with troubleshooting, a year later, the majority of time was taken with configuration, performance, and accounting tasks. This was a welcome indication that tactical, survival-level troubleshooting was under control and more strategic, longer-term challenges were receiving attention.

Time-consuming Tasks   Learn what the time-consuming tasks are in each part of the environment. These are good guideposts for selecting the most effective tools or processes. Freeing staff for other tasks is good for productivity and for morale. If possible, find the frequency and duration of these tasks to estimate the staff time spent. Sometimes, important tasks such as inventory are neglected since they are difficult and lengthy.

Critical Tasks   Find out tasks the management staff consider to be critical; often this gives a good insight into the overall management level they are currently operating from. Frequency and duration are also important parameters that give you an estimate of the staff expense for each task.

Difficult Tasks   Other tasks are just considered to be odious or difficult; they are easy to postpone or defer, especially when other things intrude. This is an area that is often correlated with a cluster of problems. A few years ago, the software distribution process was manual and difficult; most administrators avoided it as long as possible. There was a cluster of problems after each installation. The disruption and lost time justified buying a software distribution package that had been considered too expensive.

Frequent Tasks   Other tasks become a burden to the management staff because they combine unchallenging tasks that must be performed an inordinate number of times. These tasks are good automation targets; they free up time and let staff work on more important activities.

Neglected Tasks   It is also very useful to find out what the management staff members neglect. My experience is that many staffs are so consumed fighting the day-to-day battles that they just haven't the time to tackle other tasks that always seem like they can wait. Many strategic tasks such as long-term planning, evaluating new technologies, tuning the management system, optimizing networks and systems, and profiling are cited frequently.

Tuning the management system itself is an important task. Evaluating instrumentation—its coverage, bandwidth consumption, and intermediate agents—ensures that the appropriate resources are covered adequately. Frequently, administrators have the information they need for these tasks; what they lack is the time and the tools to exploit it. Capacity planning and performance optimization use information that is routinely collected. Profiling also uses collected information in order to determine the trends in utilization, application activity, and other factors.

This task information can point you toward places where their is the most opportunity. As a case in point, the same task frequently appears as a critical, time-consuming and difficult task. Also, examine the frequency/duration products for each task to identify areas where staff time is spent.

Platforms

Current customer platforms may have to be integrated into a proposed solution; they might also be assigned different functions.

Find out which platforms the customer may be using currently. It is also important to understand what is not being managed with platforms since those resources will be more difficult to integrate on a stand-alone element manager.

It is important that legacy platforms are incorporated and considered. There is a tendency to dismiss anything that is not SNMP-centric; however, the legacy platforms have several strengths. They integrate a wide array of management information and transform it into a common format. They also activate management procedures when certain events occur. Legacy platforms are interconnecting with SNMP platforms and will support a majority of the organization's networking and computing resources.

Process Tools

Process tools span the managed environments; an example is asset and inventory management. Information is collected from many sources and is assembled into an integrated view of the enterprise network and systems from an inventory-oriented perspective.

The Help Desk is another management tool (perhaps a service?) that spans environments. The Help Desk should receive inquiries from any user and handle them appropriately. Help Desks route problems to the appropriate specialists, educate users, and track problems.

Problem management is another process tool. Problems are often effectively solved by using an effective process to attack them. For example, a report of poor performance between a client and a server is most effectively addressed by quickly determining if the likely source of the problem is in the network, server, or client. Then the staff can focus their efforts and restore service quickly. The problem management, or trouble-ticketing, tools guide and record the problem resolution process to reduce downtime and increase staff productivity.

The problem management tools can accept a problem report from any source. Agents in devices may report failures while other agents report that a threshold has been exceeded. Other problems may be managed with this type of tool: a system that consistently violated configuration policies could be flagged and the problem routed to an administrator for investigation.

Other tools will span part of the managed environment. Systems management frameworks are examples of spanning tools. They integrate and control a set of tools for managing distributed systems. LAN management frameworks such as Bay Networks Optivity support sets of LAN management tools for path tracing, device management, monitoring, and troubleshooting.

Procedures

Well-managed environments have established procedures or processes they follow. Procedures should be clearly defined, with the appropriate supporting material. Often these procedures are only oral, or informal, which leads to exposures to mistakes by the management staff. As much as 20% of the troubleshooting time consumed in several organizations we have worked with has been traced to mistakes in procedures or unauthorized management activities.

Other organizations write their procedures down and keep them near the management console. More progressive organizations are building on-line procedure databases that provide information on demand. This simplifies keeping the information current and consistent between different management sites.

Look for the essential elements when you check procedures. Make sure there are clearly defined branching, exit, and escalation points. Staff must know what decisions they need to make, the criteria involved, and the next steps to take. In a similar way they need to know how to tell when they have completed a particular procedure. Finally, they need clear escalation instructions that tell them what to do when nothing has worked as expected. Escalation instructions should include the person to contact and any steps to take while awaiting more assistance.

Procedures should ultimately be embedded within the management system itself. The management system can guide the steps and in the best situations actually execute large portions of a procedure without human intervention.

Policies

Policies should also be evaluated; they are at a higher level of abstraction than procedures. A policy defines a goal of the management system, such as allocating resources based on the criticality of the activity. Policies are used to select appropriate procedures; there may be circumstances where the procedure is dictated by the appropriate policy. For example, a network device failure may cause different procedures to be executed based upon the time of day, critical applications activity, or other criteria.

Determine if policies are clearly stated and what they cover. For example, is there a policy concerning access control for the management staff? Is it clear which staff have responsibility and access to different managed resources? Other policies may determine the bandwidth that the management system consumes. Find out if there are policies that identify the critical resources and determine the relative priorities for allocating the resources to support them. Other organizations may have policies that constrain changes to the topology or the inclusion of new systems. Other policies may dictate that secured activities are separated from the rest of the enterprise. Organizations with policies in place are more likely to accept the concepts of automated, policy-based management as a long-term goal.

Both procedures and policies will be defined by rules that are created by administrators. These rules will be applied at several junctures, beginning with the event management system. An arriving event is processed to determine its relative priority. Flexible rules determine the priority as a function of other parameters and select the next step. Rules are also applied whenever an individual management tool completes its function. Rules determine if other tools are to be activated, staff to receive notifications, or trouble tickets to be closed. Unfortunately, the frameworks for achieving this level of control are immature and much work must be done by the customers themselves.

Cross-check the procedures with the task breakdowns. Determine if the most critical, time-consuming, difficult, or frequent procedures are well documented and easy to understand. This often identifies areas that need attention instead of deploying more technology.

Procedures that have many tedious steps are also strong candidates for further automation, or at least a review to determine if they are actually effective. The testing of rules and procedures is also a concern. How will we determine if the procedure actually does what we intend? It is impossible to break different devices or applications and to watch the procedure unfold. We need tools that let us simulate an event. We need to follow the procedure steps without changing any behavior as a result. This dry-run facility is not readily available in off-the-shelf products.

Covering Each Environment

Each managed environment has its own characteristics that must be understood, The common categories discussed above are used along with specific information to build a complete (as much as possible) picture of the environment we are managing.

LAN Management

Determine the number of LANs managed by an operator as a good metric to measure increased management staff productivity. Spend more time on those LANs that have been identified as critical.

Instrumentation   Determine if all critical segments are covered with permanent instrumentation. Look for wide area links and groups of LANs attached to backbones as places to use intermediate agents to advantage.

Determine the frequency of polling, the information collected, and the intelligence of agents in the networking devices. This survey collects the necessary information for making the appropriate design decisions and explaining them to the client.

Tools   Each customer will use various sets of management tools; many have no choice and must use an equipment vendor's management application. Look for completeness of the toolset: Are there any glaring omissions, such as no traffic monitoring at all? Of course, even the best toolset goes unused if the staff are undertrained or committed to the old ways. If the customer has primitive tools, it may signal extra training as part of an upgraded solution.

Legacy Management   Most customers will have legacy equipment that uses proprietary management protocols and procedures. These must be supported for an indefinite time. Gather information about all legacy equipment and current management capabilities. Some legacy equipment is managed by an element manager that may offer a reasonable level of functionality. Legacy element managers will need to be integrated with the rest of the management systems. Other legacy equipment may be managed with one of the legacy platforms. If a legacy platform exists, it might serve as the focus for incorporating other legacy equipment.

Many vendors of legacy equipment are now offering SNMP proxy agents. Find out if these agents are available. Proxy agents may simplify the integration of legacy equipment into the rest of the management framework.

Systems Management

Collect metrics that determine the number of desktops and servers managed by each staff member. Focus on critical workgroups. Be sure to include information about tasks, such as configuration, software distribution, and inventory, that are infrequent and time-consuming. If these tasks are currently done manually, be sure to get good baselines for comparing future improvements.

Instrumentation   Determine the instrumentation that covers desktops and servers, especially its diversity. Many desktops may use different agents and protocols. Assess the coverage of critical desktops and servers.

Tools   Collect the information about tools used for each environments such as NetWare, Unix, or Windows. Also determine the coverage or scope: Are all UNIX systems managed with the tools or only those in a single workgroup?

Management Structure   Determine the management structures that are currently used. Are computer systems managed locally, by a group in each campus, or by each business unit?

19.3   PUTTING IT ALL TOGETHER

Now we can evaluate alternatives and determine some guidelines to make specific recommendations. The first thing to examine are the impacts of failures and disruptions to the customer today. The information collected from earlier phases gives you estimates of outages with their frequency and duration. The duration/frequency product gives an outage as a number of hours per month, for example.

You also need to determine the impact of various types of outages. If you have detailed information, you can apply the procedure to individual LANs, workgroups, or campuses. If the information is sketchy, you may have to use enterprise-wide averages.

Weighted User Costs

Use the customer's networking user population to calculate a weighted average of the cost per hour to use the network. This is a simple calculation that sums the products of each category's relative amount with their basic costs per hour. This is a simple metric for sizing your calculations. It can be applied at any scale.

The first set of impacts will focus on outages and productivity losses since they are simpler to calculate. You need to consider the impacts of LAN and WAN outages as well as server failures.

LAN Outages

Determine the users supported by each LAN to assess the impacts of a LAN outage. The number of outage hours multiplied by the weighted user costs indicates lost productivity. In many organizations, of course, users will not sit idly by while their network is broken; they will perform other tasks. Other enterprises have a higher dependence on network availability. Use a dependence factor ranging from 1.0 (total dependence) to 0 (no dependence at all) to scale the calculation. I use a dependence factor of 1.0 to illustrate worst case and the customer factor to show a more normal impact.

Server Failures   Determine the server failure duration/frequency product to estimate the total outage. Use the average number of users per server to estimate the impact on the user community. Use an approximate dependence factor to scale the answer. The loss in productivity is the product of the number of servers, the frequency/duration product, the number of users per server, the weighted user cost, and the degree of dependence.

WAN Outages

The impacts of WAN outages are a little more complicated to derive. Most WANs use a partial mesh topology, so that failures of a link or switching element do not isolate attached LANs. The impact may be decreased performance since some of the WAN capacity is lost. It is usually simpler, as a first approximation, to look at failures at the WAN/LAN interface.

A failure at the LAN/WAN interface isolates a set of users from the rest of the enterprise. The same metrics are used to estimate the impacts: frequency/duration, the number of users, and the degree of dependence. If the customer has multiple LAN/WAN interfaces, a failure results in lowered performance, which can be incorporated into the calculation as another term that shows a degradation of effectiveness.

Productivity Impacts

These calculations can be accumulated to give an overall picture of productivity losses caused by outages. Customers are usually surprised by the totals, which grow very rapidly. This is also the place to use the projected growth rates for LANs, servers, users, and LAN/WAN interfaces.

The estimated growth demonstrates what the customer can expect if nothing is done. Usually, the impacts continue to grow and indicate the need for a better management solution.

Customers may object that productivity is a "soft" metric that is difficult to quantify. This is in part true; however, a great deal of time can be wasted waiting for networked services during an outage. Revenue loss gains the attention of other customers.

Revenue Impacts

Some customers know exactly what their exposure from outages means. For example, a credit card firm knew that it processed about 2,000 transactions a second with an average value of $77. This leads to a revenue loss of over $150,000 per second. Financial institutions may move hundreds of millions in funds in a matter of minutes. These types of stories are rather common and represent the high end of exposure. These customers need no convincing about sound management solutions.

Other organizations are more challenging when it comes to investigating revenue loss. This is where explicit identification of revenue producing portions is essential. The duration of outages can be applied to revenue generating activities if the basic information is available.

If the customer lacks explicit information about revenue generating activities, then the only resort is to use a rough metric of revenue per employee per hour and to produce a very rough estimate. It is also important to know if the revenue is truly lost; most shoppers will use another credit card rather than wait for validation, for instance. In other situations the revenue capture is deferred until a later time. Some businesses are more customer-centered than others and poor service exposes them to risks of future losses as well.

Outcomes

Usually these simple calculations reveal that new measures are needed. For example, a common outcome is that projected growth will outstrip staffing and budget increases if they are applied linearly. Instead, a new level of solution that offers higher scalability and management staff productivity must be introduced. Automation and integration are the key ingredients.

Many factors must be considered and balanced against each other when a management solution is being assembled or reviewed. The current reality is that an effective solution must be built from separate parts; there is no single source for a complete solution. Systems integrators are alternative for many organizations since they take on the burdens of delivering a turnkey solution.

These sections discuss some of the major steps, concerns, and areas that need to be considered when assembling components into a comprehensive solution.

19.4 CHOOSING A MANAGEMENT STRUCTURE

Choosing the appropriate management structure depends on several factors. The proper structure sets the foundation for future developments as the management solutions mature. Considering the properties of centralized, distributed, and hybrid structures is the first step toward defining a technical approach. Several trends are defining the new management structures: distributed management processing, centralizing staff, and introducing domain management. There are some trade-offs and political issues that must also be considered.

Distributed Management Processing

Chapter 6 illustrated the advantage of local intermediate agents that collect information and select some portion of it for further attention at a remote site. Intermediate agents also offer future opportunities for more sophisticated local analysis. Eventually, management tools will be placed in the same systems that support intermediate agents. Silicon is cheaper than bandwidth and the intermediate agent is a very scalable solution.

Centralization

Centralization will be driven by several factors such as manageable products, remote monitoring, and distributed processing. More manageable products are entering the market. These trends reduce the need for skilled on-site management staff. Local staff presence is only required for switching or adding hardware modules.

Distributing processing also facilitates the centralization of tools and staff. Adding functionality to a set of agents (through direct agent enhancements or through intermediate agents) reduces the need for on-site management staff since data collection and reduction are automatically performed.

Economic forces are driving more centralization. Centralized management structures provide the maximum leverage of tools and staff resources. Consolidating staff into fewer management sites increases their span of control and utilizes scarce expertise more effectively. It is important to remember that centralized management structures are used to increase the span of control; all staff members do not need to be in a single location. Rather, they need access to any information they need to manage any part of the distributed computing environment.

Politics

The technical trade-offs between the different structures are only one dimension of reaching an optimum design. Expect that any changes to the structure of the management system will also raise political issues. Unfortunately, politics cannot be ignored since they are frequently a pivotal part of building an acceptable solution. Many LAN workgroups were created because they were local departmental budget items that did not fall under corporate-level controls. LANs were installed, in part, as a reaction to the frustration of dealing with a centralized MIS operation which was not responsive to users and their networking requirements.

Many of these departmental or campus management environments have become fiefdoms in their own right and the management staffs do not welcome a return to a centralized management structure. Ironically, other local groups are exhausted by the demands of managing and are looking for someone else to take up their burdens. Building the needed consensus and buy-in is as essential as creating the right technical frameworks. Political factors may also dictate the speed at which consolidation actually happens.

Local access to centralized management information may satisfy administrators through the transition phase. Many local administrators are not thoroughly trained and do not actually want to be involved in the complex details of troubleshooting or performance optimization. However, they are also uncomfortable if they have no access to information that lets them understand the status of the environment they are responsible for.

Our experience has found that the local administrators need information so they can answer questions from their users and keep themselves informed about the status of networks, systems, and applications. At the same time, they are usually glad to turn over the more complex tasks to those who have the appropriate training and tools at the central site. Providing remote access to management information is a good transition strategy to consider when local management environments are accustomed to a fair degree of autonomy and independence.

Domain/Distributed Structures

Distributed management structures have received a great deal of attention in trade press articles, technical journals, and vendor literature. The scalability and flexibility of domain-based management is attractive, although it is very difficult to realize today.

A distributed solution breaks a complex, large environment into more manageable pieces (domains) and provides the means for coordinating a set of domain managers. One attraction is simplification and scaling gracefully. New domains are added without unduly increasing the loads on existing domains. Domains that become too large can be subdivided whenever necessary.

Fault tolerance can be incorporated, with domain managers monitoring each other and providing minimal management coverage if one domain manager fails. Enterprise control can be transferred between domain managers to suit organizational policies.

However, the reality is that robust distributed frameworks are still several years away. Planners can set their strategies accordingly and be in a position to adopt and exploit domain management at their convenience.

Defining Domains   Administrators should begin to define the domain structures they will use as distributed management technology becomes more widely available. Early determination of functional boundaries for systems, LAN, and WAN management operations allows time for adjustments and integration of disparate management groups. The exercise of determining domain boundaries is useful to check the criteria against the expected gains. Applying the methodologies that are necessary for a future transition to a fully distributed environment helps to delineate the potential problems.

One factor to consider in choosing domain boundaries is conserving scarce backbone bandwidth for applications rather than management traffic. Domains should be selected so that most of the management traffic is localized to high-speed LAN links. Interfaces to the WAN backbones are good choices for domain boundaries. Some management traffic will flow across these WAN links, but it should be minimized. Transferring control between domains introduces other factors; for instance, the flows across WAN links may change as the management center changes. These transitions must be accommodated in overall backbone bandwidth planning.

The domain managers need the mechanisms to signal each other and transfer control if fault-tolerance is required. Management protocols and shared information are needed for smooth transitions. Planners must also consider the staffing requirements and complements of tools that each management site requires.

Early consolidation within domains should be undertaken as soon as possible. The economic advantages of consolidation should be exploited as quickly as possible. Selecting a single domain for consolidation is often useful since the experience from the initial effort will serve to guide further consolidation efforts.

Consolidation   As domains are defined, administrators can still provide higher-quality solutions by beginning to consolidate operations within each of the potential domains. The introduction and deployment of intermediate agents or subdomain platforms, where required, will enable much of the work and value of this type of consolidation to be achieved even without full domain-level integration. Very large domains may require several other management sites to handle appropriate portions of the management workload; nesting subdomains within domains requires some careful consideration and consideration of the alternative of creating separate independent domains, which will be integrated at a later time.

Administrators can choose to use a simple integrator or legacy management platform where all the information from the domains can be collected and displayed. This first step would provide an enterprise-level monitoring and activity view, but would probably be reasonably weak in terms of providing an enterprise management site.

Picking a Winner

Some organizations are picking likely platform winners and waiting for the distributed solutions to roll out over time. They are betting heavily on the vendor's ability to deliver a scalable, robust, and economical distributed management framework. This strategy allows the administrator to continue collecting the appropriate tools and designing the appropriate management processes while waiting for the infrastructure to mature.

The most likely vendors who will be offering distributed solutions include IBM, Hewlett-Packard, Cabletron, and possibly SunConnect. Betting on undelivered technology introduces a risk that a delayed introduction or poor execution leaves the administrator with limited future options. Even these established platform players may suffer delays in delivering robust distributed frameworks.

Letting the Dust Settle   Simply staying with the solutions that are in place is another option. Administrators can use their current solutions to learn and understand requirements in greater detail and to build foundation frameworks. This leverages the current investment in management platforms and applications while increasing the quality of the current solution. In many cases, improving the current management system, even as a temporary measure, can result in substantial returns in improved availability and reduced costs of ownership.

This is a more conservative approach that postpones large commitments for future technologies until there are actually demonstrable products. Evaluations of field deployments and testing laboratories can help determine which vendors have really delivered an appropriate solution. Administrators have the security of investing in demonstrated solutions. The safe choice has the drawback of extending the time before better solutions are actually deployed. Each organization must analyze the relative benefits of early adoption against higher risks.

Hybrid Structures

Many organizations today actually use a mixture of centralized and distributed management structures. Mainframe-based networks and WANs have traditionally been managed centrally because this is the most effective structure for them. Dispersed management structures for client/server environments are also found with the multiple workgroup and campus management solutions in place today.

Several factors will keep hybrid solutions in place for an extended period of time. Often, a dispersed workgroup and campus solution is the only option: without adequate remote management tools there must be local management staff.

Another issue for organizations is the fear that management centralization results in loss of local control and responsiveness. Centralized management structures have often been seen as empires in their own right, disregarding the needs of network users. A good transition strategy that allays some of these concerns is to continue providing local administrators with access to centralized management information. Local administrators can monitor the status of their workgroups or campuses while the central site takes over troubleshooting, configuration, optimization, and other operational tasks. Local administrators will still be able to track problems and keep their users informed as they did in the past.

Management structures will retain their hybrid flavor in the future, but their composition will shift. Instead of a mixture of centralized and dispersed management environments, there will be more centralization of staff and tools with a distributed structure for the collection, reduction, and analysis of management information. Consolidation will proceed from the local workgroup to the campus and onward to the domain.

Functional Structures

The differences in systems and network management tasks and skills lead some organizations to create separate management environments for them. Systems management environments are restricted to the desktops, servers, and applications while the network management team is responsible for the LANs and WANs. Any particular functional structures will have advantages and drawbacks.

Some tasks are, of course, unique to each; it is not likely that a management staff member who is skilled at configuring routers will easily troubleshoot a messaging or file transfer application problem. There are other functions, such as problem management and inventory management that are common to both. Information management concerns must be addressed. How is information from these separate environments consolidated and leveraged? Should one group manage the common tools and processes, or should they be integrated at a higher level? Both management groups will access common inventory information, as a case in point, although they will look at different portions of it.

Collaboration

Managing a client/server environment requires close collaboration between systems and network administrators. The most difficult troubleshooting problems involve interactions between networks and systems. A user may report a "network problem" because an application is performing poorly. However, a system configuration problem or a poorly chosen application parameter may be the actual cause. Administrators must be able to exchange information and cooperate to resolve these types of problems.

An end-to-end monitoring operation can be set up to collect important information for identifying the cause of the problem. Analysis programs can determine the relative impacts of network latency and system delays and identify the areas for further investigation.

Performance optimization requires the same type of close cooperation. Systems should be configured to use network resources efficiently. Using an inadequate set of buffers or a small packet size will degrade the performance of high-volume applications. Application parameters such as low time-out values can also cause poor performance by causing failed connections and excess retransmissions. Network administrators may need to add higher speed links, additional buffering capacity to network devices, or reconfigure a routing domain to keep pace with application needs.

Both systems and network management staffs must be able to access information that helps them understand particular issues that they encounter. Common data models will provide some of the needed integration since all tools can share information from the common logical repository that holds systems and network management information. Experts in different disciplines must be able to interact when they are tracking mutual problems.

19.5 A TOP-DOWN APPROACH

Overall conceptual design requires a top-down approach which begins with the more abstract (and more important and valuable) perspectives and works toward point solutions and management platforms. There are five basic things to consider: policy, process, point solutions, frameworks, and platforms. Each of these represents a different level of abstraction and viewpoint in constructing an overall solution and strategy.

Policy

A policy-based level is the natural place for administrators to spend a good deal of time honing their perspectives. The direct incorporation of policy into the management system provides tremendous value and leverage. Administrators and network management solution designers can actually ensure that the actions of the management system are consistent with the goals of the organization. A policy-based perspective describes how the resources are to be used in order to achieve enterprise goals such as keeping mission-critical applications functioning, reducing or minimizing the costs of networking, or increasing the quality of service. These global policies keep the management solutions aligned with the needs of the organization.

Other policies are more local and affect all other management solution levels. They are embedded to control and constrain specific functions and operations. There are many options for selecting policies. Some of the more common ones will be described briefly below.

Data Collection   Policies for data collection can be used in several ways. For example, policies can define when large volumes of collected management information should be transferred to analysis sites. These policies help to minimize the impact of data collection activities on normal networking operations since accounting data can be moved

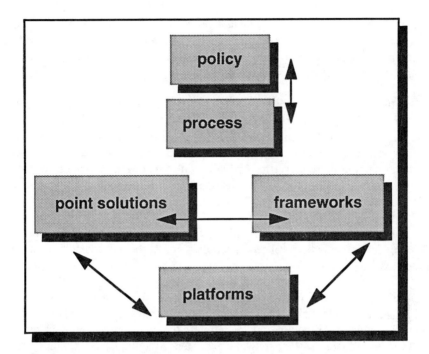

A top-down solution begins with policy constraints before moving on to describing the necessary processes. Point solutions and frameworks are evaluated to support the processes and policies.

FIGURE 19–1 Top-down solution

when utilization is low. A low-level policy of this type can be overridden if that same information is needed for fixing a critical problem.

Another data collection policy uses adaptive collection operations to improve the quality of the information collected. Administrators set triggers and define data collection and discard rules for different situations. A bandwidth constraint policy may also be implemented to monitor and control the volume of management information on the network. Such a policy usually forces the introduction of intermediate agents as the environment grows.

Troubleshooting There may be policies to constrain the actions taken by management staff during troubleshooting activities. Drastic changes to a network device or server within a single workgroup have minimal impacts (excepting the affected workgroup members), while doing the same thing to a critical server, a backbone router, or other essential resources may affect a much wider community of network users.

Troubleshooting policies could include restrictions about changing critical elements in the client-server environment or may require permission or consultation with other management staffs before these actions are undertaken. These policies can have time of day restrictions to offer more freedom in off-hours shifts.

Configuration   There may be configuration policies put in place to protect the production environment. For example, many servers support multiple protocol stacks, such as TCP/IP and IPX. Troubleshooting a particular protocol-related problem in a server may lead to a conclusion that the server should be reinitialized. However, other communities sharing those server resources must also be protected from a sudden server shutdown. Policies would prevent these actions without taking further steps to protect work in progress.

Other configuration policy constraints would be used to protect mission-critical activities. Functions such as network reconfiguration; moves, adds and changes; or adding and deleting devices may be restricted to certain hours of the day where their impact will be minimized.

Bandwidth Management   More sophisticated bandwidth management is needed as we move into the switched environment. Connection Management Systems (CMS) will find paths through the switching fabric for each application. Each application may have its own characteristic bandwidth and latency requirements. Administrators will apply constraints on users and applications so that the appropriate services are delivered to each user.

Other policy constraints will come into play when there are failures. Link and switch failures reduce the capacity of the switched fabric to varying extents. Policy rules will define the reassignment of routes and bandwidth to mission-critical activities. Less important activities receive what is left or are suspended until more bandwidth is restored.

Security   Policies for security include written policies that network users sign. Users need to be aware of their responsibilities concerning maintaining the appropriate levels of security. Other policies need to be defined for detected security breaches. Staff need to know whom to contact and what steps to take.

Tasks   Management tasks themselves can be handled with a policy-based perspective. Collecting information for accounting purposes, for example, is an ongoing task that must be carried out in a uniform and consistent fashion, if the data is to be meaningful. Policies can ensure that the appropriate tasks are activated and the appropriate information is delivered as needed in a timely fashion. Other tasks, such as continuous profiling of selected key elements, can be placed under policy control to ensure that they are carried out regularly. Still others, such as backup or software distribution, may also require policy constraints or guidelines so that they do not affect ongoing operations.

Coordination   We may need policies that coordinate sets of background tasks, such as profiling, backup, and software distribution, to ensure that they do not interfere with each other, nor adversely impact the rest of the community. Many of these types of tasks can be done at night or when the network is not congested. Congestion may occur if backup and software distribution are activated when another application was transferring large databases. Policies can define the sequence of the activities or reassign priorities when needed.

All policy-based constraints, decisions, and guidelines must be incorporated into the very fabric of the management solution so that the policies are automatically carried out at the appropriate times and with the appropriate resources and tools. The policies oversee the behavior of different management processes.

Processes

Automated processes are the basic mechanisms that will drive the real "machinery" of the managed environment. Processes will be used to coordinate individual steps, to make decisions, and handle alternative actions. The management situation and the policy interact and determine which actions and notifications are carried out. Management processes will be designed from the policy perspective in the best of all cases. Particular processes can

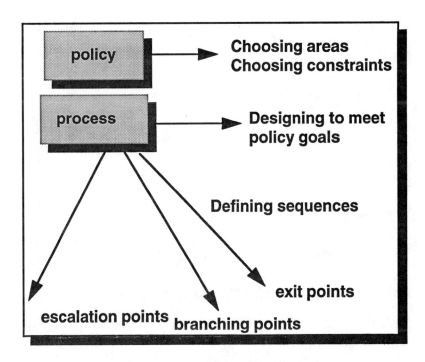

Policies drive the design of appropriate processes with decision points and defined exits.

FIGURE 19–2   Policy/Process interaction

be designed once an administrator or a designer determines that functions such as bandwidth management or backup management require policy constraints.

Each process must be designed by choosing the appropriate sequence of steps, the decision points, calibration points, escalation points, and exit points, as previously described. Once the process has been laid out and constructed, the administrator can move to choosing the appropriate staff and point solutions with which to implement the process.

Automated Management Processes: An Example

An example of a process that has been constructed might prove useful at this point. A process is defined as a sequence of actions taken by management tools and management staff. Administrators can leverage their technologies and staff with automated processes.

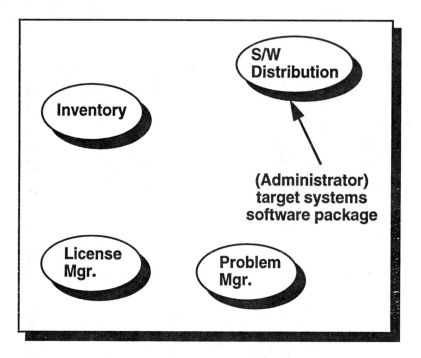

The Software distribution *process* uses several tools. The administrator presents a target list, and the software packages to be installed. A good software distribution tool allows dependency descriptions.

FIGURE 19–3   Process design: Software distribution

In this example, software is distributed to a set of target systems. There are actually a set of tools needed for building a software distribution process including software distribution, problem management inventory, and licensing tools.

The process begins with a target list—defining all the systems scheduled to receive the new software. One attribute of the tool is incorporating a list of dependencies. The new software will not install successfully without a certain amount of RAM, disc space, versions of the operating system, or special add-on boards.

These dependencies are fed to the inventory management tool along with the list of target systems. The inventory manager checks each system for the necessary resources. At the same time, the license manager is activated with the list of target systems. The license manager checks the number of licenses based on total numbers, departmental allocations, or other limits.

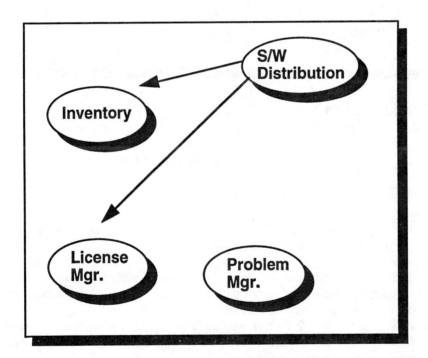

The inventory tool is used to determine if the target systems have the necessary resources for successful installation. The license manager checks to see that licensing agreements are maintained.

FIGURE 19–4   Software distribution: Step 2

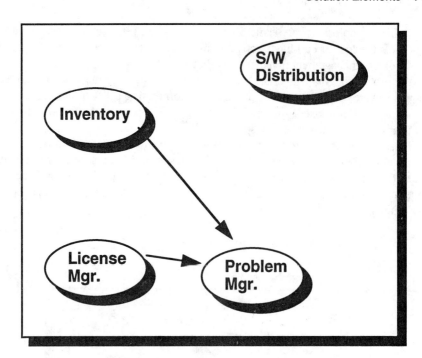

If any tools find a potential problem it is reported to the problem management system where it can be resolved.

FIGURE 19–5   Software distribution: Step 3

The inventory tool can respond in two ways: it can report that all is ready for delivery or it can issue trouble tickets to the problem management tool. After all, a system lacking the necessary memory or video card is as much a problem as a broken device.

The license manager also issues trouble tickets if there are any licensing violations detected. The problem management system tracks and clears each problem when the resources are added, or the licensing limits are adjusted appropriately.

The software is distributed after all problems are cleared. The process is finished after the inventory and licensing management tools are updated to reflect the current resources assigned to each computer system.

The event management system was used to build the sequences of tools. The software delivery tool activates the inventory and problem management tools. They may, in turn, activate the problem management system.

Information is shared through shared files that are passed between the tools. An integrated repository is not yet available.

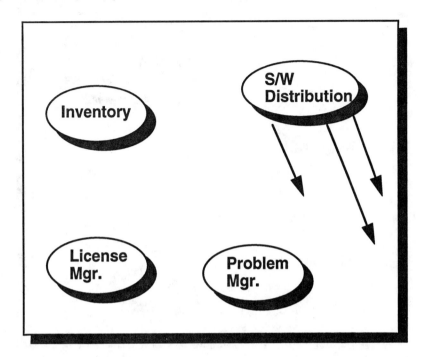

The software distribution tools deliver the software to the target systems.

FIGURE 19–6   Software distribution: Step 4

Point Solutions and Frameworks   Point solutions are used to carry out the individual process steps. And, as discussed earlier, many of these point solutions are not actually chosen; rather, they are dictated by the particular kinds of devices, applications, and systems that must be managed. In any case, point solutions frequently should not exit in a vacuum, they should be tied to other point solutions and frameworks.

Frameworks have been offered as a way of coordinating various point solutions. Designers and administrators may need to choose an appropriate framework, such as Optivity from Bay Networks or Hewlett-Packard's OperationsCenter. The framework supports a set of point solutions. Frameworks allow a more modular approach and increase the ability to share information and coordinate point solutions. Frameworks include management platforms and specifically targeted products for transport network management, systems management, and other functions.

A conceptual description of a management process includes the set of point solutions, a possible framework, and the necessary staff.

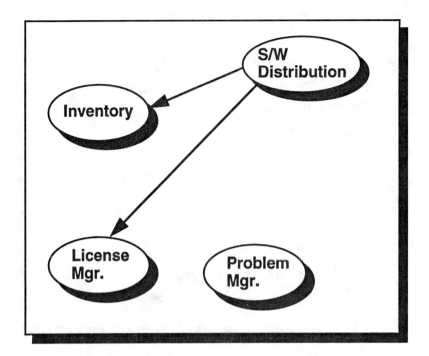

Successful delivery updates the inventory and
licensing information automatically.

FIGURE 19–7   Software distribution: Step 5

This is a useful time to identify gaps in the process structure due to lack of appropriate point solutions or staff personnel with the appropriate training and background.

Platforms

The management platforms are the foundation for all the previously described levels. Both the frameworks and the point solutions must be compatible with the chosen platform or, conversely, the platform must be chosen in order to support the types of frameworks, point solutions, and processes that are needed.

Platforms must also be evaluated to determine their suitability in the areas of common data models, distributed repositories, and other technology that supports the management tools. Easy integration and a large choice of point solutions and frameworks are also important.

Once this process has been completed, we have a fairly coherent conceptual top-down design. However, solutions will be built from the bottom up.

19.6 BOTTOM-UP SOLUTIONS

Building a solution from the bottom up is the most practical way to proceed. The bottom-up process proceeds most effectively when the dependencies for the higher levels of abstraction have already been identified through the top-down process. Also, a bottom-up approach accepts the realities of the limited solutions available in particular areas. Actually, an iterative process that alternates between top-down and bottom-up approaches may be needed: lack of a particular element may require a change in the top-down strategy that depended upon it.

Practical Perspectives

Make sure that all critical elements are as manageable as possible. Determine if they are equipped with redundant power supplies, have hot-swappable modules and environmental

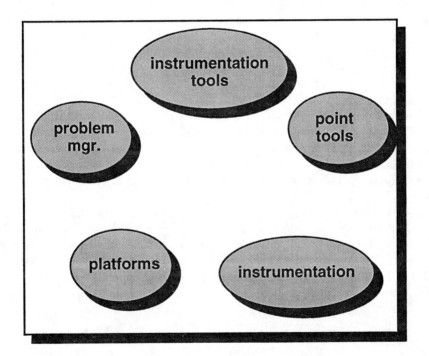

The basic requirements are: the set of point tools for the managed elements, a problem manager, and instrumentation tools. Platforms and instrumentation are the basic infrastructure.

FIGURE 19–8   Bottom-up elements

monitoring. Make certain that critical servers have power sharing, hot-swapped modules, and mirrored disks for critical data.

Use the calibration points to ensure basic physical redundancy. Are critical connections to corporate backbones and server farms protected with redundant devices or links? Are key servers and databases protected? Is critical information stored at another site? How is it synchronized?

Building a solid foundation and then moving up to incorporate the elements required to carry out the conceptual designs created in the top-down exercise will pay dividends and quickly converge on an appropriate management solution.

The Foundation

The foundation is the minimal complement of elements upon which a more sophisticated management solution can be constructed. The **collection of point tools** for managing devices, systems, and applications is supplemented by the foundation components. The **management platform**, a **problem management tool**, and **basic instrumentation** capabilities are the basic components.

The platform provides the ongoing support and infrastructure as more tools, frameworks, processes, and policies are added to the management solution. A platform must be capable of dealing with today's environments and have the capacity to support new applications and services in the future.

A problem management system is necessary to track, catalogue, and analyze problems. Collecting information on trends and significant problems facing the administrators is important. A sophisticated problem management tool is a sound investment since it provides higher levels of correlation and access to historical data to find similar patterns. Analysis tools can also provide the feedback for designing more effective management processes.

Instrumentation is necessary, of course, for monitoring and understanding the behavior of the many elements in a distributed client/server environment. Instrumentation itself includes remote monitors for key segments and critical elements, as well as applications that allow the easy collection, manipulation, presentation, and analysis of the collected data. Larger environments also require early consideration and selection of the appropriate intermediate agents for scaling purposes.

Frameworks

Many frameworks are available for collecting tools into more functionally grouped and integrated areas, such as network or systems management. Frameworks must be compatible and supported by the management platform in order to provide maximum integration and leverage of the information. Over time, some frameworks may merge with the platforms as they mature, but at this stage, selecting an appropriate framework can provide long-term benefits for building a solution.

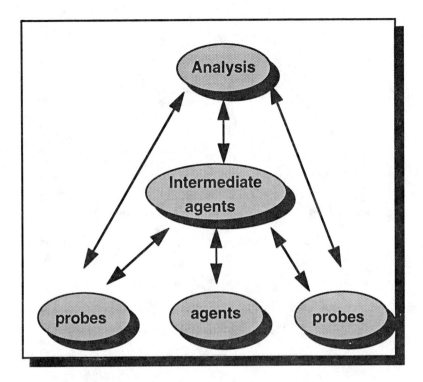

Point tools can be obtained from a device or system
vendor, others are provided by third parties for specific
environments. Tools can be deployed separately or as
part of a framework.

FIGURE 19–9   Point tools

Point Solutions

Point solutions are tools that are specific and limited to a small set of functions. There are
basically three categories of point tools that should be considered: vendor-specific, target-
specific, or neutral. Vendor-specific tools are usually supplied by the provider of a particular element or device. These tools take advantage of the proprietary MIB extensions and
quite often, the administrator has no choice but to deploy them.

Target-specific tools are emerging in the systems management area. For example,
multiple vendors provide tools for managing the Novell NetWare environments. System
administrators have a choice among target-specific tools, although all the features and
functions are not necessarily consistent between different products.

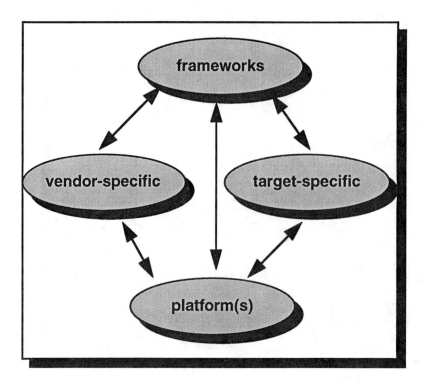

Instrumentation must be designed with intermediate agents in mind for scalability. Out-of-band access must be considered for critical sections.

FIGURE 19–10   Instrumentation

Neutral tools do not depend upon specific elements, instead they span a set of elements. Accounting tools use data from many managed elements and produce information about resource utilization. General management reporting tools incorporate data from various sources and provide summary reports on network and system health, availability, and other metrics.

Administrators start with the mandated point tools for their elements. They can supplement these tools with target-specific and neutral tools identified in the top-down design. These tools can be organized into the management processes.

Process Tools

Process tools can be selected or constructed to coordinate and manage the processes designed in the top-down exercise. Process tools, of course, must work with the frameworks, platforms, and individual point tools. Special types of software that we have been calling "integrators" may also be required. These special purpose applications are used to "glue" different elements together when designing and building a sequenced process. An example of an integrator might be a simple application that receives information from a point tool, converts it into a form required by another tool, and then triggers the appropriate event to activate the next tool in the sequence. Many integrators can be found in initial solutions; hopefully, over time, many of these will disappear as the appropriate integration technologies find their way into frameworks and platforms.

19.7   USING THE CALIBRATION POINTS

The calibration points can be used to target the specific attributes of a proposed solution, or they can be used to prioritize a phased introduction. The calibration points collected for failures can be used to select the tools that can reduce downtime. Better monitoring may be the first alternative to consider: Are failing devices, systems or applications adequately monitored? Adding permanent probes, more intelligent agents, or an intermediate agent may allow for closer tracking and earlier notification of potential problems.

Critical Resources   Make sure that critical devices, servers, and systems have the features that minimize the impacts of failures; make sure that they can be restored to service quickly with hot-swappable modules, for instance. Sometimes devices may need to be moved in order to get the highest availability features on the key elements.

Identify key LAN/WAN interfaces—usually routers—and determine if they have the necessary features. Use the productivity and revenue loss estimates to determine if a redundant interface is justified.

Carry out the same analysis for critical servers; make sure they have adequate manageability support. Use the productivity and revenue loss estimates to evaluate the options of adding redundant servers. Remember that redundant servers also add to management tasks in terms of keeping consistent information on several servers. Databases with shadowing and replication may be needed as well.

Management Tasks   The task breakdowns help you to prioritize the problems that should be addressed. For instance, some tasks may appear in several of the categories. Organizations frequently report, for example, that moves, adds, and changes are among the most difficult, critical, and time-consuming tasks they perform. This particular problem may be addressed by suggesting intelligent hubs with port and module switching, switches, or better planning, training, or procedures.

Tasks that consume large amounts of staff time or require high skill levels are the ones that offer the largest potential payback. They should be given a high priority in a phased solution whenever possible.

Impacts   Make sure that any identified productivity and revenue impacts are included if they are significant. Attention to these issues can deliver large returns for the effort.

Collecting all the information gives you a good idea of the customer's current environment—the pressing problems, the rates of failures, the impacts of failures, and projected growth rates. Now we can start to build a solution that moves the customer from the current position toward the desired outcomes.

19.8 SUMMARY

The iterative cycle of top-down and bottom-up design and implementation approaches allows planners to define a current solution and ensure they have left room for evolving towards a more sophisticated and effective solution with time. The top-down strategy identifies high-value functions at a level of useful abstraction that is not enmeshed in a volume of details. Top-down approaches allow administrators to define overall policies and discover opportunities to insert them throughout the solution. Some policies may not be automated (or even possible to automate), but considering them usually opens new areas to exploit.

Bottom-up approaches build from actual basic components and work toward higher-levels of abstraction. Basing each level on actual components provides a safe, phased implementation scheme. Continued checking between the approaches is common as the actual details are filled in. Some assumptions or goals will be exposed or modified in the harsh light of practicality.

19.9 GENERAL WIDGETS

The company began work early on the set of policies that might be beneficial for managing their enterprise computing environment. They identified policies for such areas as security management, baselining networks, Help Desk intakes, problem escalation, responding to a security breach, responding to failures, responding to users, consuming network bandwidth for management, making changes, and many others. Some of these policies were directly translated into processes—steps, staff, and tools that would be needed to implement and enforce each policy.

Many of these policies cannot be automated yet, unfortunately. Wherever possible, policies are displayed on screens when certain events occur. This helps acquaint the management staff with the goals of policy-based management and also gives them some guidance when they must take action. Some simple scripts that incorporate some policy distinctions have been implemented. For instance, a script checks for the time of day before selecting other steps. There is a policy that restricts certain topology changes during peak productive hours.

An ongoing effort is underway to move management solutions from technology to General Widgets business processes. The goal is to make the transition from managing for efficiency to managing for effectiveness. This process is centered around the identification and management of the mission-critical applications. The first phase consists of identifying this set of applications. This is not a static set of applications; others will join the set over time. Further refinement is needed to actually identify those clients and servers that are involved in these critical applications. Once this step is completed, the underlying infrastructure can be mapped according to the applications it supports.

A static mapping is not sufficient since it is behavior that causes the problems. Monitoring tools are needed that provide the insight into application behavior. Administrators want to know: Who uses it? Where are they located? What kinds of traffic volumes and response times are being delivered? Where are the performance bottlenecks? Answering these questions will lead to more effective management decisions.

For example, fault correlation will be used to identify business impacts associated with management events. A server failure can be associated with those critical applications the server supports. Appropriate project managers can be notified to update them on conditions that affect their ability to carry out a business task. This type of correlation also simplifies the handling of events—one failure that impacts critical activities is more important than another that doesn't.

Failures can also reduce the availability of service. Management information can identify the critical applications that are using the network and ensure that operators give them precedence. Automated processes will carry out these decisions in the future. Less important applications should be throttled back or suspended while the critical applications maintain their quality of service.

Of course, all the less exotic issues must also be addressed. General Widgets carried out a basic evaluation of their network topologies to identify critical areas that required redundant facilities. Additional routers and links were incorporated where there was vulnerability to a single failure. The same process was carried out with critical servers; they were evaluated and some equipment was rearranged as a result. The key servers got uninterruptable power supplies, mirrored disks, redundant controllers, and other features that kept the key information available.

The implementation of intelligent intermediate agents was a key step in the strategy. These agents off-load the platforms and filter the information closer to its source. Remote configuration switches the flow of events from any management center to any other center. Today's robustness also offers future options. Most SNMP platforms still lack distributed capabilities, and the intelligent agents insulate the platforms from the instrumentation underneath. Intelligent agents can forward events and control to different platforms as instructed. Introducing correlation and local actions will allow a single platform to oversee more distributed activities.

The General Widgets strategy is moving forward with intelligent instrumentation, consolidated management at the four centers, and laying the groundwork for more centralized management when products mature. The consolidation of management functions is already paying off with increased staff productivity and more uniform services. Configuration management policies are also showing strong payoffs in reduced troubleshooting time, easier software distribution, and better security. Integrating more information is the next challenge. Solving this problem opens the way for centralized policy oversight of a distributed management team.

Critical application information can be used in the planning process as well. Topology changes can be evaluated in terms of the applications they disturb or improve. Monitoring can be targeted toward keeping the key services operating as long as possible.

19.10 CHECKLIST

There are two kinds of information that need to be collected. **Data points** are used for calculations to determine further steps. For example, the numbers of devices and systems are necessary for calculating the amount of management traffic for remote polling. **Calibration points**, in contrast, are used to guide your solution and to check its direction. Knowing the most time-consuming management tasks will point you toward solutions that free management staff. Having accurate information (data points) on the amount of time consumed by a task is useful for demonstrating quantifiable savings after a solution is deployed.

Often the information you need is not available or may not be very precise. That is the nature of the problem—a well-managed environment that has the information you need is already in good shape. The organizations that need the most help usually have the poorest quality information. You can only do the best you can—often estimates and educated guesses will be your guidelines when information is poor.

1. Finding Out Where You Are Going

   Desired customer outcomes

   Competitive: time to market, customer service, etc.
       can management's contribution be demonstrated?

   Technical: availability, service quality, etc.
       are metrics available? can the outcomes be measured?

   Policy areas
       identifying key applications
       appropriate support for key applications
       quality of service
       span of control
       access control and security
       data collection impacts
       data collection intelligence
       management scheduling
       disaster recovery
       configuration and changes, etc.

2. Finding Where You Are Starting From

   High Level Information

   This information is used to make sure the business goals and environment are considered early and often. The data points are used for rough estimates of productivity and revenue if better information is not available.

   calibration points
       markets
       share
       volatility

    competitive strengths
    competitive weakness
data points
    revenues
    employees

A Census

This is where a lot of good information can be collected. Often, the quality may vary, estimates may need to suffice. The identification of all resources is key to understand the scale of the solution. Two-year projections help to estimate future capacities of the solution. These projections also help to demonstrate the current and future problems that customers are facing. Identifying key applications and critical elements insures that attention and efforts are invested appropriately.

calibration and data points
    numbers, types and distribution of LAN segments
    identified critical segments
    projected growth rates for each
    numbers, types and distribution of LAN switches
    identified critical switches
    projected growth rates for each
    numbers, types and distribution of WANs
    identified critical WAN interfaces
    projected growth rates for each
    numbers types and distribution of internetworking devices
    identified critical devices
    projected growth rates for each
    numbers, types, and distribution of legacy equipment
    identify critical legacy equipment

    number of supported users
    numbers, types and distribution of desktops
    identified critical desktops
    projected growth rates for each
    numbers ,types, and distribution of servers
    identified critical servers
    projected growth rates for each

    numbers, types and distribution of applications
    identified critical applications

    revenue producing LAN segments identified
    revenue produced = $ / hour

    revenue producing servers identified
    revenue produced = $ / hour

revenue producing clients identified
revenue produced = $ / hour

revenue producing applications identified
revenue produced = $ / hour

calculate the average number of users/segment
obtain an estimate of degree of dependence on the segment

calculate the average number of users/server
obtain an estimate of degree of dependence on servers

calculate the average number of users/WAN interface
obtain an estimate of degree of dependence

3. Current Management Environment

Calibration points

Documented management strategies?

Budget
    hardware
    tools
    platforms
    staff
    training

Staffing
    skill levels
    key staff

Coverage
    business hours
    24×7 fully staffed on-site
    24×7 staff on call

Reports
    health
    availability
    response time
    throughput
    service levels

Failures—*focus especially on critical resources and applications, otherwise use available data as typical*
    frequency
    duration
    staff requirement
    identify most frequently failing devices or components

Critical elements identified in census
    are manageability features incorporated?

Volume of user complaints

Management tasks
  most frequent
  most critical
  most time consuming
  most difficult
  most neglected

Procedures
  availability—written—on-line
  escalation ?
  clarity and degree of automation?
  identify missing procedures,
    i.e., response to a security breach

Check against task breakdowns
  are most pressing procedures clear?

Policies
  check for defined policies
  security and access control
  management bandwidth
  identifying critical elements
  availability of critical services and applications
  changes to the environment

Instrumentation
  coverage of critical resources?
  extended coverage?
  permanent or dispatched instruments
  intermediate agents?
  out-of-band access?

Management structures
  centralized
  distributed
  dispersed

Platforms

Tools
  completeness
    toolset
      span of servers
      span of clients
    stand-alone
    platform resident
    client/server

4. Impacts

> evaluate productivity losses
> project future losses based on growth
>
> evaluate revenue losses
> project future losses based on growth
>
> estimate staff operational loading in terms of segments/LAN staff member, etc.
>
> incorporate two-year projections to estimate staffing growth
>
> compare with estimated management budget

5. Solution elements

> Using calibration points
>> critical devices
>>> manageability features
>>> strengthen key devices by moving, upgrades
>> critical LAN/WAN interfaces
>>> redundant LAN/WAN interfaces
>
> Are key servers manageable?
>> mirrored discs, etc.?
>> redundant servers
>> data shadowing and replication
>
> Remotely managed systems
>> agents
>> NICs
>> flash memory
>> operating system instrumentation
>> application instrumentation
>
> Management tasks
>
> Identify most promising management tasks to tackle
>> high criticality to the organization
>> high staff time consumed
>> high skill levels required
>
> Choose management structures
>> maximum consolidation of staff and resources
>> remotely managed products
>
> Centralized
>> deal with projected growth rates for scalability
>> intermediate agents for additional scaling
>> robustness must be addressed
>> policy centralized as well?
>
> Distributed
>> design domains
>> bandwidth conservation at WAN

transfer of control?
hand-offs and signaling
staffing requirements at each management site

Use Instrumentation checklist

Use event management checklist

Use platform checklist

Tool selection

Prioritize by business impacts
addressing revenue losses
minimizing productivity losses

Prioritize by task
difficult tasks
frequent tasks
critical tasks
time consuming tasks
neglected tasks

Prioritize by rare skill levels on staff

Constraints
frameworks required
availability on chosen platform

Phased introduction
platforms
instrumentation
intermediate agents
processes and tools

CHAPTER 20

Conclusion

Parts of this book have probably been discouraging, since some areas of client/server management are still short of what we need. However, encouraging developments continue to tantalize us with hopes for future relief.

20.1   REMAINING HURDLES

Some of the key requirements for more effective management solutions are still missing. Technical impediments aren't the barrier at this point; the understanding of the problems and the potential solutions have been extensively researched. The issue seems to be that no vendors have actually pursued any solutions aggressively.

Data Integration

Management solutions fall short because the tools do not have the information they need to improve the breadth and depth of analysis. Better information provides the traction for correlation engines, knowledge bases, and sophisticated analysis.

Sharing information between management tools depends upon a common data model—ways of naming, locating, and accessing the needed information. Object-based models will simplify some tasks, but the data model is not emerging.

This is an area where the management platform vendors were expected to step up, but they have actually slowed the efforts by withdrawing from the Management Integration Consortium—a group of software vendors addressing the data integration issues. Instead, we are likely to see the appearance of proprietary models that will not interoperate. If this occurs, the Independent Software Vendors will be forced to adapt their applications

348

to each specific data model, hardly a mark of progress. The alternative is that a dominant vendor will force a de facto standard by pulling through more vendors to their model.

Systems management vendors are also moving forward by building their own frameworks that do not depend directly on the SNMP management platforms. Companies such as Tivoli are opening their frameworks to other tool vendors. Data sharing is moving forward at this level.

Toolset Integration

Despite the developments of systems management frameworks, the integration between management tools is poor. Building automatic sequences of tools is difficult and staff time must be utilized instead. The prospects for immediate improvement are not bright, unfortunately.

Common event signals would help move the process forward. Sequencing occurs through the event management system itself and common signaling would make it simpler to interconnect various tools.

The basic question is, Who steps up to solve the problem? Some tool vendors build management tools that facilitate sales of network devices, for example. Their competitive focus is on staying ahead of the competition rather than integrating the pieces. The platform vendors have been slow to build the promised infrastructure, but they cannot integrate the products that use their platforms.

It seems that customers, or those they hire, will need to step up to this issue. Each administrator will want to adapt the toolset to a specific set of requirements. Administrators need a simple way to "snap in" tools to meet their requirements.

Domain Management

True scalability for the enterprise-level management cannot be delivered without some type of domain-based management system. The basic infrastructures have emerged from most of the SNMP management platform vendors, but much remains undone—most of the basic pieces such as object brokers, repositories, and client/server frameworks, are not available yet.

The pace seems to be slow; however, the deployment of large-scale integrated platforms is still rare.

20.2   EMERGING TRENDS

Distributed Intelligence

The trend toward distributed, intelligent collectors is well underway. Products from vendors such as Bridgeway Corporation, Legent Corporation, Hewlett-Packard, IBM, Network Intelligence, SSDS, and Tivoli Systems are offering distributed collection, filtering, topology, discovery, and other management functions. More products will be introduced, offering the breadth of options that will strengthen the move toward distributed processing.

Client/Server

Client/server architectures have been introduced by Cabletron, SunSoft, NetLabs, and IBM. These infrastructures are in different stages of maturity, and all need to be completely fleshed out.

The influence of DCE—the Open Software Foundation's Distributed Computing Environment—is being felt. More vendors are announcing DCE-compliant products or adapters that interface to other client/server offerings. The DCE infrastructure supports many of the elements needed for effective management solutions. This, of course, was the goal of the DME (OSF Distributed Management Environment), an effort that never seemed to catch hold. Ironically, the need still exists and the DCE technology may yet emerge as a foundation for converging management architectures for distributed management.

More Leverage

Management tools are beginning to offer benefits of object-oriented technologies. For example, companies such as Tivoli Systems use objects to encapsulate configuration profiles or policies that can be applied to sets of resources. These types of features offer better control, simpler management, and reduced staff effort and time.

Applications Management

This is the area where much remains to be done. Applications are the ultimate stressor of our networks and computer systems; we can't really control and manage everything else without gaining better control of the applications.

The main need is for instrumentation—building applications that provide the remote access and control needed for effective management. Unfortunately, many current applications lack the necessary access. This is where tools such as the CoroNet Management System come into play; the application "probe" extracts useful application information from the network traffic.

Other approaches add special agents that extract information from applications. BMC Software, for instance, has introduced Patrol, another systems management framework that focuses on database management. The main components of Patrol include a Console, Intelligent Agents, and Knowledge Modules. The console provides a centralized administration site with the ability to collect information from multiple intelligent agents and display it.

The Intelligent Agents are embedded in individual systems where they can monitor systems parameters, file systems, processes, security, overall resource utilization, and the system kernel itself. Agents can automatically baseline information about normal operation and use this to detect anomalous behavior. Administrators can set thresholds for forwarding notifications of potential problems. Automatic correction mechanisms can be specified for the Intelligent Agents so that local actions can be initiated to resolve problems as quickly as possible.

The Knowledge Modules are used to provide a set of embedded recovery and monitoring routines optimized for particular types of databases. The Knowledge Modules can discover all of the databases in the managed environment by interrogating the resident intelligent agents. Knowledge Modules can monitor database parameters including performance, disk activity, queue waiting times, and space consumption. Individual sessions can also be monitored to track their performance, thereby allowing administrators to keep an eye on mission-critical database or transaction processing applications.

Automatic configuration routines can be used to apply standard configurations to other databases in the managed environment. The Knowledge Module also contains stored knowledge so that automatic responses to resolve problems are incorporated into the management environment. Stored knowledge is basically scripts and other types of small programs that are activated when various types of errors are detected. Administrators have the ability to extend and customize the stored knowledge to reflect their own experience as well as to clone expertise from other sources.

More applications management tools are still needed. Better application design will be key for general management. Database management was an early target because of criticality and the easy access to database statistics and operating information. Other key applications such as groupware and messaging are receiving stronger attention now. Systems management tools such as workload management and scheduling automate the control and management of the application. Storage management, backup, and fault-tolerant environments also improve applications manageability.

Extensions to the Business Process

Much of the basic technology used for managing distributed systems is the foundation for an intelligent business process management infrastructure. The key elements are instrumentation, intelligent agents, event management, automation, and data integration.

Extending management technologies to business processes creates new opportunities to automatically monitor business activities, react intelligently to business problems, and manage the business for competitive advantage. Selected business metrics are tracked, and automated responses are invoked to correct problems. For the first time, the enterprise has an ongoing, accurate real-time picture of how it actually operates and behaves.

Enterprises also have the **feedback** they need for optimizing their business processes. Weak spots are identified and changes are measured. Resources and staff are allocated efficiently while automation takes over repetitive tasks. Business managers keep their fingers on the pulse of their organizations.

Using management technologies in this way makes enterprises stronger competitors because they literally **incorporate** these corporate-wide mission critical business processes and resources into an intelligent management infrastructure.

Business processes use enterprise management system services. For example, an employee leaving the organization activates a business process that closes accounts, transfers benefits, and clears up other matters. This process can send a notice to the network management system to change all the appropriate network and system access codes.

The integration of business processes is a step beyond network and systems management. Network and systems administrators are already shifting their perspectives to process-related problems rather than simple failures.

SSDS has provided Intelligent Enterprise Management solutions to large organizations for several years. THEdesc is **intelligent middleware** that supports a set of functions including:

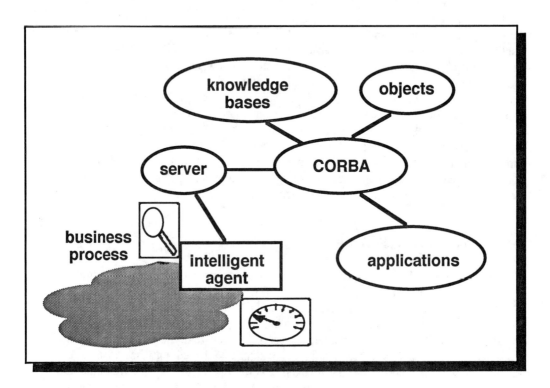

SSDS incorporates business processes into the management framework. Intelligent agents collect information from business processes and feed it into the management system.

FIGURE 20–1   Managing business processes

- ➡ information exchange between agents and management applications
- ➡ rule-driven event management with task automation
- ➡ integration of all management data
- ➡ naming services for locating objects
- ➡ security and authentication services
- ➡ a vendor-neutral framework that allows customers to choose their own products
- ➡ integration with other management platforms and applications

Standards such as DCE and CORBA provide an object-oriented environment that incorporates networks, systems, and business processes. Intelligent agents are able to measure the attainment of goals, such as responding to customer inquiries within a given time. The agents use THEdesc's services to exchange messages with other business process managers, as well as human staff.

This opens the definition of enterprise management to incorporate a broader view of the solutions we are trying to build. Technology problems can be related to business processes and the management system becomes another asset for increasing internal effectiveness and competitive strength.

20.3   CONCLUSION

The administrator still has too much work, and the many trends mentioned above will be making matters easier. In the meantime, there is much to do to determine the policies and processes that will exploit the technologies and tools that can be obtained. Network and systems management will remain an art that demands creativity, willingness to change, and adaptivity. There are practical steps and products that move us toward our goals.

Index